A Nonviolent Theology of Love

A Nonviolent Theology of Love

Peacefully Confessing the Apostles' Creed

Sharon L. Baker Putt

FORTRESS PRESS
MINNEAPOLIS

Contents

Acknowledgments

Many conversation partners engaged and challenged me as I wrote this book, among them Eric Seibert, Richard Crane, and Shelly Skinner. Eric's dedication and conviction concerning a nonviolent God continue to inspire me. Richard's artesian fountain of theological information and little golden nuggets always made me think and laugh. And Shelly's insistence on reprising the fundamentals of the faith kept me grounded. I thank each of them wholeheartedly for extending their scholarship, expertise, encouragement, and friendship. Additionally, I express my deepest gratitude for Robin Collins, whose creative theological interpretations relating to atonement, evil, and the human person significantly improved this book. I must also express deep appreciation to my good friend Fisher Humphreys, who read the entire manuscript in its roughest form and offered invaluable critique and suggestions. Undoubtedly, the quality of this book would be much poorer had Fisher not contributed his inspired guidance.

Of course, I must also acknowledge my students, who motivated and encouraged me by asking tough questions with open minds, consistently volunteering their critiques, and insistently challenging me with the biblical witness. Among my students, I must give special recognition to Becca Fedor, my TA, who spent hours reading and editing the manuscript, and to Austin White, whose artistic talent provided a beautiful image of the global church. Thank you as well to the many students who served as conversation partners throughout the process, particularly Kiersten Smeal, who, thankfully, took on the thankless job of helping with the index, as well as Kortnei Confer, Sami John, Joshua Orsi, and Kylie Kosko. Many thanks also to Kathy and Jack Caputo for making space for me to write in the comfort and quietness of their home and for their friendship and encouragement during the years it took to write the book.

Many thanks to my editors at Fortress Press, who have contributed significantly to this text. I am very grateful to Rebecca Adams, my developmental editor, for the hours and hours she spent editing, enhancing content, offering ideas, and, at times, improving my prose. Without her expert editorial guidance, this book would not be what it is today. Her professional proficiency, unending patience, and discerning eye made the publishing process a pleasure. Emphatic thanks to Heidi Mann, whose careful copy editing caught my many typos and *faux pas*.

Finally, I give my special heartfelt thanks to B. Keith Putt, my closest, dearest friend—and husband—for editing this manuscript, offering insights, listening to my endless complaints, and proving once again that, although he is a philosopher, he sometimes knows theology better than I do!

The Apostles' Creed

I believe in God, the Father almighty,
　　creator of heaven and earth.

I believe in Jesus Christ, God's only Son, our Lord,
　　who was conceived by the Holy Spirit,
　　born of the virgin Mary,
　　suffered under Pontius Pilate,
　　was crucified, died, and was buried;
　　he descended to the dead.*
　　On the third day he rose again;
　　he ascended into heaven,
　　he is seated at the right hand of the Father,
　　and he will come to judge the living and the dead.

I believe in the Holy Spirit,
　　the holy catholic church,
　　the communion of saints,
　　the forgiveness of sins,
　　the resurrection of the body,
　　and the life everlasting. Amen.†

---

* Or, "he descended into hell," another translation of this text in widespread use.
† Apostles' Creed, *Evangelical Lutheran Worship* (Minneapolis: Augsburg Fortress, 2006), 105. This wording first published by English Language Liturgical Consultation in *Praying Together*, 1988.

Preface

A perfect Introduction to Theology text does not exist. I know because I've spent years searching for one. This book is a result of that search. To write a work of theology risks forcing the reader to wade through an ocean of perplexing academic jargon, complicated arguments, and long, content-filled footnotes describing the plethora of research that went into the project—all components that academicians typically expect. I do hope academic theologians will find this book useful, especially in the classroom, but I write primarily for pastors, church lay persons, and undergraduate students; the everyday people who want to learn theology; those who preach, teach, or simply wish to live life as close to the gospel message as possible. I've written the text I always wanted to use—what I hope is an accessible, engaging introductory text with a philosophical and theological sophistication that does not overwhelm its readers.

The Approach

Every text needs an organized structure that serves as the "skeleton" for the entire content of the book. What does a skeleton do? It supports and shapes a body. It gives an organism its backbone and enables it to stand on solid ground. In like manner, this book needs a backbone, a strong structure that shapes it and gives it support. Therefore, I have chosen the Apostles' Creed, as a foundational document of Christian theology, for the book's skeleton.

In a world dominated by many religions and belief systems, the Apostles' Creed characterizes the identity and beliefs of Christians from as early as the second century CE. As an early Trinitarian, ecumenical statement of faith, the Apostles' Creed presents the Christian tradition with broadly defined assertions that allow freedom for multiple expressions of the doctrines of our faith. In contrast, many later creeds and confessions lock their adherents into one narrow theological viewpoint to the exclusion of other significant and valid doctrinal expressions of thought. Fortunately, the Apostles' Creed maintains for us a connection with our historical Christian roots while, at the same time, allowing some room in which to reinterpret and reexpress traditional doctrines in ways relevant to our constantly changing cultures.

Christian traditions throughout history have always worked to construct relevant theological perspectives that preserve the spirit of their particular ancient creeds. This book continues that endeavor, engaging and reinterpreting traditional doctrines for the benefit of the church and for the furtherance of the kingdom of God. I firmly believe that learning many different perspectives not only helps us appreciate the thoughts of others throughout history, but also provides us with fodder for our own theological views. In order to provide a broader landscape of Christian thought for the various topics we will explore, I survey many church doctrines throughout church history, along with the classical and contemporary theologians and thinkers who have grappled with them. I then develop my own constructive theological stance within each chapter.

The Vision

As does anyone who strives to understand God through theological reflection and discourse, I come to the discipline with a certain interpretive lens; I have my own particular perspective on God and God's dealings with us and the world. My starting point for the theological endeavor is the biblical statement "God is love." I discuss this in more detail in chapter 2, "Hermeneutics" (the art of interpretation). Although introductory texts do not usually cover the subject of hermeneutics, I include it because of the necessity of interpretation for constructing theology. We all have (even if implicitly) a way of interpreting the biblical text and come to the text with presuppositions. This volume significantly engages the theological peace tradition, attempting to put into dialogue the currents and concerns of this tradition with historical, classical resources such as those found in Eastern Orthodoxy, along with more prophetic and liberation traditions such as Black and feminist theologies. I have attempted to write a historically grounded, relatively comprehensive introductory text that constructively builds upon traditional theological expressions and focuses on God's love, divine blessing and justice, and the implications of extravagant grace. I want this book to communicate authentic good news to its readers in ways that motivate spiritual and practical transformation and appeal to their deepest moral and spiritual intuitions. I hope this book will restore in us a sense of the sacred and inspire a positive vision of what it means to live the Christian life. I hope readers find that this book applies relevantly to everyday life and encourages them to walk in Spirit-inspired love so that, through them, others will come to know the God of love. For me, this is what theology is all about.

At the same time, this book directly challenges certain doctrines and currents of theology. I believe the impetus behind the ease with which the church has periodically justified violent behavior lies in our conceptual image of God and our presuppositions surrounding how God acts in the world. Our theology tends to dictate our behavior. If we can justify God's violence, the next step is to justify our own. My eagerness to write this book, therefore, emerges out of a passion to think differently—albeit biblically—about the character of God. I want to help my students and the church rethink theology outside of what theologian Walter Wink calls "the myth of redemptive violence." According to Wink, the myth of redemptive violence "enshrines the belief that violence saves, that war brings peace, that might makes right. It serves as one of the oldest continuously repeated stories in the world" and pervades the Christian tradition as an archetypal myth.[1]

I do not suggest we throw away two millennia of Christian traditions in favor of the newest trend in theological studies; on the contrary, I suggest that some of our theological traditions may stem from a misinterpretation of God's revelation in Scripture, or from faulty, unexamined presuppositions. In many cases alternative interpretations—some of them historic, venerable, and profound—deserve careful consideration. I want to revisit and reinterpret Christian traditions to help us be more faithful to the God disclosed in Jesus of Nazareth and to offer a theology more relevant to contemporary cultures so we can partner with God in transforming the world with the good news of forgiveness and new life in Jesus Christ. To this end, in the last pages of every chapter I offer a constructive theological perspective that begins with my defining characteristic of God as nonviolent love and that carries all the way through the book from the Trinity to the Last Things.

Students of theology need a fresh glimpse of the love, mercy, and redemptive power of God through Jesus. Christians need to recommit themselves to the call of God to be "ministers of reconciliation" and lovers of both neighbors and enemies even while, at times, responding to violence with nonviolent resistance (2 Cor 5:11–21; Mark 12:31). I am aware, of course, that one book will not fully accomplish this turn toward creative peacemaking that the church so desperately needs; however, it will add to the good work being done by scholars, pastors, teachers, and lay workers in the wider church. I pray that this text will further the academic discussion of many issues in peace theology and in theology in general, and introduce readers anew to the good news of a nonviolent, loving, peaceable God.

1. Walter Wink, "Facing the Myth of Redemptive Violence," *Ekklesia*, November 15, 2014, https://tinyurl.com/2gqsml.

1. Revelation and Theology

I believe . . .

> The . . . theologian who does not find that his work drives him to pray frequently and urgently, from his heart: "God, be merciful to me a sinner," is scarcely fit for the job.
>
> —Emil Brunner, *The Christian Doctrine of God*

> Our theology, since it is a human enterprise, needs to be constantly revised and reformed.
>
> —Donald Bloesch, *Essentials of Evangelical Theology*

How many times have we seen a TV show or read a book with a big "reveal" at the end? The author or producer finally discloses the deeper meaning or the real story or the true identity of a character. This unveiling of the truth surprises us and gives new meaning to the story. The "reveal" always enlightens us with its clearly defined answers and "aha" moments.

Many of us believe divine revelation is God's "big reveal" that finally gives us total understanding of the divine character and way of working in the world. We may believe that revelation only comes through official pronouncements from religious authorities or perhaps through a sacred text such as the Bible, with clear instructions for life that we must simply read and obey. But is the Bible that clear? Does God reveal the divine nature completely through church doctrines and Scripture? Or does God still keep something hidden from us as a mystery? What do we do with revelatory experiences that somehow communicate God to us? And what does it all have to do with theology?

The word "*theology*" describes our way of making sense of revelatory experiences. We always seek to understand and apply what we gain from revelation, whether we realize it or not. In this chapter, I talk not only about the nature of revelation—how God comes to us in our finitude and human history—but also about the task of theology—its definition and purpose. When we "do" theology, we strive to construct a coherent picture of God's character and ways of acting in the world. Most importantly, we do theology to know God. We find out, however, that God is knowable and unknowable at the same time. Our encounter with revelation and our theological task will never end, because we can never fully plumb the depths of God's mystery or exhaust God's revelatory resources. But such knowledge and understanding will always surprise, renew, challenge, and transform us.

The Nature of Revelation

Contemplating divine revelation reminds me of the work of the abstract expressionist artist Mark Rothko. My husband and I have traveled to various places just to stand in front of Rothko's paintings and catch glimpses of the depths of color and layering deep within the pigments. The Rothko Chapel in Houston, Texas, is one of our favorite places to see his work. The artist painstakingly designed the space that would hold his work and engineered the placement of his paintings. He did not want people to come and merely walk around the chapel looking at each canvas as a separate piece, although we do that too. He desired that we first soak in the atmosphere of the entire room as a consecrated space and experience the works as one whole. Rothko hoped each person would find the art an experience that communicated something profound and previously undisclosed to them.

As soon as I stepped into the chapel the first time, I felt the hushed and holy ambiance, a peaceful tranquility. The paintings that dominated each wall appeared as gigantic, silent black sheets of canvas. But as I moved closer and gazed carefully at each piece of art, I noticed they were not black. The longer I stared at these masterpieces, the more colors, patterns, and undulating layers emerged from the paint, interrupting my initial preconceptions. At one moment, I thought I saw red entangled in the black. At another moment, I detected stripes forming a pattern under the darkness. As I stood before each painting, the light shining in from outside changed, and then, so did the paintings, surprising me again with new colors, patterns, and depths of hue. My husband, who had visited the chapel many times before, explained that each time he stood in that room, the shifting light infiltrating the space revealed new and surprising visions of the paintings. He could never completely plumb their depths, never with absolute certainty know what the paintings "really" looked like, and never fully understand Rothko's creative message lying (un)disclosed in each piece.

God discloses the divine self to us in a similar way by revealing a message previously unknown and unexpected. We translate the Greek word *apokalyptein* as "revelation," meaning "a striking disclosure," "an unexpected uncovering," or "an unveiling." Just as the Rothko paintings surprised me with their complexity and the depth of their message, God surprises us by revealing the divine character, actions, and desires for us and the world. Just when we think we understand God, when we believe we have it all figured out, God "changes the light" or interrupts our status quo by revealing something new and unexpected. When God communicates to us, that divine "voice" comes uninvited and as an intrusion that shakes up our preoccupation with ourselves, awakening us from our dogmatic slumbers, challenging and calling us to something new. Philosopher Merold Westphal explains that the silent and revelatory "voice" of God has the "power to break through our prejudices, to disrupt and unsettle them, to call them into question, to show that they need to be revised or replaced, that they are always penultimate and relative, never ultimate or absolute."[1]

God breaks through all obstacles to heal, liberate, and save us. The Hebrew word for "to break through" (*perets*) literally means "to break through a wall" or "to burst through" something hardened into inflexibility. We can apply this notion to our theological task. God breaks through our limitations, our prejudices, and our lack of intellectual humility, revealing something new and previously unknown. We can look to medieval theologian Meister Eckhart to take us even a step farther. He believes that, through divine revelation, God breaks through to us, but in response, we break through to God and lead transformed lives as participants in the life of God. In other words, God comes down to us, breaks through our conceptual walls, and reveals the divine character and will. This revelation, when we truly receive it, raises us up to God, enabling us to live lives transformed by the Spirit of God. So revelation includes both "hearing" and "doing," both a communication from God and a response from us.

We need to remember, however, that God's self-disclosure to us through revelation is never a set of divine propositions that dictate doctrinal belief systems. Instead, as theologian Ray Hart says, revelation serves as the "fundament from which, and against which, and toward which theology thinks."[2] As the foundation from which theology merely *begins* its thinking process, revelation does not give us thoroughly thought-out, totally complete, full-blown doctrines. Rather, revelation unveils facets of God's character and will. It acts as a motivator to heal us and transform us into participants in the work of God in the world.

Revelation never gives us total knowledge of God. It hinges on the fact that despite the surprising moments of self-disclosure, God still remains hidden, shrouded in mystery, and inaccessible to finite creatures of dust. So, like the changing light that precludes total comprehension of the Rothko Chapel paintings, the cloud of unknowing[3] that surrounds God ensures we will never completely clear away the fog. God self-reveals; yet, at the same time, God hides. We "know" God through what God reveals to us, but we live with only partial knowledge. This paradox—divine revelation residing in the midst of divine mystery—keeps us in the game, so to speak. It keeps us seeking, knocking, and asking for more of God. It makes our relationship with God dynamic and alive because the hunt takes precedence over the capture. In order to maintain a dynamic, growing, and intimate relationship

---

1. Merold Westphal, *Whose Community? Which Interpretation? Philosophical Hermeneutics for the Church* (Grand Rapids, MI: Baker Academic, 2009), 153.
2. Ray L. Hart, *Unfinished Man and the Imagination: Toward an Ontology and a Rhetoric of Revelation* (New York: Seabury, 1979), 87.
3. This phrase comes from the title of a mystical text written anonymously in the fourteenth century. *The Cloud of Unknowing* is a major work in the *apophatic* theological tradition, or the "way of the negation," which stresses how we can only speak of God in terms of what God is not or what we cannot say. The *cataphatic* theological tradition, or the "way of affirmation" of images, in contrast, emphasizes positive statements we can make about God, such as "God is love." We need both paths.

with God, we want to keep on hunting, seeking, and catching glimpses of the elusive mystery that we call Father, Son, and Holy Spirit. Because knowing God is a form of union with God, we want to know all we can, while knowing we cannot know everything.[4] So we live on the dash between the year of our birth and the year of our death, seeking to know God in our time, for our context, and within our circumstances.

To be effective, revelation needs to find a conduit that connects it to our brains, to travel the eighteen inches or so (at least figuratively) into our hearts, and then to work its way back out of us into our transformed actions. Every form of communication needs some sort of transmitting medium. Landlines use wires; cell phones and radios use waves; the internet as reached on my computer uses a wireless digital signal. Since revelation is a communication from God, it needs a conduit to get from God to us. We know it must be wireless communication, but what is it exactly? Garrett Green believes that our imaginations, fueled by the image of God in us, serve as the conductors that enable us to receive revelation.[5]

We use our imaginations all the time. Unfortunately, we most often use them when we daydream or worry. But we also use our imaginations when we think about God. Obviously, we cannot audibly hear or visually see God. We cannot examine God under a microscope, send a text or email to God, or call God on the phone. Consequently, we use our imaginations when we think about God and how God acts in our lives and in the rest of the world. In fact, our capacity to reason is intimately connected to our ability to imagine. When we dream, invent, write, think theologically, or do anything creative, we use our imagination. The Protestant Reformer Martin Luther, minus an imagination, would never have moved the medieval church into a new age of reformation. Rev. Dr. Martin Luther King Jr., without an imagination, would never have pushed the nation toward civil rights for black Americans. By *imagination* I do not mean daydreaming or thinking up images of unicorns or other fantastic objects that have no purchase in reality. I am talking about our minds' creative ability to map out theological expressions of the ineffable God we see described in narrative and poetic form in Scripture and experienced in our day-to-day lives. In fact, the imagination serves as the key or the medium that connects us to God, and as the conduit through which God reveals the divine mind and character to us.

The image of God, which we will discuss at length in chapter 10, serves as the point of commonality and connection between divinity and humanity and makes God accessible to us through our imaginations. It enables our imaginations to interpret revelation and to imagine God correctly so we can gain real knowledge of God.[6] We see that God's imagination connects to us through *our* imagination,

---

4. Paul Tillich, *Systematic Theology*, vol. 1 (Chicago: University of Chicago Press, 1973), 153.
5. For a helpful treatise on the imagination and its connection to God and the *imago Dei*, see Garrett Green, *Imagining God: Theology and the Religious Imagination* (San Francisco: Harper & Row, 1989).
6. Green, *Imagining God*, 84–87. Green argues that the imagination is the *imago Dei* in us.

opening up channels of communication that enable us to work together to transform the world for God's glory.

Yes, God has an imagination! The second creation story in Genesis 2 reveals the reality of the divine imagination. You know the story: God creates the human being from the mud. The Bible says, "Then the Lord God *formed* man from the dust of the ground and breathed into his nostrils the breath of life; and the man became a living being" (2:7; emphasis mine). The word we translate "formed" (*yatsar*) means "to squeeze something into shape," but another form of the verb (*yetser*) carries the notion of a "mental impulse" or "imagination"—in this case, the divine imagination intentionally playing in the dirt and creating a human being for mutual partnership in taking care of the world and working with God for God's purposes.

Jewish theologians talk about how in using the divine *yetser* (imagination) to create humanity, God gifted us with the *yetser hatov* or the good imagination, the ability to imagine the good, to know the good, and to know the good God fully. Before spiritual ignorance and infection through sin set in, the image of God worked in us and enabled us to know God completely, without taint or corruption. With the entrance of sin, however, the *yetser hatov* lost its luster and became dulled by corrosion so that human beings can no longer imagine God clearly or determine the divine will without error. Our spiritual ignorance dimmed the image of God so we can no longer see the divine light clearly. Due to our spiritual ignorance, our humanity made in the image of God found itself saddled with an imagination infected by a *yetser hara*, or an imagination prone to imagining evil. The *yetser hara* drew us farther and farther from God as we began to imagine ways of life without God. Consequently, we doomed ourselves for an existence separated from God. Christians believe our salvation through Jesus Christ results in our transformation; we are made new creations, redeemed from the *yetser hara* and, through sanctification, we are enabled again to imagine God in valid ways.

That said, God has gifted us with the ability to imagine, to participate with God in imagining a new creation, to be a "creative vicar of God" as those created in God's image.[7] The imagination functions as a point of contact, a conduit through which God discloses God's self to us and enables us to explore God, the world, and ourselves in new and creative ways. So our imaginations play a significant role in receiving divine revelation.

General Revelation

Equipped with the image of God in us and outfitted with our imaginations, we gain access to divine self-disclosure from outside of us through what theologians have termed "general" and "special" revelation. These two modes of revelation developed

---

7. Richard Kearney, *The Wake of Imagination: Toward a Postmodern Culture* (London: Routledge, 1994), 65–71. See also Pope John Paul II's papal encyclical on our co-creative abilities with God called *Laborem Exercens* (On Human Work), 1981.

in Christian thought in order to answer one of the major questions that has haunted theologians for millennia: At what point does divine revelation make *effective* contact with humans? The word "effective" refers to revelation complete enough to lead people to salvation, to redemption in Jesus Christ. In Michelangelo's fresco *The Creation of Adam*, God and Adam reach out to each other, *almost* making contact. The narrow space of air between their outstretched fingers speaks volumes and leads us to ask the question, Where and how do the divine and human effectively and salvifically "touch"? Theologians have spent decades arguing over the validity of general revelation for salvation. Some, such as John Calvin and Karl Barth, claim that the divine and the human cannot make effective contact through that form of revelation at all—the fingers do not touch. Others, like Thomas Aquinas, John Wesley, and Paul Tillich, make the opposite claim. So which is it?

Before we answer that question, we need to define the terms. *General revelation*, sometimes called "natural revelation," comes to us first through the natural created world. Through general revelation, God discloses the divine character and nature through generic or natural means to everyone at all times in every place through the multiplicity and diversity of all natural phenomena. In fact, Tillich notes, "The mediums of revelation taken from nature are as innumerable as the natural objects."[8] Even stones can mediate something about God when we look at their enduring qualities and then metaphorically see God as the "rock of ages." We gaze into the night sky and see the stars, planets, and vastness of space and imagine how it all came into existence, eventually coming to the conclusion that this could not have happened by chance. And as we have already seen, in interpreting nature we are using our imagination, which is also part of the created order.

We see support for the divine communication through general revelation in Scripture as well. Psalm 19 tells us, "The heavens are telling the glory of God; and the firmament proclaims his handiwork. Day to day pours forth speech, and night to night declares knowledge. There is no speech, nor are there words; their voice is not heard; yet their voice goes out through all the earth, and their words to the end of the world" (vv. 1–4). In other words, all of creation, the entire universe, communicates with us and reveals something to us about God. Creation does not speak to us in an audible voice, but the majesty of the heavenly expanse, the grandeur of the bright stars and planets, and the mystery of the dark unknown all attest to the existence and character of God. Another passage in the Psalms points us to the earth itself as a testimony that reveals God: "The voice of the Lord is over the waters; the God of glory thunders, the Lord, over mighty waters" (29:3–4). The psalm goes on to describe God's power seen in roaring fire, magnificent forests, flowing waters, and raging winds. Nature, in its glory, reveals God to us. In fact, Romans 1:20 tells us that God's "eternal power and divine nature, invisible though they are, have been understood and seen through the things he has made."

8. Tillich, *Systematic Theology*, vol. 1, 189.

The creation of the universe and of our beautiful small planet all mediate to us a revelation of God as creator.

Our conscience serves as the second conduit for general revelation. It can mediate an understanding of the Divine to us through our inner moral convictions, when we "instinctively" know the right thing to do or the most loving way to treat someone. In Romans 2:14-15, Paul explains that when gentiles, "who do not possess the law, do instinctively what the law requires, these, though not having the law, are a law to themselves. They show that what the law requires is written on their hearts, to which their own conscience also bears witness." Our conscience acts as the medium through which we can receive divine revelation concerning the morality set forth in God's law: do not murder, steal, covet, worship false gods, commit adultery, and so forth. Most of us seem to possess some inner, innate sensitivity that communicates right and wrong and also drives us to seek and to find God. So, general revelation provides us with a basic foundation for gaining knowledge of God, a starting point that motivates us to dig deeper, seek more, and fill in the gaps. The knowledge gained through nature and conscience is not *complete* knowledge. Yet we receive the part and thus are lured to seek the whole.[9]

Although we have only discussed the two most significant mediums of general revelation, we can point briefly to others. Many Christian theologians believe we can come to know God more fully through seeking to understand other faith traditions and through secular literature, music, art, and films—all of which use imagination, feeling, and reason. If all truth is God's truth,[10] as some claim, that truth can reveal itself to us in manifold ways, with a multitude of resources. Instead of being afraid we only understand in part, we can have confidence in our ability to connect with God through these faculties, though in ways that leave room for mystery and further growth.

Special Revelation

Can general revelation lead us to know and understand the Christian message of salvation through Jesus Christ? Most theologians believe not, because it only provides a basic perception of the reality and existence of God and not the more specific knowledge of Jesus. In other words, it cannot lead to salvation. They would argue that in order to receive saving knowledge of Christ, we need more specific revelation from God. *Special revelation* refers to the activity of the triune God in creating, redeeming, and sanctifying the world, but especially with Jesus Christ and his life, teachings, death, and resurrection as the center. We comprehend this

---

9. I have not dealt with general revelation mediated through other religious traditions. That is the topic of a future book.

10. This phrase was coined in a well-known book of the same name: Arthur F. Holmes, *All Truth Is God's Truth* (Grand Rapids, MI: Eerdmans, 1977).

saving work of God through Scripture and tradition, but also through historical events, personal experience, and the proclamation of the Word.

Revelation through Scripture. Scripture expresses a double nature: classical literature written by human authors *and* a divinely inspired sacred text. Ordinary human beings wrote the books in the Bible, but Christians traditionally claim that God spoke through ordinary people and still does so today. So when we read and interpret the Bible, we need to ask a double question: What did the author mean to say culturally, historically, and circumstantially? And what does God intend to disclose to us, through this text, about the divine character, salvation, and holy living? The Bible speaks to us with a human voice as authors communicate their own contexts, issues, and beliefs. But it also breaks into the mundane life on earth with the divine voice that clears the fog concealing God, and makes the transcendent deity immanent to us by gracing us with something new and transformative.

Scripture consists of many genres: prophetic, narrative, prescriptive, wisdom, and hymnic literature. First, in *prophetic* discourse, the author speaks the words of another, a voice behind a voice, so to speak.[11] The Nicene Creed reflects the idea of a double author, stating, "We believe in the Holy Spirit . . . who has spoken through the prophets."[12] For the most part, we interpret this form of revelation as an unveiling of the future, the divine plan for history and, especially, for the last days. Interpreting the prophetic books as merely pointing to the future, however, risks reducing them to apocalyptic predictions that have no currency in the present. Instead, we need to understand that these books reveal much to us about the promises and faithfulness of God for fulfilling the divine plan for all creation. But we should not limit or reduce revelation to the genre of the prophetic.

Second, *narrative* discourse, which composes most of the Pentateuch (the first five books of the Hebrew Bible), the Gospels, and Acts, recounts the history and experiences of a people and their God. Through these texts we can trace the hand of God in key events and significant circumstances. Narrative literature functions as a community's confessions of faith that enable us to learn of the divine character, nature, and will. This literature reveals to us the faith of a people and the faithfulness of their God and, in so doing, provides the church with an important witness for a future of hope in our own journeys with God.

Third, *prescriptive* discourse reveals the "will of God" as seen, for instance, in the books of Leviticus and Deuteronomy. But this form of literature does not only dictate law and command. Beginning with the liberation from slavery in Egypt, it also unveils the heart of the divine covenant with God's people—obedience

---

11. Paul Ricoeur, *Essays on Biblical Interpretation*, ed. Lewis S. Mudge (Philadelphia: Fortress, 1980), 75–76.
12. Nicene Creed, *Evangelical Lutheran Worship* (Minneapolis: Augsburg Fortress, 2006), 104. This wording first published by English Language Liturgical Consultation in *Praying Together*, 1988.

not to the letter of the law, but to the spirit of love instilled in their hearts. In Deuteronomy 6:4–6, we read the great *Shema*, the most significant command for the Hebrew people and, in fact, one that remains just as important today: "Hear, O Israel; The Lord is our God. The Lord alone. You shall love the Lord your God with all your heart, and with all your soul, and with all your might. Keep these words that I am commanding you today in your heart." Jesus proclaims the covenantal intent of this law in Matthew 22:37, basically repeating the same words found in Deuteronomy, transferring the movement of faith from an external obedience to an internal obedience born from the love of God that works through the Spirit. The apostle Paul carries this internal heart condition toward God and others into his theology as well, stating that

> you show that you are a letter of Christ, prepared by us, written not with ink but with the Spirit of the living God, not on tablets of stone but on tablets of human hearts. Such is the confidence that we have through Christ toward God. Not that we are competent of ourselves to claim anything as coming from us; our competence is from God, who has made us competent to be ministers of a new covenant, not of letter but of spirit; for the letter kills, but the Spirit gives life. (2 Cor 3:3–6)

The passages of prescriptive discourse throughout the Bible reveal God's will for a faith based on the internal attitude of the heart, a love-based rather than a rule-based faith.

Fourth, according to philosopher Paul Ricoeur, *wisdom* discourse "brings to light the overwhelming question of the sense or nonsense of existence."[13] It reveals the link between human action and the world, teaching us how to endure suffering and find meaning in the inevitability of chaos in our lives. Wisdom literature shows us how to behave in trying circumstances and as God's people. The signature text for this form of literature is the book of Job. After all his suffering, his adamant inquiries to God, and the constant question of "Why?" on Job's lips, God finally appears in a whirlwind and reveals the divine character and might for Job to see. Because of God's self-disclosure, Job learns and experiences a fresh, new intimacy with God. And through Job, we receive the divine revelation and can apply it to our lives. Divine revelation via wisdom literature discloses, clears the fog, and allows us to discover God anew in every circumstance. It teaches us how to negotiate the vicissitudes of life.[14]

Finally, we come to *hymnic* discourse. The songs of praise and prayers of supplication, such as those found in the Psalms and elsewhere, reveal to us the heartfelt emotional response of God's people as they celebrate triumphs and suffer tragedies.

13. Ricoeur, *Essays on Biblical Interpretation*, 86.
14. Ricoeur, *Essays on Biblical Interpretation*, 56–58.

Hymnic discourse reveals a God who listens and who acts on our behalf, and a God who both celebrates and grieves with us. We listen in on a community's extolling of God as creator, protector, comforter, and deliverer, knowing that through their experience and the words on the page, God reveals God's self to us too.

Each of the modes of scriptural discourse reveals God through various means. Theologian Karl Barth (1886–1968) organized the revelation of God through Scripture into three categories: the *revealed* word, the *written* word, and the *proclaimed* word. We might put it another way: revelation comes through the incarnate Son of God as the *living* word, through the Bible as the *written* word, and through preaching as the *spoken* word. All of these forms of scriptural revelation hinge on the Trinitarian understanding of God: the Father has "spoken" through the Holy Spirit, "animated with the Spirit of Christ" the Son.[15] And the triune God still speaks to us today. The Holy Spirit who was active in composing the Bible all those centuries ago remains active in helping us understand it in our present time.

But what is the goal of special revelation through Scripture in all three of its forms? I think the Bible itself reveals its goal. First, Jesus speaks to his disciples, revealing the purpose for his instruction, which we have in Scripture: "I have said these things to you so that my joy may be in you, and that your joy may be complete" (John 15:11). The writer of 1 John echoes this purpose, stating, "We are writing these things so that our joy may be complete" (1:4). But John 20:31 reveals what I believe remains the most significant purpose of Scripture: "But these are written so that you may come to believe that Jesus is the Messiah, the Son of God, and that through believing you may have life in his name." The words of Jesus and the Johannine writer reveal God's desire for us to love God, to love each other, and to proclaim the gospel message of the kingdom of God and eternal life through Jesus Christ. As a result, we all reap the benefit of a restored relationship with God and a mutual partnership with the divine community in transforming others with this message of hope. God's revelation through the written, living, and spoken word always points us to Jesus Christ and the salvific message of redemption and the transformed life on earth to follow.

Revelation through tradition. Although opinions and even doctrines differ depending upon the stream of Christianity, the Christian tradition also serves as the medium through which God reveals the divine character, will, and plans. Although those in Protestant denominations tend to make a broad division between Scripture and tradition, the Scriptures actually form the foundation of tradition. The New Testament was the first written expression of the Christian tradition after the death of Jesus and the apostles. Furthermore, the church existed for centuries before it actually recognized the Bible as its own canon of Scripture. So the writings

---

15. Thomas A. Hoffman, "Inspiration, Normativeness, Canonicity, and the Unique Sacred Character of the Bible," *Catholic Biblical Quarterly* 44 (1982): 457.

of Scripture, presided over by the Holy Spirit, first articulated the tradition of the church. The Bible itself, therefore, is a product of tradition.

Of course, we also see the work of tradition in our imaginative construction of creeds, doctrines, liturgies, hymns, devotional practices, commentaries, and theological treatises. But we do not pull our theological traditions from thin air. The Holy Spirit guides and teaches us to contribute to Christian tradition through these varied expressions. We can believe that God reveals God's self to us in the work of the church as it develops, grows, and continually reinterprets the Christian tradition. In fact, for the Roman Catholic and Eastern Orthodox churches, Scripture and tradition hold almost equal value and authority as conduits through which God reveals the divine character to us. They believe that the Holy Spirit not only inspired the Bible, but also plays a significant role in the handing down of doctrines, creeds, and liturgies that people still use today. So for these denominations, tradition flows seamlessly from Genesis to Jesus and from Jesus to our present moment.

Many Protestants, on the other hand, with their historical motto of *sola scriptura*, or "Scripture alone," believe that the Bible alone serves as the authoritative tool that reveals God to us. They believe that no other text, doctrine, or creed is needed to lead them to salvation through Jesus Christ. In this case, tradition, although important to the church, takes a back seat to the Bible as the most significant source of divine revelation. Most Protestants appreciate tradition and regard it as essential for understanding and articulating their faith, but tend to claim that it does not serve as a medium through which we receive any substantive revelation of God. A notable exception is the Anglican idea of the *Three-Legged Stool*, consisting of Scripture, tradition, and reason, and the further elaboration of this called the *Wesleyan Quadrilateral* (meaning "four components"), which adds experience to the mix as well. These Protestant approaches recognize that even if we claim to receive revelation from "Scripture alone," we do in fact use other faculties in reading and interpreting it. We will discuss these approaches more in the following chapter.

The Nonviolent Nature of Revelation

Revelation through both Scripture and tradition always requires responsible interpretive skills. As part of our interpretive task, we must try to distinguish between a) the personal human witness to various events in the Bible, with their historical predicaments, contexts, and belief structures, and b) the self-disclosure of God in Jesus Christ with the message of redemption, peace, and goodwill to all people. As Christian theologians, we must make a fundamental distinction in our approach to understanding the Bible as revelation—a distinction stressed most strongly in Eastern Orthodoxy: our theology and interpretive habits should always point to Jesus Christ as the center of our faith. If we believe that God most fully and clearly reveals the divine character and will in the person of Jesus of Nazareth, then we need to maintain a theological consistency and interpret the revelation of both the Hebrew Bible and the New Testament through the life, teachings, death, and resurrection of God's fullest revelation, Jesus Christ. And since the purpose of the Bible, as we saw above, serves as a witness that leads us to the fullness of joy and eternal life through Jesus, then interpreting divine revelation through the lens of Jesus will keep us from irresponsible errors of judgment about what general and special revelation say about the human condition.

We have, unfortunately, seen these errors throughout our Christian history with the participation of the church in such things as crusades and inquisitions, slavery and the oppression of minority groups. God gives us the responsibility to receive divine revelation and to listen first of all to the voices of the widow, the orphan, and the stranger, the oppressed, and others who make unconditional claims on us for mercy, justice, and love. This emphasis has a strong history throughout both the prophetic tradition of the Hebrew Bible and Jesus's teachings. The revelation of God through Jesus specifically rejects violence, oppression, and abuse of others so that any interpretation of revelation that tries to marry doctrine to violence against others makes for an unholy alliance.[16] In addition to understanding revelation consistently through the lens of Jesus, we must seek to understand both general revelation and the special revelation of the Bible through what has been called "the revelation of the victim." Philosopher and literary critic René Girard goes as far as to claim that Jesus most fully reveals the suffering and innocence of this world's perennial victims, and he further believes that the Bible uniquely and clearly champions the perspective of the victim. We see, with both the prophetic tradition and Jesus as our lens, that Scripture emphasizes the liberation of captives and the inbreaking of the alternative to violence in God's kingdom of mercy, justice, and love. With this understanding, we can begin to do theology that adequately reflects the gospel message of true "goodwill" toward all humanity in light of a God of infinite love.

What Is Theology?

Now that we have thought about revelation, we can begin to talk about theology. The task of theology, according to theologian Paul Tillich, "is to explain the contents of the Christian faith."[17] Consequently, this book attempts to explain what we believe and why we believe it so we can better understand our faith and the God in whom we place that faith. *Theology* is from the Greek word *theos*, meaning "God," and *logos*, which means "words about" or "the study of," so theology is the study of God, words about God, or, to be true to the philosophical tradition, "reasoning

16. Westphal, *Whose Community?*, 150–54.
17. Tillich, *Systematic Theology*, vol. 1, 61.

about God." Simply put, theology is talking about God. The theological enterprise encompasses a study of much more than God, however; it includes everything under the divine realm—subjects such as Trinity, Jesus, the Holy Spirit, salvation, creation, humanity, sin, the church, and the end times. Consequently, as we work our way through this book, we will explore these various topics in turn.

Theological Task and Purpose

Of course, we do not enter into the theological arena without a task and purpose in mind. Theology requires careful thought and critical analysis of the truths and revelation in Scripture, tradition, and our already formulated beliefs so that we can continually develop and articulate models of faith that address relevant issues in our relationship with God, in the life of the church, and in the divine mission to transform the world into a place of love, justice, and righteousness. So we might say that theology traverses the distance back and forth between two poles—the divine truth of revelation and the everyday life in which we receive God's truth. We find we must continually reinterpret Christianity's foundational truths in clear, comprehensive language that diverse cultures and peoples find relevant for accomplishing God's purposes.

Our continual reinterpretations keep our relationship with God dynamic and intimate as we persevere in our search for the fullness of God's truth especially revealed to us in Jesus Christ. In fact, the task of theology is to keep on asking questions and pursuing answers in order to nurture and sustain our faith. So theology is a questioning endeavor rather than an exercise in standardizing and reifying official doctrine. We never finish the theological task, never find all the answers, and never experience absolute certainty. Nevertheless, our faith drives us to understand the things of God, and the more we understand the things of God, the more we know God. Consequently, we enjoy a more intimate relationship not only with God but also with each other as we continually live out the most significant purpose for our theological endeavors—transformed lives for God's glory and the furtherance of God's kingdom.

Some students protest the amount of work that reading, praying, thinking, interpreting, reasoning, and constructing our theological belief system require, often asking, "What is the purpose?" I always answer with one word: "Transformation." We do the hard work of theology so that God through the Holy Spirit can transform us into the image of Jesus Christ. Theology transforms us into the life of Christ, changing how we perceive the world, how we treat others, and how we list our priorities. When students ask about how to begin this transformative theological process, three characteristics or virtues come to mind: faith, humility, and love. Let us look at each in turn.

First, faith. Fourth-century theologian St. Augustine of Hippo says, "Do not seek in order to believe, but believe that you may understand," expressing a dynamic faith that restlessly and persistently pursues a deeper understanding of and intimacy with God.[18] Seven centuries later, Anselm of Canterbury echoes Augustine and says basically the same thing: "Faith seeks understanding." The lure of understanding the one in whom we believe drives our faith with an *eros* kind of craving to know the nature and character of God, to comprehend how God operates in the world, to catch a glimpse of what pleases God, what motivates God, and what God desires. Our faith hungers unceasingly for the God in whom we put our faith. In other words, our faith in God generates an unquenchable thirst to understand God in every way humanly possible so we can say with the Psalmist, "As the deer pants [longingly] for the water brooks, so my soul pants I pant [longingly] for You, O God. My soul (my life, my inner self) thirsts for God, for the living God. When shall I come and see the face of God?" (42:1–2 AMP). *Panting* and *longing:* these are words that describe strong desire, so strong that nothing can satisfy us except the one we desire to know and understand fully—God. So we study theology, not to gain knowledge for the sake of knowledge, merely to feed our intellects. We study theology in order to understand God, to feed our souls, and to draw nearer to the divine presence as an act of love.

In addition, we study to make our faith our own—not the faith of our parents, pastors, Sunday school teachers, youth leaders, or college religion professors. Struggling through the theological issues, questioning what we have always believed, agonizing over decisions between doctrines, and constructing beliefs for ourselves enable us to remain strong in our faith during momentous events, life's lows, and especially life's highs. Our faith becomes more significant as we go through the process of figuring it out for ourselves; when we can own our faith, we seem more inclined to invest our lives in it.

We often mistake a sense of certainty about what we believe we know about God as faith in God. But absolute certainty and faith are opposites. In fact, they are downright incompatible. Remember why God claimed to be Abraham's friend? Not because Abraham had absolute certainty, but because he had *faith*. Abraham *believed God* (Jas 2:23 AMP). Faith and doubt as questioning actually work together. They complement each other, walking hand in hand as companions. Doubts about God and the theological issues surrounding God make faith necessary. So never fear your doubts. Instead, know that doubt strengthens faith and motivates us to search for the truths about God. Doubt opens our minds to learn and keeps us humble.

The second characteristic for a transformed life involves humility—humility both theological and practical in nature. "Lay first the foundation of humility," says

---

18. Augustine, "Tractate 29, John 7:14–18," *Tractates on the Gospel of John* (New Advent, n.d.), https://tinyurl.com/yagp4efc.

St. Augustine of Hippo.[19] Why do we need to approach the theological endeavor with humility, you might ask? Because we are not God; we are finite creatures with no unmediated access to God. We cannot physically touch, see, hear, smell, or taste God. We cannot put a piece of God under a microscope and examine the divine substance. We cannot email God and get a response, or call God on the divine hotline and have a one-on-one auditory conversation. We cannot meet God for coffee or take God out to dinner and linger long over dessert exchanging ideas. Now don't get me wrong—I am *not* saying we cannot communicate with God or that God does not communicate with us. But we have only mediated access to God—access through indirect means. In other words, our access to God occurs through many forms such as Scripture, our imaginations, people in our lives, experiences, circumstances, music, art, stories, historical events, and so on.

Because all our information about God is mediated (as opposed to direct knowledge), we never achieve absolute accuracy in what we think we know; now we "know only in part" (1 Cor 13:12). Although God reveals to us the divine nature and will, God still remains shrouded in mystery, veiled with incomprehensibility. For now, we "see in a mirror, dimly" and therefore need to remember that even our best interpretations do not quite allow us to fully apprehend the totality of God. Consequently, we cannot know anything about God with absolute scientific certainty (and even scientific knowledge is uncertain!). This lack of complete, direct knowledge should generate in us a sense of theological humility. We could be wrong about how we have interpreted the evidence that provides us with knowledge of God. Someone else that we vehemently disagree with could have it right. Or we may all be wrong! As finite creatures with limitations on knowledge, we have the obligation to interpret responsibly and to examine the evidence, to hold our interpretations with openness to new evidence and viewpoints. We must always cultivate humility of heart and maintain a teachable spirit.

The third and most important characteristic of a transformed life is love—love for God and for others as Jesus commanded. The apostle Paul also says, "With all humility and gentleness, with patience, [bear] with one another in love" (Eph 4:2). We cannot overstate the importance of love. Jesus makes it clear when he boils down all 613 of the *mitzvot* from Jewish law into just two commandments: to love God and to love others, including ourselves. And Scripture tells us to do *all* things with love (1 Cor 16:14). But we especially need to practice loving others when it comes to interpreting the Bible and doing theology. If we do theology merely to show off our newfound knowledge, we waste our time. Christian theology is always about showing others the love of God as revealed in Jesus. So we work through our personal theological systems, praying that God will use our knowledge and beliefs

---

19. Augustine, "Confessions," in *Saint Augustine's Childhood: Confessions*, book 1, trans. Garry Wills (New York: Viking, 2001), 7.10.

to transform us into the image of Christ. Hopefully we will get to a point where we can say with Paul, "For to me, living is Christ" and "It is no longer I who live, but it is Christ who lives in me," and with John the Baptist, "He must increase, but I must decrease" (Phil 1:21; Gal 2:20; John 3:30).

Some Christians get very upset with those with whom they disagree, often to the detriment of the gospel message and the proclamation of the kingdom of God. We tend to cast judgment on others, sometimes with vitriol and venom, bringing shame to the name of Christ—the one sent to redeem the world through the love of God and the one we are told to imitate. I tell my students to remember that if they are judging a person, they are not loving him or her. Furthermore, if we all are only partially right at best and possibly totally wrong, who are we to judge another person's theology? We will better serve God by acting according to 1 Peter 4:8, which exhorts us to "maintain constant love for one another, for love covers a multitude of sins." All of us who interpret the Bible and attempt to understand God through our theological constructions are in the same boat, floating on the same unfathomable ocean, trying to scan the depths of God's riches for us (Rom 11:33). So let us try, through prayer, receptivity, discernment, and the rigor of careful thought, not only to seek to understand God, but also to learn to give others the benefit of the doubt in love—even if we think they are wrong. Permit faith to motivate your lust for God, allow humility to permeate the path of discovery, and let love cover the sins of error—both ours and others'.

2. Hermeneutics

I believe . . .

> In an attempt to simplify, we try to force the Bible's cacophony of voices into a single tone, to turn a complicated and at times troubling holy text into a list of bullet points we can put in a manifesto or creed. More often than not, we end up more committed to what we want the Bible to say than what it actually says.
>
> —Rachel Held Evans, *A Year of Biblical Womanhood*

> The moment of interpretation . . . is also the moment of the hermeneutical circle between the understanding initiated by the reader and the proposals of meaning offered by the text.
>
> —Paul Ricoeur, *Hermeneutics and the Human Sciences*

Every semester, some of my students ask innocently why we have to interpret the Bible. "Can't we just read it and easily understand what it means (especially with those words of Jesus printed in red)?" Yet in our libraries, literally thousands of books line the biblical and theological studies shelves, implying that, most likely, the contents of any two of these books do not agree completely. Why the conflicts between interpretations? If Christianity bases its beliefs on one book, the Bible, why do interpretations of its content vary so drastically? And where do we begin in the search for the "correct" interpretations?

My answer: we should begin at the beginning—with the science of interpretation, called hermeneutics. The word *hermeneutics* derives from the Greek word *hermeneuein* and means "to interpret" or "to translate." The noun form of that word, *hermeneus*, means an "interpreter" or "translator." The more interesting etymology of the word, however, derives from the name of the Greek messenger god, Hermes. As the inventor of language, he delivers important messages back and forth among the gods and between the gods and human beings. He is, however, a tricky divinity, one who does not always communicate his messages clearly. At times he may even lie. He likes to speak in riddles; in the very revealing of his message Hermes often intentionally conceals the true meaning of his communication. He delights in the confusion his messages bring to bear on the recipients. His confounding communiques demand interpretation, hermeneutical skills that enable us to disclose the mystery inherent in any message. And we certainly need to practice these skills when reading the Bible.

Methods for Interpreting the Bible

Ever since the tower of Babel when God confused the languages, human beings have had to exercise hermeneutical skills to understand one another and the texts they write and read. Indeed, throughout Christian history hermeneuts, or interpreters, have provided readers with various methods to interpret, to understand, and to apply the Bible.

Early and Medieval Hermeneutics

Early Christian theologians grasped the notion that the Bible contains deep spiritual truths, often overlooked if read in a narrow, literal sense. These early hermeneuts applied the ideas of the threefold body, soul, and spirit to the Bible and distinguished between the a) *literal* (body), b) *moral* (soul), and c) *spiritual/allegorical* (spirit) senses of a given passage of Scripture. In the medieval period a fourth category, the anagogical sense, was added to this list, which we now know as the *Four-fold Method*. (Jewish medieval interpreters used similar methods, and even extolled the overflowing of many different meanings of scriptural texts as a blessing rather than a problem!)[1]

To determine the *literal* sense of Scripture we look at the "plain meaning," or what the text says directly. To determine the *moral* sense, we look for the ethical message of the text, the part that tells us how to live godly lives. For the *spiritual or allegorical* sense of Scripture, we explore the meaning of deep theological truths buried in the text. Many ancient and medieval theologians believed this method produced the deepest truths found in the Bible. The *anagogical* sense of Scripture explores the mystical interpretations, seeking to explain future events, the human soul, and the life to come. Even though we still implement some of these ancient and medieval methods, at the time of the Reformation the most radical Protestants largely renounced use of any but the literal sense. Since then, however, theologians and biblical scholars have investigated ways to understand the Bible responsibly, including using all four of these approaches.

Reformation and Protestant Hermeneutics

The English Reformation took a different turn from the radical Protestantism of Calvin and Zwingli, who allowed only the literal sense of Scripture. The Anglican priest Richard Hooker (1554–1600) used Scripture, tradition, and reason to construct and define theological beliefs. This approach, called the *Anglican Three-Legged Stool*, comes from the idea that three legs will provide a firm footing. Neglecting the use of one leg leads to the "stool" of interpretation falling over—a metaphor

---

1. Gerald L. Bruns, *The History of Hermeneutics* (New Haven, CT: Yale University Press, 1992).

for irresponsible theological hermeneutics. Later, interpreting the thought of John Wesley (1702–1791), Methodists added a fourth category, the experience of God, to the Anglican Three-Legged Stool to make up what we now call the *Wesleyan Quadrilateral*: Scripture, tradition, reason, and experience as tools for constructing theology. Because these methods apply directly to the process of theological construction, we will unpack this method of interpretation later in this chapter.

Modern and Philosophical Hermeneutics

The nineteenth-century philologist and philosopher Friedrich Schleiermacher first emphasized the circular motion of biblical interpretation. In a concept that became commonly known as the *Hermeneutical Circle*, he articulated how readers of texts try to understand the parts in reference to the whole, and the whole in reference to the parts. In Schleiermacher's words, we seek "to find the spirit of the whole through the individual, and through the whole to grasp the individual."[2] For example, we have already mentioned how Christian theology understands the whole of Scripture through the person of Jesus (a foundational tenet of Eastern Orthodox hermeneutics) and we, in turn, understand Jesus best through a holistic reading of the entire Bible. Another circular method of interpretation, called the *Hermeneutical Spiral*, focuses on pre-understanding, exegesis, explanation, and understanding. According to this method, we believe we already understand the meaning of a text. Consequently, we study and exegete the text, and that in-depth exploration enables us to explain its meaning. This process either confirms our pre-understanding, denies and corrects our pre-understanding, or enhances our pre-understanding in ways that extend our knowledge and application of the text. Modern hermeneuts have contributed to a growing philosophical movement in the nineteenth and twentieth centuries that seeks to understand hermeneutics scientifically and continues to influence modern theologians and biblical scholars today.

Liberation Hermeneutics

In this book, I draw upon the modern philosophical tradition as well as another significant modern development that arises out of the strong prophetic tradition within the Hebrew Bible and New Testament: liberation hermeneutics. This hermeneutical approach requires us to read the Bible through the eyes of the oppressed and poor. Liberation hermeneutics bases its interpretations upon the attitude of God toward those who live on the margins of society and find themselves condemned, avoided, ignored, or abused by the people in power. Using the

---

2. Quoted in C. Mantzavinos, "Hermeneutics," in *The Stanford Encyclopedia of Philosophy* (Spring 2020 Edition), ed. Edward N. Zalta, https://tinyurl.com/yb5decpd.

Bible, the *hermeneutics of suspicion* (see below), and personal experience, liberation perspectives purposely produce theology that is relevant and helpful to people in socially and politically oppressive contexts. Liberation theologian Leonardo Boff offers this definition: "The liberation theologian goes to the Scriptures bearing the whole weight of the problems, sorrows, and hopes of the poor, seeking light and inspiration from the divine word." He says that "once they have understood the real situation of the oppressed, theologians have to ask: What does the Word of God have to say about this?"[3] The word of God, as we shall see, says plenty about justice for the poor and oppressed. This prominent theme occurs not only in the prophets of the Hebrew Bible but also in the words of Jesus, who indicates that those whom society rejects, God accepts. Black theology similarly interprets the Bible in light of the experience of slavery and racial oppression, opening the Scriptures in ways that speak to both oppressed and oppressors. It offers a critique of abusive structures that harm God's creatures as well as new, hopeful ways of thinking that stress the importance of justice, grace, and practical application in striving for the reign of God.

Thrownness and Presuppositions

Even when implementing one or more of these hermeneutical methods, we do not pull our diverse interpretations from thin air. They emerge from somewhere; we think, interpret, believe, and act in certain ways for several reasons. Scholars who work in the area of hermeneutics identify at least two major hindrances that limit our ways of perceiving the world and that may distort how we interpret texts.

Thrownness

Twentieth-century philosopher Martin Heidegger, echoing the nineteenth-century Danish philosopher Søren Kierkegaard, uses the term *thrownness* to describe the fact that people are born into the contexts of family, society, culture, and world-views that predate their existence.[4] For example, I was born in Niscayuna, New York, into a lower middle-class Lutheran family of immigrants from Denmark. My family held particular views on God, work ethics, family values, politics, and human rights. I absorbed these perspectives and eventually took them as my own. As a child raised in the North in the 1960s and '70s, I grew up thinking that people from the South dressed in overalls and straw hats and chewed on pieces of hay. Because of how they spoke, I had the impression they were a bit lacking in intelligence! Of course, TV shows like *Hee Haw* helped form these perceptions. My husband, on the

---

3. Leonardo Boff, *Introducing Liberation Theology*, trans. Paul Burns (Maryknoll, NY: Orbis, 1987), 32.
4. Søren Kierkegaard, *Repetition*, trans. Walter Lowrie (New York: Harper Torchbooks, 1941), 104. The term *Geworfenheit* is translated as "thrust" instead of "thrown" in this translation.

other hand, grew up as a Baptist in Mississippi in the 1960s and believed that New York was filled with cold, unfriendly people living in a tangle of barren concrete, asphalt, and tall buildings. Of course, we both now know that the South cultivates very smart people, that the North abounds with natural beauty and grandeur, and that people who wear overalls and chew on hay live in both the North and the South! Nonetheless, neither one of us had a choice about where we were born, our family of origin, or the views held by the society into which we were thrown. For better or for worse, these factors both formed and informed our thinking about the world. And because we are all so entirely immersed in our cultures and traditions, we cannot merely set them aside and think differently. They remain a part of who we are, yet the voices we hear in our heads are not our own; they belong to those from whom we have inherited our perceptions, ideas, and beliefs.

Presuppositions

Fortunately, however, we can educate ourselves beyond our narrow perceptions. In fact, with this book, I hope to open us up to ideas beyond the field of perceptions and beliefs our thrownness has dictated to us, by making us realize we must maintain a steady awareness that we are embedded in a culture that profoundly influences our hermeneutics. Awareness comes when we can pinpoint our presuppositions. To have a presupposition means "to assume or suppose beforehand," "to think or believe something in advance of actual knowledge or experience," or "to take something for granted." It implies believing something before researching, studying, and applying good hermeneutical methods. Theologians, teachers, and writers throughout history have all inherited presuppositions that infiltrate their hermeneutics, their theology, and their written works. Awareness of our preconceived ideas is the key to responsible hermeneutics.

The significance of presuppositions applies just as much to the authors of the Hebrew and Christian Scriptures. Although many Christians believe human authors composed the biblical texts under divine inspiration, those divinely inspired human authors still wrote from within their own context, through the lenses of human languages and worldviews, human cultures and belief systems. Their native countries and social norms saddled them with certain presuppositions about how God and the world work, and those presuppositions were woven into the fabric of the texts they wrote. Every author writes (and reads) already jaundiced by his or her own culture—even those who were inspired by God to write the biblical texts. For instance, ancient authors wrote with early creation stories, Jewish doctrine, Greek poetry, and Roman household codes swirling around in their minds, which then became ingredients the Holy Spirit used to inspire Scripture. Writers of Scripture also presupposed a certain cosmology, a certain way of determining God's actions and dealings with people. For example, they believed the sun circled the earth, and that every natural disaster, every war, every famine, every child born, every crop that grew, every rainstorm, every pellet of hail—all—came from the hand of God; nothing happened that God did not control, administer, or will.

Some of my students ask me, "If biblical authors wrote with their own context in mind, how do we determine the cultural content from the divinely inspired content?" Theologian Mary O'Neill suggests that we not be surprised to find evidence of the author's culture in a biblical text but, instead, seek to discern the revelation of God in the midst of these influences. She writes, "To recognize revelation it is necessary to identify the 'inbreaking,' that which confounds cultural expectations and raises human sights to possibilities that are rooted in God's vision and will for humankind."[5] We can see how this works out over time. In many cases, ancient authors' presuppositions carried over into later theological traditions. For example, before Galileo, the Roman Catholic Church believed in an Aristotelian view of a geocentric universe, that the sun and all the planets revolved around the earth. Not only did the ancient philosopher Aristotle confirm this idea for them, but their interpretation of certain biblical texts did as well.[6] When Galileo studied the night sky and determined that the earth and all the planets must revolve around the sun, he was brought before the Inquisition. They charged him with heresy, arrested him, and banned his writings. Their presupposition that the sun revolved around the earth blinded them to a new interpretation of natural phenomena. Later, the Roman Catholic Church apologized and made amends for their treatment of Galileo, and today, virtually no one believes the geocentric theory of the universe. Cultural ideas simply changed in the face of new evidence from both the natural world and new ways of interpreting Scripture.

Before we use this example to indict the Roman Catholic Church for the initial error of its ways, we need to remember that we all hold to certain presuppositions— none of us is immune. At one time in our history, many good Jesus-loving, Bible-believing Christians presupposed the inferiority of people with dark skin and interpreted Scripture in ways that supported slavery. It seemed obvious to them that God willed the practice, and they could find Scripture verses to prove it! We see throughout history and right up to the present time how similar presuppositions have led to the marginalization and sometimes even abuse of women, children, LGBTQ+ people, and various minority groups. However, there were always other ways to read these same passages, taking into account Scripture as a whole and the deep underlying principles about God's most fundamental nature. Eventually, these more liberating interpretations held theological sway. Very few people currently defend slavery, especially theologically, even though the Bible still contains

5. Mary Aquin O'Neill, "The Mystery of Being Human Together," in Catherine Mowry LaCugna, *Freeing Theology: The Essentials of Theology in Feminist Perspective* (San Francisco: Harper SanFrancisco, 1993), 142.
6. For example: "The world is firmly established; it shall never be moved" (1 Chr 16:30) and "You set the earth on its foundations, so that it shall never be shaken" (Ps 104:5).

those verses that supposedly supported it. God's nature does not change; the Bible does not change. But our perceptions of God's work in the world and of how to interpret that work biblically do change. Through the power of the Holy Spirit, God breaks into our rigid ways of thinking and leads us to understand over time that God ultimately wills love and flourishing for every human being.

Nonviolence, Power Dynamics, and Hermeneutics

Because of the biases generated by our thrownness and presuppositions, we should always approach our beliefs and doctrines with what Paul Ricoeur calls the "hermeneutics of suspicion," asking ourselves if our particular theological viewpoints benefit one particular group over another, either intentionally or unintentionally.[7] We employ a good hermeneutics of suspicion when we ask who holds the power, and who, therefore, endures marginalization, gets left out, or suffers oppression on account of this interpretation or that theological idea. For instance, as a white female I might easily advocate a theology that ignores or undermines people of color. Why? Because I am white. Therefore, I am blind to certain things, such as the experience and suffering of black women. Their experience adds a perspective I cannot see. If I were a white man, I might have no ethical problem holding to a particular doctrine that subjugates women, without even thinking about it. For instance, the medieval "Great Chain of Being" advocated an order of creation that elevated men over women and granted men divinely appointed authority to rule over all those perceived as inferior in the cosmic scheme of things. Arguing that Scripture could never support the ordination of women is another example of this type of theology. Accepting slavery, as we have seen, is another. Although minority voices have gained some momentum and appreciation in recent years, those in power, the dominant leaders of the church (read mostly white, male Westerners here), constructed the theological belief systems we still hold today. And those doctrines have often served, supported, and secured the positions, power, and prestige of white, male (sometimes celibate) clerics.

For the most part, I believe classical Western theologians and biblical scholars were products of their own contexts, cultures, thrownness, and presuppositions and remained largely unaware of the prejudices and denigration of females and non-white people their theologies caused. Some theologians most likely constructed oppressive theological beliefs without malice, innocently ignorant of the damage to others; their presuppositions blinded them to it. But in other cases, we have reason to suspect that human greed, ego, and self-serving agendas motivated certain theological ideas. In fact, all of us should remain suspicious of our own motives in constructing theological belief systems, since we may easily hold to a doctrine

---

7. Paul Ricoeur, *Freud and Philosophy: An Essay on Interpretation* (New Haven, CT: Yale University Press, 1970), 27, 32–36; Paul Ricoeur, "Biblical Hermeneutics," *Semeia* 4 (1975): 33.

that would place us in a privileged position over others, or simply leave the life experience of others out. Before we accept a certain theology, we should always ask ourselves, "Who benefits from this doctrine or belief, and can we interpret it differently in ways that benefit humanity as a whole?"

Of course, not all presuppositions lead to negative or unbiblical beliefs. For instance, the American Baptist church I attended as a young child taught me that God loves everyone. My pastor and Sunday school teachers drilled that image of God into my head so completely that I have always believed that "love" defines God best. "God is love" has become my defining presupposition about God and has motivated and influenced everything I write and teach. When I open the Bible, I am predisposed to read the canon of Scripture through the lens of that "canonical" presupposition; it functions as my "canon within the canon," meaning that not every idea in Scripture holds the same importance as every other, and one might take some theological ideas or scriptural texts as more authoritative than others. In my case, every doctrine I hold must remain consistent with the one positive, primary presupposition that "God is love" (1 John 4:8).

My focus on God as nonviolent love reveals not only my primary presupposition but also my deep concern about the violence that Christians have sometimes justified through certain interpretations of Scripture and various Christian doctrines. At times, certain interpretations and doctrines have allowed the church to rationalize the abuse of women and children, the physical torture of unbelievers and "heretics," various forms of bigotry and racism, and even the jingoism inherent in contemporary political rhetoric. For example, pastors have informed women that remaining with their abusive husbands is consistent with Christ's idea of bearing his cross. Or, as another example, some years ago several evangelical leaders signed the so-called Land Letter to President George W. Bush, urging him to engage in the Iraq War, a war that was later proved to be based on false presuppositions about whether Saddam Hussein had weapons of mass destruction (he didn't). These types of acts by Christian leaders should lead us to ask serious questions about the ethical implications of holding to a classical doctrine of God as a violent deity. Certain classical doctrines of God, as we shall see, pose wide-reaching ethical problems. Some of these doctrines may be based on faulty presuppositions influenced by culture and unexamined power dynamics, ending up contradicting very basic Christian teachings such as "God is love."

The implications of love as a defining characteristic for God reach far into what we believe about God's nature, how God interacts with the world, and how we live our lives. Our theology determines our behavior; what we believe about God informs what we do. For example, I believe that love and violence are incompatible, so my focus on divine love leads me to question any theological idea or system that paints a picture of a violent God. After years of trying to understand the unfortunate Christian propensity to condone, advocate, and participate in outrageous injustices throughout the millennia, I have come to the conclusion that our doctrines, the way we imagine God, can lead us to agree to be willing participants in such atrocities, either actively or through the silence of assent. What we believe about God makes a difference—it is literally a matter of life or death. If we could ask the victims of the various inquisitions and crusades, domestic violence, slavery, religious wars, and other kinds of horrific oppression and violence, I am fairly confident they would agree. To remain consistent with my presupposition about God, therefore, I also have to believe that God, whose very nature constitutes love, never condones or advocates violence. Instead, God remains true to the revelation of Jesus Christ to love enemies, extend grace to all, forgive sinners, redeem all creation, and transform the world into a kingdom of kindness, mercy, and compassion.

In summary, our views of God and our world issue from our presuppositions given to us through the context we are thrown into. We gain an awareness of our own blind spots and bless others by empathizing with their contexts, listening to their perspectives, and appreciating their theological voices. A well-known poem helps us understand the significance of context. It describes five blind men who go into the same room and feel the same elephant. Yet they all interpret the elephant differently, depending on where they stand. One, feeling its side, thinks it feels like a rough wall. The second, feeling the tusk, says it feels like a spear. The third touches the trunk and argues that it feels like a snake. Upon finding a leg, another man says the elephant feels like a tree, and the last grabs the tail and chimes in, saying he feels a rope. The blind men then argue about who is right! We, too, look at the same texts and, blinded by our presuppositions, interpret the texts differently from one another. Although we are not feeling an elephant, we all look in the dark for God (for we see now through a glass darkly, according to 1 Corinthians 13). We see God while embedded in different cultures with very different presuppositions that form us and influence us, often under the radar of our awareness, especially with regard to power dynamics implied within them. And for the most part, unless we research and study, as well as listen to the stories and perspectives of others, we will remain unaware of the contextual/cultural ingredients that so profoundly impact our beliefs.

Lest we be intimidated by all this theory and the many warnings, let's remember we all already engage in the practice of hermeneutics, every day. Every communication, verbal or not, is a hermeneutical issue, and we interpret everything in life—every event, every word, and every text. That's why taking everything we have discussed in this chapter into consideration is so important. We must remember what philosophers call the "hermeneutics of finitude."[8] Basically, as *creatures* of God, and not God ourselves, we exist in the state of finitude, vulnerability, and ignorance. Because of our finitude, we can, at best, be partially right and, at worst, totally wrong! We can never attain full disclosure from God, complete knowledge

---

8. Hans-Georg Gadamer, *Truth and Method*, trans. G. Barden and J. Cummings (New York: Crossroad, 1980), 88–89, 414.

for theological construction, or total accuracy in what we believe. Moreover, we cannot escape our thrownness or the presuppositions we hold; they come naturally as a result of living in our culture, during our present age, in our certain families and churches and schools. As we interpret and construct our theological belief systems, we simply need to do so with as much awareness of our presuppositions as possible, open to the "inbreaking" Spirit of God speaking to us, because we can only remove blinders we know about. The parable of the blind men and the elephant also suggests we need the humility to learn from one another's perspectives, listening deeply instead of merely arguing.

Sources for Doing Theology

Now that we have explored the basic methods for doing theological hermeneutics, we need to focus on the next step in the interpretive and constructive process—the sources upon which to practice our hermeneutical skills. We cannot understand what we believe and formulate our doctrines without resources that provide us with the material for our theological task. I think we find the most useful configuration of resources in the work of eighteenth-century Methodist minister John Wesley, who provides us with a significant method for constructing theology responsibly. He believed that theological discourse should, first and foremost, find its footing in the Christian Scriptures. But, that said, Wesley also knew that the centuries of church traditions make an extremely significant contribution to the theological undertaking. So for him, doctrine derived from Scripture must harmonize with tradition. Moreover, he knew that we can never understand Scripture or ecclesiastical traditions without the capacity to think through the ideas, languages, and constructions of doctrine, so Wesley added reason to his list of sources for doing theology. Additionally, as a practical theologian who believed faith must be lived out in daily life and divine truth must be brought to life through experience, he added experience as the fourth source for his methodology. Although Wesley himself never used this terminology, his four-source method has become known as the *Wesleyan Quadrilateral*, using Scripture, tradition, reason, and experience for the theological enterprise of constructing doctrine.

Scripture

According to Wesley, Scripture bears a heavy burden as the source that carries the most authority. The Bible serves as the primary text for theological discourse and the development of doctrine. When we open the Bible and begin to read, we also begin the process of interpretation. No matter what view we hold on the inspiration of Scripture, we as human beings find ourselves thrown into a certain culture that inescapably influences how we interpret the words on the page. The biblical authors wrote the words of Scripture millennia ago, in cultures and countries vastly different from our own, and in entirely different sets of circumstances. Often their cultures differed drastically from one another as well. Consequently, since Scripture has been read and reread and, therefore, interpreted and reinterpreted by thousands of faithful believers throughout centuries of Christian (and Jewish) history, we should not be surprised that multiple interpretations and applications of biblical truths have accrued through the evolution of various Christian traditions. In actuality, a multiplicity of interpretations for a single passage of Scripture is the rule rather than the exception.

This diversity of interpretations raises questions of concern for those who believe in the inerrancy (errorlessness) of the Bible. Let's examine this problem. First, the term *inerrancy* itself means no one single thing: diverse views on the authority of Scripture range from seeing it as trustworthy for matters of "faith and practice" (as Roman Catholics and many Protestants do) all the way to insisting on its authority in matters of history and science (as some conservative evangelicals and fundamentalists do). Second, the idea of a formal doctrine of inerrancy is a product of the last two centuries. In fact, "there have been long periods in the history of the church where Biblical inerrancy has not been a critical question."[9] So Christians, including the church fathers, have held views of Scripture and read particular passages very differently from one another. In reality, we could have a totally inerrant Bible, but as soon as we opened the text and began to read, the idea of inerrancy would not make any difference whatsoever to determine meaning and practice. Why? Because we are finite human beings who make mistakes, not inerrant readers or interpreters, and we must interpret the Bible. We simply cannot escape the necessity of interpretation, and because of the vast number of interpreters, we also cannot escape the potential for error.

So an idea of biblical inerrancy by itself does not suffice; we still need an inerrant interpreter—an impossibility for sure. Naturally, the Roman Catholic tradition recognizes this dilemma and opens up the possibility of an inerrant interpreter— the pope speaking *ex cathedra* (which, by the way, rarely occurs). In Protestant life, the notion of an inerrant Bible, along with an emphasis on the "priesthood of all believers," obligates every reader to be an inerrant interpreter. But who has the authority to claim inerrant interpretation? If you search through a library's biblical studies shelves (call letters: BS), several of the authors of those books may hold to scriptural inerrancy; yet we would find extensive differences in their interpretations. Consequently, the idea of inerrancy does not inoculate us against our thrownness and presuppositions. Even if the biblical writers went into a trance and wrote exactly what the Holy Spirit dictated so that Scripture remained unaffected by human culture or characteristics, we as contemporary readers still must interpret the texts under the influence of our own, often errant, thrownness.

---

9. J. J. Coleman, "Biblical Inerrancy: Are We Going Anywhere?" *Theology Today* 31 (1975): 295.

Unfortunately, all too often, arguments about inerrancy spread dissension and divide the church. Due to the accompanying attitude that an inerrant Bible must have only one valid interpretation—the one I say is correct—we fight with one another rather than love one another. At times, Christians have gotten so caught up in their arguments over inerrancy of the Bible that they have forgotten to ask, What is Scripture for? The more emphasis we put on the "true" propositions concerning Scripture and the subsequent beliefs about God, the less emphasis we put on doing what Jesus actually clearly commands us to do—to love God and love others by feeding the hungry, clothing the poor, standing with the suffering other, and liberating the oppressed. What good do arguments about the inerrancy of the Bible do for those who struggle for mere survival, "who are not interested in the abstract truth, 'infallible' or otherwise"?[10] We do more for the kingdom of God when we set aside "wrangling over words, which does no good but only ruins those who are listening" and causes "stupid and senseless controversies" that "breed quarrels" (2 Tim 2:14, 23). We need to realize that interpretation is inevitable, that we do not have the corner on God's truth, and that our interpretations may not always be the right ones.

Although many adherents to doctrines of inerrancy claim that the authority of Scripture is at stake, I believe we can hold to a rigorous belief in the authority of Scripture without the intrusion of the divisive language of inerrancy. Note that the Apostles' Creed, the most foundational statement of Christian belief, nowhere articulates an explicit statement about Scripture and inerrancy, even though it is implicitly *about* Scripture. Nor, as we have seen, does the Bible make these claims about itself. The Christian church did not even have the canon of Scripture as we know it today until the fourth century after Christ, yet early Christians believed they had authoritative evidence about Jesus's life, death, and resurrection through oral and, later, written stories in the Gospel narratives. They also wrote down additional narrative accounts (the Acts of the Apostles) and pastoral letters that they believed were of value. The Gospel accounts themselves speak with four voices, no one of which is the "right" one. In conveying the central story of Christianity—the life, teachings, death, and resurrection of Jesus—they offer four different versions, each subject to many interpretations.

After I explain to students the plethora of possibilities when interpreting the Bible, they inevitably ask, "How are we to know when we have interpreted correctly—or, worse, incorrectly?" Although the Christian tradition can lay claim to an overabundance of wrong biblical interpretations, I am not sure we need to use the language of "correct" and "incorrect" when trying to understand Scripture and apply it to our lives. Instead, let's discuss "responsible" and "irresponsible" or "valid" and "invalid" interpretations. If Scripture is the most important and authoritative source for doing theology (and I believe it is), how do we interact

10. James H. Cone, *Black Theology of Liberation* (Philadelphia: J. B. Lippincott, 1970), 152.

with it in a responsible way? Let's look at a few helpful pointers beyond what we have previously discussed concerning the personal understanding of our contexts, our presuppositions, and our finitude.

Authorial intent and historical era. Both the reader and the author are thrown into and immersed in cultural contexts and have formed presuppositions and beliefs accordingly. In order to interpret responsibly, then, we must consider the context in which the author wrote the biblical text and the reason for the particular content of a book of Scripture. When we read the Bible, we journey back thousands of years into cultures, customs, and beliefs of people far removed from us. The opening lines of *Star Wars* aptly apply to us when we study Scripture—"A long time ago in a galaxy far, far away"—because when we enter the worlds of the Bible, we may as well be traveling to another galaxy. We cross the threshold into a foreign land with thousands of years and just as many miles separating us from the texts and the authors who wrote them. So, the more we can learn about the historical eras we study, the more valid our interpretations of Scripture.

In addition to gaining access to biblical cultures, customs, and beliefs, we need to figure out the authorial intent of a book or passage. Of course, even discerning an author's intended meanings does not ensure a good interpretation, for at least two reasons. First, we still cannot rid ourselves of our own thrownness and presuppositions. They will always infect any search for meaning. At the same time, however, we can get closer to the author by studying the *culture* in which he or she lived, the *languages* in which the text is written, the *meaning* of words from that time period, and the *purpose* for which the text was written. Once we understand as much as we can about what the text said back then, we can ask the question, "What does the text say to us now?" The answers, tempered with the author's intent, the historical context, and cultural understanding, enable us to apply the text to our lives—a significant step since the purpose of studying and interpreting Scripture is to embark on the path of holy living.

Second, we can never get into an author's head far enough to determine their intended meaning. In fact, the author is often unaware of alternate meanings written into his or her own text. Readers can pick up a text and understand the words and ideas in ways the author never envisioned. So meaning develops and expands, sometimes in ways the author would approve of and sometimes not. Furthermore, once a text reaches us, we read it absent the author. The author has left the room, so to speak, and leaves us with a text to decipher in the midst of our own cultural and social contexts. A document separated from the author and his or her historical context opens up the possibility for a heterogeneity of interpretations, valid or invalid. In order to eliminate potential irresponsible hermeneutical errors, we need to attempt as best we can to understand the author and his or her context and purpose for writing a text. Remember, however, our best attempt to understand authorial intent is itself always a product of the reader's interpretive process. In other words, we can only access the author's agenda by reading and interpreting the author's text, which means, of course, that we make such determinations under the influence of our own contemporary thrownness.

Context. Context is king! At least that is the first lesson I learned when I began to read the Bible. We must always place the passage of Scripture within the context of the chapter that surrounds it, the book that encompasses it, and the entire Bible that contains it. No verse of Scripture is an island; in order to interpret responsibly, we should interpret every part in light of the whole, and the whole in light of its parts. In fact, according to another form of the Hermeneutical Circle we discussed earlier, we have two ways to do this: *between* the books of the Bible (*intertextuality*) and *within* a certain book of the Bible only (*intratextuality*). Because the Bible is a conglomeration of sixty-six different books, we often research the meaning of words and themes by comparing them throughout the various books. We can assume the validity and relevance of comparative words and themes in other books of the Bible, knowing that God inspired all of Scripture. For example, a number of years ago I wanted to gain all the information I could about divine justice. Rather than merely camping out in Deuteronomy 28 (intratextuality), a chapter well known for its slant toward retributive justice (tit-for-tat justice), I practiced intertextuality and searched out *all* the Hebrew and Greek words in the Bible most often translated into English as "justice." By doing so, I gained a more complete understanding of what the entire body of Scripture says about divine justice, which resulted in a more valid interpretation of how God interacts with the world. Had I only taken my information from one book of the Bible, I would have missed significant characteristics that define God and justice. I would have seen only a small part of the picture and misinterpreted the notion of divine justice. So we need to do the hard work and interpret parts of Scripture within the context of the whole. I am also practicing intertextuality in this current volume by interpreting Christian thought in light of the Apostles' Creed, not only using it as the structure of this book, but also consulting it as a valid source for constructing doctrine. That is to say, I am interacting with both the texts of Scripture and the text of the creed.

When we try to understand a certain passage in a single book of the Bible, we can also study that *book* intratexually. This means we look at all the words and ideas in our chosen passage and compare them to how those same words (if any) are used in the rest of the book. By reading the book as a whole, we make note of the flow of ideas, exhortations, and issues. We read the passage in light of the ideas, purpose, and main goal of the book so that our interpretations do not contradict the author's message in other passages. We need to remember, however, that verse and chapter divisions are not divinely inspired, so often a passage will split off into another chapter, separating the central message from its whole. For example, some scholars believe that Isaiah 52 should end with verse 12, connecting verses 13–15 instead to chapter 53, all of which describe the exalted and suffering servant. When we study those passages of Isaiah, we can too easily disconnect the message of God's servant from one chapter to another. Reading within and across verses, chapters, and books of the Bible helps us interpret responsibly, reducing the potential for harmful misinterpretations.

Genre. The word *genre* derives from a French word meaning a "kind" or "classification." Accordingly, when we consider genre in light of the biblical texts, we split the books into classifications such as law, poetry, wisdom literature, historical narrative, prophecy, apocalyptic literature, gospels, and epistles. We need to distinguish among these various literary forms because the Bible is not one text written in one generic style. Different types of literature require different methods of interpretation.

For example, we would not read and interpret historical narrative in the same way we would a poem. We read and understand poetry as figurative language, rich with metaphor, typology, simile, hyperbole, and symbolism, whereas the language of historical narrative tells a more straightforward story of circumstances that occurred in the past, using language that engages us with one-to-one correspondence between words and events. We know that when we read in the book of Isaiah (55:12) that "the trees . . . clap their hands" in praise, we are reading figurative language—trees do not clap their hands; they do not *have* hands. We know we cannot take poetic forms of writing as literally as we do the historical narrative accounts in Scripture. Referring back to our discussion of Scripture as divine revelation in chapter 1, we see that the different literary genres of Scripture reveal God's discourse with us in different ways.[11]

Whatever the genre, we must approach our interpretive task with prayer and meditation. God's Spirit does teach us if we listen. Our rigorous, responsible study, in partnership with the Holy Spirit, will lead us toward learning the truths of God's revelation through Scripture. Take time to meditate prayerfully on a passage or verse; keep it in your mind; read it over and over, always open to the inbreaking of new thoughts and ideas.

Tradition

When I was a child, my family always celebrated Christmas Eve at my Aunt Carol's house with all my cousins, aunts, uncles, and grandparents. Aunt Carol always wore a gorgeous green velvet gown and made lobster bisque. She was beautiful (still is) and it was delicious! My aunt handed that rich tradition down to me. When I grew up, got married, had children, and moved out of state, I continued the tradition of making lobster bisque on Christmas Eve. (Unfortunately, I didn't have the gown.)

---

11. Paul Ricoeur, *Essays on Biblical Interpretation*, ed. Lewis S. Mudge (Philadelphia: Fortress, 1980), 73–85.

We can all think about traditions we practice over and over again for holidays, birthdays, special events, or as a daily routine. For example, every morning before sending my boys off to school, we sat together, read Bible stories, memorized Scripture, and prayed. That was our tradition, and we did it faithfully through all their school years.

Traditions are important reminders of significant beliefs, events, or people in our lives. They are rich legacies we hand down or hand over to another. In fact, the word we use comes from the Latin, *tradere*, a proto–Indo-European word that may at one time have been spelled *trado*. Regardless of the vowel change over the centuries, the word maintains the Indo-European root, *do*, which means "to give." The Greek word *paradosis*, usually translated "tradition" in the New Testament, also retains the root *do*. So to have a tradition actually connotes "to give something over" or "to hand something down" to others. You may have already thought about other common words formed from the root *do*, such as "donate," to give a gift, or "pardon," to forgive an offense or debt.

In our theological context, we hand down doctrines, ways of perceiving God and our faith. As I discussed above, we all come from a certain tradition that has constructed its own belief system. Those ways and doctrines differ so widely that *many* different traditions, denominations, and doctrines make up what we know as Christianity. In most cases, the traditions passed down by various Christian theological systems provide us with beautiful, rich, and beneficial conceptions of God, salvation, and the world that we hope our children and their children will value enough to repeat and reenact for generations. I have structured the theological content of this book around one of the oldest and most beloved traditions of the church, the Apostles' Creed. So even as we explore new ideas in each chapter and build upon the work of those who have come before us, the framework of our construction remains firmly rooted in an age-old Christian tradition. And just as I have received the gift of the Apostles' Creed, I am using this gift for this present theological endeavor, hoping to pass it on to the next "generation" of Christians.

Obviously, as the millennia-old Apostles' Creed affirms, our traditions do not appear out of thin air; they develop over time within specific communities. Theologian Ray Hart describes tradition as the "linguistic debris" that accumulates over the centuries as each new community searches for language to make theology relevant for its culture and society.[12] These traditions give us a sense of belonging and comfort, a space we can call home. They provide us with a place to put our feet and take a stand. We also need to realize that traditions are always plural. Many different traditions converge in our lives from our churches, communities, families, educational institutions, friends, and workplaces and mold us and enable us to understand life and faith in certain ways. These many traditions affect how we

---

12. Ray L. Hart, *Unfinished Man and the Imagination: Toward an Ontology and a Rhetoric of Revelation* (New York: Seabury, 1979), 28.

interpret Scripture, understand God, and apply theological concepts to our lives. But because we belong to these traditions, because they give us a home, a place to stand, we prejudge traditions that differ from our own. Belonging to a theological tradition usually means we exhibit prejudice against doctrines, beliefs, and practices that diverge from the place we call home. That is why Hans-Georg Gadamer refers to what we have called presuppositions as "prejudices," which positively or negatively separate our traditional doctrines from other doctrines.[13]

We know, then, that traditions benefit us, adding richness and beauty to our lives. At the same time, we cannot blindly trust our theological traditions without question; we cannot simply believe what we have been taught about God, salvation, and the created world without thinking through the implications of those beliefs. We can love our doctrinal tradition, but we must also use our brains! In fact, the word *tradition* provides us with its own warning. The Greek *paradosis* in the New Testament has another meaning we need to take into consideration. In John 18:2, Judas "was *betraying*" Jesus (emphasis mine) to the political leaders. In other words, Judas betrayed Jesus when he "handed [him] over" to the authorities, when he "gave" Jesus to the political powers. The word many of our Bibles translate "betray" is the verb form of the noun *paradosis* (lit. *paradidous* from the verb *paradidomi*), the word usually translated "tradition"! The word implies that with tradition, we hand something over to someone else, as Judas did! We learn from this that our traditions either enrich us with the wisdom of the past or betray us, as with the folly of Judas against Jesus. We can hand down doctrines and beliefs to our children that are, at best, partially correct and, at worst, totally wrong. So we need to decide if we will act as Judas, betraying our next generations with faulty doctrine, or as Jesus, handing over a rich legacy of faith, beliefs, and practices. Because of this difficult balancing act, the church must adopt a certain sense of suspicion surrounding tradition; must think against it, deciding (prayerfully) what to salvage, reinterpret, and reapply. Through rigorous study and careful contemplation, we need to identify which of our traditions' doctrines have betrayed us, and reinterpret them not only for our benefit but also for the benefit of those who come after us.

When I talk about the reality of our Christian doctrinal tradition betraying us and, therefore, the necessity of continual reinterpretation, inevitably a student will protest that we cannot change what the Bible says. That student is correct: we cannot change the Bible. But our understanding and application of it change all the time. Throughout the history of the Bible's composition (lasting many centuries), and for the last two thousand years, the Christian community has been constantly about the business of reinterpreting Scripture. Layers of interpretation in both the biblical texts and the history of Christian doctrine reveal that the *tradition* is to

---

13. Gadamer, *Truth and Method*, 272; Hans-Georg Gadamer, *Philosophical Hermeneutics*, trans. D. E. Linge (Berkeley: University of California Press, 2004), 31, 291.

continually reinterpret the tradition! As I have written in another text, we "reinterpret continually, repeatedly, with a repetition of reinterpretation that preserves the relevance of the living and active word of God."[14] Remaining faithful to the past (tradition), relevant to the present, and hopeful toward the future become our tasks as we read and interpret the Bible and apply it to our lives of faith.

Reason

Since our faith seeks to understand God and the world, doing theology requires a lot of thought. Every time we open the Bible, read a theological text, or undertake the task of interpretation, we use our capacity to reason, think through differing concepts, consider the options, and discern between choices. In fact, the word *reason* comes from the Latin word *reri*, which later became *ratio* and indicates engaging in discussion, thinking logically, and taking into account differing perspectives in a "rational" way. Without reason, we would not be able to process our thoughts, speak coherently, understand what we read, use our imaginations, construct our belief systems, and order our world. So our ability to reason plays a vital role in the theological task. Reason drives our making sense of the world. We constantly attempt to order our world, to seek patterns, traditions, and neatly outlined instructions for living life, and for knowing what to believe and how to apply those beliefs.

The poet Wallace Stevens beautifully expresses this propensity for order in the last two stanzas of his poem "The Idea of Order at Key West."[15] In this poem, Stevens describes a harbor in which sea captains can drop anchor and float idly in the calm water until they once again sail to other ports. At first, he sees no order, no neatly lined docks with slips for each vessel—just boats bobbing in the water in seemingly random and reckless abandon. But after staring long enough at the lights as the boats lazily oscillate on the gentle waves, Stevens sees a pattern, a certain order to the way they "portion out the sea." Even in the midst of the chaotic alignment of the sea crafts, his mind seeks order there. We have a "blessed rage for order" built into our brains: we automatically order our worlds.

But just as we saw with our discussion on tradition, a hard-nosed adherence to objective reason can get us into trouble. Even Stevens issues just such a caution in a second poem, "Six Significant Landscapes."[16] In the last stanza he writes:

> Rationalists, wearing square hats,
> Think, in square rooms,

14. Sharon Lynn Baker, *Razing Hell: Rethinking Everything You've Been Taught about God's Wrath and Judgment* (Louisville, KY: Westminster John Knox, 2010), 154.
15. Wallace Stevens, "The Idea of Order at Key West," in *The Collected Poems of Wallace Stevens* (New York: Knopf, 1990). See the full poem online at https://tinyurl.com/yyeufstk.
16. Wallace Stevens, "Six Significant Landscapes," in *Collected Poems*. See the full poem online at https://tinyurl.com/st6wow7.

Looking at the floor,
Looking at the ceiling.
They confine themselves
To right-angled triangles.
If they tried rhomboids,
Cones, waving lines, ellipses—
As, for example, the ellipse of the half-moon—
Rationalists would wear sombreros.

Stevens warns against the angularity of rationalism, the nice, neat structure of systems. We might periodically need to soften those angles with curves or admit that definitive systems leave things out, that the uncertainty of ellipses always haunts us. Theologically, this would admonish those of us who think we have all the answers through reason not to confine ourselves to one view of God, Jesus, the Holy Spirit, creation, humanity, redemption, and the church. We can get so caught up in our neatly reasoned "square room" that we never entertain the mysteries and beauty of God. We put God into our square box, not realizing we cannot so conveniently package God. We need to loosen up (put on a round hat, like a sombrero), think outside the box, and open our hearts and minds to experience something new from God!

Experience

Now, newly outfitted with our "sombrero thinking," let's move on to Wesley's fourth and final source for doing theology—experience. The etymology of the word stems from the Indo-European root *peira*, which means "to try," "to risk," or "to take a chance." We actually get our word *peril* from the same root. So according to its etymology, experience is an experiment in living, a risky enterprise for the hale and hearty, not for the faint of heart. It takes courage to venture out into a life of faith without knowing with absolute certainty the character of God and the truth of our belief system. We face constant unforeseen events that threaten to wash us up on the rocks, shipwrecking and stripping us of a solid place to put our feet. Nonetheless, philosopher Jacques Derrida exhorts us to live into the peril, to take the "leap of faith" into the uncertainty of existence, with but two caveats.[17] First, we should always take risks that enable us to identify meanings and belief structures that offer security. I would take it a step farther and say we find that security in the gospel message of redemption and reconciliation to God through Jesus Christ. Second, Derrida encourages us to embrace risk with a willingness to welcome new

17. Jacques Derrida, *Psyche: Inventions of the Other*, Meridian: Crossing Aesthetics 1, ed. Peggy Kamuf and Elizabeth Rottenberg (Stanford, CA: Stanford University Press, 2007), 36, 45. See also B. Keith Putt, "Indignation toward Evil: Ricoeur and Caputo on a Theodicy of Protest," *Philosophy Today* 41, no. 3 (Fall 1997): 460.

ideas, the in-coming of something that shocks us, stirs us up, knocks us free from the status quo, and opens our hearts and minds to loving the diverse "other." I would add to that and ask us periodically to take a leap out of our status-quo thrownness and presuppositions to consider fresh revelations of the living God, unique experiences of faith that mold us more deeply into imitators of Christ.

Scripture gives a glimpse into what can happen when we leave the security and comfort of home and commit ourselves to the adventure and risk of experiencing God. Picture the young virgin Mary, sitting quietly and securely in her home, sewing her outfit for the village dance or making candles so she can read at night. And into the calm of comfort the angel Gabriel comes, disrupting her status quo, interrupting her complacency and monotony with an offer she very well could have refused—were she not a risk-taker. Fortunately for the church, she took the leap into peril and joined God in the experience of her lifetime. We can say the same about the paralytic lowered through the roof—he experienced the God of experience and was healed. Or think about Peter, James, John, and Jesus ascending Mount Tabor for a campout. As they sit singing songs or telling ghost stories in front of the campfire, Jesus gets up to take a short walk and bright light splits open the night sky. Blinking their eyes and trying to adjust to the sudden change in ambience, they see Jesus talking with Moses and Elijah. Although at first they fear for their lives, when Jesus approaches them, they lean into the experience, allowing it to both shock them and shape them as they follow him down the mountain back into the perils of life with their Lord.

Philosopher and theologian John Caputo claims that "anything that falls short of God will not have the bite of experience."[18] Through the risky business of experience, we meet up with the God of experience, who lends the divine self to us in the form of new and surprising revelation. Without the ability to experience the revelation of God, we would not understand the Christian message, be able to participate in the life of the church, or deal with matters of faith. We know and can reason because we experience. In fact, experience serves as the channel through which the other theological sources connect and interact with us. We receive the content of our theology through experience. When we read the Bible, we experience joy, sorrow, conviction, hope, peace, grace, and love. We experience God in certain ways, which then influence how we think of God theologically. Various theologians articulate the content and expression of our experiences of God. For example, Friedrich Schleiermacher believes we experience God as a feeling of absolute dependence with an immediate awareness of "something" unconditional that transcends our intellect and our will.[19] Twentieth-century theologian Paul

18. John D. Caputo, "The Experience of God and the Axiology of the Impossible," in *The Experience of God: A Postmodern Response*, ed. Kevin Hart and Barbara Wall (New York: Fordham University Press, 2005), 25.
19. Friedrich Schleiermacher, *The Christian Faith: A New Translation and Critical Edition*, trans. Terrence N. Tice and Catherine L. Kelsey (Louisville, KY: Westminster John Knox, 2016), 85.

Tillich places a significant emphasis on experience, arguing that it is not only the medium through which we receive the contents of our theology but also something we actively participate in through the revelation of the Holy Spirit.[20] So, one of the essential ingredients to valid theological construction is our ability to experience God and put that experience into words.

We need to remember, however, that all our experiences are formed in the crucible of our thrownness and presuppositions, which then form biases that influence the way we interpret those experiences. When we think about theology, therefore, we should always keep in mind that our own biases significantly infect the construction of our theological beliefs, always remembering that human experience varies widely and that we need to consult many different perspectives, especially those of the least fortunate of society, to inform a valid theology. And we must always remember that Jesus Christ's life, death, teachings, and resurrection remain our primary criteria for evaluating any experience or theological system, and our safeguards in this perilous journey through experiencing God.

20. Paul Tillich, *Systematic Theology*, vol. 1 (Chicago: University of Chicago Press, 1973), 64.

3. The Trinity

. . . in God . . .

> But you, beloved, build yourselves up on your most holy faith; pray in the
> Holy Spirit; keep yourselves in the love of God; look forward to the mercy
> of our Lord Jesus Christ that leads to eternal life.
>
> —Jude 20–21

> Oh mystic marvel! The universal Father is one; and one the universal Word;
> and the Holy Spirit is one and the same everywhere . . .
>
> —Friedrich Schleiermacher

Do you want to dance? God does. In fact, Zephaniah describes the delightful divine dance for us, saying that God "will rejoice over you with gladness, he will renew you in his love; he will exult over you with loud singing as on a day of festival" (3:17–18). These verses provide us with a profound word picture in which we see the almighty God of the universe dancing around God's beloved people—us!—jumping and turning and spinning with great pleasure. Then God stops and lovingly meditates on us, much like a mother would gaze upon her newborn baby and look with awe at the little fingers and toes, taking in all the minute details of such an inexpressible miracle. Suddenly, not able to sit still in the excitement of divine love, God springs into action and begins the dance once again, circling and leaping around us, singing with joy and exultation because we are God's own beloved treasure.

In the divine community dancing symbolizes the creative, flowing movement of love-in-action among God the Father, God the Son, and God the Holy Spirit. And as an extension of divine extravagant grace, infinite love, and unfathomable benevolence toward the world, God invites us into the sacred space of divinity and urges us to join this mystical, eternal dance. Indeed, dancing is not only allowed—it is strongly encouraged! C. S. Lewis believed we all have a place reserved for us on the dance floor. None of us needs to sit on the outskirts of the ball as mere spectating wallflowers. All of us have our names on the Trinitarian dance card and can take our place on the floor as active partners with the Father, Son, and Holy Spirit in the beautifully choreographed kingdom waltz (or even the boogie, samba, jitterbug—your free choice—God knows all the steps to every dance).[1]

---

1. C. S. Lewis, *Mere Christianity*, in *The C. S. Lewis Signature Classics: An Anthology* (New York: HarperOne, 2017), 183–84.

This extended metaphor of the dance actually points us to a theological term—*perichoresis*, a Greek word that describes the flowing movement among the three members of the Trinity. This concept within Trinitarian theology is so important that philosopher Richard Kearney cites the sacred divine "dance-play" of perichoresis as one of the most profoundly significant and powerful images of God.[2] Broken down etymologically, the word literally means to dance (*choros*) around (*peri*), and it refers to the circular divine dance movements we discussed in Zephaniah. So when we reflect on perichoresis, a beautiful image arises of the circular dance of the Father, the Son, and the Holy Spirit as they move in relation to one another in the reciprocal choreographic sway of eternal intimacy. The three belong together as one, yet they remain distinct partners in an interplaying movement of love. An even more beautiful image surrounding perichoresis is the idea that, by sending the Son and adopting us as children, the triune God invites all of us to join in the "great dance of creation and rebirth" in which we, too, experience the loving intimacy of the Father, Son, and Holy Spirit.[3]

The Trinity in the Bible

As majestic and delightful as the notion of perichoresis sounds, and although the concept is biblical, this word does not actually appear in Scripture at all. But then, neither does the word *Trinity*. The Bible alludes to the revelation of the Trinity without using the word itself. So, we need to ask not only where the idea of a Trinitarian dance comes from, but how the Christian tradition formed a doctrine of the Trinity at all. Even though the Trinity as traditionally conceived does not appear in the Bible, the concept of the threeness of God does. The Hebrew Bible prepared early Jewish Christians for thinking about God in Trinitarian terms in passages portraying God as spirit, wisdom, and word (Ps 143:8–10; Gen 1). The spirit of God (third Person of the Trinity) empowers creation, teaches skills, and guides God's people. The Wisdom of God (first Person of the Trinity), a more personified vision of the divine, calls the people to lead lives devoted to God and to heed the counsel of God's laws. And the Word of God (the Son, or the second Person of the Trinity) speaks forth new life and, through the mouths of the prophets, exhorts God's people to live up to divine standards. This trio also presents itself in Isaiah as he speaks of the "spirit of the Lord" and refers to the "shoot [that] shall come out from the stump of Jesse," which Christians believe foreshadows Jesus as the Messiah (Isa 11:1–3).

Moreover, the first creation story in Genesis 1 describes the Holy Spirit hovering and brooding over primordial chaos during God's process of creating the universe. Then God the Father speaks through God the Son/Word, making cosmos out of

2. Richard Kearney, *The God Who May Be* (Bloomington: Indiana University Press, 2001), 109.
3. Kearney, *God Who May Be*, 109.

chaos, form out of the formless void, and new creation out of no creation at all. And of course, we may say that the Trinity makes an appearance when Abraham entertains three strangers who identify themselves later as the Lord (Gen 18:1–15). As these few examples show, the Hebrew Bible often portrays God as three distinct persons who deal personally with the universe in order to create new life, extend grace, teach wisdom, reveal truth, and redeem a broken people.

When we look at the New Testament, we see that it mentions the Father, Son, and Holy Spirit quite frequently without any explanation at all, to the point that the early Christians may have taken the concept of the threeness of God for granted.[4] Indeed, we can pinpoint close to 120 passages where the Bible mentions all three persons of the Trinity together. For example, during Jesus's baptism all three persons in the Godhead appear: the Son in the water, the Father speaking, and the Holy Spirit descending (Matt 3:16–17; Mark 1:10–11). Again in Matthew, Jesus tells his disciples to baptize believers in the name of the Father, the Son, and the Holy Spirit (Matt 28:19). In Acts we see the stoning of Stephen, who, close to death, utters a Trinitarian description of his vision. He gazed into heaven and in the power of the Holy Spirit sees Jesus standing at the right hand of God (Acts 7:55–56). And Jude tells us, "Build yourselves up on your most holy faith; pray in the Holy Spirit; keep yourselves in the love of God; look forward to the mercy of our Lord Jesus Christ that leads to eternal life" (Jude 20–21). Paul also uses patterns of Trinitarian language to express the one God in threeness, stating that "There is one body and one Spirit, just as you were called to the one hope of your calling, one Lord, one faith, one baptism, one God and Father of all, who is above all and through all and in all" (Eph 4:4–6). Paul professes the activity of the Trinity in the bestowal of spiritual gifts: "Now there are varieties of gifts, but the same Spirit; and there are varieties of services, but the same Lord; and there are varieties of activities, but it is the same God who activates all of them in everyone" (1 Cor 12:4–6). Triune terminology also appears in greetings and benedictions: for example, "The grace of the Lord Jesus Christ, the love of God, and the communion of the Holy Spirit be with all of you" (2 Cor 13:13).

From Genesis to Revelation (Rev 1:4–5, for example) the experience believers have of God forms triadic patterns that give voice to a divine/human relationship with a God described as Father, Son, and Holy Spirit. So we see that the Trinitarian language reflected in the New Testament translated easily into the life of the early church for worship, preaching, practice, and doctrine, eventually becoming the conventional and unifying description of the Christian God. In fact, some theologians believe that the interaction between Father, Son, and Holy Spirit expressed in the

---

4. Fisher Humphreys, "The Revelation of the Trinity," *Perspectives in Religious Studies* (September 2006), 292.

Bible serves as the foundation for understanding the nature, character, attributes, and work of God both eternally and within the bounds of history.[5]

The Trinity in the Early Church

The church in its earliest decades never developed a formal or official doctrine of the Trinity; nonetheless, Christians were Trinitarian long before we had a Trinitarian theology.[6] Those first- and second-generation Christians maintained a commitment to the Jewish belief in one God but, at the same time, did not see the worship of Jesus as a violation of that belief. Those first believers never thought the notion of a Trinity or of a God who functions in three persons, as the church would eventually articulate the divine threeness, was incompatible with the monotheism out of which the Christian tradition arose. Indeed, the early church consistently incorporated the Father, Son, and Holy Spirit in their worship, liturgies, prayers, and articulations of the faith. So, although not emerging explicitly from the pages of the Bible, understanding God as Trinity arose from a century or more of scriptural interpretations, community worship experiences, and theological language that described God in triune terms. In fact, in the late second century, Irenaeus (130–200 CE), the bishop of Lyon, affirmed that the belief in a triune God originated with the earliest Christians: "Now the Church, although scattered over the whole civilized world to the end of the earth, received from the apostles and their disciples its faith in one God, the Father Almighty, who made the heavens and the earth, and the seas, and all that is in them, and in one Christ Jesus, the Son of God, who was made flesh for our salvation, and in the Holy Spirit, who through the prophets proclaimed the dispensations of God."[7] Trinitarian thought sprang from their attempts to talk about God and the relationship they saw in Scripture between the Father and the Son of God, the Holy Spirit and the Son, and the triune God's relationship to all creation.

Because of its conceptually abstract nature, Trinitarian thought remains one of the most difficult theological constructions in the Christian tradition; yet it is also one of the most important theological doctrines. So we have to work to understand the historical development and technical terms of this doctrine as it has been formulated in both East and West, up until the present day.

In an attempt to explain more adequately the nature of God as "three," the early church father Tertullian (160–220 CE) proposed the word *Trinity* (*trinitas* in Latin) to speak about the threefold God. He used the term *person* (*persona* in Latin) to articulate the differentiation between the three—Father, Son, and Holy Spirit. Some decades later the Eastern theologian Origen (185–254 CE) further

---

5. Richard J. Plantinga, Thomas R. Thompson, and Matthew D. Lundberg, *An Introduction to Christian Theology* (Cambridge: Cambridge University Press, 2010), 109.
6. Humphreys, "Revelation of the Trinity," 292.
7. Irenaeus, *Against Heresies*, 1.10.1 (Peabody, MA: Hendrickson, 1994).

elucidated the triune distinction between the individual existences of each person with the Greek word *hypostasis*, which alludes to the eternal "begottenness" of the Son and the eternal "procession" of the Holy Spirit. That is to say, the Son and the Holy Spirit always existed as the Son and the Holy Spirit from all eternity—they are co-eternally God with the Father; the three share, and actually *are*, the same divine reality.[8] These Latin and Greek words expressed concepts that, because of their very loftiness and inexplicability, defied articulation and, at the same time, were significant in explaining the deity of the human Jesus. So the early church continued its quest to define the Trinity and to construct official doctrine.

As the centuries progressed and Christianity became more widespread, the new emperor, Constantine, and other church leaders began to see the need for the development of a more formal theological expression of what they had always accepted in worship.[9] These conversations and the forging of new doctrine that took place, most significantly in the fourth century, largely dictate what we believe today about the Trinitarian God.[10]

But these new doctrines did not come quickly or easily. Church leaders battled over the issue of the Trinity and how the human Jesus could participate fully in the divinity of the one God. The Council of Nicaea in 325 CE, called by Emperor Constantine, brought together several hundred bishops from regions in both the East and the West to discuss, among other things, the nature and make-up of the Trinity. In order to simplify a complicated argument, we will discuss two main players in what became known as the "Trinitarian Controversy."

First, the priest and theologian Arius (256–336 CE) believed that Jesus was not fully divine, but was a non-eternal, preeminently created, superior human being—the "firstborn of all creation" (Col 1:15)—yet inferior and subordinate to the Father. Arius and his followers worshipped Christ as a mediator between God and humans, but never gave him divine status. Arius thought of Jesus as of *similar* substance (*homoiousios*) with the Father, meaning that Jesus is not of the same essence as God but is of a different, more humanlike essence and, therefore, *not* God.

Athanasius (296–373 CE), bishop of Alexandria, contested Arius and proclaimed the full divinity of the Son, claiming instead that Jesus was of the *same* substance (*homoousios*) as the Father. This means that, because Jesus eternally was, is, and always will exist as the same essence as God, Jesus *is* God—not similar to God, but in essence, actually, truly God.

Before we conceptually execute Arius, who lost the argument, and applaud Athanasius, who won, we need to remember that these theologians and their followers did not try to construct doctrine outside the bounds of scriptural accounts. They

---

8. Plantinga, Thompson, and Lundberg, *Introduction to Christian Theology*, 120–21.
9. Stephen R. Holmes "Classical Trinity: Evangelical Perspective," in *Two Views on the Doctrine of the Trinity*, ed. Jason S. Sexton and Stanley N. Gundry (Grand Rapids, MI: Zondervan, 2014), 31, 33–34.
10. James R. Payton, *Light from the Christian East: An Introduction to the Orthodox Tradition* (Downers Grove, IL: IVP Academic, 2007), 69.

did not want to deceive Christians who seriously sought answers to the question of Jesus's divinity. And as far as we know, they did not have a major personal or political agenda for holding to certain doctrines. Instead, these early theologians developed their theology based on certain significant concerns. For example, Arius wanted to keep God safe from the all-too-earthy vicissitudes of life. He and his followers believed that the transcendent, incomprehensible, omnipotent, omniscient, perfect, and holy God could never touch foot on earth, walk in the dirt, or suffer hunger, thirst, fatigue, insults, or pain. His concerns, therefore, led him to emphasize an image of God as untouchable, too holy to condescend to the level of humanity in all its impurities. So for him, Jesus remained defined as *homoiousios* (of similar substance) with the Father, which kept the divine substance free from impurities. Athanasius had different concerns involving salvation. He believed that the efficacy of the atonement depended completely on the full divinity of Jesus Christ as well as on his full humanity. In other words, he believed that if Jesus were not fully divine, there would be no fully effective salvation. So for Athanasius, Jesus is *homoousios* (of the same substance) as the Father, so that God both authors and accomplishes salvation for all creation.

Although the argument between the *homoousian* and the *homoiousian* Christians continued for decades, the formula developed by Athanasius and his followers held sway and largely still dictates what we believe today—God is one substance or essence (*homoousios*) in three persons (*hypostasis* or *prosopon*).[11] We see this "same substance" theological construction articulated in the Nicene Creed (325 CE), which states that Jesus is "the only Son of God, eternally begotten of the Father, God from God, Light from Light, true God from true God, begotten not made, of one Being with the Father."[12] Because of continued conflict, however, we see an attempt to solidify theological claims surrounding the doctrine of the Trinity with the so-called Athanasian Creed, most likely written in the fifth century, a hundred years after the death of its namesake. It clearly states that "the Father is God, the Son is God, and the Holy Spirit is God; and yet there are not three gods, but there is one God." Ever since Athanasius won the debate, many Christians believe that Jesus is *consubstantial* with (*homoousios*, or of the same essence as) the Father: Jesus is God in the flesh. And, of course, the Apostles' Creed, likely written formally in 390 CE and very Trinitarian in its structure, states the divinity of Jesus in its own terms. Starting with a statement about God the Father, the creed moves to the next person in the Trinity and says: "I believe in Jesus Christ, God's only Son, our Lord, who was conceived by the Holy Spirit, born of the virgin Mary. . . ." The phrases "God's only Son," "our Lord," and "conceived by the Holy

11. Because the words *homoousios* and *homoiousios* do not offer clear and distinct explanations of the relationship between Father, Son, and Holy Spirit and fail to define the distinction between each, Gregory of Nyssa developed a more consistent way of talking about the Trinity. He used the words *hypostasis* and *prosopon* to explain God's three persons and *ousia* to explain God's one essence.
12. Nicene Creed, *Evangelical Lutheran Worship* (Minneapolis: Augsburg Fortress, 2006), 104. This wording first published by English Language Liturgical Consultation in *Praying Together*, 1988.

Spirit" are all assertions of divinity. The following stanza of the creed affirms belief in the Holy Spirit. The Apostles' Creed serves as a statement of belief in God and, in its very framework, describes God as Father, Son, and Holy Spirit, hence declaring the divinity of each. As we will see, however, none of these creeds spells out exactly *how* the *three* persons of the Trinity could possibly constitute *one* God. To complicate matters even more, the East and West differed on the pathway to theological precision.

The Split between East and West

Theological disputes between the East and the West primarily over the Trinity eventually led to the Great Schism in the church (1054 CE), an event that divided the major sectors of Christianity into Orthodoxy in the Greek-speaking East and Roman Catholicism in the Latin-speaking West. Out of this split, two major theories of the Trinity emerged, most popularly articulated by Augustine of Hippo and Thomas Aquinas in the West and by the Cappadocian Fathers in the East.

Augustine of Hippo and the Western Classical Trinity

Drawing from Tertullian, the patriarch of Western theology, Augustine of Hippo (354–430) aligns his Trinitarian theory with the formula one substance/essence (one being) in three persons (*una substantia, tres personae*). Because of his classical views of God as simple (divine unity) and uncompounded (not mixed with any other substance), he begins his theological construction with the transcendent, incomprehensible one God we have discussed under classical theism and then progresses to the threeness of God. This starting point, according to Eastern theologians, accentuates the significance of the "one God" over and above that of the "three persons."[13] Augustine was uncomfortable with the word *person*, which seemed to him to divide God into separate entities, a plurality inconsistent with simplicity. But although Augustine focused on the transcendent simplicity of the one God, he believed the "persons" amounted to relations within the one divine essence, so that the Father expresses the characteristic of fatherhood; the Son expresses the characteristic of sonship; and the Holy Spirit expresses the characteristic of the exhalation of God into the world.

Augustine took his cue from the idea that humanity is created in the image of God, indicating an affinity between God and humans in which we exhibit similarities to the Trinity. He explained it using metaphors from human existence, such as the bond between lovers and the components that constitute the human psyche. Since *love* describes God, the Trinity exists as God who loves (Father), God who is

---

13. Stanley J. Grenz, *Rediscovering the Triune God: The Trinity in Contemporary Theology* (Minneapolis: Fortress, 2004), 9–11.

loved (Son), and love itself (Holy Spirit). We might express this same concept with the terms *the Lover, the Beloved,* and *the bond of Love.* In other words, love cannot exist without something or someone to love. If God is love, then God naturally and eternally loves the Son, and the Holy Spirit of love binds the two together in a Trinity of divine persons.[14]

Augustine also borrowed the imagery of the rational human mind to articulate the Trinity. He divided it into three parts: memory (Father), understanding (Son), and will (Holy Spirit).[15] All of these are contained in one essence or substance, yet are three different capacities of the human brain. Augustine says that one mind contains its whole memory, its whole understanding, and its whole will; yet, they each reference the others as separate functions of the one mind. For instance, my understanding and my will remember; my memory understands my will; and my will remembers my understanding. So even though the mind functions in three interrelated ways, the mind is one mind, one essence, united in all its activities. "Therefore," Augustine states, "since they are each and all and wholly contained by each, they are each and all equal to each and all, and each and all equal to all of them together, and these three are one, one life, one mind, one being."[16] So under Augustine's influence classical theists in the West continued to emphasize the *one* substance of God, and only after establishing that fact did these theologians begin to think about the distinct threeness of that one God.

This Western emphasis on oneness and transcendence developed into what is called the doctrine of *the immanent Trinity*—understood as the Father, Son, and Holy Spirit as they live and move and have their being within the Godhead—as distinct from the *economic Trinity*—the Father, Son, and Holy Spirit working in history to bring about salvation. Because of their reliance on Western classical images of God, theologians from this time period needed to make a significant distinction between God's Trinitarian activity in eternity (within God's self) and God's Trinitarian activity in history.

Naturally, because God within the immanent Trinity remains so distant and distinct from creation, mere humans cannot know or understand this aspect of God. God functions in three persons in transcendent bliss, outside the realm of human cognition, human history, and human activity. The outcome of the church's focus on the one transcendent, simple (unchanging) God over and above the distinct plurality of the persons led to a view of the Trinity as somewhat detached from reality. This detachment caused the worship and prayers of the Christian community to concentrate on metaphysical and theoretical doctrines of God, and the more relational aspects of the three persons—Father, Son, and Holy Spirit—took a

14. Plantinga, Thompson, and Lundberg, *Introduction to Christian Theology,* 127.
15. Another formulation of the same idea is mind, knowledge, and love.
16. Augustine, *On the Trinity,* trans. Edmund Hill, ed. John E. Rotelle (Brooklyn, NY: New City, 1991), 298–99.

back seat. Fortunately, Eastern Christian theology picked up the relational slack in Western thought.

The Cappadocian Fathers and the Eastern Social Trinity

Basil of Caesarea (330–379 CE), his younger brother Gregory of Nyssa (335–394 CE), and fellow bishop Gregory of Nazianzus (329–390 CE) heavily influenced the outcome of questions surrounding the Trinity—at least in the East. In fact, these three theologians may have made the most significant impact on Trinitarian theology of anyone in the Eastern Orthodox Church. Beginning with the threeness instead of the oneness of God, they focused on the members of the divine tri-unity and highlighted the role of the Father as the source of the other two members—emphasizing the Son's "begottenness" and the Spirit's "procession" from the Father.[17] In other words, these early theologians explored the question of how God the Son and God the Spirit come "out of" or are related to God the Father. The focus on three rather than one emphasizes the relational aspects of the triune God as Father, Son, and Holy Spirit as they work together throughout salvation history. We see God less as essence and more as relationship, less as transcendent unknowability and more as intimate relatability. So, although the Eastern church holds strongly to the idea of the oneness of God, it believes just as strongly that the genuine nature of the One is to be Three. Consequently, only after grounding the conception of the Trinity in the participatory outworking of the three "energies" of God does Eastern Christian thought make the move toward God's unity as "being" or "essence."

The Eastern church interprets the Western concept of the immanent and economic Trinity a bit differently by making quite a bold distinction between the "essence" and the "energies" of God. Eastern theologians claim we cannot know the incomprehensible, incomparable, and ineffable God in God's essence or being, since God is, apart from creation and connection with creatures. John of Damascus (675–749 CE) explains the divine mystery and our capacity to comprehend it by saying: "It is plain, then, that there is a God. But what He is in His essence and nature is absolutely incomprehensible and unknowable."[18] Because God remains unknowable and ineffable, we need a way to talk about God, to "see" God, and to know God, which leads Eastern theologians to make a clear distinction between God's *essence*—God's being, above and beyond the realm of human knowledge and comprehension, and God's *energies*—God's actions in the world to bring about redemption.[19] For example, God's activities in creating, saving, and sustaining a fallen creation involve an intimate and deeply involved participatory relationship

---

17. Grenz, *Rediscovering the Triune God*, 8–9; Vladimir Lossky, *The Mystical Theology of the Eastern Church* (Crestwood, NY: St. Vladimir's Seminary Press, 1976), 52, 56.
18. John of Damascus, *An Exposition of the Orthodox Faith*: 1.4.
19. For a good explanation of God's essence and energies, see Payton, *Light from the Christian East*, 79–84.

based upon love between God and all that God has made. God accomplishes this divine work through what Eastern theologians term "divine energies."

In fact, these energies *are* God—not feelings, influences, or mere action, but God in God's self as Father, Son, and Holy Spirit acting within history and within the bounds of human existence.[20] So, as contemporary Orthodox theologian Vladimir Lossky asserts, "God is transcendent in his essence . . . but God proceeds outside his essence. He continually bursts forth from his hiding place, and this bursting forth . . . [is] a mode of existing in which the Divinity can communicate itself to created beings."[21] When God bursts forth, God does so by "begetting" the Son of God, Jesus Christ, and by sending forth the Spirit of God, both of whom reveal the divine inner life that desires to redeem, to give new life, transform, and include all creation in the loving embrace of the triune God. Even though each of the three energies functions in ways distinct from the others, one does not exist without the other two because together all three are God in perfect unity of will, action, and love. From the essence of the Father comes the begetting of the Son, who reveals God through the incarnation. From that same essence of the Father comes the procession of the Spirit, who continues the work of God in the name of Christ through indwelling, teaching, comforting, and giving gifts.[22]

The Eastern Orthodox Church beautifully expresses the energies of God as loving relational activity inside and outside of the Trinity. With a common will, mission, and goal, the Father, Son, and Holy Spirit interact in perfect accord. Filaret of Moscow (1783–1867) expresses this triune integrative intimacy, writing of "the love of the Father crucifying, the love of the Son crucified, and the love of the Holy Spirit triumphant in the invincible power of the cross."[23] All three persons of the Trinity participate in the redemptive deeds that effect the reconciliation and restoration of all creation to God. And in addition, we know and understand God through the unity of the distinct three. For example, as John of Damascus says, "The Holy Spirit is the image of the Son; for no man can say that Jesus is the Lord, but by the Holy Ghost. Thus it is by the Holy Spirit that we know Christ, who is both Son of God and God, and it is in the Son that we see the Father."[24] The Son is begotten by and the Holy Spirit proceeds from the Father, and the Father is communicated in the Son

20. Payton, *Light from the Christian East*, 81.
21. Vladimir Lossky, *In the Image and Likeness of God* (Crestwood, NY: St. Vladimir's Seminary Press, 1974), 40.
22. Vladimir Lossky, "The Procession of the Holy Spirit in Orthodox Trinitarian Theology," in *Eastern Orthodox Theology: A Contemporary Reader*, ed. Daniel B. Clendenin (Grand Rapids, MI: Baker Academic, 2003), 175–77. Eastern and Western theologians argued over whether the Holy Spirit proceeded from the Father or from both the Father and the Son. In the attempt to remain consistent to the Trinity existing with one common will, the East believed that the Holy Spirit proceeded from the Father only. Western theologians, who believed that Jesus has a human and a divine will, insisted that the Holy Spirit proceeded from the Father "and the Son" (*filioque* in Latin).
23. Filaret (Metropolitan of Moscow), *Oraisons funèbres, homélies et discours*, trans. A. de Sturdza (Paris, 1849), 154. "*Charité du Père qui crucifie; charité du Fils qui est crucifié; charité du Saint-Esprit qui triomphe par la vertu efficace de la crucifixion.*"
24. John of Damascus, *De imaginibus*, III, 18, 1340 AB. Also quoted in Lossky, *Mystical Theology*, 84.

and the Holy Spirit. The Father is made manifest through the Son and Spirit, while the Son and Spirit act through the divine energies of the Father, all three united in the bond of love. Consequently, Gregory of Nyssa can assert with confidence that "the source of Power is the Father, the Power of the Father is the Son, the Spirit of Power is the Holy Spirit."[25] So we see that in Eastern Christian thought the Father, Son, and Holy Spirit exist in social accord, eternally harmonious, in mutually loving relationship, distinct from one another in energies and activities, yet completely united in essence and power. But the beauty of the Trinity does not end there. God graciously extends the loving divine social accord to those outside of God, all of whom are made in God's image. This language of social accord brings us to the next Trinitarian metaphor: "the social Trinity."

The Social Trinity

The Relational God

The Eastern Orthodox tradition provides us with a dynamic image of the Trinity that hinges on our experience of the divine in the world. Eastern theologians believe that abstract ideas of God, such as pure Being (*purum esse*), omnipotence, omniscience, immutability, impassibility, and *actus purus* as articulated in the classical theistic tradition, sterilize and remove God from human experience. Consequently, they sought more concrete concepts that would express the loving, creative, and all-inclusive personality of God found in their own experience of salvation and sanctification. For them, experience of something or someone automatically includes a relationship. So an experience of God is also a relationship with God. The creative conception originally developed by Eastern theologians understood God as "person" rather than as "substance," so that "personhood, being-in-relation-to-another, was secured as the ultimate originating principle of all reality."[26] As a result, the move away from essence to experience, and from substance to personhood, compelled theologians to understand God in relational terms, even as relationality itself.

These theologians started this thought process by looking at God at work in their own lives, through salvation, healing, worship, and prayer. They encountered God in Scripture and in the words and deeds of Jesus, God in the flesh, who loves unconditionally, who welcomes all into God's kingdom, and who lovingly desires to share with us the divine life. They believed the power of God's Spirit removes ethnic and social boundaries and builds bridges where walls once existed. They experienced the hope of a new creation in the drawing together of a new

25. Gregory of Nyssa, *Adversus Macedonianos, De spiritu sancto*, 13', P.G., EXV, 1317 A.
26. Catherine Mowry LaCugna, "God in Communion with Us: The Trinity," in *Freeing Theology: The Essentials of Theology in Feminist Perspectives*, ed. Catherine Mowry LaCugna (San Francisco: HarperSanFrancisco, 1993), 86–87.

people for God in Christ. For them, the Trinitarian God manifests the divine life and love through experience.[27] Consequently, if we know God through experience, we must have a relationship with God, and therefore, God must be relational. Furthermore, we can think about each person of the Trinity as constituted not by abstract terms, such as *pure essence* or *ultimate being*, but by relationality—eternally within God and externally with us in the world.[28] In fact, channeling Western theologian Friedrich Schleiermacher, Paul Tillich states that the doctrine of the Trinity finds expression most fully in God's relationship to humanity and the world. He believes that each person of the Trinity represents a way in which God relates to us, especially regarding "sin and forgiveness, creation and death, and eternal life, the presence of the Spirit in the church and in the individual Christian," the relationship with creation, redemption, and life in the Spirit.[29] In other words, the kingdom of God manifests itself as each member of the Trinity actively participates in the salvation history of the world, as God hands on to Jesus the task of saving, and Jesus hands on to the Spirit the task of sanctifying—each handing on to the other the next step in the divine process of redemption. Because it encompasses the entirety of the Godhead and God's work to redeem the world, the doctrine of the triune God serves as the foundation for all Christian theology.[30]

Twelfth-century Scottish theologian Richard of St. Victor (d. 1173) conceived of the Trinity as persons in love. He asserted that the process of redemption set in motion by a relational triune God begins with the notion of "supreme goodness"—a goodness energized by supreme love.[31] He echoed St. Augustine of Hippo with the notion of the Trinity as love, arguing that the assertion "God is love" (1 John 4:8) automatically implies a love relationship between loving "persons." The very nature of love requires one who loves and one who is loved, a shared experience of reciprocal relationship between lovers that both gives and receives, each loving and each loved.[32] Other theologians in the West have developed analogous ideas. For twentieth-century theologian Wolfhart Pannenberg, this Trinitarian love actually constitutes the essence of the divine life as Father, Son, and Holy Spirit in eternal communion, bound together in a communal dance of mutual love. For those who hold to a social or relational view of the Trinity, God's very being consists in personal, loving communion.[33] For medieval Franciscan theologian John Duns Scotus, God is perfect love. For that to remain the case, God must love within God's self,

---

27. Paul Fiddes, "Relational Trinity: Radical Perspective," in *Two Views on the Doctrine of the Trinity*, ed. Jason S. Sexton and Stanley N. Gundry (Grand Rapids, MI: Zondervan, 2014), 163.
28. See Gordon Kaufman, *In the Face of Mystery: A Constructive Theology* (Boston: Harvard University Press, 1993), 415; Paul D. Molnar, "Classical Trinity: Catholic Perspective," *Two Views*, 76, 79; Fiddes, "Relational Trinity," 179.
29. Paul Tillich, *A History of Christian Thought: From Its Judaic and Hellenistic Origins to Existentialism*, ed. Carl Braaten (New York: Simon & Schuster, 1968), 408.
30. Grenz, *Rediscovering the Triune God*, 21–22, 80, 99.
31. Richard of St. Victor, *The Trinity*, ed. Ruben Angelici (Eugene, OR: Cascade, 2011), 2.13, 18; 3.6.
32. Grenz, *Rediscovering the Triune God*, 11.
33. Grenz, *Rediscovering the Triune God*, 120, 147.

among the persons of the Trinity. In fact, for Scotus, the Father, Son, and Holy Spirit love one another with friendship love (*amor amicitiae*), a love that naturally reaches willfully out to others for inclusion in the divine love triangle.[34]

Some theologians, such as Karl Rahner in the twentieth century, hold more closely to dominant Western theological traditions and assert that emphasizing love between the persons of the Trinity diminishes the unity of essence (*homoousios*), but I believe we need not throw unity out in favor of the distinction between persons. In the words of contemporary theologian Cornelius Plantinga:

> The Holy Trinity is a divine, transcendent society or community of three fully personal and fully divine entities: the Father, the Son, and the Holy Spirit or Paraclete. These three are wonderfully united by their common divinity, that is, by the possession of the whole generic divine essence.... The persons are also unified by their joint redemptive purpose, revelation, and work. Their knowledge and love are directed not only to their creatures, but also primordially and archetypically to each other. The Father loves the Son and the Son loves the Father . . . and the Trinity is thus a zestful community of light, love, joy, mutuality, and verve.[35]

Brazilian theologian Leonardo Boff tries to bridge the gap between East and West. He suggests that in the perichoretic dance between Father, Son, and Holy Spirit, each person both gives and receives everything from the other persons all at the same time. They all emerge from one another in a unified triadic relationship of love and redemptive purpose—distinct in persons yet unified in divinity and purpose.[36] The distinction of persons loving one another in a perichoretic dance harmonizes beautifully with the unity of the one divine essence that is love. Interestingly, the animated symbol for the Rio 2016 Olympics helps us imagine this beautiful image of the divine dance. Three abstract figures, connected by hands and feet, dance in a circle of living color. The three figures flow together in a seemingly undulating dance of intimacy and love, eternally connected to one another while allowing enough open space for others to join in.[37]

Any discussion on the Trinity should also include the thought of contemporary Franciscan theologian Richard Rohr, who says that "whatever is going on in God is a *flow*, a *radical relatedness*, a *perfect communion* between Three—a circle dance

34. Thomas H. McCall, "Relational Trinity: Creedal Perspective," in *Two Views*, 125.
35. Cornelius Plantinga Jr., "Social Trinity and Tritheism," in *Trinity, Incarnation, and Atonement: Philosophical and Theological Essays*, ed. Ronald J. Feenstra and Cornelius Plantinga Jr. (Notre Dame, IN: University of Notre Dame Press, 1989), 27–28. The word *paraclete* describes the Holy Spirit as an advocate or a helper.
36. Leonardo Boff, *Trinity and Society*, trans. Paul Burns (Eugene, OR: Wipf & Stock, 2005), 146–47.
37. See the image here: https://tinyurl.com/w6r88uf.

of love."[38] And fortunately for us (and for all creation!), God invites us to participate in that communion of love.

The Invitational God

We see that the Trinitarian God exists as relational, as one whose very essence is love. God discloses to us an eternal life of divine sharing, of participating in all movements of life in and outside the Godhead. The very nature of love compels God to extend the divine relationality outward into the life of the world. We find one of the more beautiful expressions of the relationality of God and the divine hospitality toward the world in Andrei Rublev's fifteenth-century icon *The Trinity*. This famous Russian iconographer included the colors gold, blue, and green in his artistic expression. The gold represents the Father as the ultimate source of perfection and wholeness. The blue indicates the incarnated Son in which the sky (heaven) and the sea (earth) unite humanity and divinity together for the sake of redemption. The green in the icon portrays the Holy Spirit's continual fertility manifest in giving life and making all things new in a "divine photosynthesis that grows everything from within by transforming light into itself."[39] Interestingly, art historians assert that a mirror once embellished the table at the front of the icon, suggesting there is room for other people at the feast—us! Rublev's creative image provides insight into the character and will of God, who invites us to participate in the divine inner life, to enter the dance as partners in mutual love and purpose.

As God makes space at the table (and on the dance floor) for us in the communion of Father, Son, and Holy Spirit, we live and move and have our being in God. The Father delivers the Son into the world to redeem, and sends the Spirit into the world to gather all creation together in unity with the divine. This results in an eternal dance of choreographic kingdom creativity that makes us partners in the work of transforming the world. As theologian Lesslie Newbigin aptly explains, "The Church's mission to all the nations is a participation in the work of the triune God, and we are invited to become, through the presence of the Holy Spirit, participants in the Son's loving obedience to the Father."[40] So as we participate in the divine communion of love, we work with God to bring all things back to God. We might consider it a circular motion that begins with the dance between Father, Son, and Holy Spirit, who then, out of the urging desire of love, invite us to join in as partners, raising us into the presence of God (Eph 2:6) and sending us back into the world to invite others to the heavenly ball (Matt 28:19–20).

38. Richard Rohr, *The Divine Dance: The Trinity and Your Transformation* (New Kensington, PA: Whitaker House, 2016), Kindle digital edition, loc. 361.
39. Rohr, *Divine Dance*, Kindle digital edition, loc. 416.
40. Lesslie Newbigin, *The Relevance of Trinitarian Doctrine for Today's Mission* (Edinburgh: Abingdon, 1984), 78; see also the excellent essay by Humphreys, "The Revelation of the Trinity," previously cited.

Just as in creation, everything flows out from God, and in the divine dance God brings all things back to God in choreographed compassion.

The Participational God

The divine invitation always stands open, urging us to live God's life through the new humanity given to us in Christ in the dynamism of the Spirit, who continually empowers us to do the work of the kingdom. But that's not all. God exists with us, in us, and through us as the divine life flowing through all things, circling and dancing, re-creating and redeeming, reconciling and restoring as our partner in the work of transforming the world. Carl McColman puts this Trinitarian conception into words poetically:

> God is in us, because we are in Christ. As members of the mystical body, Christians actually partake in the divine nature of the Trinity. We do not merely *watch* the dance, we *dance* the dance. We join hands with Christ and the Spirit flows through us and between us and our feet move always in the loving embrace of the Father. . . . We see the joyful love of the Father through the eyes of the Son. And with every breath, we breathe the Holy Spirit.[41]

Our participation in God's kingdom work can take various forms, such as prayer, forgiveness, and sacrifice. Union with the Trinitarian God comes alive in prayer. We pray to the Father, through the Son, in the power of the Holy Spirit—a relational movement that includes us as agents of change in the world. Theologian Paul Fiddes says that "as we pray, we can add the persuasive power of our love to God's. That is, in praying for others we are expressing our love and concern for them, and God takes that desire into the divine desire for their well-being, wanting to exercise the influence of created as well as uncreated love."[42] In addition, forgiveness unites us with the Son through the Father in the Spirit: we, much like Jesus as he hung on the cross suffering because of human sin, can say, "Father, forgive them; for they do not know what they are doing" (Luke 23:34). Every time we forgive someone, we participate in the life of the Father, Son, and Holy Spirit, who made forgiveness the coin of the realm, offering free admission into the life of the divine dance. Again, we turn to Fiddes, who says, "Even where our forgiveness is not accepted or the offender is not present to us, we are making a journey in God, enhancing a persuasive divine love that will have incalculable effects in the lives of others."[43] And we participate in the dance with God whenever we give of ourselves sacrificially. By so doing we imitate God's movements in the world,

41. Quoted in Rohr, *Divine Dance*, loc. 1108.
42. Fiddes, "Relational Trinity," 184.
43. Fiddes, "Relational Trinity," 184–85.

as children sent on a mission by their father or mother. We share the love of God made manifest by the life, death, and resurrection of Jesus Christ. Wherever we see the movement of an act of kindness, an offer of help in time of need, a stance of solidarity with the oppressed, a giving of resources to relieve suffering, we also see the truth and grace of the Trinitarian God. These sacrificial moments participate in the potently charismatic flow of the life and love of God.[44]

As we participate in the divine dance, invited by the Father, raised to the God-head by the Son, and empowered by the Spirit, we engage with God in *homoagapic* love—that is, a sharing with God and with each other of the same (*homo*) love (*agape*) that flows between the Father, Son, and Holy Spirit. This means that the love existing in the immanent Trinity is the same love in the economic Trinity, infiltrating everything in the world. This notion might lead us to ask not only how we behave in the world as homoagapic God-lovers, but also how *God* behaves in the world within which the homoagapic love of God freely flows.

God, as eternal love, embraces the world in its entirety—good and evil, joys and sorrows, positive and negative. And with us as divine partners, God suffers these contradictions and triumphs over them.[45] Consequently, we participate in union with the suffering God and share the movements of joy and heartache, hope and love. With God, we stand against corruption, oppression, hatred, and greed as we work in the power of the Spirit to create and promote God's goodness and love.

The Nonviolent Trinity

One of the first questions to consider as we explore the implications of God's behavior in the world concerns God's behavior within the Trinitarian relationship itself. In theological terms, we must study the immanent Trinity before examining the economic Trinity. Although historically both Western and Eastern theologians make some sort of separation between the two Trinitarian ways of communion and make broad distinctions between the activity of the immanent and economic Trinity, Karl Rahner believes that the economic Trinity *is* the immanent Trinity and vice versa (theologians often label this theory "Rahner's Rule").[46] This brings what has been separated back together. What God is in God's self is what God is in the world, Rahner asserts. If God appears to us as triune, then God is triune in God's very being, within the Godhead. The same applies to love. If God is love in God's self, then God is also love in relationship to the world. In other words, the transcendent, mysterious God is the same communal, triune God of love within the relationship between Father, Son, and Holy Spirit as God as Father, Son, and Holy Spirit is to the world.[47] Latin American theologian Leonardo Boff agrees

---

44. See also Fiddes, "Relational Trinity," 182.
45. Grenz, *Rediscovering the Triune God*, 79.
46. Karl Rahner, *The Trinity*, trans. Josephy Donceel (London: Continuum, 1970), 38, 49.
47. Grenz, *Rediscovering the Triune God*, 59, 126.

with Rahner, to a point. He will admit that the economic Trinity is the immanent Trinity, but not the other way around. Because he holds strongly to the notion that God remains an unfathomable mystery the depths of which we can never completely plumb, Boff does not believe that the way God works in the world (the economic Trinity) can ever totally manifest the transcendent God. So for him, "the economic Trinity is the immanent Trinity but not the whole of the immanent Trinity." There is always more of God than we can know.[48]

Theologian Catherine LaCugna appreciates the language of "immanent" and "economic" when referring to the Trinity, but she exhorts us to part ways with that language when we think about God in relationship with creation. Instead, she would rather talk about "the one ecstatic movement of God outward by which all things originate from God through Christ in the power of the Holy Spirit, and all things are brought into union with God and returned to God."[49] This movement suggests a divine invitation to the dance, which, once accepted, raises us up to God (Rom 6:5-11; Eph 2:6; Col 3:1) in union with Father, Son, and Holy Spirit, and enables us to live the life of God in the power of the Spirit on earth. LaCugna believes that "there is neither an economic nor immanent Trinity; there is only the *oikonomia* [household] that is the concrete realization of the mystery of *theologia* in time, space, history, and personality."[50] She believes the Trinity expresses the "household" or "comprehensive plan" of God in the history of the world, working to redeem, reconcile, and restore all creation to God—a dance of God that includes us as partners, existing with God in the mystery of love and communion, fulfilling the divine purposes.[51]

Discussions on the immanent and economic Trinity have everything to do with nonviolence as a fundamental principle. If the economic Trinity is the immanent Trinity, then God's way of acting in the world is consistent with who God is in God's self—in the Godhead, where Father, Son, and Holy Spirit relate to one another in loving communion. If the Godhead exists *as* love, then no violence or disharmony exists between Father, Son, and Holy Spirit. In fact, the Bible never alludes to any sort of violence between the persons of the Trinity. The Father does not do violence to the Son or the Spirit. The Son does not do violence to the Father or the Spirit. And the Spirit never does violence to the Son or the Father. They make love, not war! Consequently, if God does not act in violence within the Godhead, we can assert that God does not act violently in the world either. A God who exists *as* love cannot exercise that love in violent ways either between persons of the Trinity or between God and humanity. Scripture makes this concept quite clear.

---

48. Boff, *Trinity and Society*, 215.
49. Catherine Mowry LaCugna, *God for Us: The Trinity and Christian Life* (San Francisco: HarperSanFrancisco, 1973), 223.
50. LaCugna, *God for Us*, 223.
51. LaCugna, *God for Us*, 223.

For instance, Jesus tells us to love our enemies and pray for those who treat us badly. Why? So we can be children of the Father in heaven (Matt 5:43–48). Children of the Father imitate the Father who loves all enemies. In this way, we can be perfect as God is perfect—a statement made in the context of loving enemies and not dealing with them violently. It seems, therefore, that God's "perfection" is in loving, rather than in having to control everything by doing violence. We gain that loving perfection when we imitate the actions of a God who loved us enough to redeem us even while we were still God's enemies. This loving God makes a way for nonviolent reconciliation rather than for violent retribution (Rom 5:8–10). Jesus did not utter from the cross, "Father, smite these sinners." Instead, he prayed, "Father, forgive these sinners" (Luke 23:34, paraphrased). When God sent the Son into the world, the first message given to explain his presence was "Glory to God in the highest heaven, and on earth *peace* among those whom he favors" (Luke 2:14). God sent Jesus, the divine Son, to establish peace on earth as in heaven. Since God continually exercises (with us) the divine dance of love, there is no room for violence—not in the immanent Trinity, or in the economic Trinity, or in heaven, or on earth. The nonviolence of the immanent Trinity extends also to the economic Trinity.

Conclusion

As we think about communion with God, it may sound too good to be true—the creator of the universe summoning *us* to the dance. German theologian Jürgen Moltmann reflects upon the Rublev icon of the Trinity and paints for us a beautiful picture of the relational, dancing, triune God who invites us into the divine life. He says that "the relationship of the divine persons is so wide that it has room for the whole world."[52] Richard Bauckham asserts the same when he says that the divine invitation expresses "the uniting of all things with God and in God."[53] Through the work of the Son and by the power of the Spirit, the Father gathers all creation into the divine community, united in history and for all eternity. Moltmann believes that without such an inclusive dance, God would not be God. We worship an "open Trinity" that excludes violence.[54]

As we can see, the doctrine of the Trinity not only reveals the nature of God as nonviolent but also teaches us that God creates us to share in the divine life of nonviolent love. God makes room for us in the divine dance as redeemed partners in the work of the kingdom. God imparts the divine self to us through the incarnate Son who makes atonement for the world. The Holy Spirit continues the work of the Son by joining us in union with the Father and Son and transforming us more and more into God's likeness of living and loving in nonviolent ways. So the doctrine

---

52. Jürgen Moltmann, *The Church in the Power of the Spirit* (New York: Harper & Row, 1977), 60.
53. Richard Bauckham, *The Theology of Jürgen Moltmann* (Edinburgh: T & T Clark, 1995), 17.
54. Grenz, *Rediscovering the Triune God*, 82.

of the Trinity remains extremely relevant as we learn to behave in more Christ-like, peaceful, hope-bearing ways.[55]

Even though controversies still surround the doctrine of the Trinity and its continual development, I believe that the Trinity remains the most "distinctive feature of the Christian conception of God"[56] and that "it matters more than anything."[57] Theologian Paul Tillich asserts that if we talk meaningfully about God at all, we simply cannot get away from the Trinity.[58] According to Catherine LaCugna, "The doctrine of the Trinity is in fact the most practical of all doctrines," because it teaches us to articulate the gospel message, provides insight into transforming relationships, and provides the church with the language for worship.[59] The Trinity shapes our lives as Christians, enables us to understand how God works to redeem the world, and engages us in a divine/human relationship in order to fulfill God's purposes for all creation. Consequently, the doctrine of the Trinity remains one of the most significant ingredients for a uniquely Christian theological articulation with powerful transformative potential. And how we talk about God really matters.

55. McCall, "Relational Trinity," 135–36.
56. Kaufman, In the Face of Mystery, 412.
57. Lewis, Mere Christianity, 185.
58. Paul Tillich, Systematic Theology, vol. 1 (Chicago: University of Chicago Press, 1973), 251.
59. Catherine Mowry LaCugna, "The Practical Trinity," Christian Century 109, no. 22 (July 15–22, 1992): 679.

4. God

. . . the Father almighty . . .

[While] everything around me is ever changing, ever dying, there is underlying all that change a living power that is changeless, that holds all together, that creates, dissolves and recreates. That informing power or spirit is God. . . . And is this power benevolent or malevolent? I see it as purely benevolent. For I can see that in the midst of death life persists, in the midst of darkness light persists. Hence I gather that God is Life, Truth, Light. He is Love. He is the supreme Good.

—Mahatma Gandhi

God. The Father. Almighty. What do we mean by those words? Is "God" a name? Or a description? Does it point to something or nothing, male or female, a material or an immaterial reality, a person or an energy? Different faith traditions and religions have different answers. As much as we hate to admit it, we do not know the answer to these questions with any sense of absolute certainty. Our language does not come close to explaining God—it says either too little or too much. Although many people claim to experience God, how do we know it is God we are experiencing? And as we experience God and talk about God, we remain in constant danger of setting up conceptual idols and worshipping those instead of the true God, the God who remains a mystery to us.

In fact, the ancient Hebrew people felt the same way. They expressed the mystery of God through clay objects called "cult stands." Thousands of these stands have been discovered in archaeological sites in Israel dating from the twelfth to the tenth centuries BCE. An article in *Biblical Archaeology Review* features an image of a "Taanach Cult Stand" in which two figures serve as bookends framing an empty space. Although scholars do not know for certain their exact use in worship, some believe that, for worshippers of YHWH (the name of God in Exod 3:14), the space between the figures represents the seeming absence of the very present mystery they called God.[1] Likewise, we as Christians worship a God we cannot see, who dwells in a cloud of unknowing, an absent yet present divinity that eludes us in our attempts to describe the divine nature, actions, and attributes.

---

1. LaMoine F. DeVries, "Cult Stands: A Bewildering Variety of Shapes and Sizes," in *Biblical Archaeological Review* 13, no. 4 (July/August 1987): 26–37; a copy of this article can be found here: https://tinyurl .com/ut9pza5. Elizabeth Bloch-Smith, "Cult Stands, 12th–10th Century BCE," in Center for Online Judaic Studies, https://tinyurl.com/see8x5p.

Yet, we must verbalize our thoughts surrounding God in our worship, prayer, Bible study, and everyday conversations. Although we may not think so, how we talk about God is extremely important. Because the Christian message exhorts us to imitate God, our view of God and God's actions very often forms the structure for our own ethics and actions. If we believe that God acts violently, then we can justify our own violence toward others. If we see God's justice as retributive and punitive (concerned with punishing the offender), we could very well justify our own acts of retribution toward those who have harmed us. But if we view God's justice as merciful and restorative (seeking to restore the offender), we may treat others with mercy and seek to restore broken relationships. Knowing God begins with our words that form concepts that influence our behavior.

The question we have to ask ourselves is, Can we know God? If we answer yes to that question, we need to ask, How? We do know that we can't know with absolute certainty whether we have it right. But since our faith seeks understanding, we must try. We do that by studying the Bible, researching our tradition, using our ability to reason, and interpreting our experience in a spirit of prayer, with a critically engaged mind.

So, let's do a little brain exercise. Write down all the words you can think of that describe God—words such as *rock*, *Lord*, *redeemer*, *just*, *love*, and so forth. Write down as many as you can. Now draw a big box around all your words. Notice that if we limit our perception of God to what we have enclosed in our box, we are putting God in a box and actually constructing our own conceptual idol. So we might want to draw a dotted line around our words about God so that new ideas can enter in and other ideas can exit the box if they do not hold up to the evidence of Scripture, tradition, reason, and experience, mediated by our imagination. It is important to remember that most of who God is and how God acts in the world remains hidden outside the box. Which means, of course, that those who think outside the box—those who think differently than the words we have in our box—might have discovered truths about God we haven't yet uncovered.

The Bible contains many images of God that give us an idea about who God is and how God acts in the world. We need to remember, however, that the language used to describe God is metaphorical. That doesn't mean it isn't true; in fact, quite the opposite! Metaphorical language about God communicates profound truths. For instance, Scripture refers to God as a rock (Deut 32:4). Is God really a hunk of granite? Of course not. But the metaphor of a rock tells us the truth that God is strong, a refuge for those who need protection. We also see God referred to as an eagle or a large bird under whose wings we find safety (Isa 40:31; Ps 91:4). In the face of danger, large birds spread their wings and hide their young under them. This is a beautiful metaphor that gives us a picture of God as a protector.

Scripture also depicts God as a mother who gives birth to, nurtures, and nurses her children (Deut 32:18; Isa 42:14; 49:15). In fact, the Hebrew word *raham*, one the Bible uses often to speak about God, literally refers to a mother's love for her children. We see this word in 1 Kings 3 in a famous story about two women disputing over a son in front of King Solomon. One woman's baby has died, and she takes the live newborn of the other woman and claims it as her own. The two women go before Solomon so he can cast judgment and determine who the baby belongs to. He finally says, "Split the child in two and give one half to each woman" (1 Kgs 3:25, paraphrased). The woman whose child it wasn't—the one who stole the child—agreed. "But the woman whose son was alive said to the king—because compassion [*raham*] for her son burned within her—'Please, my lord, give her the living boy; certainly do not kill him!'" (1 Kgs 3:26). The real mother had such compassion and love for her child that she was willing to give him up to the other woman so he could live. Thus, Solomon knew who the true mother was and gave the child back to her. God has that same kind of motherly love for us. Indeed, the word *raham* in Scripture most often describes God. Does that mean God is a woman? Absolutely not! God is not a woman. Neither is God a man. God is not a rock or an eagle either. But Scripture can't describe God's characteristics in any other way than to use language that comes from everyday life so we can understand through these metaphors the character of God.

Keeping in our minds the danger of idolatry and the significance of metaphorical language for God will motivate us to a sense of humility and hospitality toward new ideas. It will require us to live by faith and not by absolute certainty. Remember, absolute certainty often leads to violence because we are so certain about what we think about God that we willingly justify doing violence to those who do not see things our way. With all that said, let's get into some major ways people have thought about God.

Classical Theism

As we have seen, we don't develop our theological beliefs *ex nihilo* (out of nothing). All our doctrines emerge out of sociocultural circumstances, worldviews, and already established traditions. Our notions surrounding the character, attributes, and actions of God come from ideas in place long before Christians started constructing their own theological belief systems. So, where do our thoughts about God arise?

Neoplatonism

The system of thought most familiar to early Christians was the Neoplatonism of Greek philosophy and culture, which Christian theologians appropriated as the framework for Christian doctrine. In fact, when Paul first preached the gospel to the people in Greece and Rome, he purposely used the ideas and language of the Greek philosophers to relate to and reach his hearers. He employed great rhetorical skills by crafting a message that answered questions posed by Plato, Socrates,

Aristotle, and others. Paul taught that through faith in Jesus Christ, people's souls "would finally grasp the timeless wisdom that every previous philosopher had said was the key to happiness."[2] Greek thought provided a foundation for Christian doctrine and made it relevant and respected in a broadly Hellenistic culture. Put another way, "while Judaism and the Bible gave Christianity its weight and matter, its flesh and blood so to speak, Plato and Neoplatonism became its conceptual spine."[3] Church father Clement of Alexandria (ca. 150–ca. 215 CE) and those in his society believed "Christianity was not the enemy of philosophy, but its finest and last expression."[4] Because of its connection to the prevailing philosophy of the day and the familiar streams of Judaism in the Hebrew Bible, Christianity spread swiftly and, hidden within its theological foundation, so did Greek philosophical concepts. Starting in the second century, the thought of the early Christian scholars, often referred to as Patristic scholars or church fathers, competed with the prevailing theisms (ideas about God) of the age in which the popularity of the Greek and Roman pantheon of gods occupied the minds and hearts of most people. The "new" way of thinking as Christians enabled theologians to claim that the God of Jesus "was the fulfillment of the God sought by the philosophers"—not some tribal deity, but the universal God who sees all, knows all, and has power over all creation.[5]

Western philosophical thought claimed that God must have certain attributes such as "perfection" and "simplicity." Perfection, in this case, meant that God cannot move or change because only an imperfect being moves or changes. In other words, God, in this view, has no need for any additional growth, change, knowledge, power, emotion, or potential: God is a totally complete, perfect being. For these early thinkers steeped in Western philosophical thought, God is *immutable, impassible, incomprehensible, omnipotent, omniscient*, and *actus purus*, or *pure actuality* (we will define these terms in the next section). In this view, God does not feel any kind of passion or pain and never experiences weakness or ignorance, because all of these constitute a change of some sort, which would indicate the existence of imperfection.[6] These theologians also understood God to be omnipresent, transcendent, and eternal in what became known as the tradition of *classical theism*. Together, these conceptions have significantly influenced Christian doctrine since the inception of the church and have formed the foundation for many theological traditions throughout the centuries.

2. Arthur Herman, *The Cave and the Light: Plato versus Aristotle, and the Struggle for the Soul of Western Civilization* (New York: Random House, 2014), 150.
3. Herman, *The Cave and the Light*, 152.
4. Herman, *The Cave and the Light*, 153. Jesus's teachings epitomized the Platonic notions surrounding beauty, nature, truth, justice, forms, and being.
5. John Sanders, *The God Who Risks: A Theology of Providence* (Downers Grove, IL: IVP, 1998), 141.
6. Sanders, *The God Who Risks*, 142–43.

Attributes of God according to Classical Theism

Classical theism uses the following concepts to define God:

Actus purus, Latin for "pure actuality." All God's work always was, is, and will be complete. As a result, God has no potential because all God's work is already completely and fully actualized. Often scholars who hold to a view of God as *actus purus* cite Exodus 3:14, where God says, "I am who I am." If interpreted in this way, the verse could indicate the non-potential of God. God is, period. God needs nothing else, is nothing else, will be nothing else, other than this same, one God for all eternity—without beginning and without end.

Immutability. That God is immutable means God cannot change, at all, for any reason. Because God is characterized by pure actuality and has no potential, God cannot change God's mind or knowledge or attitude or actions. Of course, the Bible does contain verses that speak of God's immutability, such as Malachi 3:6, where God says, "For I the Lord do not change." Numbers 23:19 reminds us that "God is not a human being, that he should lie, or a mortal, that he should change his mind." James 1:17 tells us that in God there is "no variation or shadow due to change." So we see that in some instances, Scripture supports the image of God as immutable.

Impassibility. God is impassible, meaning God cannot suffer because suffering involves the change from not suffering to suffering. Any type of emotion or pain would bring God all too close to the human condition, where the messiness of life might infect the divine purity. The idea of an impassible God stems from the Platonic theologians who thought any change meant imperfection. So the Christian God, as total perfection, must never suffer emotion or pain. Finding scriptural support for divine impassibility is nearly impossible—indeed, we find only the opposite! But because of their fixed ideas surrounding the divine attributes, classical theists explain scriptural passages in which God grieves or experiences joy as mere anthropomorphisms—the use of human language, attributes, and characteristics to describe a nonhuman being.

Omniscience. In Latin, *omni* means "all" and *scientia* means "knowledge." So, God knows everything, past, present, and future. God knows the number of hairs on your head. In fact, God does not have to count them—God already, always, knows. Scripture supports this attribute in some cases. For example, the Psalmist tells us that God's understanding is "beyond measure" (147:5) and that before we speak a word, God knows it (139:4). Isaiah voices a similar sentiment, saying that God's "understanding is unsearchable" (40:28), God's purpose will stand, and all God's intentions will come to pass (46:9–10). Remember, Scripture never uses the word *omniscient* for God's knowledge, but we can interpret these verses to indicate its depth and breadth.

Omnipotence. Again, in the Latin, *omni* means "all" and *potens* means "powerful," so the word indicates that God can do all things. Furthermore, everything God does has always, already, eternally been done. Remember, in classical theism, God has no potential, so God does not act in the moment in response to our actions or thoughts. God's action always has been already acted out from all eternity. Although the Bible never explicitly mentions the word *omnipotence* to describe God, we can find some verses that would lead us to believe that God is all powerful. For example, Daniel tells his audience that God "does what he wills with the host of heaven and the inhabitants of the earth" (4:35). Isaiah speaks for God, saying that no one can deliver from God's hand; God works and no one can hinder God (43:13) and that "the Lord of hosts" has made plans and no one can change them (14:27). Job cries out to God that no divine purpose "can be thwarted" (42:2). Genesis, Jeremiah, Luke, and Matthew attest that nothing is too difficult for God.[7] We can interpret these verses to imply God's omnipotence even though they do not directly claim it.

Calvin and Classical Theism

One of the most significant theological developments that arose out of classical theism comes from the sixteenth-century Reformer John Calvin (1509–1564). Disenchanted with the corruption he saw in the Roman Catholic Church, he used the classical theology handed down to him from theological greats such as St. Augustine and Thomas Aquinas to write the *Institutes of the Christian Religion*, constructing a theology that remains extremely popular in some streams of Christian thought today. Calvin's followers continued to develop his theology in what we now know as "Calvinism." Later Calvinists and other theologians made his theology easier to remember by making up an acronym for his thought—TULIP.[8] See if you can detect the streams of classical theology in what follows:

T = Total depravity. Calvin taught that the image of God in human beings is crusted over to the point that sin has totally infiltrated their hearts, minds, souls, and bodies, so that they cannot choose on their own to desire God or seek

---

7. Gen 18:14; Jer 32:27; Luke 1:37; Matt 19:26.
8. Although not specifically stated identical to the TULIP pattern, the tenets of these five points are found in the Canons of Dort (1618). See also Roger E. Olson, *The Mosaic of Christian Belief: Twenty Centuries of Unity and Disunity* (Downers Grove, IL: InterVarsity, 2016), 308.

redemption through Christ. Only through the work of the Holy Spirit and the election of God can people be redeemed. Human agency plays no part.

U = Unconditional election. Calvin thought God elected (preordained) all humans to either heaven or hell. Some Calvinists argue that Calvin himself held to what is called "single predestination," meaning God elects a few people to be saved and go to heaven, while all the others automatically suffer condemnation in hell because of their sin. Other theologians interpret Calvin as holding to "double predestination," the idea that God elects some people to salvation based on no conditions other than the fact that God desires to save some of us, and elects all the rest to hell. In other words, God does not foreknow that someone will be good or will choose God—that would be a condition. Rather, God elects someone merely out of grace, simply because God wants to.

L = Limited atonement. Calvin believed that Jesus died *only* for the elect, not for those predestined to hell. So, for him, God limits the work of Jesus to redeeming only those God elects to salvation.

I = Irresistible grace. Calvin believed that those God has elected will not be able to resist the saving grace mediated through the Holy Spirit. If God elects someone to salvation, that person will never, ever be able to resist that grace or refuse salvation.

P = Perseverance of the saints. Calvin believed that an elect person will always, no matter what, persevere in that state of saving grace until he or she dies. Because the saving grace of the Holy Spirit is so effective and irresistible, not one of the elect will fall away.

Not only does God randomly predestine some people for salvation; Calvin also taught that God preordains everything that happens in the universe. He calls this God's "providence," defined as God's rule and power over all creation. God governs heaven and earth with total control, omnipotence, and omniscience. Calvin writes that God "is deemed omnipotent, not because he can indeed act . . . but because, governing heaven and earth by his providence, he so regulates all things that nothing takes place without his deliberation. For when, in The Psalms, it is said that 'he does whatever he wills' [Ps 115:3], a certain and deliberate will is meant."[9] Contemporary Calvinist pastor John Piper takes very seriously this doctrine of providence. He wrote a sermon after 9/11 asserting that God not only allowed the terrorists to murder over three thousand people but caused those

9. John Calvin, *Institutes of the Christian Religion*, ed. John T. McNeill, trans. Ford Lewis Battles (Louisville, KY: Westminster John Knox, 1960), 1.16.3, 4; also at https://tinyurl.com/ybbz8qkv.

events to occur.[10] I believe, however, that we must carefully examine the presuppositions leading to any theology that endorses the violence of God. Theologian Roger Olson writes, "I believe someone needs finally to stand up and in love firmly say 'no!' to the egregious statement about God's sovereignty often made by Calvinists . . . I have gone so far as to say that this kind of Calvinism, which attributes everything to God's will and control, makes it difficult (at least for me) to see the difference between God and the devil."[11]

If the theology of Calvinism remains unsatisfactory to those holding views of a nonviolent God, perhaps the theology of Calvin's student Jacobus Arminius will sound more plausible. Some say he presented a type of "cure" for Calvin's hard-nosed determinism. So, not to be outdone by Calvin's TULIP, late Arminians crafted the acronym DAISY to condense Arminius's arguments against Calvin's theology. But since various forms of the DAISY exist and none of them adequately defines Arminius's theology, we will forgo that acronym and instead look for "A CURE" for Calvinism. Here are Arminius's views:

A = Almost total depravity. Arminius believes that although sin has almost completely tarnished the image of God in humanity, God's image still shows through, working in the community alongside that sin. Human beings participate with the Holy Spirit to desire God, and respond freely to God's urgings to receive divine redemption.

C = Conditional election. God elects people to salvation based on God's foreknowing the choices they will make (called "middle knowledge" in philosophical arguments). If God knows someone will accept Jesus as savior, then God elects that person to be saved.

U = Unlimited atonement. Arminius taught that Jesus died for the forgiveness of *all* people. By the grace of God through the Spirit working in their lives, human beings choose whether they want to receive that salvation through Jesus Christ—a beautiful image of the Trinity at work to redeem creation.

R = Resistible grace. Through freedom of choice, people can resist God's saving grace and refuse salvation.

E = Evanescence of believers. Arminius believed that once people receive faith, they can easily remain faithful. But they also have the capacity to fall away from

10. John Piper, "Why I Do Not Say, 'God Did Not Cause the Calamity, but He Can Use It for Good,'" Desiring God, September 17, 2001, https://tinyurl.com/uu3blhe.
11. Roger E. Olson, *Against Calvinism* (Grand Rapids, MI: Zondervan, 2011), Kindle digital edition, loc. 293.

grace and lose their salvation. This assertion has proved controversial in the debate between Calvin and Arminius.

Arminius's thought softens Calvin's TULIP slightly, but has theological problems of its own, which we will discuss later. Although both Calvin's and Arminius's theologies have significant issues, their motivations for constructing their views centered completely upon the desire to preach the good news and bring glory to God through Jesus Christ. The fact that Greek philosophical ideas and classical theism formed the foundation for their doctrines may never have entered their minds. Steeped in their own cultures and the inherited worldview of Greek thought, they, like many theologians before them, developed their theology based on classical views of God and interpreted Scripture through that lens.

Note, however, that the classical view of God in Greek philosophy that formed the basis for the pre-understanding of the Christian God in these views causes some significant problems for the interpretation of Scripture. Some of the passages describing God cohere with these classical notions, but many others do not. Classical theologians, therefore, have either ignored scriptures that describe God as angry, loving, repentant, and sad or explained them away as anthropomorphisms that we cannot take literally.[12]

The Hebrew/Biblical View of God

This brings us to the second most influential way, historically, of viewing God. Theologians over the centuries have questioned the classical view of God because incidents in the Bible contradict that view. For instance, if God has no potential and, therefore, cannot change, how did God change God's mind about destroying Nineveh? How could God change the divine mind about wiping out the Hebrew people when Moses prayed and asked God to spare them after they worshipped a golden calf in the wilderness? We actually see God changing God's mind in Genesis 6 when God brought the flood. God had regretted creating humans! So, God changed the divine mind and wiped them all out, except for Noah and his family. (We will address the problem of God seeming to be violent in cases like this in future chapters.) Fourth-century bishop Gregory of Nyssa affirms a more dynamic view of God than the static God described by classical theism. For him, God is involved in time and responds to humans relationally. Our prayers, worship, words, actions, and attitudes affect God.[13] Gregory of Nyssa and other theologians desiring to remain faithful to the biblical witness hold to more of a Hebrew/biblical perspective in their views. So let's see how this perspective bears up under biblical scrutiny.

---

12. Justin Martyr, *First Apology* 13; *Second Apology* 6; Origen, *De principles* 2.4.4; *Contra Celsus* 4.37; 6.53.
13. Gregory of Nyssa, *Against Eunomious*, 1.42. See also Sanders, *The God Who Risks*, 146.

The Hebrew/biblical view nuances classical theism and views God in the following ways:

Potentiality. The Hebrew people and, later, the Israelites viewed God as having potential. As we have seen, the Bible reveals that God has the potential to change God's dealings with the world. Divine potentiality makes for a God who relates to us, intervenes in the affairs of the world, and acts spontaneously in response to our actions. People who hold this view of God believe that God answers prayer; so when we pray, God has the potential to answer according to what we ask. Of course, Scripture abounds with evidence of God answering prayer, relating to us, intervening in the world, and responding "in the moment." So the next logical step is to believe that God changes. This ties directly into the next point.

Nuanced immutability. Multiple passages in the Bible attest that God can change, but in certain instances, God does *not* change. So what do we do with those seemingly contradictory ideas? We examine them in context. As we have seen in the section on classical theism, some verses indicate that God does not change. In contrast, however, God changed God's mind about destroying the inhabitants of Nineveh in Jonah 3:10. In Amos, God relents and does not destroy the house of Jacob (7:3, 6). Of course, the most significant event in which God changes God's mind is in Genesis 6. God saw the wickedness of humanity and changed God's mind about creating them. The NRSV says, "The Lord was sorry that he had made humankind on the earth, and it grieved him to his heart" (Gen 6:6). The word translated "sorry" (*nacham*) means "to repent," indicating a change of mind and direction. God created; then God repented of that creation and destroyed it. We also see that prayer changes God's mind. For example, while Moses visited with God on the mountain in Exodus 32, the Hebrew people built a golden idol to worship. Because of this act of disobedience, God decided to destroy the people. But Moses prayed to God and asked God to spare them. God heard Moses and "changed his mind about the disaster that he planned to bring on his people" (Exod 32:14).[14]

In the Hebrew/biblical view of God, the power of prayer has a significant impact on God, and we see in Scripture that prayer changes God's dealings with the world. So what about the passages that demonstrate that, in some ways, God does not change? Notice that the verses pointing to God's immutability are in the context of divine faithfulness to keep promises and remain faithful to the divine covenant. We can affirm that God's faithfulness to God's covenant never changes; God's faithfulness to keep promises and to be with God's people never changes. Lamentations 3 beautifully expresses this: the writer laments all the hardships he

---

14. Other passages in which God changes God's mind: 1 Sam 15:10–11; 2 Sam 24:16; Jer 26:13, 19; 42:10.

has suffered and then declares, "But this I call to mind, and therefore I have hope: The steadfast love of the Lord never ceases, his mercies never come to an end; they are new every morning; great is your faithfulness" (Lam 3:21–23). Additionally, the verse in James typically used by classical theists to support divine immutability appears in the context of the unchanging character of God's goodness: "Every generous act of giving, with every perfect gift" comes from God, who never changes in goodness and the giving of good gifts to God's people (Jas 1:17). So, does God change? Yes—God changes in response to God's people and when circumstances warrant it; God changes God's *dealings* with the world because authentic relationships require the dynamics of change, the give-and-take type of relationality that responds to the other. But does God change? In another sense, no. God's *faithfulness* never changes. God's promises never change or fail. Consequently, when we speak about immutability, we need to nuance it in this way.

Passibility. Impassibility makes no sense in the Hebrew/biblical view of God. God can suffer. Suffering indicates change—emotions change, and pain changes our attitudes and behaviors. God suffers in many ways in Scripture: God is grieved in God's heart about creating human beings (Gen 6:6). In Isaiah 63:9, God sees the afflictions of the people, feels their affliction with them, and redeems them with love (another emotion!). God weeps and laments that creation is laid waste (Jer 9:10, var. in NRSV notes), and wails and mourns for Moab (Jer 48:31–32). We ourselves can grieve the Holy Spirit through our disobedience (Eph 4:30). Indeed, God's passion for creation motivated God's redeeming action in the world: "For God so loved the world that he gave his only Son, so that everyone who believes in him may not perish but may have eternal life" (John 3:16). And if we believe in the divinity of Jesus, to be theologically consistent we also have to believe that, because Jesus suffered during his life and death, God suffered as well. In fact, German theologian Jürgen Moltmann emphasizes the significance of the cross in revealing the suffering of God, writing, "When the crucified Jesus is called 'the image of the invisible God' the meaning is that THIS is God, and God is like THIS."[15]

In light of the many passages of Scripture that attest to God's love, grief, anger, joy, and desire, we are hard pressed to view God in any way other than as a God who suffers with the divine creation. Granted, those who hold to the classical theistic view of God have asserted that the descriptions of God feeling human emotions are anthropomorphisms or metaphors but do not truly describe the perfect, immutable, impassible God. We need to remember, however, that these anthropomorphisms and metaphors point the way to something (someone) real,

---

15. Jürgen Moltmann, *The Crucified God: The Cross of Christ as the Foundation and Criticism of Christian Theology* (New York: Harper & Row, 1974), 205. Emphasis on "THIS" is in the original source.

to an ultimate reality who feels pain and emotion—to the God most fully revealed through the suffering Christ.[16]

Nuanced omniscience. The Hebrew/biblical view affirms that God is omniscient, and that God is not omniscient. As we saw with immutability, the scriptural evidence requires us to nuance divine omniscience. The classical theists accurately describe the knowledge of God, but when we read those passages in context, we see that God's omniscience extends to the plans God has for salvation history. God knows exactly what God will do in response to human disobedience as well as what God will do in order to redeem all creation. God knows all of God's plans for the world and how God will act in every situation. In other words, God knows everything God will do. But the scriptural witness indicates that God does not know what we will choose to do before we choose it. We see this in Deuteronomy 8:2, where God tested the people to see if they would remain faithful. The same "non-knowing" occurs in Genesis 22:8–12, when God tested Abraham to see if his faith was strong enough to offer his son as a sacrifice. Did God know what choices these people would make before they made them? If so, why would God test them? What's more, since God has gifted humanity with free choice, the Bible seems to suggest that God doesn't know with certainty the choices we will make before we make them.

We can think about this in terms of a parent knowing her child. I have four sons and I know them well enough to "know" what they would choose to do in certain situations. Do I know with absolute certainty? No. But I have a close enough relationship with them that I can make an educated guess and usually guess correctly. Applied to God, we can say that God knows us intimately (Ps 139)—so intimately that God "knows" what we will choose before we choose it. Can we surprise God with a different choice? If we have an authentic and freely chosen relationship with God, then, yes, in theory that is possible. That said, how omniscient is God? For classical theology, God either plans all events, including our choices, before the creation of the universe or God's foreknowledge of events and choices enables God to know all things before they happen. Either one of these ways of knowing compromises the exercise of authentic human freedom. Once God knows something, it is done, written in stone, and cannot change. Many people like this view of omniscience because it brings them comfort. If God knows everything, nothing happens that surprises God—God knew Hitler would rise to power and have six million people killed; God knew before the foundation of the world that you would be born in a certain place at a certain time and had already planned your entire life. And God knows when the next world war will occur; God knows who the next president will be; God knows the entire future from beginning to end, and for

---

16. See Gregory A. Boyd, *The Crucifixion of the Warrior God: Interpreting the Old Testament's Violent Portrayals of God in Light of the Cross* (Minneapolis: Fortress, 2017), 1:17; Eric A. Seibert, *Disturbing Divine Behavior: Troubling Old Testament Images of God* (Minneapolis: Fortress, 2009), 185–87; Moltmann, *Crucified God*, 204–5.

some, God has even preordained it all. But that train of thought raises other questions and problems. If God knew Hitler would start a world war and kill so many innocent people, why did God let it happen? Worse yet, if God preordained this event, what does that say about God? That actually seems to make God complicit, if not responsible for the violence, catastrophes, and evil in the world.

If, however, we hold to the view that God knows everything that *can* be known, such as God's plans for salvation history and the choices we have before us, including the consequences for each of those choices, God does not bear responsibility for the evils of the world. Instead God works to overcome evil with good; God interrupts the evil with the fresh breath of love, redemptive activity, and good news.

But what does this type of knowledge look like? Picture a web with God in the middle. Every strand of the web is a choice that each person has to make. Extending off each strand is another strand that represents all the consequences for each choice; every consequence produces more choices, which then produce more consequences. What a complicated and tangled web we weave! Now multiply our webs of choices and consequences by billions and billions of people who all have their own webs. And God knows it all—every set of choices put before us (but not which choice we will make) and every consequence based on the choices we could make. Not only that, but God knows how God will respond to every single choice and consequence so that when we do choose, God knows how God will respond. Which seems like a more knowledgeable God? The God who either preordains or knows what we will choose ahead of time? Or the God who knows the entire web of possible choices and consequences for every person who ever lived and knows how God will respond in each instance? Certainly the second view of divine knowledge is more relational. Does the Hebrew/biblical view believe in God's omniscience? Yes. God knows all of God's plans to bring about the redemption of all creation. Is God omniscient? In a certain sense, no. God gives us authentic freedom to make potential choices and responds to us as those choices become actualities. We must nuance the idea of omniscience according to the evidence found in Scripture.

Nuanced omnipotence. In the Hebrew/biblical view, God is omnipotent, and God is not omnipotent. Again, as with the other attributes we have discussed, classical theistic images of God hold to a strong omnipotence; God's power is unlimited. But in the Hebrew/biblical view of omnipotence, God is all powerful and has the power to bring about God's final plan to redeem all creation. But God also takes a risk and limits some of the divine power in order to give human beings authentic freedom to act. For example, in Genesis 2–3, right in the beginning, God gives humanity the power to make a significant choice—to obey God or not to obey God. Unfortunately, they choose the latter, and God responds to them by making them clothes and making sure they do not live forever in their sin by barring their way to the tree of life.

In fact, all throughout Scripture God gives human beings the power to make their own choices and the freedom to suffer their own consequences. We also see the divinely given power of free choice in Deuteronomy 28. As the Hebrew people stand on the cusp of entering the land God promised them, God gives them a choice: they can choose a life of obedience and receive many divine blessings, or they can choose the path of disobedience and suffer the consequences.

In fact, almost the entire Hebrew Bible follows the same pattern: God gives the people the power of free choice, and they choose wrongly; they suffer the natural consequences, and God, unchangingly redemptive, unfathomably compassionate, rescues them. Could God overrule the freedom of choice so the people did not have to suffer the consequences of their disobedience? Yes. But the scriptural evidence leads us to believe that God does not. So, is God omnipotent in this view? Yes. Although the Bible does not explicitly attest to the omnipotence of God, it suggests the greatness of God's power for certain events. For example, Jeremiah affirms God's power in creation, saying: "Ah Lord God! It is you who made the heavens and the earth by your great power and by your outstretched arm! Nothing is too hard for you" (32:17). Paul exhorts the Romans that God's power to save will never fail, saying that the gospel "is the power of God for salvation" (1:16). Through the mouth of Isaiah God proclaims God's power to fulfill the divine plans: "My purpose shall stand, and I will fulfill my intention. . . . I have spoken, and I will bring it to pass; I have planned, and I will do it" (46:10–11). And according to the Psalmist, God's power extends to the divine capacity to understand. He writes: "Great is our Lord, and abundant in power; his understanding is beyond measure" (147:5). On the one hand, these verses give us the evidence to say that God exercises divine omnipotence in the acts of new creation and salvation, in fulfilling plans for the future, and in the ability to understand all things.

On the other hand, Scripture provides us with the evidence to conclude that God limits divine omnipotence by giving human beings the freedom and the power to make their own choices and suffer their own consequences. It seems, therefore, that the instances in which God gives up divine power are those surrounding God's authentic relationship to us. You have heard the old saying "If you love something, set it free; if it comes back, it's truly yours." We might say that God desires an intimate and voluntary relationship with us; God sets us free so we can choose to love God and serve as partners in an eternal relationship with the divine.

Contemporary proponents of these nuanced views of God's attributes, often labeled "open theists," believe that God designed the universe and created humanity with the authentic freedom to make choices out of a desire for a dynamic, authentic, and flexible relationship with us. Rather than fixing the future in some eternal reality ordained before the existence of the universe, God allows the future to remain open for human beings to take part in creating the future, and for a dynamic divine responsiveness to human activity. Not only does this image of God open up the possibility of a more relational God, invested in making humanity partners in bringing about the divinely planned salvation of creation, but openness-of-God theologians claim that it has stronger scriptural support than do classical theistic notions of God.[17]

The Case for a Nonviolent God

Open theism leads us to focus more on the dynamically relational character of God as revealed in Jesus as a God of love, self-sacrifice, mercy, peace, and redemptive justice rather than on metaphysical attributes that put distance between us and a remotely transcendent, static God. Consequently, instead of focusing on all the "omnis" and classical qualifications of the divine attributes, let's focus on the character of God revealed in Jesus, who embodied these divine characteristics. In Luke 15:3-7, Jesus tells the parable about the shepherd who drops everything and searches for the one lost out of one hundred sheep, not willing to let even one go. Jesus ate with sinners and abolished the dividing lines between peoples from every class, color, and culture (Eph 2:14–15). Jesus taught that the "law of love is the law of life in the kingdom," the law of unlimited forgiveness that transforms hearts.[18] The law of love that Jesus reveals precludes violence—we do not do violence against those we love, nor even against our enemies. If Jesus manifests God in this way, we need to answer these questions: Is God violent? and does God ever condone our violence?

But before delving into a theology of the nonviolent God revealed to us by Jesus, we will benefit from a quick glance at how we have traditionally justified the horrific divine violence in the Hebrew Bible. Yes, it is there! God often appears as a deadly dictator who uncompromisingly lays down the law, decreeing that "Whoever curses father or mother shall be put to death" (Exod 21:17). As biblical scholar Eric Seibert points out, God orchestrates the mass killing of thousands in Sodom and Gomorrah (Gen 19), in the plague that wiped out 14,700 people in the time of Moses (Num 16:49), in the death of the firstborn males before the exodus from Egypt (Exod 12), and by murdering all but a few of the human race in a great flood (Gen 6–8).[19] God instantly executes Uzzah for putting a hand on the ark of the covenant to keep it from tipping over onto the ground (2 Sam 6) and punishes thousands of people because David obeyed the divine command to take a census (2 Sam 24). These events and many others really do appear in the pages of the Bible, and for millennia, most Christians accepted this view of God largely without

---

17. Although I do not usually allow my students to reference Wikipedia as a legitimate source, the site's article on Open Theism is actually quite good: https://tinyurl.com/rxt72sy. For further study see Sanders, *The God Who Risks*; Clark Pinnock et al., *The Openness of God: A Biblical Challenge to the Traditional Understanding of God* (Downers Grove, IL: InterVarsity, 1994); Gregory Boyd, *Satan and the Problem of Evil: Constructing a Trinitarian Warfare Theodicy* (Downers Grove, IL: InterVarsity, 2001); and Gregory Boyd, *God at War: The Bible and Spiritual Conflict* (Downers Grove, IL: InterVarsity, 1997).
18. Boyd, *Crucifixion of the Warrior God*, 1:183.
19. Seibert, *Disturbing Divine Behavior*, 15–90.

question. How do we justify these divine deeds that, according to our own justice system, are extremely unjust? There are several ways biblical scholars and theologians have sought to answer this problem. Following are just a few:

Just cause. We defend God's violent behavior by claiming God has just cause to afflict a person or a nation. But does this argument hold up under scrutiny? Did Uzzah really deserve to die because he saved the ark from falling?

Greater good. Although God acts in questionable ways, these events, we could argue, serve the greater good. We might ask, however, do the ends justify the means?

Divine immunity. We defend God by asserting that everything God does must be right. All God's actions are righteous. We may even believe that God transcends our moral compass, that God's ways are higher than our ways. But is genocide ever a righteous act?

Divine permissive will. We defend God by saying, "God allows bad things to happen, but is not ultimately responsible for them." That sounds better: it makes humanity accountable for their choices. Yet, Scripture tells us that God orders mass murders, such as the command to Saul to wipe out an entire nation, including men, women, children, and animals. When Saul kept some of the animals alive, God removed him as king (1 Sam 15). So, does the idea of God's permissive will really get God off the hook for violence?

Progressive revelation. We can defend God by saying that God actually acted differently in the Hebrew Bible than in the New Testament. As time progressed, so did God's self-revelation, from a seemingly violent divine character to the peace-making one seen in Jesus. Nonetheless, the biblical narrative does not conform to such a simple chronology of violence to peace. And we must ask the question, Is God consistent in character throughout the ages?

For many biblical scholars and theologians, none of these justifications adequately explains the difference between the violence of God in the Hebrew Bible and the most complete revelation of God through Christ in the New Testament. Through responsible interpretation, however, we can imagine a solution to this major problem.

How do we interpret these passages in light of a theology of a nonviolent God? First, we have to own them. After all, the Bible includes them, so we cannot ignore them. Second, we need to recognize that, although the Christian tradition affirms the divine inspiration of Scripture, the human authors, nonetheless, wrote from inside a very human culture with worldviews, presuppositions, traditions, languages, and social systems as the ingredients that structured their worlds.

These ingredients found their way into Scripture. For example, the authors of the Hebrew Bible believed that God causes fortune and misfortune; God opens and closes wombs; God controls the weather; God punishes the wicked and rewards the righteous; God commands warfare and causes victory or defeat; God created a four-cornered, flat earth supported by pillars; and God created the sun to revolve around the earth.[20] These views explained the world the people of those times lived in. Because the writers of the Bible were steeped in their culture with their own set of presuppositions, they could not have thought any other way. So they sincerely thought that God told them to go into battle, that God won their wars for them or caused their defeat. They truly believed that whatever misfortunes befell them came from God acting as the causal agent.

We do not have to believe everything the ancients believed, however. This does not signify the inaccuracy of Scripture; rather, it merely points to the fact that the Bible comes from both human and divine sources. Literary critic and philosopher René Girard views the Hebrew Bible as a "text in travail," meaning that it has a dual view of God as sometimes violent and sometimes completely opposed to violence.[21] Indeed, as time goes on (especially in the words of the prophets), people come to understand the true nature of God better and better. God has not changed, but our understanding of God does. I believe God allowed the Scriptures to be a "text in travail" in these difficult passages to teach us something important about how (or how not) to live life as God's people. We are in a long process of learning what God is really like, and gradually we learn that the violence we once ascribed to God really originates from humans interpreting God in a certain way. It arises from our human tendency to project onto God what we ourselves do. As the full revelation of God, Jesus causes us to question these justifications of divine violence and to attempt to rethink our perceptions of God. Jesus undoes our misconceptions and gives us the privilege of participating fully in the revelation of God through his life, death, and resurrection. Through Jesus, God embraces us as partners in communicating through human language, limited as it may be, the nonviolent divine character and plan for bringing peace to the world.

How do we know, then, which passages of Scripture reveal the true nature of God? As we have mentioned before, we practice a christocentric hermeneutic. To start with, because we believe that God's moral character is most fully revealed through Jesus, we read and interpret the Bible through the lens of Jesus. Although Scripture teaches us that Jesus laid aside some of the ethereal divine attributes such as omnipresence, our method for interpreting Scripture focuses on moral characteristics like justice, goodness, mercy, love, and forgiveness—all inherent in

20. For example: 1 Sam 2:6–8; Gen 25:21; 30:2; Jer 10:13; Job 5:10; Deut 28; Judg 11:23–24; Josh 10:10–13; Isa 11:12; 38:8; Ps 50:1.
21. René Girard, "Generative Scapegoating," in *Violent Origins: Walter Burkert, René Girard, and Jonathan Z. Smith on Ritual Killing and Cultural Formation*, ed. Robert G. Hamerton-Kelly, (Stanford, CA: Stanford University Press, 1988), 141.

the life, teachings, death, and resurrection of Jesus. In other words, Jesus allows us to see God in action in the world.[22] To see what God is really like, therefore, we look at what Jesus taught and how he acted. Our rationale for this line of thought comes from the pages of Scripture. For example, we see that God took on flesh and lived among us (John 1:14). The Bible says that all the fullness of deity dwelled in Jesus in bodily form (Col 1:19) and that "he is the reflection of God's glory and the exact imprint of God's very being" (Heb 1:3). In fact, Jesus himself tells his disciples, "Whoever has seen me has seen the Father" (John 14:8–9). In the contemporary Bible version called *The Message*, Jesus says, "You have your heads in your Bibles constantly because you think you'll find eternal life there. But you miss the forest for the trees. These Scriptures are all about *me!*" (John 5:39–40).[23]

Theologian C. S. Cowles writes, "In the New Testament, Jesus is not defined by God; rather, God is defined by Jesus. Jesus is the lens through whom a full, balanced, and undistorted view of God's loving heart and gracious purposes may be seen."[24] C. S. Lewis simply states that Jesus is what the Father has to say to us.[25] In addition, virtually all early Christian theologians emphasized the christocentric interpretation of the Bible.[26] We do not privilege a christocentric hermeneutic because we have sold out to a "feel-good God" or a sappy form of the gospel. We interpret Scripture in this way because Jesus reveals to us the moral character of God. The heart of Jesus reveals the heart of God and should always be our guide "to a truer understanding of the character of God."[27]

A truer understanding of the divine character should, in turn, lead us to believe in the consistency of God's character. If the Holy Spirit served as the guide for writing all Scripture, and God the Spirit cannot contradict God, then Scripture should never contradict itself, especially surrounding depictions of God.[28] God's moral compass and heart of unending love, compassionate mercy, restorative justice, and unconditional forgiveness do not change over time. God's faithfulness to creation does not wax and wane—it remains eternally consistent.

Perhaps one of the most significant reasons to read Scripture through the lens of Jesus has to do with Trinity. God is Father, Son, and Spirit. The three are the same—one God. Consequently, the Father cannot act in ways the Son or Spirit would not act. If the Son is nonviolent, the Father and Spirit are nonviolent as well.

---

22. See Seibert, *Disturbing Divine Behavior*, 185–87.
23. From *The Message*, trans. Eugene H. Peterson (Colorado Springs: NavPress, 1993). The italics are in the source.
24. C. S. Cowles, "The Case for Radical Discontinuity," in *Show Them No Mercy: Four Views on God and Canaanite Genocide*, ed. C. S. Cowles et al. (Grand Rapids, MI: Zondervan, 2003), 22.
25. C. S. Lewis, *Mere Christianity*, in *The C. S. Lewis Signature Classics: An Anthology* (New York: HarperOne, 2017), 182.
26. Boyd, *Crucifixion of the Warrior God*, 41, 425.
27. David Janzen, "The God of the Bible and the Nonviolence of Jesus," in *Teaching Peace: Nonviolence and the Liberal Arts*, ed. J. Denny Weaver and Gerald Biesecker-Mast (Lanham, MD: Rowman and Littlefield, 2003), 57.
28. M. F. Wiles, "Origen as a Biblical Scholar," in *From the Beginnings to Jerome*, ed. Peter R. Ackroyd and C. F. Evans, CHB 1 (Cambridge: Cambridge University Press, 1970), 480.

Trinitarian theology dictates that the three remain totally consistent, in perfect harmony, and in one accord in every thought and deed. Indeed, scholar David Janzen affirms that "how God acts at one time is consistent with God's action elsewhere"; given that, "the character of God cannot differ fundamentally from God as revealed in Jesus Christ."[29] When we try to comprehend God, we gain a consistent image of God's character, actions, and judgments through what Scripture reveals about Jesus. Jesus is the standard by which we interpret all of Scripture.

Given our christocentric hermeneutics, then, what does Jesus teach us about God? First, Jesus reintroduces us to God. By challenging our commonly held view of God, "he demonstrates how [our] view of God [is] fundamentally flawed in certain respects; it [is] much too exclusive and far too violent."[30] We see this in our encounters with Jesus in the New Testament, starting in the book of Matthew when the angel tells Joseph Jesus's name: Emmanuel—literally, "God is with us." This means God is fully revealed to us in Jesus of Nazareth. This "God with us" will save the people from their sins. But even more incredibly, this Savior, this "God with us," came as a baby, born in a humble abode to a poor family.[31] What does this tell us about God? It tells us that the almighty creator God humbled the divine self by letting go of the privileges of the "omnis." By trading the rich glory of heaven for the impoverished humility of humanity, God emptied God's self into a human body and lived life as a humble servant. If we take time to focus on certain passages, the Hebrew Bible also expresses a God who serves the world. For example, in Deuteronomy, God encircles, cares for, and guards the people. Like a mother with a baby, God provides them with food and drink (32:10–14). Isaiah encourages the Hebrew people, telling them that God sits in the heavens longing to shower them with graciousness, strongly desiring to serve them with compassion (30:18). We can find many more passages in which God serves the needy, but the point remains—Jesus, who came to serve and give his life as a ransom for many, reveals God as a humble servant (Mark 10:45).

Second, Jesus loves his enemies (Matt 5:44; Rom 5:10) and asks us to do the same "so that [we] may be children of [our] Father in heaven" (Matt 5:45). We are God's children if we take after God, if we mirror God's actions in the world by loving our enemies and praying for those who persecute us. In other words, we love like God loves. How do we know how God loves? We look at Jesus, who loved and ate and drank and partied with sinners, touched lepers, and defended prostitutes—all considered God's enemies (Mark 2:15–17; John 8:2–11). Jesus actually reverses the culturally ingrained, Hebrew/biblical notion of the law of retribution (*lex talionis*), which gave offended parties the right to respond to a wrong with retaliation. When originally given, this seemingly punitive law actually served to limit the amount of violent retribution one could bring against another person. So it was life-giving in

29. Janzen, "The God of the Bible," 61. See also Seibert, *Disturbing Divine Behavior*, 185–87.
30. Seibert, *Disturbing Divine Behavior*, 188.
31. Matt 1:21–23; 2:1; Luke 2:1–7.

its day, even tending toward nonviolence in its original cultural context—a context in which unlimited violent retribution for offenses occurred often. But Jesus goes further and tells his listeners to "turn the other cheek," to go the extra mile, and to "not resist an evil doer," all of which amount to loving enemies (Matt 5:38–41).[32]

Paul tells us that while we were still God's enemies, God loved us extravagantly and, therefore, sought to redeem and reconcile us through the work of Jesus (Rom 5:10–11). Paul tells us there is no longer enmity not only between God and humanity but also between male and female, and between slave and free (Gal 3:28)—which would have been quite a controversial concept in first-century cultures.

Even today, the notion of radically tearing down boundaries and eliminating enmity riles up some Christians! It seems so contrary to how we think. We tend to keep our boundaries, sometimes by violent means. But in the Bible, Jesus reveals that love precludes violence and that God loves enemies rather than killing them, heals sinners rather than hating them, and defends prostitutes rather than condemning them. These are all acts of nonviolence. Moreover, in his reading of Scripture, Jesus omits a verse portraying divine violence. Luke tells the story: Jesus goes to the synagogue in Nazareth and, as a respected rabbi, stands up and reads the scroll of Isaiah, which says: "The Spirit of the Lord is upon me, because he has anointed me to bring good news to the poor. He has sent me to proclaim release to the captives and recovery of sight to the blind, to let the oppressed go free, to proclaim the year of the Lord's favor." He then rolls up the scroll and sits down, omitting the next phrase: "and the day of vengeance of our God" (Luke 4:16–21; Isa 61:1–2).

In another instance, Jesus rejects Moses's laws commanding retributive justice and initiates a new, nonviolent command to love our enemies—a command echoed by Paul's exhortation to "overcome evil with good" (Matt 5:38–44; Rom 12:21). Contemporary theologian C. S. Cowles asserts that the command to love our enemies "represents a total repudiation of Moses' genocidal commands and stands in judgment on Joshua's campaign of ethnic cleansing."[33] In addition, by forgiving the woman caught in adultery, Jesus subverts the Levitical law that calls for a death penalty and opts for nonviolence instead (John 8:2–11; Lev 20:10).[34] Obviously, Jesus reinterprets Scripture—much like we are doing right now—and leaves out the violence. His focus on the redemptive, restorative, and healing portions of Isaiah reveal the heart of God to redeem without violence. In fact, Jesus expresses the desire of God when he says, "Indeed, God did not send the Son into the world to condemn the world, but in order that the world might be saved through him" (John 3:17). Jesus shows us that God seeks to save, not smite, the lost; God

---

32. See Cowles, "Case for Radical Discontinuity," 33.
33. Cowles, "Case for Radical Discontinuity," 33.
34. See also Sandor Goodhart, *The Prophetic Law* (Lansing: Michigan State University Press, 2014). Goodhart asserts that the Jewish prophetic law supports nonviolence.

works to forgive, not to fight, sinners; God yearns to give eternal life to us, not to take life from us (Luke 19:10; 5:17–32; 7:48; 23:34; John 3:16).

In addition, Jesus reveals God's rejection of violence when he sets off for Jerusalem and stops in a little Samaritan town. The people would not allow him to stay there, so the disciples offer to call down fire from heaven and smite the villagers, but Jesus refuses to react violently. So whereas the Samaritans rejected Jesus, Jesus reveals God's heart to them by rejecting violence (Luke 9:51–55). Again and again, Jesus refuses violence in favor of peace, refusing to use his power to protect himself or his disciples. And if Jesus is the "exact imprint of God's very being" (Heb 1:3), then God, too, must reject violence. It should be noted that when Jesus says, "I have not come to bring peace, but a sword" (Matt 10:34), he is not encouraging violence but is saying metaphorically that people will have to choose to follow his narrow way of nonviolence or the broad way of violence—the one that leads to death. This stark choice will tear even families apart.

In the Hebrew Bible we see testimony to the nonviolent God. Right from the beginning in Genesis 1, God does something no other known god in the ancient world did: God creates the universe nonviolently. Rather than gods rebelling against other gods, killing them, and cutting up body parts to create the universe, as we see in the ancient *Enuma Elish*, God peacefully speaks the stars, planets, worlds, and creatures into being. Moreover, when Cain killed Abel, God did not seek retribution or wipe Cain off the face of the earth. Instead, God rejected a violent response and arranged for Cain's safety, allowing him to live in peace with those around him (Gen 4).

Interestingly, although the writers of the Hebrew Bible often interpret God commanding them to take violent action against others, Scripture also attests to the fact that God hates violence. For example, Isaiah speaks God's words and says that the people's "hands are defiled with blood. . . . Their works are works of iniquity, and deeds of violence are in their hands. Their feet run to evil, and they rush to shed innocent blood. . . . The way of peace they do not know, and there is no justice in their paths" (59:3, 6–8). Similarly, Ezekiel proclaims God's displeasure, saying that the people have "become guilty by the blood that [they] have shed" and that their violence only begets more violence (22:1–13). God accuses Israel through the mouth of Hosea and says that the people keep the cycle of violence in play and that "bloodshed follows bloodshed" (4:2). Micah cries out in despair, "The faithful have disappeared from the land . . . they all lie in wait for blood, and they hunt each other with nets" (7:2), indicating that *had* the people remained faithful, they would *not* lie in wait for blood but would live peacefully in the land. We see this peace brought to fruition by God in the last part of the chapter—the people do violence, and God works to redeem and bring peace. Remember, David was not allowed to build God's house because of the violence he had wrought during his years as king (1 Chr 28:3). Moreover, the Psalmist attests that God hates violence

(5:6) and instead "makes wars cease to the end of the earth; he breaks the bow, and shatters the spear; he burns the shields with fire" (46:9).

We see, then, that even in the Hebrew Bible God works toward and desires peace. In many of the passages we have discussed, God chastises the people for their violence: not only the kind of violence that sheds blood but also the kind that shreds character and spreads deceit. And at the end of these lament passages, the prophets always speak about God's desire to redeem and restore, to forgive and forget.

Let's look at one more significant text. The only sin mentioned in the flood story is violence: "And God said to Noah, 'I have determined to make an end of all flesh, for the earth is filled with violence because of them,'" (Gen 6:13a). This passage implies that humanity has caused God's grief and change of mind due to their violence. Obviously, Scripture teaches that God abhors violence. But what about verse 13b, where God says to Noah, "Now I am going to destroy them along with the earth"? We need to ask the question: If God hates human violence, would God do violence as an act of justice?

It seems paradoxical that in the Hebrew Bible God often threatens violence against disobedient people. But is this a paradox? Remember the age in which the Hebrew Bible was written. People thought everything around them came from the hand of God, including the flood. They may be attributing things to God that did not actually come from God. Context is everything. Yet, we cannot simply dismiss these violent images of God in the Bible; all Scripture has a purpose, even the passages that may provide inaccurate images of God. But we do need to use responsible hermeneutical methods when interpreting these difficult passages. And for Christians, it all comes back to our principle of christological hermeneutics. So when we confront seeming inconsistencies surrounding the character of God in the Bible, we search the depths of Scripture for context and glimpses of Jesus in the text, for images of God that reveal the self-sacrificial love of Christ.[35] For that, we turn to Origen, one of the early church fathers.

Origen (184–253) taught that only those truly dedicated to a relationship with God deserved to glean the richness of the divine meaning in the Bible. Furthermore, he believed that Scripture has levels of truth analogous to the body (literal) and to the soul (moral) and the spirit (allegorical/figurative). (We touched on this understanding of Scripture in chapter 2.) He believed that the literal level contains surface truths and is the result of humans writing under the guidance of the Spirit. The moral level provides guidance for living life. The spiritual level communicates the deeper meanings of Scripture and requires us to dig beneath the surface of the text to discern the more profound truths that the Holy Spirit reveals—truths that always point to the life, death, and resurrection of Jesus Christ, who through

---

35. Boyd, *Crucifixion of the Warrior God*, 418.

Scripture dwells among us still.[36] So Origen teaches us to search the Scriptures to find there "something worthy of the expressions of the Holy Spirit"—in other words, something worthy of the teachings, actions, and revelation of God in Christ.[37] Remember that Jesus "is the interpretive key to the Bible," so as we set about the interpretive task we begin by asking, "How does this passage of Scripture . . . testify to Christ?"[38] We may need to privilege some images of God over others in order to remain faithful to the biblical witness that proclaims the Prince of Peace alongside the Father of Mercy.

We see the divine relational testament to Christ in the Hebrew Bible when God visits Abraham and sits with him to eat a meal (Gen 18:1–15), when God takes the time to wrestle with Jacob (Gen 32:22–32) or calls Samuel from his bed (three times) to have a conversation (1 Sam 3:2–14). We also see how God appears and speaks with Moses face to face (Exod 33:11), and later comes to Elijah in the still, small breeze instead of in a hurricane (1 Kgs 19:11–13). We recognize the divine Christ-like purpose and determination to save when the Psalmist cries, "Where can I go from your spirit? Or where can I flee from your presence?" (Ps 139:7). God, in harmony with Jesus, goes wherever it takes to win one person back into a restored relationship. We see in God the mission of Jesus to rescue us from our trials in Psalm 46:1, which says: "God is our refuge and strength, a very present help in trouble." The character of God expressed in Psalm 40:1–3 testifies to the witness of Jesus who hears our prayers and rescues us from sin: "I waited patiently for the Lord; he inclined to me and heard my cry. He drew up from the desolate pit, out of the miry bog, and set my feet upon a rock [note that Jesus is sometimes described as a rock], making my steps secure. He put a new song in my mouth, a song of praise to our God." We could keep on with many more examples, but you get the point. Scripture is packed full of passages that portray a nonviolent God in ways that harmonize with the God Jesus reveals to us.[39]

---

36. R. P. C. Hanson, *Allegory and Event: A Study of the Sources and Significance of Origen's Interpretation of Scripture* (Richmond, VA: John Knox, 1959), 193. Quoting Origen, Hanson writes: "We see in a human way the Word of God on earth, since he became a human being, for the Word has continually been becoming flesh in the Scriptures in order that he might tabernacle with us." He also echoes Origen when he indicates the levels of interpretation as "ordinary" and "superficial"—that is, the surface level that can contain some discrepancies surrounding the character and actions of God. He corresponds the higher, deeper level of interpretation to "the Word transfigured on the mountain" (193).
37. Origen, *Homilies on Joshua*, 8.6. See also Boyd, *Crucifixion of the Warrior God*, 429.
38. Graeme Goldsworthy, *Preaching the Whole Bible as Christian Scripture* (Grand Rapids, MI: Eerdmans, 2000), 33, 21. For an excellent volume on how to read the troubling Old Testament texts in a nonviolent way and glean from them images of the nonviolent God, see Eric A. Seibert, *The Violence of Scripture: Overcoming the Old Testament's Troubling Legacy* (Minneapolis: Fortress, 2012).
39. I realize the problems with reading the Hebrew Scriptures purely through Christian eyes and seeing Jesus on every page or in every story, and I am not by any means whatsoever a "supersessionist." Even though I advocate a christocentric hermeneutic in general, I would also stress the importance of interpreting passages in the Hebrew Bible on their own cultural terms. But these ancient words belong also to the Christian tradition as Christian Scriptures. In this book, at least, I treat them as such.

But what about the violent passages? How do we find purpose in those, and how should we interpret them? Again, we turn to Origen for some answers. He believes that the treasures of God's wisdom are hidden from slothful people who do not want to take time to dig for it. As with Matthew's "treasure hidden in a field" (13:44), we need to sift through all the different kinds of plants—weeds, flowers, grasses, and edibles—to find the nourishment necessary to feed the soul with divine wisdom, knowledge, and truth. Origen believes God uses the difficulties of Scripture as a tool to help us grow in faith. As we seek out the purpose of these violent stories, we dig deeper than the surface layer to find the treasure concealed underneath. For example, when we read about God commanding Saul to kill all the Amalekites—men, women, children, and animals—we should feel repulsed in light of what Jesus teaches and how Jesus treats enemies. The wisdom of God in such passages may be in showing the horrific consequences of war in order to reveal that God actually rejects the violence of killing (1 Sam 15). We should, instead, find other ways to break down barriers between enemies, ways that promote peace. The alternative, as Scripture makes clear, is grave indeed. During the height of its popularity, WWJD ("What would Jesus do?") paraphernalia made Christian bookstore owners a lot of money, but there might be something to this common phrase when we take up the task of interpreting Scripture. Ask yourself: What would Jesus teach us concerning these stories, that passage, or this concept? I believe that Jesus always comes out on the side of a nonviolent, loving, forgiving God who gives us the Bible in order to teach us how to live.

We have spent a bit of time discussing the nonviolence of God, so you may be wondering: Why does the image of a nonviolent God matter? This question demands an urgent response from the church, given the violence that prevails in the world today, because violent notions of God may well have contributed to the "warmongering tendencies in human society, which have led to a perpetration of incomprehensible evil."[40] We all know about the many historical crusades and inquisitions that resulted in the murder of thousands under the guise of the idea that "God wills" violence. But let us look at just a couple other, more modern examples out of hundreds at our disposal. In his second Inaugural Address, President Lincoln used his interpretation of the divine will to justify war, stating that if God wills it, no matter the amount of bloodshed, we must acquiesce because "the judgments of the Lord are true and righteous altogether" (Ps 19:9 KJV). And in 1979 the group The Moral Majority actually lobbied *against* reducing US nuclear arms, advocating for American dominance in the world, pushing in favor of the use of nuclear weapons, violence, and war. They believed that pro-nuclear resolutions were in line with the biblical message and were God's will for America. I will never forget the late Rev. Jerry Falwell's comment during a CNN interview after the terror attacks

40. Terence F. Fretheim, *The Suffering God: An Old Testament Perspective* (Philadelphia: Fortress, 1984), 15. Richard Kearney asserts that "tyrannical Gods breed tyrannical humans" in *Anatheism: Returning to God after God* (New York: Columbia University Press, 2011), 138.

on 9/11; speaking of the terrorists, he said we should "blow them away *in the name of the Lord*." In other words, his theology led him to believe we should launch our own contemporary crusade.[41] Shamefully, polls show that 77 percent of American evangelical Christians supported the misguided (and violently preemptive) war in Iraq. Professor Merrill Unger, a contemporary theologian, has endorsed a violent God, writing that "if God permits men to use atomic warfare, it will be to accomplish His purpose and to glorify His name." In the same vein, Baptist pastor Charles Jones asserts that "someday we may blow ourselves up with all the bombs. . . . But I still believe God's going to be in control. . . . If He chooses to use nuclear war, then who am I to argue with that?"[42] These kinds of disturbing statements should make us seriously reexamine our theology and its basis in Scripture.

Advocating for war and violence on the grounds that God "wills it" directly violates the most fundamental teachings of Jesus and the Christian exhortation to love our enemies. Taking into consideration the oneness of the Trinitarian God, if violent actions violate the teachings of Jesus, then war and violence also violate God's will.[43] Conceiving God as violent, warmongering, and punitive allows us to justify our own horrendous acts, unleashing unconscionable violence, killing at will whenever we think God ordains it. Scripture instead exhorts us to imitate Jesus, God's exact representation and the imprint of God's very being (Heb 1:3). In these very Scriptures, God calls us to be a sweet aroma of Christ in every place, love our enemies, and be at peace with all people (2 Cor 2:15; Matt 5:44; Rom 12:18). When we do, others will know we are followers of God in Christ.

Both the Hebrew Bible and the New Testament give witness to the nonviolent God as revealed in Jesus and to the responsibility God's followers have to live into that divine nonviolence by spreading the love of Jesus Christ in every place as the ministers of reconciliation we have been called to be (2 Cor 5:18–19). Let us always be aware of how our theological presuppositions about God's very nature inform our ethics so we can avoid the worst errors of the past.

41. Bob Allen, "Falwell on Terrorists: 'Blow Them Away in the Name of the Lord,'" EthicsDaily.com, October 29, 2004, https://tinyurl.com/uj6qnou. See Sharon L. Baker, *Razing Hell: Rethinking Everything You've Been Taught about God's Wrath and Judgment* (Louisville, KY: Westminster John Knox, 2010), 62.
42. Paul Boyer, *When Time Shall Be No More: Prophecy Belief in Modern America* (Cambridge, MA: President and Fellows of Harvard College, 1992), 135, 150.
43. Richard Hughes, *Christian America and the Kingdom of God* (Chicago: University of Chicago Press, 2009), 18.

5. Creation

. . . creator of heaven and earth.

There is not one blade of grass, there is no color in this world that is not intended to make us rejoice.

—John Calvin

There is something to be said about the vastness of the earth, as well as the vastness of the heavens, in reminding us how small we are and how great God's creation is.

—Aleksandra Layland

Scientist Carl Sagan says we live on a "pale blue dot." In the divinely created theater of grace, in the seemingly infinite cosmic expanse, with its billions and billions of galaxies, each with hundreds of billions of stars, we live on that pale blue dot brought to light by the last vestiges of a sunbeam, reaching out to the very edge of our solar system.[1] As Sagan attests:

That's home. That's us. On it, everyone you ever heard of, every human being who ever lived, lived out their lives. The aggregate of all our joys and sufferings, thousands of confident religions, ideologies and economic doctrines, every hunter and forager, every hero and coward, every creator and destroyer of civilizations, every king and peasant, every young couple in love, every hopeful child, every mother and father . . . every 'supreme leader', every saint and sinner in the history of our species, lived there—on a mote of dust, suspended in a sunbeam.[2]

Such knowledge may make us feel insignificant, unimportant, and alone in such a boundless, immeasurable expanse. But we are not alone. As Christians we believe that God is infinitely aware of our pale blue dot. We believe that God intervenes in the workings of that pale blue dot. And out of the countless googolplexians[3] of pale dots glimmering faintly in the vastness of space, Jesus inhabited this existence, this pale blue dot, in this solar system, in this galaxy. What amazes me more, however,

1. Looking back toward us from the very edge of our solar system, the space craft *Voyager* 1 took this photo of the earth, appearing in a ray of sunlight as a pale blue dot, barely visible in the vastness of the cosmic expanse: https://tinyurl.com/y7k43ojg. Image credit: NASA, February 14, 1990.
2. Carl Sagan, *Pale Blue Dot: A Vision of the Human Future in Space* (New York: Random House, 1994), 6.
3. The largest number in the world with a name.

is that not only did God create the entire universe—all of it; God also, somehow, created our small blue planet—a planet that resounds with divine beauty and goodness—specifically for life, redemption, and relationship with the Creator.[4]

But before we proceed any further on the beauty and goodness of creation, we need to start "in the beginning" with Genesis 1. The Bible does not give us a date or any indication of when the beginning began (Gen 1:1). Yet while reading the first few verses in Genesis, we get a sense of timelessness, that in the boundless, ageless, eternal nothingness, God formed the universe from the formless void and, simultaneously, created what we call "time." St. Augustine helps us understand the timelessness of God's creative activity when he states that "the world was not created in time, it was created with time."[5] So from this timeless creative act, God created the space in which to place the universe and the time in which it exists. In other words, in the very act of bringing the universe into being, God created space-time along with it.[6] The first creation story, in Genesis 1, emphasizes the creation of time as something new, stating six times, "And there was evening and there was morning" (vv. 5, 8, 13, 19, 23, 31). Does this declaration of days suggest or require a literal reading of the story? Did God truly create the universe in six days?

The questions surrounding the beginnings of creation, space, and time have plagued the church for millennia and have served to divide the body of Christ into disparate groups who have argued unnecessarily about hours and days, evolution or creation, and the literal versus nonliteral interpretation of the texts in Genesis. Let us, therefore, briefly discuss possible ways of reading these significant texts in order to glean from them some important theological truths.[7] Most biblical scholars and theologians talk about the two creation passages in Genesis as "myths," a term much misunderstood by nonacademic Christians. Theologian Langdon Gilkey defines a religious myth as "a symbolic story expressing the religious answer to man's ultimate questions."[8] Karl Barth, however, refuses to use the word *myth* because of the negative baggage surrounding this term. Similarly, when some of my students hear the creation stories referred to as myths, they immediately think "falsehood" or "fairy tale." That may well be what the word means in secular arenas, but not in academic, religious, theological, or biblical contexts, where it has a technical meaning. Some readers may, like Karl Barth, prefer the word *saga*

---

4. This statement affirms the purpose for life on our small blue dot of a planet, but does not in any manner preclude the potential for some other "pale blue dot" out there somewhere in the vastness of space that God also created for life, love, and redemption.

5. Augustine, *Confessions*, 11.

6. Hans Küng, *The Beginning of All Things: Science and Religion*, trans. John Bowden (Grand Rapids, MI: Eerdmans, 2005), 121; James Leo Garrett Jr., *Systematic Theology: Biblical, Historical, and Evangelical*, vol. 1 (Grand Rapids, MI: Eerdmans, 1990), 293.

7. Of course, the creation accounts in Genesis are not the only Scriptures that describe the making of the universe. The Bible contains many other passages that communicate God's work of creating. Here is a sampling: Gen 14:19, 22; Deut 4:32; Isa 40:28; 42:5; 45:18; Amos 4:13; Prov 8:22–31; Ps 19:1–6; Job 38; John 1:3; Acts 4:24; Rom 4:17; Eph 3:9; Col 1:16–17; Rev 4:11.

8. Langdon Gilkey, *Maker of Heaven and Earth: A Study of the Christian Doctrine of Creation* (Garden City, NY: Doubleday, 1959), 34.

to describe Scripture's prehistorical narratives that describe realities within the confines of time and space, such as the creation of the world.[9] Both the term *myth* and the term *saga* refer to a story that may or may not be literally true or historically accurate but that, nonetheless, reveals profound truth. And often the term *myth* refers to a culture's stories of origin, tales of creation, or first events that reveal truths about the beginnings of the earth and its human inhabitants.

Middle Eastern culture very often uses the storytelling method to communicate truth. Rabbis, both ancient and contemporary, teach difficult concepts through story. Everyone in these cultures knows that these narratives do not serve as literal, historically accurate, step-by-step accounts of what actually happened. That perception of truth typically defines the modern Western way of thinking rather than the Middle Eastern mind. Those in Middle Eastern cultures also know that these texts express profoundly significant truths about God, humanity, the world, and redemption. So as we talk about the creation accounts in Genesis, we need to remember that these narratives fall under the category (or genre) of myth or saga—they tell the truth through stories. We see Jesus teaching his followers in this same manner through parables—another term we can apply to the creation myths. So, whichever term we use for these stories, and whether we believe God created in six literal days or over billions of years, we can know that they reveal significant truths about both God's creative action and the created universe. In fact, as scholar Luke Timothy Johnson proclaims, "Everything that exists is capable of revealing God simply by its existence."[10] So let us examine and reflect on a few of these truths.

Creation as Revelatory of the Characteristics of God

As we read the stories in Genesis 1 and 2, we find they reveal profound insight into the character of God and God's expectations for all creation. These truths should matter more to us than trying to determine how long (scientifically) it took God to create everything. These texts arise out of ancient, not modern, cultures without any connection to modern scientific knowledge. It's not that these questions do not matter; they do, but we need to engage the ancient texts on their own terms. Let's see what they tell us theologically.

Creation Reveals God as the Creator of Everything That Exists

A couple of arguments surrounding the creation of the universe have plagued Christian doctrine for a very long time. The first one, as we mentioned, discusses

9. Karl Barth, *Church Dogmatics*, vol. 3.1, ed. Geoffrey W. Bromiley and Thomas F. Torrance (Edinburgh: T & T Clark, 1956), 80–81.
10. Luke Timothy Johnson, *The Creed: What Christians Believe and Why It Matters* (New York: Doubleday, 2003), 96.

the issue of time. Yes, Christians have argued about this over the centuries, coming up with diverse answers (which implies that no one of them has the corner on truth). But is this a necessary dispute given the more significant truths found in these passages? Whether God created the universe in six twenty-four-hour periods or over many billions of years, or merely provided the energy to begin the process and left it to continue on its own, we can agree Scripture clearly reveals that God created everything that exists, both seen and unseen. Modern and scientific theories about creation and evolution, though important, create controversies that can serve to spread dissension and divide the church. So instead of focusing here on various possible positions regarding evolution, theistic evolution, young-earth creationism, old-earth creationism, or progressive creationism, in Genesis 1–2 we can, instead, focus on the idea that God willingly and voluntarily created the universe.[11] Theories of *how* God did things import scientific categories foreign to the ancient worldview that produced these stories. Consequently, scientific arguments can distract us rather than lead us toward the main points these texts make surrounding the divine act of creation. Trying to think like the ancient authors, we can concentrate more on the revelation that God created order and harmony out of disorder and chaos, that God created the universe very good—not perfect, but good—and that God created human beings in God's image and breathed into them the breath of life.[12] This keeps us focused on profound theological ideas that can be expressed in these truth-filled creation texts.

Another historical argument among Christians concerns the ideas of *creatio ex nihilo* (creation out of nothing) or *creatio ex materia* (creation out of something or out of preexisting material). The Latin phrase *creatio ex nihilo* means that God created the universe not out of some unformed, fluctuating particles swirling around in the dark chaos of primeval space—that would indicate a "something"—but out of absolute nothingness, from no material cause whatsoever.[13] This view gained popularity around 200 CE in response to Platonic and Gnostic[14] notions that God created the universe out of eternally preexisting matter. In the Christian tradition, proponents of the idea of *creatio ex nihilo* believe it protects the doctrine of creation against Greek philosophical dualism in which eternal matter and an eternal God coexist and together cause the creation of the universe.[15] Such

---

11. These questions are important but outside the scope of this book. For those interested in these matters, a good place to start is a comparative study of these different creation positions in Deborah B. Haarsma and Loren D. Haarsma, *Origins: Christian Perspectives on Creation, Evolution, and Intelligent Design* (Grand Rapids, MI: Faith Alive, 2011).
12. John Hick, like Friedrich Schleiermacher, talks about an original "perfection" as a way of speaking about how created things have the possibility for development. See *Evil and the God of Love* (London: Palgrave Macmillan, 2010), 225–41.
13. Küng, *Beginning of All Things*, 121–22.
14. Gnosticism, deemed heretical by the church, claimed that salvation comes through esoteric knowledge and that matter is essentially evil.
15. Paul Tillich, *Systematic Theology*, vol. 1 (Chicago: University of Chicago Press, 1973), 253.

thoughts, some have feared, might indicate the presence of a competing deity and would contradict monotheism.

Although specific references to *creatio ex nihilo* do not exist in the biblical text, ancient and modern theologians who hold to this doctrine find support in Scripture.[16] For example, Revelation 4:11 says of God, "You created all things, and by your will they existed and were created." Romans 4:17 teaches God "gives life to the dead and calls into existence the things that do not exist." This could be interpreted to mean all things exist only by the will and the word of God, not by any preexisting matter. So, "out of nothing" means that God alone served as the cause of everything that exists—God needed no other cause than God's self. This doctrine says something about God's sovereignty, but it also describes God's relationship to God's creatures: all creatures owe their existence only to God. Karl Barth teaches that *creatio ex nihilo* also emphasizes the fact that God rejects the "nothing" in favor of the "something." God willingly says "no" to nonexistence and "yes" to life.[17] Just as God said "no" to the nothingness in creating the universe, God also says "no" and annihilates the nothingness of sin and death through Christ, whose work provides for the "yes" to eternal life in the new creation, in the new heavens and new earth.[18]

Creatio ex materia counters the theory of creation out of nothing, claiming that God created the world from some sort of preexisting matter. This stance coheres well with the ancient Greek philosophers who believed that God, through a lesser being and mediator called the "demiurge," created the universe out of matter that exists eternally. Early theologians such as Justin Martyr and Clement of Alexandria taught according to Plato's doctrine that God's creative material came from preexistent matter—things you cannot see, that have no form and, therefore, are *no*-thing until God made them *some*-thing.[19] In fact, Hebrews 11:3, used often to support *creatio ex nihilo*, can also support *creatio ex materia*. It says that "by faith we understand that the worlds were prepared by the word of God, so that what is seen was made from things that are not visible." In other words, what we now see as the created world was formed by God from "things" we cannot see, such as unformed, preexistent matter. But, speaking of "matter," no matter what we decide about the "nothingness" out of which God created, we may all be able to agree that what truly matters is that the triune God of love created the universe and gives human beings the responsibility to care for it.

16. *Creatio ex nihilo* is taught explicitly in 2 Maccabees 7:28. The phrase appears there in the Latin Vulgate.
17. Barth, *Church Dogmatics*, vol. 3.1, 330–34.
18. Jürgen Moltmann, *God in Creation: A New Theology of Creation and the Spirit of God* (San Francisco: Harper & Row, 1985), 90.
19. *Stromateis* 5:14; 1 Apol. 59.

Creation Reveals the Trinitarian Nature of God

Theologian Richard Plantinga asserts that "the triune God is the principal protagonist of the Christian story. The second main character is creation."[20] Although the writers of Genesis did not have any notions of a Trinity, we may interpret Genesis 1 as representing the three persons of the Trinity at work in the creation process from the very beginning of the Bible: "In the beginning while God created, the heavens and the earth were formless and void, and darkness was over the surface of the deep; and the spirit of God was hovering over the face of the waters. Then God said, 'Let there be light'; and there was light" (1:1–3; my translation). These verses reveal that the Trinitarian love relationship does not stay forever isolated within God's self but that the triune God extends that love "beyond the Trinitarian life in order to bring into existence a universe which is other than God."[21] The presence of God the Father creates (v. 1). As the source and foundation of all existence, the Father acts directly as the creative agent, and by the Father's will all things come into being. The Spirit of God hovers, broods, and moves over the surface of the waters. We can also translate the Hebrew word for "hover" or "move" as "fertilize," which I find provocative.

So the eternal Spirit of God works in the universe by sweeping over the primeval waters, breathing life into the world of creatures. Reformer John Calvin fittingly says that "it is the Spirit who, everywhere diffused, sustains all things, causes them to grow, and quickens them in the heavens and in the earth."[22] So God the Spirit provides the life-giving breath, the provision of life to all creation, and allows every creature to participate in the eternal life of God.[23] The Son, as the Word of God, actively speaks the words "Let there be light." John attests to the same activity of the Son in creation: "In the beginning was the Word, and the Word was with God, and the Word was God. He was in the beginning with God. All things came into being through him, and without him not one thing came into being" (1:1–3). Colossians affirms the Son's role in creation, stating that "in [God's beloved Son] all things in heaven and on earth were created" (1:16).

Consequently, we see that God the Father creates everything through the word of the Son. Indeed, right from the start, the triune divine community of Father, Son, and Holy Spirit forms the foundation for the creation of the universe. Characterized by love, the Trinity itself creates something wholly other than God from the outflowing of the love that defines the Trinitarian relationship.[24] In fact, God first thought of sending the Son into the world to extend love and grace well before

---

20. Richard J. Plantinga, Thomas R. Thompson, and Matthew D. Lundberg, *An Introduction to Christian Theology* (Cambridge: Cambridge University Press, 2010), 147.
21. See Stanley J. Grenz, *Theology for the Community of God* (Grand Rapids, MI: Eerdmans, 2000), 98.
22. John Calvin, *Institutes of the Christian Religion*, ed. John T. McNeill, trans. Ford Lewis Battles (Louisville, KY: Westminster John Knox, 1960), 1.13.14.
23. See also Job 26:13; 33:4; Gen 2:7; 6:3, 17; 7:22; Ps 104:30.
24. See Grenz, *Theology for the Community of God*, 101, 105; Moltmann, *God in Creation*, 98.

any act of creation (Rev 3:14). That means when God created the worlds, God wove grace and love into the very fabric of the universe through Jesus. In the words of Richard Rohr, "God's first 'idea' was to pour out divine, infinite love into finite, visible forms."[25] And God "in-Spirited" the matter of all creation with an outflow of love that invites our participation in the constant process of creating new life in the world through such things as birth, artistic expressions, scientific discovery, agriculture, and preaching the gospel.

Creation Reveals God as Love

We use the word *love* in many ways for a variety of feelings, such as "I love ice cream" or "I love my husband" or "I love my cat." But what does it mean to love when we apply that word to God? The Greeks have several words to talk about love compared to our one word in English. A few of these Greek love words describe God and help us understand the divine desire to create and sustain the universe. The first word, *agape*, the love we typically apply to God, means to love selflessly. To say that God loves us with *agape* love describes God as a selfless, self-giving lover who puts no conditions on that love—nothing we do or say or think weakens the divine love for us. C. S. Lewis called *agape* the "gift love" because God gifts it to us without any reason.[26] God loves the creation unconditionally, no matter what, come what may (John 3:16; 1 John 4:8).

The second word, *philia*, indicates the love implicit in a deep friendship. The Greeks often considered *philia* as one of the more significant types of love because of its loyalty, tenderness, and camaraderie. It expresses the intimate knowledge that accompanies true friendships. Indeed, Scripture reveals that God loves creation in this manner, with tenderness and intimacy, as partners in maintaining the good creation. For example, John 5:20 uses *phileo* (the verb form) to describe the intimate partnership love between the Father and Son, while Jesus calls us *philous*, friends who love and are loved intimately by God (John 15:15; 16:27).

The third word, *pragma*, describes a practical type of love that pursues the means to make a relationship work well. This type of love enables partners to understand one another on a deep emotional, psychological, physical, and spiritual level. We see in Scripture that God strives to develop and maintain a deep relationship with creation not only through the process in which God worked to create a universe, but also in how God works to bring humanity back to God in a redeemed, reconciled, and restored relationship. In fact, the story of the Bible depicts the divine endeavor to knock down the boundaries that obstruct and hinder our love relationship with God, with each other, and with all creation.

---

25. Richard Rohr, "Christ Since the Beginning," *Richard Rohr's Daily Meditation* (email subscription), February 17, 2019.
26. C. S. Lewis, *The Four Loves* (New York: Harcourt Brace Jovanovich, 1960), 17.

The fourth word, *storge*, means the kind of instinctual, affectionate love a parent has for a child. No one has to teach most parents how to love their children—they just do. In most cases, a typical parent's love for a child remains steadfast, supportive, and warm. Of course, we know from the Bible that God has this type of love for us, God's children (1 John 3:1-2). God even allows us to call God the intimate and informal "Abba" or "Father" (Rom 8:15).

The fifth word, *eros*, is my personal favorite and, I believe, serves as the motivating force behind the divine creation of the universe. *Eros*, often thought of simply as "lust," actually describes the type of love that drives a person to pursue the love of another. It desires the other with a strong and insatiable longing and, therefore, stimulates the lover to go to any lengths to obtain a meaningful relationship with the other person.[27] Surprisingly, God loves us in this manner! We see the essence of *eros* at work in Isaiah, who says that "the Lord longs to be gracious to you. And therefore He waits on high to have compassion on you" (30:18 NASB). This verse portrays God as having a strong desire to love us and the will to wait, if need be, to shower us with that love. Throughout the Bible we see instances in which God pursues human beings for intimacy, partnership, and love (Ps 139; Jer 31:3; Luke 13:34; John 3:16; 17:24-26; Eph 5:25; 2 Pet 3:9; Rev 3:20). This *eros* love drives God to create something totally other than and outside of God—something for God to love, cherish, nourish, and invite into intimate relationship with the divine Trinitarian community.

As Christians, we believe that God is love, and we can further see that such extravagant love, by its very self-giving nature, loves unconditionally (*agape*), intimately (*philia*), practically (*pragma*), instinctively and affectionately (*storge*), and longingly (*eros*). This authentic love, God's love, requires an object to love (1 John 4:7-19). The Father, who loves eternally within the Trinitarian relationship, reciprocates that love in the creation of the universe. So we can say that all creation exists as a manifestation and product of God's love. The dynamic love, active in all its forms, among the Father, Son, and Holy Spirit naturally flows out of the Trinitarian God into the universe, freely giving life to something wholly other than God—namely, God's good creation. As theologian Daniel Migliore says, "The triune God who eternally dwells in loving communion also welcomes into existence a world of creatures different from God."[28] God's nature, as self-giving love, willingly creates the external universe to be the recipient of and the participant in the free-flowing, boundless love of the triune God.[29]

---

27. *Eros* describes the drive toward a desired object as well as toward another person.
28. Daniel Migliore, *Faith Seeking Understanding* (Grand Rapids, MI: Eerdmans, 2004), 92; Moltmann, *God in Creation*, 92.
29. Grenz, *Theology for the Community of God*, 101.

Creation Reveals the Nonviolent Divine Character

The Hebrew creation myths in the Bible reveal that, contrary to ancient accounts popular in surrounding cultures, God exerts nonviolent energy to create the universe. The Hebrew creation stories do presuppose the typical Middle Eastern conceptions of the world, such as the primeval chaos of the oceans, the waters under the earth and above in the heavens, and the multilayered physical construct of the cosmos, all ideas common at the time. Nonetheless, they differ significantly in that the stories of the surrounding regions described the making of the universe as a violent endeavor involving struggling, murderous gods strewing severed body parts into the heavens to create the world. Walter Brueggemann asserts that the stories in Genesis 1 and 2 propose "a critical alternative to creation-by-combat ideology."[30] For the God of the Hebrew people, violence plays no part. This God peacefully spoke the universe into existence—"Let it be," and it came into being. We have no violence, no murdered mother god, no cosmic battles for power, but, instead, a calm divine command bringing life where once life did not exist. Rather than creating through a bloody brawl with familial deities who demand and coerce creation, God peacefully invites the creative elements into a beautifully ordered existence. Although the nonviolent act of creation carries significant weight for the case for a nonviolent God, it also points toward another characteristic of God as a sovereign ruler.[31]

Creation Reveals the Sovereignty of God

Sermons, hymns, liturgies, creeds, and catechisms almost always include statements testifying that God is sovereign over all creation. But what does that mean? The Oxford English Dictionary defines *sovereign* as "supremacy or rank above or authority over others. A superior; a ruler; a governor, lord, or master over others. Frequently applied to the deity in relation to created things." Taking this definition into consideration, we can say God rules, governs, and serves as Lord over all creation. God is supreme and superior to all things. God alone wills what to create and how to create it. Divine sovereignty over creation clearly rules the day in the biblical accounts of creation and beyond.

The creation story emphasizing God's sovereignty over all of the cosmos made the Hebrew people different from all the surrounding nations, who believed that their gods could not control or harness the mysterious, chaotic waters of the sea or the destructive forces of nature battering them with wind, rain, thunder, lightning, and hail. The Hebrew God, instead, spoke all such forces into existence in Genesis. This God played with sea monsters, constructed storehouses for the

---

30. Walter Brueggemann, *Genesis*, Interpretation (Atlanta: John Knox, 1982), 32.
31. J. Richard Middleton, *The Liberating Image: The Imago Dei in Genesis 1* (Grand Rapids, MI: Brazos, 2005), 266.

wind, rain, and hail, and aimed every bolt of lightning according to the book of Job. Only a truly sovereign God could accomplish such incomprehensible and magnificent feats.

In addition, God exercises sovereignty by creating according to the kind intention of the divine will and the loving character of God. Stanley Grenz articulates this concept beautifully, writing: "Although free to govern creation according to his own purposes, God always acts in accordance with his own character, which is love. Indeed, the freedom of God as Creator is the freedom to fulfill his loving purposes for his handiwork. Consequently, in all he does, God seeks only what is best for the universe that he fashioned as the outflow of divine love."[32] God, out of the love that defines the divine nature and character, voluntarily creates the universe and then rules over it all with loving compassion and kind intentions.

Thinking about God as sovereign leads to the next term often found in theological texts—*providence*. God's providence in relation to God's sovereignty reveals that not only does God rule majestically over all creation, but God also cares for and protects all creation. So with these two words—*sovereignty* and *providence*—we have an image of a supreme Lord whose rule lovingly nurtures, sustains, guards, and cares for the universe and everything in it. God's purpose for the good creation takes into consideration the divine goal for all things: "So that at the name of Jesus, every knee should bend, in heaven and on earth and under the earth, and every tongue should confess that Jesus Christ is Lord, to the glory of God the Father" (Phil 2:10–11).

Creation Reveals the Purpose of God

God would not have created the universe without a purpose. As we discussed earlier, all creation is the physical manifestation of the Trinitarian love of God flowing out into the world. Since God desires to create loving communion with something other than God, we should also believe that God's main purpose for creation involves our participation in the divine community of love. Indeed, God raises us (and eventually all creation) up into the triune relationship to dance with God in dynamic partnership in caring for the cosmos. Consequently, we might say that all creation dwells in and is transformed by communion with God, according to the divine purpose.[33]

God's purpose is also eschatological, or having to do with the future. Ultimately, God desires to unite all creation in Jesus Christ. We could say that all of God's activity in creation and in history hastens toward the final *telos* (end or purpose) when all are one in Christ. Paul reveals the divine vision for a united creation, a vision we now see only partially, when, speaking of God's renewed creation in Christ,

---

32. Grenz, *Theology for the Community of God*, 106.
33. James R. Payton, *Light from the Christian East: An Introduction to the Orthodox Tradition* (Downers Grove, IL: IVP Academic, 2007), 97.

he writes: "In that renewal there is [truly] no longer Greek and Jew, circumcised and uncircumcised, barbarian, Scythian, slave and free; but Christ is all and in all" (Col 3:11). With the will of God the Father, the redemptive work of Jesus the Son, and what some theologians have described as the "luring" presence of God the Spirit, all creation will finally experience its release from slavery into the freedom and redemption of God (Rom 8:21) and will enjoy the glory of the divine presence for all eternity in a new heaven and a new earth.[34] So, wrapped up in the drama of creation is also the promise of a new creation and the hope of salvation.

Creation Reveals the Freedom and Generosity of God

According to Paul Tillich, "God is creative because he is God. Creation is God's freedom and God's destiny."[35] Indeed, creation results from God's free and voluntary will. Nothing outside the divine will forces God to create; instead, the triune love of God drives and inspires God to create new life, new community, new partnerships, and new relationships. Because of the nature of divine love as *eros*, the erotic drive that stimulates God to love the wholly other, the creation of the universe harmonizes with God's true character. The triune God freely gives the gift of creation and life, enabling those outside the Godhead to live in fellowship with God in love.[36]

All of creation also speaks of the generosity and love of God. The triune God gives creation to us as the gift of life, beauty, community, purpose, and partnership with the sovereign Lord of the universe. For example, Psalm 145 extols the divine generosity, saying of God, "You open your hand, satisfying the desire of every living thing" (v. 16), a verse Reformer Martin Luther recommended as an everyday table blessing for families. But I like best the translation of this verse in *The Message*, which says: "Generous to a fault, you lavish your favor on all creatures." Look around at the world—the beauty in a flower, the majesty of the mountains, the power of the ocean waves, the splendor of a rainbow, and the awe of the heavens. God generously provides us with rain to grow crops, sun to warm us, stars to guide us, food to nourish us, and living creatures to love us—everything needed for life to continue abundantly.

Characteristics of Creation

The Goodness of Creation

Scripture attests to the goodness of creation. The divinely orchestrated creation of the universe serves as the very first "sermon" ever preached, proclaiming the good news. Theologian Jürgen Moltmann asserts that the entire creation sings

---

34. Moltmann, *God in Creation*, 94–95.
35. Tillich, *Systematic Theology*, vol. 1, 252.
36. Migliore, *Faith Seeking Understanding*, 100.

out a "joyful paean" of praise that affirms the goodness and beauty of God's creative artistry.[37] Scripture attests to the grandeur, majesty, fertility, and beauty of God's creation. For instance, the Psalmist declares that "the heavens are telling the glory of God; and the firmament proclaims his handiwork" (19:1). In addition, three full chapters in the book of Job extol the power and majesty of divine grace in the creation of the universe, emphasizing the delight God takes in the goodness of all creatures (39–41). Despite creation's limitations of finitude, vulnerability to disease, powers of destruction and oppression, and the very real existence of evil, God created the universe, including our small planet, and pronounced it "very good" (Gen 1:31).[38] Nothing can ever change that.

Creation's Difference and Dependence

We also see in the creation accounts that God created a universe radically different and distinct from the divine triune reality. The universe is not God, but a totally different, diverse entity separate from God. Karl Barth explains that "creation . . . is the beginning of all the things distinct from God."[39] So, although creation demonstrates the first of God's mighty acts in and for the universe, that same creation remains different from God. It actually reveals the divine desire for diversity, otherness, and intimacy with something that is not God. It shows that the triune God affirms difference and, in loving communion, creates a space for the finite other. Theologian Jürgen Moltmann expresses God's plan for difference, aptly asserting, "The harmony of unity and difference in the triune creator is reflected in the creation of a cosmos richly differentiated. It is the triune God, creator, redeemer, and consummator, present in the world by Word and Spirit, who provides the basis and the vision" of a diverse community.[40] In addition, the creation of the universe articulated in Genesis 1 and 2 affirms that difference is good, and that the diversity of the animals, birds, fish, insects, geography, and human beings originates in God's delight and desire for difference.

Although the transcendent God and the material universe are different from one another, creation remains utterly dependent upon God for its continued existence. We depend upon God for the gift of life in all its forms. Acts 17:28 attests to this life-giving dependence, stating, "In him we live and move and have our being." Our very existence is God's gift to us, and that existence depends upon God for the continual process of new creation. With God, we carry on the creation process through birth, agriculture, art, music, architecture, and much more.

---

37. Moltmann, *God in Creation*, 97. See also Migliore, *Faith Seeking Understanding*, 92; Payton, *Light from the Christian East*, 96.
38. Migliore, *Faith Seeking Understanding*, 103–4. See also Gen 1:12, 18, 21, 25.
39. Barth, *Church Dogmatics*, vol. 3.1, 42. See also Payton, *Light from the Christian East*, 89.
40. Moltmann, *God in Creation*, 12.

In addition to creation's dependence on God, all the components in creation coexist and are interdependent. God never meant for us to exist alone and independently. Instead, as we see in Genesis 2:18, God said that it is not good for human beings to be alone. Human beings coexist with each other, with the animals, with the soil, with rivers and lakes and oceans, and with all the forms of life that make up our world. We can expand the context of this passage to take in not only the human need for other humans, but all of creation's need for the rest of creation. Human beings, with all the rest of creation, make up a community of harmonious interdependence, of give-and-take, and of mutual respect and reciprocity. More importantly, however, nothing can exist without dependence upon God. This reality forms a beautiful image of intimacy and interdependence that reflects the glory, purpose, and goal of the triune God in bringing all things together so that all are in God and God is in all (Eph 4:6; Col 1:17; 1 Cor 8:6; 1 John 4:16).

The Responsibility of the Human Race

When we think about humanity's dependence upon all of creation, we also think about God's command in Genesis that the newly created humans "have dominion over the fish of the sea and over the birds of the air and over every living thing that moves upon the earth" (1:28). God's sovereignty and providence work hand in hand with God's exhortation to humanity to have dominion over the creation. We participate together with God in a true partnership. "Human beings are given the responsibility of caring for the whole of creation as God cares for it. It is a 'dominion' of care and protection rather than of domination and abuse."[41]

That care and protection include working to preserve the earth's natural resources, to make space for the nonhuman "other," for plants, animals, rivers, lakes, oceans, ice caps, air, soil, mountains, meadows, and even microbes to flourish and fulfill their God-given purpose. In order to succeed at this partnership with God, we need to consider every other part of creation as important as we are. The moment we thoughtlessly destroy either human or nonhuman, sentient or non-sentient matter, we fail in our duties as divinely appointed protectors of the world. We need to realize that God did not create the universe for humans to use merely for our own selfish reasons or benefit. Instead, as partners with God in the continual process of re-creation, we nurture creation in ways that allow for healthy new life to grow season after season, year after year, until the end of time. After all, our human destiny is tied up with the fate of the rest of the earth.

41. Migliore, *Faith Seeking Understanding*, 98.

Theological Models of Creation

Theologians have offered a variety of models when talking about God's methods for creating the universe. These metaphors each capture something different about God's work and purposes. In the *classical theistic model*, God creates from outside the universe and, although the presence of God's Spirit freely infiltrates the world and the Son lives among us, God remains separate from the creation. Most Christians are familiar with this model, and we have discussed it at length already. But we need to discuss several other models as well.

Pantheism is the belief that everything is God. *Pan* means "all" and *theism* comes from the Greek word *theos*, for "God." So, pantheism expresses the theory that in some sense, the universe actually *is* God. Sometimes theologians talk about all creation as the first "incarnation" of God, when God materialized and exposed God's body (or divine substance) for all to see. Creation, then, in this view is the very body of God, and through this body, "God has chosen to communicate God's very Self in multitudinous and diverse shapes of beauty, love, truth, and goodness, each of which manifests another facet of the Divine."[42] So every created thing, as a part of the divine body, expresses the beauty and goodness of God.

Panentheism is a variant of this idea, with some important differences. *Pan*, again, means "all," and *en* means "in," so panentheism expresses the idea that everything is *in* God. Although the specific beliefs within this model differ, panentheists hold to belief in a God greater than the universe and different from the universe. At the same time, God infiltrates and contains the universe in God's self. We can describe the universe as existing inside "the womb" of God, so to speak. In this articulation of panentheism, God acts as the mother of the universe who nurtures, sustains, and protects creation, for in God "we live and move and have our being" (Acts 17:28). All things depend upon God for existence and the continuation of life.[43] God calls the universe into being by making room inside God's self, by stretching out the heavens (Job 9:8; Zech 12:1) and placing the entire creation inside God.[44] This forms a beautiful image of God's intimacy, love, and relationship with the world—like a mother with a child in the womb. The child could not exist without the mother, and the mother would never be a mother without the child.

Some theologians find compelling the metaphor of God as a *builder* or *artist*. We might sometimes refer to God as a builder to explain the creation of the universe, in that God forms, fashions, or fabricates everything that exists. God builds families (Ps 127:1) and acts as a potter to fashion the divine community (Isa 64:8; Rom 9:21). Scripture provides us with a beautiful image of God forming and fabricating in

---

42. Richard Rohr, "Creation Reflects God's Glory," *Creation*, Week 2, Center for Action and Contemplation, February 18, 2018. https://tinyurl.com/y8ovwdvl. See also Sally McFague, *The Body of God: An Ecological Theology* (Minneapolis: Fortress, 1993), 184; Job 38–39; Rom 1:20.
43. Moltmann, *God in Creation*, 300.
44. Moltmann, *God in Creation*, 88.

Genesis 2:7, when the divine hands play in the clay to form human beings out of the ground: the word *yatsar* means "to form" or "to mold." It applies both to fashioning objects from clay and, interestingly, to forming ideas in the mind—a direct reference to the imagination (as *yetser*). So the image expressed in this verse describes God using the divine imagination to form and mold us into persons in the divine image—beautiful imagery of intimacy and love.

Similar to the model of God as a builder, we might think of God as an artist. This metaphor defines God as a creative person at play. Whether an artist is painting a picture, sculpting a pot, creating a poem, or writing a book, think about the imagination, intimacy, and care they put into their work. They ponder what to make, what the object will look like, and what message it will portray to the world and then, with loving attention, begin creating a masterpiece. When finished with the project, they leave behind a piece of themselves; they typically sign or place their mark on the work of art so everyone who looks at it knows who has created it. And sometimes artists simply play with paint or wood or words just to see what happens. For example, I "write" icons, which really means I paint them. But when working on one, I take my time, think through the pigment choices and brush strokes, sometimes using very small utensils to paint in great detail. I also paint abstract art, which often means I randomly "throw" paint on a canvas and play with the colors flowing in interaction with one another, experimenting and moving the lines and shapes to make something pleasing to the eye. No matter the method employed, artists create works of love with a goal in mind for each piece.

When we imagine God as an artist, we might think of God carefully crafting a human being, paying attention to detail, using the divine imagination to form a creature. I see God thoughtfully creating the placement of suns, moon, and planets and creating microscopic sea creatures. I can see God at play creating a giraffe with a long neck, a baboon with a red bottom, and an elephant with its long nose. Moreover, when we look at a beautiful sunset or a majestic mountain range or a serene body of water in the quiet of early morning, we sense that God the artist has been at work creating for a purpose and for our pleasure according to the divine will.

Eastern Orthodox Views of Creation

The Eastern Orthodox Church adds an interesting and significant twist to the doctrine of creation. As we discussed in the chapter on God, Orthodox theologians make a distinction between God's *essence* and God's *energies*. The divine essence as the transcendent nature of God actually is God the Father, Son, and Holy Spirit within the Godhead. Because the divine essence remains out of our reach, beyond our abilities to comprehend, and bound up within the Trinitarian community of love, these theologians stress that we cannot know God in God's essence. They think, however, that we do know God through the divine energies, and through these energies, God creates the world.

The distinction between the essence and energies of God make sense in light of our previous discussion on the immanent and economic Trinity. God's essence describes the immanent Trinity in its exclusive, totally transcendent Father, Son, and Holy Spirit relationship, while the divine energies describe the Father, Son, and Holy Spirit in relation to the world. In Eastern Orthodox thought, through the divine energies God connects intimately with all creation and suffuses it with Trinitarian grace. So through God's energies, the Father creates the universe, the Son communicates the divine will and work of redemption, and the Holy Spirit cultivates the continuing renewal of creation moment by moment, day by day, until the end of time, forever.

No less God than the divine essence, the creative power of the divine energies ensures that God is never distant, never aloof, but is totally involved in the universe.[45] Through Trinitarian energies, God intimately expresses the divine will for each creature, sending forth God's *logos* (word or will) so that every creature receives God's energies deep within it. Contemporary Eastern Orthodox theologian James Payton describes this beautiful divine work, writing that "there is a distinctive *logos* [an inner shape or purpose] for trees, flowers, dogs, and human beings, and each individual representative of each created nature has the *logos* within himself, herself, or itself. This divinely implanted *logos* defines each created nature . . . and indicates what the ultimate purpose of that ought to be."[46] We see, then, that God implants the divine will in each creature through the divine energies, and that God creates everything as a gift and for a specific purpose.[47] Medieval theologian Hildegard of Bingen (1098–1179) describes the act of creation as the divine "greening" in which the Spirit of God exerts "greening power" to give life and fertility to all of creation in an outpouring of love. She says that all of creation is "showered with greening refreshment, the vitality to bear fruit."[48]

Creation by a Nonviolent, Loving God

The Nonviolence of Creation

As in any doctrine in theological discourse, I cannot overemphasize the significance of connecting theories of creation with theories of the nonviolent God. We can do this with ease. First, we discussed earlier in the chapter that the creation narratives prevalent in ancient Middle Eastern cultures recount stories of "creation-by-combat," in which power-crazed deities fight each other and scatter

---

45. Payton, *Light from the Christian East*, 91, 97.
46. Payton, *Light from the Christian East*, 95.
47. Payton, *Light from the Christian East*, 95.
48. Hildegard of Bingen, *Illuminations of Hildegard of Bingen*, commentary by Matthew Fox (Rochester, VT: Bear and Company, 2002), 43–44.

amputated body parts around to form the universe as we know it.[49] In contrast, in the Hebrew creation story, God creates the universe peacefully with a mere few words—"Let there be," and there it is. This nonviolent activity of God that calls the worlds into existence "signals the Creator's original intent for *shalom* [peace, but see below] and blessing at the outset of human history, prior to the rise of human (or divine) violence."[50]

If God's original intent in creating the universe was to bring forth the shalom actively present within the Trinitarian relationship, we need to explore more fully the meaning of this biblical word. Shalom means much more than "peace," as we often translate it. This simplistic interpretation of the word misses the profound meaning implicit in the notion of shalom. In addition to indicating a profound peace, shalom conveys expressions of wholeness, well-being, good health, safety, prosperity, rest, harmony with all creation, trust, and tranquility. Theologian Randy Woodley asserts that in a world infused with shalom, "historic wrongs would be righted; former enemies would come back together in love; through restitution, justice would be served to those who had been wronged for years; people with physical, emotional, mental, and spiritual afflictions and anguish would be healed; people would be at peace with one another . . . ; pollution would cease; climate change would be thwarted; there would be no wars; and everyone and everything would be happy with the Creator and all creation."[51] Peace in its fullest sense would permeate every aspect of the universe, which God created with peaceful power.

Practically speaking, a theology of a shalom-impregnated creation should always inform our interpretation of an allegedly violent God found in various passages in Scripture from Genesis to Revelation. The peaceful, creative opening of the entire biblical canon serves as the interpretive framework for determining the legitimacy of the divine and human violence that infiltrates much of Scripture. The entire narrative of the Bible—creation, fall, and redemption—frames God's fundamental purpose to bring about shalom on earth and goodwill toward all people, and if we want to interpret responsibly, we need to take the divine desire for shalom into consideration when reading these texts.[52] The nonviolent, loving God creates a nonviolent universe through nonviolent means, and into this very good creation, Genesis 3 tells us, humanity brings sin, corrupting God's peaceful creation with continual violence. Once we understand the divine plan and purpose for the universe articulated in the creation passages, we may reasonably conclude that the moral violence we see in the world, both then and now, is ours, not God's.

49. J. Richard Middleton, "Created in the Image of a Violent God? The Ethical Problem of the Conquest by Chaos in Biblical Creation Texts," *Interpretation* 58, no. 4 (October 2004): 355. See also Grenz, *Theology for the Community of God*, 100.
50. Middleton, "Created in the Image," 355; Middleton, *The Liberating Image*, 269.
51. Randy S. Woodley, *Shalom and the Community of Creation: An Indigenous Vision* (Grand Rapids, MI: Eerdmans, 2012), 11.
52. Middleton, *The Liberating Image*, 269; Darrin W. Snyder Belousek, "God, Evil, and (Non)Violence: Creation Theology, Creativity Theology, and Christian Ethics," *The Conrad Grebel Review* 34, no. 2 (Spring 2016): 157.

But what about natural violence that comes about through animal instinct? This is a difficult question. Students often ask about the violence of "Nature, red in tooth and claw" (a phrase from the Victorian poet Alfred, Lord Tennyson) evident in creation. Yet when we look at the creation accounts in Genesis theologically, we do not see killing of any sort. God tells humanity they can eat from any tree, but *not* that they can eat any animal. God gives every green plant to all the animals and humans alike, implying that animals had no place in God's original food chain. Remember, these stories tell profound truths about God and creation. The divine plan for creation in these ancient texts seems to preclude violence of any kind. In fact, in the biblical text God does not tell humans they can eat animals until after the flood story—animals did not even appear to fear humans until after the flood (Gen 9:1-3).

Yet, we see what seems to be violence, or at least pain and suffering, in the natural world. Fortunately, in Scripture God promises to make all things new again, to bring all creation into its original divine intent for shalom so that the universe, once again, will exist without violence. The Bible describes a future peace-filled creation:

> The wolf shall live with the lamb, the leopard shall lie down with the kid, the calf and the lion and the fatling together, and a little child shall lead them. The cow and the bear shall graze, their young shall lie down together; and the lion shall eat straw like the ox. The nursing child shall play over the hole of the asp, and the weaned child shall put its hand on the adder's den. They will not hurt or destroy on all my holy mountain; for the earth will be full of the knowledge of the Lord as the waters cover the sea. (Isa 11:6-9)

This passage reveals God's ultimate plan for peace for all creation—one in which enemies such as children and poisonous snakes, lions and their typical prey, will all live and love in peace. In this vision, the entire creation serves as a doxology that praises God's extravagant love and generosity (Ps 19:1; Job 38:7). The beauty of the sunrise and sunset "shout for joy" (Ps 65:8); the hills rejoice with thanksgiving (v. 12); the meadows and valleys sing with delight (v. 13); and the trees of the field clap their hands in joy (Isa 55:12)—all in exultant appreciation for the divine love, care, and creativity.[53] Medieval mystic and abbess Hildegard of Bingen expresses the nonviolent love of God toward creation: "As the Creator loves His creation so creation loves the Creator. Creation, of course, was fashioned to be adored, to be showered, to be gifted with the love of the Creator. The entire world has been embraced by this kiss."[54]

---

53. Brueggemann, *Genesis*, 27.
54. Quoted in Norman Wirzba, *The Paradise of God: Renewing Religion in an Ecological Age* (New York: Oxford University Press, 2003), 1.

This profound theological vision from the Bible requires that we do the hard work of trying to understand its relationship to what we have discovered about the world in our modern scientific age. If we choose to believe in an evolutionary universe, especially, we may need to account for the violence we see in the natural world (animals eating each other, volcanoes and earthquakes) as something creation is growing out of as it moves forward in the evolutionary process. Or we could understand "natural" pain and suffering as somehow harmonizing with a sacred, shalom-based view of the world (as some Native American cosmologies seem to do in the way they think about the animal, plant, and mineral world).[55] But even those who interpret the biblical narrative literally and believe that all natural evil originates because of the "fall" (as most people did prior to Darwin) have to explain how the fall could actually redesign the entire created order, seemingly overnight. So we must wrestle with these questions whether we are literal creationists or subscribe to some kind of theistic evolution.[56] We will talk more about the problem of evil and suffering in chapter 10, "Humanity."

The Continuity of Creation

From our study of the creation texts, we can affirm that God, out of infinite love and peaceful purpose, works to redeem, reconcile, restore, and transform the universe into its intended goodness through Jesus. So God continues the process of creation by creating all things new—new persons and new life. In fact, the word create—bara in Hebrew—indicates present and future action. The Bible expresses the continual creating process and supports the view that the divine creative power works something new every day. For example, the Psalmist writes, "When you send forth your spirit, they are created; and you renew the face of the ground" (104:30).[57] Psalm 102:18 expresses the idea of a future creation in its mention of "a people yet unborn." Each individual, one by one, is created by God in a continual process. And God continually works to create in us clean hearts, as we see in the prayer of David in Psalm 51. God continually creates new life, as articulated in 2 Corinthians 5:17: "If anyone is in Christ, there is a new creation: everything old has passed away; see, everything has become new."

We can see, therefore, that modern theories of evolution can harmonize well with the divine process of a continuing creation. Paul Tillich clearly expresses this

55. For this position and a treatment of evolutionary theology in general, see John F. Haught, *God after Darwin: A Theology of Evolution*, 2nd ed. (New York: Routledge, 2019). See also Haught's essay on animal suffering and theodicy, "Teilhard and the Question of Life's Suffering," in *Recovering Teilhard's Fire*, ed. Kathleen Duffy (Philadelphia: St. Joseph's University Press, 2010), excerpted at Metanexus: https://tinyurl.com/y9ku6jx9; and Keith B. Miller, ed., *Perspectives on an Evolving Creation* (Grand Rapids, MI: Eerdmans, 2003).
56. Robin Collins makes this point in "Evolution and Original Sin," in *Perspectives on an Evolving Creation*, Keith B. Miller (Grand Rapids, MI: Eerdmans, 2003), 489–99. Or see the serialized version online (introduced by Ted Davis): https://tinyurl.com/y8pyoowb.
57. Johnson, *The Creed*, 94.

same notion of a continual creation when he writes that "God *has* created the world, he *is* creative in the present moment, and he *will* creatively fulfill his *telos*" (end or purpose).[58] In other words, creation did not happen like a fairy tale's "once upon a time"; instead, God started the process of creation that we read about in Genesis 1 and 2 but expressed the divine desire for an ongoing relationship with the world by continually creating new life. Some theologians believe God creates a dynamic universe, open to "change, novelty, and indeterminacy as well as continuity, order, and coherence."[59] So science and the Christian faith should keep working together to inform us about the universe God created and to influence our actions to keep that good creation healthy.

The Unity and Diversity of Creation

God created the universe with peace and harmony in mind. In fact, we could say that all creation ideally reflects the divine plan for universal shalom in which all creatures live in unity, peace, and partnership with all things. That unity includes the interconnectedness of everything God makes. Every ingredient that makes up the material world bears the mark of the creator, has its life in the divine, and contributes to God's purposes. Consequently, each creature relates significantly in some way to every other created thing. In other words, we are incomplete without the entire universe; we depend on all other elements in order to live life fully.[60] We can learn from Native Americans (and others in various indigenous cultures) who see everything as connected in a great web of life, in which each part is an expression of the whole.[61]

At the same time, the biblical texts represent God creating all things "according to their kinds" (Gen 1:21 NIV; Gen 6:20 NRSV) as unique entities within the harmony of the whole. In Genesis 1, God creates many different bodies that light up the night sky. God forms a plethora of living creatures—butterflies, mice, lions, tigers, bears, birds, fish . . . you get the picture. Each one looks and acts different from the others. Indeed, we can appreciate God's creative diversity while sitting in an airport or on a park bench watching people. No one person looks or behaves or talks the same as another. Even identical twins are not identical! With ten thousand new species of animals discovered each year and scientific projections claiming a total of up to fifty million species worldwide, how can we deny the divine propensity toward creative diversity? While at times challenging, the world's diversity mirrors God's

---

58. Tillich, *Systematic Theology*, vol. 1, 253.
59. Migliore, *Faith Seeking Understanding*, 116–17.
60. Woodley, *Shalom and the Community of Creation*, 42.
61. Quantum physicists now believe in the interconnectedness of the entire universe through what they call "quantum entanglement," a theory that Einstein introduced as "spooky action at a distance." See Jeffrey Bub, "Quantum Entanglement and Information," in *The Stanford Encyclopedia of Philosophy* (Spring 2019 Edition), ed. Edward N. Zalta, https://tinyurl.com/y9qsy2rx.

nature as love and includes God's intention for unity without uniformity, harmony in the midst of diversity.

The Human Responsibility to Creation

Let's look at human responsibility within the context of shalom. As we have seen, God tells the first human beings to "rule" or "have dominion" over all creation (Gen 1:26). Western theologians as sophisticated and influential as St. Thomas Aquinas and St. Augustine (the heavy hitters of the Western classical tradition) interpreted "dominion" in anthropocentric terms, arguing that human beings have primacy and could do what they liked with the created order. As products of their own preconceptions, times, and cultures (perhaps even gender?), they believed that the earth existed purely for human consumption. Aquinas wrote that "the life of animals and plants is preserved not for themselves but for man," and Augustine argued, "By a most just ordinance of the Creator, both their life and their death are subject to our use."[62] These teachings went largely uncontested for centuries. Unfortunately, they also have served to give human beings permission to harm our natural environment by carelessly clear-cutting our forests, polluting our air, and dumping poisons in our rivers, lakes, and oceans. Climate change is advancing on us so quickly that scientists now predict that if we do not change our ways, by 2050 we will destroy our world to the point of challenging our own ability to exist.[63]

Clearly God does not intend this form of "dominion" by human beings. We need to remember that, contrary to the opinion of some of our earlier theologians, "ruling" does not mean creation exists solely to serve our needs; such a view is shortsighted and misses the profound interdependence between us and the created order. Dominion does not give us *carte blanche* permission to do as we want with God's creation, heedless of where it will lead. Instead, it functions as a command to guard, preserve, nurture, and sustain the gift of creation. Ecologist Fred Bahnson and eco-theologian Norman Wirzba express this picture of dominion: "God takes the first human being freshly formed from the soil and says, 'Take care of the garden. Learn to serve and protect the ground. Commit to loving the soil, and in this loving work catch a glimpse of who I am and what I do.'"[64] Through loving and caring for the earth, we get a glimpse of God in us, the God who cares for and nurtures the good, divine creation and partners with us in carrying out that godly work. Consequently, we are called to make peace with all of creation, not wreak havoc and do violence to ourselves and other created beings. Our very own well-being depends on this stewardship.

---

62. Thomas Aquinas, *Summa Theologica* 2.2, q. 64, a. 1; Augustine, *City of God*, 1, 20 (quoted in Aquinas).
63. Chris Mooney and Brady Dennis, "The World Has Just Over a Decade to Get Climate Change under Control, U.N. Scientists Say," *Washington Post*, October 7, 2018, https://tinyurl.com/y4n9jp72.
64. Fred Bahnson and Norman Wirzba, *Making Peace with the Land: God's Call to Reconcile with Creation* (Downers Grove, IL: IVP, 2012), 17–18.

Having dominion over creation makes us responsible not only to appreciate the extravagant divine generosity but also to commit to working together to protect our environment. God calls us to remain faithful to the partnership we have with God and with each other to continue the divine work of shalom in creation, re-creation, and renewal.[65] Unfortunately, our careless and sometimes selfish actions have put the good health of the earth in peril. We have frustrated God's intentions and purposes for a good creation filled with shalom and have acted as masters rather than as trustees of the world. We have acted violently toward nature in ways that deny the interconnectedness of all life on earth. Our violence against the earth, in opposition to God's peaceful methods of creating it, deforms what God has formed, potentially returning us to the formless and void nothingness of nonexistence. Consequently, now more than ever, we need to remember that God has a vision for the creation in which all live in unselfish harmony in a world defined by shalom. Because God's act of creation lies solely in divine love, our acts toward creation should express that love. We serve as God's partners in propagating a new "messianic peace" that works to end violence in our relationships with God and each other, and to restore a right relationship with the created order.[66] Indeed, creation tends toward a mutually loving communion with God and each other, and we should work with, not against, that tendency.

Richard Rohr expresses the interplay of divine and human action toward creation with these beautiful words: "God is not an offended monarch on a throne throwing down thunderbolts, but a 'fountain of fullness' that flows, overflows, and fills all things. Reality is thus participatory; it is *love itself.* . . . God as Trinitarian Flow is the blueprint and pattern for all relationships and all of creation."[67] God's outpouring of love creates new things from a previously void chaos and invites us, again and again, to share in the divine purpose of creating and renewing all things, the gracious work of shalom on earth. The Trinitarian love of God, reflected by Father, Son, and Holy Spirit, reveals the divine intent to share that love by giving life to others and partnering with us in the divine plan for redemption. As God's counterparts in the universe, we exist "to be both the recipient of and the mirror of [that] divine love."[68]

Carl Sagan's "pale blue dot" emphasizes the insignificance of our position in the vast universe and, at the same time, stresses the significance of a life lived in love:

> The Earth is a very small stage in a vast cosmic arena. Think of the rivers of blood spilled by all those generals and emperors so that in glory and triumph they could become the momentary masters of a fraction of a dot.

65. Belousek, "God, Evil, and (Non)Violence," 170.
66. Belousek, "God, Evil, and (Non)Violence," 170.
67. Richard Rohr, "The Blueprint of Creation," *The Cosmic Christ*, Week 1, Center for Action and Contemplation, March 28, 2017, https://tinyurl.com/yb23o6rn.
68. Grenz, *Theology for the Community of God*, 101.

Think of the endless cruelties visited by the inhabitants of one corner of the dot on scarcely distinguishable inhabitants of some other corner of the dot. . . . To my mind, there is perhaps no better demonstration of the folly of human conceits than this distant image of our tiny world. To me, it underscores our responsibility to deal more kindly and compassionately with one another and to preserve and cherish that pale blue dot, the only home we've ever known.[69]

Even taking into consideration our incredible insignificance in the universe, as of yet we know of no other planet that supports human life. And, amazingly, God the Father, Son, and Holy Spirit, out of generosity and love, willed us into existence and invites us to be partners in the divine community of shalom love as partners. How then shall we live?

69. Sagan, Pale Blue Dot, 7.

6. Jesus

I believe in Jesus Christ, God's only Son, our Lord . . .

On the third day he rose again; he ascended into heaven,

he is seated at the right hand of the Father . . .

> How we see Jesus . . . shapes what we think the Christian life is most centrally about.
>
> —Marcus Borg, *Jesus*

> A man who was merely a man and said the sort of things Jesus said would not be a great moral teacher. He would either be a lunatic—on the level with the man who says he is a poached egg—or else he would be the Devil of Hell. . . . Either this man was, and is, the Son of God, or else a madman or something worse. You can shut him up for a fool, you can spit at him and kill him as a demon or you can fall at his feet and call him Lord and God, but let us not come with any patronizing nonsense about his [merely] being a great human teacher. He has not left that open to us. He did not intend to.
>
> —C. S. Lewis, *Mere Christianity*

Almost every summer throughout my elementary school years I attended Vacation Bible School at the local Baptist church. I distinctly remember one summer morning when the pastor came to our class to teach us about Jesus. He stood in front of us holding two glasses of clear water high over his head. In a dramatic, theatrical move he poured the water from those glasses into a jar on a table below him. And much to our amazement, the water in the jar turned from clear to red. "This," he said, "describes who Jesus is." Of course, our young minds, unable to grasp the beauty and complexity of the metaphor, focused instead on the magically transformed water-into-"wine" trick and totally missed the point the pastor was trying make about the person of Jesus. Now, decades later, I wonder if we have missed the point of the wedding-in-Cana story told in John 2:1–11. Maybe that story is less about the tricky transformation of water into wine and more about the miraculous transformation of the divine into the human. Maybe the pastor's trick and Jesus's miracle can help us answer this question: Who is Jesus?

The Divinity of Jesus

The disciple Peter calls him the Christ, which explains why, in theological circles, the study of Jesus's person and work is called "Christology." Since this chapter explores questions surrounding Jesus Christ, let's start with what Jesus himself said. Standing at the base of Mt. Hermon in Caesarea Philippi, Jesus asked his disciples, "Who do you say that I am?" Some said Jesus was John the Baptist. Others said he was Jeremiah. And yet others said he was one of the prophets. More contemporary voices, such as proponents of the scholarly working group The Jesus Seminar, say Jesus was merely a sage or a great moral teacher. But if we take Jesus's positive response to Peter's answer seriously, we might all echo Peter and say that Jesus is "the Christ [Messiah], the Son of the living God" (Matt 16:13–16). But what do all those lofty-sounding words mean? And how do they matter to us today? These questions lead us into complex and sometimes difficult terminology and concepts as we struggle to make sense of Jesus's nature.

The Eventual Heresies

Christians throughout history have tried to answer questions about who Jesus is in a variety of ways, many of which were eventually considered heresies—at least according to the doctrines arising out of fourth- and fifth-century churches and church councils. The church fathers of the fourth and fifth centuries rejected many of the beliefs surrounding the incarnation of Jesus, mainly because they failed either to stress the significance of his divinity, to emphasize adequately his humanity, or to join the two natures satisfactorily. The proponents of these different christological constructions were not trying to think up heresies; on the contrary, they were making serious attempts to understand Jesus in light of the significantly life-changing claims made about him by the early Christian communities. The first so-called heresy arose from first-century Jewish Christian thought. Referred to as the *Ebionites*, this sect of believers denied the divinity of Jesus, rejected the virgin birth, and asserted that Jesus received a supernatural endowment when he received the Holy Spirit at his baptism. *Docetists*, who generally held to Gnostic beliefs in the evil character of the physical world, denied the humanity of Jesus by saying he only *appeared* as a human but was truly, and exclusively, divine. *Appollinarianism*, named after the followers of the fourth-century bishop of Laodicea, Appollinarius, thought Jesus received a new, divine soul that replaced his human soul. Although Jesus had an animal nature, they thought, he did not possess a human spirit. Instead, they claimed that the divine *Logos* (Word of God in this context) dominated his existence. *Eutychianism*, named after Eutyches, a presbyter in Constantinople in the fourth and fifth centuries, argued that the human and divine natures were united into a third type of nature controlled by God.[1] All this sounds confusing because it is confusing! So how did the church respond?

The Council of Chalcedon in 451 CE

Much of our doctrine surrounding the person of Jesus comes from the councils held in the fourth and fifth centuries. Leaders met in several church-wide councils to investigate and establish a unifying doctrine of the person of Jesus that would also serve to unify the church. In chapter 3, "The Trinity," we discussed the council at Nicaea (325 CE), during which the church officially declared the full divinity of Jesus. This doctrine of divinity (Jesus as *homoousios* with the Father) caused all sorts of problems because not only was Jesus divine (a less obvious conclusion), but Jesus was (most obviously) human as well. But once the church decided Jesus was fully divine and one of the persons of the Trinitarian God, they needed to figure out *how*. According to the Nicene Creed, the triune God exists in three persons— Father, Son, and Holy Spirit—and Jesus is just one person. How, then, do two different natures—the human and the divine—fit into that one person? How could one person be fully human and fully divine in one body? To resolve this problem, Emperor Marcion called the bishops together to meet in Chalcedon in 451 CE to decide the issue and construct a formal doctrine to eliminate the heresies still plaguing the young church.[2]

The Chalcedonian fathers, driven by the thought of Nestorius (386–451 CE), archbishop of Constantinople, and Cyril (376–444 CE), patriarch of Alexandria, sought to determine the exact nature of Jesus, one man possessing both a human and a divine nature. Nestorians believed that Jesus could not be consubstantial (*con* meaning "with" and *substantial* having to do with essence) with both God and humanity at the same time, so they separated Jesus into two distinct persons with a divine rational mind and no rational human mind. When Jesus experienced hunger, thirst, sadness, joy, pain, and tiredness, for example, Nestorians claimed he acted out of his human nature. When Jesus performed miracles, taught, and rose from dead, he acted out of his divine nature. Nestorians thought the divine Jesus merely put on humanity as a person puts on a coat. Those on Cyril's side of the argument thought this sharp division of natures made Jesus into two persons rather than just the one person as stated in Trinitarian logic. They also argued that this line of thought led to an unfortunate diminishing of the humanity of Jesus,

---

1. Roger E. Olson, *The Mosaic of Christian Belief: Twenty Centuries of Unity and Disunity* (Downers Grove, IL: InterVarsity, 2016), 232–37.
2. Olson, *Mosaic of Christian Belief*, 225–27. The theological background and personages in this christological argument are much more complex than I have articulated in this brief discussion. I simplify for the sake of understanding the main theological issues surrounding the person of Jesus without the many complications that fall outside the scope of this introductory text.

which, for them, potentially thwarted the efficacy of the cross and, therefore, of the salvation of our souls.

Those following Cyril of Alexandria believed that Jesus has two natures, one human and one divine, each completely united to the other, yet unconfused. They constructed the theology of the *hypostatic* union—*hypostasis* meaning two natures united in one substance or one underlying existence. They also asserted that Jesus has a rational human mind. In addition, rather than Jesus merely wearing humanity as we wear a coat, they believed that God actually became human, that God made humanity God's own. In other words, Jesus existed as one fully integrated person with fully united human and divine natures. The Nestorians, however, thought this went too far in uniting the natures, making Jesus into a "one-natured" God/man, "a third something that is neither fully and truly human nor fully and truly divine."[3] These different theological disagreements arose, for the most part, due to the varying presuppositions and hermeneutical methods of the scholars involved.

Before we criticize these early Christian thinkers either for their heresy or for the impracticality of their arguments, we need to walk a bit in their shoes and discover the reasons behind their rationales. Nestorius and his followers, proclaimed heretics by the end of the council, identified deeply with the Greek philosophical conceptions of God as *actus purus*, immutable, impassible, and omniscient. Consequently, because Jesus lived as a human being who grew and learned (exhibiting mutable characteristics), who suffered, and who did not know everything (see Matt 24:36), they thought he could not be divine. In addition, the God of the "omnis" would never experience the impurities of the human condition. Only the human nature of Jesus, completely separated from the divine nature, they argued, could get his hands and feet dirty by walking the earth, or suffer hunger, thirst, fatigue, pain, and human emotions. Nestorius and those who came after him felt the need to construct a theology that kept God safe from the vicissitudes of human life. Thus, they separated the human and divine into what many consider two different persons. This served to distance God from the human condition, while providing a solution for the problems surrounding God in a human body.

The followers of Cyril, on the other hand, did not concern themselves as much with saving God from the world of human experience. Their concerns were more focused on defining the nature of salvation. Although Cyril never came out and explicitly claimed that Jesus could suffer, he came very close. He did assert that only a fully human and fully divine Jesus could save humanity from sin. His idea was that humanity sinned and needs salvation; only the divine, however, can save. Consequently, they reasoned that the Savior must fully embody both humanity and divinity in order to effect the salvation of souls. As it turns out, the church voted Cyril's thought in and Nestorius's thought out. They wrote the "Definition of Chalcedon," asserting that Jesus Christ, "Son, Lord, Only-begotten," is

3. Olson, *Mosaic of Christian Belief*, 229–35.

recognized in two natures, without confusion, without change, without division, without separation; the distinction of natures being in no way annulled by the union, but rather the characteristics of each nature being preserved and coming together to form one person and subsistence, not as parted or separated into two persons, but one and the same Son and Only-begotten God the Word, Lord Jesus Christ.[4]

In other words, the council accepted the doctrine of the hypostatic union, which describes the union of two natures in the divine Logos, who came to earth as a human being—one nature through the power of the Holy Spirit and the other nature through the humanity of Mary, his mother. Both natures existed in one fully integrated person, in a perfect union. At the same time, however, these natures remained distinct from one another, unconfused, human *and* divine, yet one—a paradox that we often describe as the mystery of the incarnation.

Articulations of the Divinity of Jesus

Although the church held several more councils to argue about and affirm previous decisions, the doctrines laid down in the Nicene Creed and the Definition of Chalcedon remain the foundational beliefs for much of Christianity today. These councils, decisions, and doctrines serve as the foundation for Christianity's central beliefs. A focus on these abstract, ontological (having to do with being or essence) descriptions of Jesus Christ, however, confuse us and distract us from the significance of the historical reality of Jesus and his work with us, in us, and on our behalf. Franciscan theologian Richard Rohr points out that after the church decided upon the "substance" and "nature(s)" of Jesus and, for the most part, answered the questions surrounding how humanity and divinity can be "one," the church fathers still left us with "cold academic theologies" that bear no resemblance to "practical and transformative implications for history, evolution, and even ourselves." Rohr reminds us that many in Christian churches routinely recite the Nicene Creed not even aware that "there are no warm or human words like 'love,' 'healing,' or 'forgiveness' in the whole text."[5]

Other theologians have struggled to articulate a meaningful Christology through approaches other than the ontological, philosophical Greek categories of the Nicene and Chalcedonian creedal statements. As early as the second century, theologian and historian Justin Martyr (100–165) attempted to express his understanding of Jesus not in Greek philosophical terms but in terms more familiar to the people. He described Jesus not as *homoousios* with the Father, but by using the titles ascribed to him in Scripture: Christ, Lord, Savior, rock, Word, wisdom,

---

4. "The Chalcedon Formula," Anglicans Online, May 23, 2017, https://tinyurl.com/yb99sdwn.
5. Richard Rohr, *Eager to Love: The Alternative Way of Francis of Assisi* (Cincinnati: Franciscan Media, 2014), 213–15.

King, priest, Son of God, and Son of Man—common metaphors easily understood by the population at large.[6] W. T. Conner, a contemporary Baptist theologian, urged the church to set aside the language of "substance" in favor of the language of "personality" and to talk about Jesus in terms of function rather than in terms describing his being. Conner invites us to think not so much about what Jesus *is* as about what Jesus *does*. He brings language about Jesus out of the abstract into the material and focuses on his personal life, characteristics, relationships, actions, and teachings. Rather than understanding Jesus as a combination of two abstract "natures" or "substances," he asks the church to contemplate him as a "creative and redemptive personality" who profoundly influences human lives.[7]

Similarly, theologian Oscar Cullmann, a colleague of Karl Barth, asks, "How does Jesus function?" rather than "What is his nature?" He maintained that Jesus's relationship to divinity lies in how he functions, or acts, to bring about salvation history.[8] In other words, the church can affirm that Jesus functioned as God and acted according to God's will. Functionally, in total unity with God, Jesus fulfilled God's tasks on earth—he actualized God in the world. The well-known black theologian James Cone also offers support for the expression of Jesus's divinity through the way Jesus functions in the lives of those who suffer. For example, the black church confesses the divinity of Christ through their encounter with him as the crucified and risen Lord. Because Jesus suffered oppression and abuse unjustly, he understands the suffering of black people. He gives these suffering people comfort and draws them into an intimate relationship through common experiences. In addition, he not only suffers with those who suffer; he also conquered suffering and death, thereby providing hope in otherwise unhopeful contexts. Indeed, our personal experiences of the presence of Jesus among us today can serve as a testimony to his divine status as Immanuel—"God with us."[9]

Interestingly, we can reach even farther back into history and see that the very early church developed common beliefs about Jesus and his divinity outside the limitations imposed by the Greek philosophical language of the fourth- and fifth-century church fathers. We look at the devotional life of early Jewish believers not only because the first communities to receive Jesus as Savior and Messiah were Jewish but also because their faith never offered them creeds to sign or formal doctrines to entertain. Instead, we understand that they expressed their beliefs not through formal doctrine (it was not yet developed on a universal level) but through devotional practices, hymns, prayers, confessions, and worship. In fact, historian

---

6. Justin Martyr, *Dialogue with Trypho the Jew* (Pickering, OH: Beloved, 2015)., 34.2; 59.1; 61.1; 126.1. See also Larry W. Hurtado, *Lord Jesus Christ: Devotion to Jesus in Earliest Christianity* (Grand Rapids, MI: Eerdmans, 2003), 641–42.
7. W. T. Conner, *A System of Christian Doctrine* (Nashville: Southern Baptist Convention, 1924), 156, 159, 163; Stanley J. Grenz, *Theology for the Community of God* (Grand Rapids, MI: Eerdmans, 2000), 321, 342.
8. Oscar Cullmann, *Christology of the New Testament*, trans. Shirlie C. Guthrie and Charles A. M. Hall, rev. ed. (Philadelphia: Westminster, 1963), 3.
9. James Cone, *God of the Oppressed* (New York: Seabury, 1975), 121–22.

Larry Hurtado argues that "in the devotional practices and attendant beliefs of the earliest Christian circles, Jesus was linked with God in an astonishing and unexpected way," even as early as twenty-five years after his death.[10] Jewish Christian proclamations of Jesus's divinity marked devotional and worship practices from their earliest moments. Consequently, we need to rethink evolutionary theories that present the belief in Jesus's divinity as a much later development. Hurtado writes that "devotion to Jesus as divine erupted suddenly and quickly, not gradually and late, among first-century circles of followers . . . the origins lie in Jewish Christian circles of the earliest years."[11] In that sense, we follow the lead of the early church and, therefore, cannot say that Jesus simply came to us as God on earth. We need to say that Jesus actually came to us as God's unique glory in human form, sent to reflect God, and who now warrants full reverence as God.[12]

The belief in the divinity of Jesus expressed in devotional practices should astonish us because the earliest Christians emerged from Jewish traditions, which, as we know, held specifically to strong monotheistic (one God) beliefs that distinctly separated them from the Romans, Greeks, and surrounding polytheistic communities. The intense monotheism of Jewish converts to Christianity prevented them from bowing down to the emperor or to Rome's gods, even when threatened with horrifying forms of death. Yet according to Pliny the Younger (61–113), an early historian, from the first century on these Christians worshipped Jesus, sang hymns to him, and prayed to him as to God. Even knowing the punishment they would suffer, they refused to curse Christ, their Messiah. Consequently, the reverence given to Jesus as God by monotheistic Jewish believers "amounted to a remarkable one-of-a-kind accommodation of Jesus to a level of reverence that the Christians otherwise freely reserved for the one God of biblical tradition."[13] The anti-Christian philosopher Celsus expressed disgust and disbelief that these early believers added Jesus to their monotheistic system. He writes that "they do not consider what they are doing a breach of monotheism; rather, they think it perfectly consistent to worship the great God and to worship his servant as God. And their worship of this Jesus is the more outrageous because they refuse to listen to any talk about God, the Father of all, unless it includes some reference to Jesus."[14] Celsus accused these Jewish Christians of making Jesus mightier than God as they worked to ensure that Jesus remained preserved as God and Lord.

Indeed, these Jewish Christians found support in the biblical texts for their belief in Jesus as God. We find evidence of this accommodation in the community's

---

10. Larry W. Hurtado, How on Earth Did Jesus Become a God? Historical Questions about Earliest Devotion to Jesus (Grand Rapids, MI: Eerdmans, 2005), 25, 27.
11. Hurtado, Lord Jesus Christ, 650, 135–36; Hurtado, How on Earth, 25.
12. Hurtado, How on Earth, 29.
13. Pliny the Younger, Epistles 10.96, in A New Eusebius: Documents Illustrative of the History of the Church to A.D. 337, ed. J. Stevenson (London: SPCK, 1974), 13–15; quotation from Hurtado, How on Earth, 14, 28.
14. Celsus, On the True Doctrine: A Discourse against the Christians, trans. R. Joseph Hoffmann (New York: Oxford University Press, 1987), 116–17.

widely used interpretation of Psalm 110. They connected the opening words, "The Lord says to my lord, 'Sit at my right hand . . .'" (v. 1), to Jesus, especially in such verses as Romans 8:34 and Ephesians 1:20 (see also Acts 2:33; 7:55; Col 3:1; Heb 1:3; 10:12; Rev 3:21). A similar, commonly used connection occurs between Isaiah 45:23 and Philippians 2:9–11. In Isaiah, "every knee shall bow, every tongue shall swear" allegiance to God the Savior. The early Jewish Christians applied those same words to Jesus, indicating his status as God in the flesh.[15] In addition, the opening of the book of John applies the term "God" to Jesus: "In the beginning was the Word, and the Word was with God, and the Word was God. He was in the beginning with God" (John 1:1–2). The disciple Thomas testifies to Jesus's divinity, exclaiming, "My Lord and my God!" when he sees and touches the resurrected Christ (John 20:27–28). Notice that Jesus says nothing to contradict Thomas's astonishing attribution. Furthermore, although we never see Jesus in the Bible standing on a mountaintop yelling at the top of his lungs, "I AM GOD!" we do see him acting in ways that only God would act. For instance, he forgave the sins of the paralytic man when everyone knew that only God could forgive sin (Matt 9:2; Mark 2:5; Luke 5:20). Some of the Jewish leaders thought he was claiming divinity by calling God his Father. Jesus's response? He tells them that God has sent him to do God's will and that he deserves the same honor they give to God. Jesus's statements, for the people listening to him in those days, amounted to an assertion of divinity (John 5:18–24). Standing with his disciples in Caesarea Philippi, Jesus asks them, "Who do you say that I am?" When Peter answers, "You are the Messiah, the Son of the living God" (another assertion of divinity), Jesus does not refute him but, instead, praises him for his insight (Matt 16:16–19). Titus, too, applies divinity to Jesus, speaking of the "manifestation of the glory of our great God and Savior, Jesus Christ" (2:13). Moreover, Jesus's actions of stilling the turbulent seas, feeding five thousand men (not counting women and children) with five loaves and two fish, healing lepers, and giving sight to the blind also point to his uniqueness, if not also to his divine status.

We see references to Jesus's divinity in the Pauline corpus as well. For example, the well-known *kenosis* passage in Philippians 2 states that Jesus existed "in the form of God" and equal to God (v. 6). Even though the passage tells us he emptied himself of that form and equality in order to be like us, he nonetheless possessed those qualities as God in human flesh (v. 7). The word for "form" in the Greek New Testament is *morphe*, which denotes an external appearance or the way a person or thing looks. Paul is saying here that God morphed into a human; God changed from divine "appearance" to human appearance. Colossians supports this understanding of Jesus, claiming that in Jesus "the whole fullness of deity dwells bodily" (2:9). The author of Hebrews also seems to agree with the Pauline texts, writing that

15. Hurtado, *How on Earth*, 26.

Jesus is "the reflection of God's glory and the *exact* imprint of God's very being" (1:3; emphasis mine). In fact, the first ten chapters of the book of Hebrews express the uniqueness and superiority of Jesus as the Father's divine Son.

Although biblical scholars have critically examined the texts that support the divinity of Jesus and some have offered various valid interpretations over the years to try to demystify or deny such thought, historical studies also reveal that the early church, birthed by Jewish converts, worshipped Jesus as God and applied Old Testament Scriptures to his life and work. The early belief in Jesus as "God with us" and the devotional practices common in the church served as the foundation for later biblical writers and for the development of doctrine as the young church expanded.

As the church grew and spread, extant historical documents record the growing belief in the divinity of Christ. Clement, bishop of Rome from 88 to 99 CE, affirms Jesus as God, writing, "We ought to think of Jesus Christ as we do of God, as 'Judge of the living and the dead.'"[16] Ignatius of Antioch (35–108) wrote various letters in which he affirms Jesus as divine, as the appearance on earth of God. For him and his Christian community, Jesus is the "eternal and invisible, yet who became visible for our sakes; impalpable and impassible, yet who became passible on our account. . . ."[17] For Ignatius and the first-century Christians, Jesus is the mind of God, the knowledge of God, and the mouth of God who speaks the truth of God without error.

In addition, Christians associated their belief in the divinity of Jesus with God's promise of a "messiah," the English translation of the Greek word *Christos*. The notion of Jesus as Messiah functioned so prevalently in early Christian thought that people took for granted the title "*the* Christ/Messiah." In fact, within twenty years of Jesus's death, the word *Christos* "lost its titular significance and became a name."[18] So these Christians believed in Jesus as God's long-awaited Messiah who also was the true Lord—a very shocking notion given the fact that Jesus died on a cross as a common criminal. The fact of such a demeaning death, however, lends credibility to their belief. That these early believers embraced such an unusual, unexpected, and undignified event for the saving actions of the Messiah, written forever in the annals of history, and forever transforming the lives of those who believe, attests to the power of their beliefs. But why did these earliest Christians make such amazing and unexpected claims about a mere human being? We can answer that question with one word—resurrection.

16. 2 Clement 1.1.
17. Ignatius, *Letter to Polycarp*, 3.2, https://tinyurl.com/y7fj43fu.
18. N. T. Wright, *The Resurrection of the Son of God* (Minneapolis: Fortress, 2003), 555.

The Resurrection

Early Christians believed in Jesus as the Messiah and as divine first and foremost because of his resurrection.[19] Even though the divinity of Jesus serves as the foundation of the Christian faith and there is much evidence for it in Scripture, its truth really lies in the reality of his resurrection from the dead. The resurrection serves as the one event that both attests that Jesus is the Messiah and confirms his divinity. Theologian Stanley Grenz argues that "in the resurrection God sounded the verdict concerning Jesus' life. . . . Through the resurrection the one Jesus called 'Father' gave ultimate and final acknowledgement to the work of his messenger. The resurrection is God's declaration that through his ministry, Jesus had indeed inaugurated the divine reign. In him God is truly at work enacting his eschatological purpose, which is the establishment of the community of God."[20]

The Apostles' Creed confesses that we believe "Jesus Christ, God's only Son, our Lord, . . . was conceived by the Holy Spirit, born of the virgin Mary, suffered under Pontius Pilate, was crucified, died, and was buried. . . . On the third day he rose again." What a claim! Who dies, gets buried, and comes back to life? And do we really believe it literally happened? The notion that Scripture and the early church attest to the historical accuracy of a literal resurrection generates vast controversy in the world of biblical and theological scholarship. For example, nineteenth-century theologian Friedrich Schleiermacher contended that the historicity of the resurrection did not matter to the early church and, therefore, should not matter to us because it has nothing to do with the redeeming work of Jesus. The resurrection, for Schleiermacher (and, he claims, for the disciples) was an outward perception of an inward experience. The importance of the inward resurrection lies in its ability to transform a person into someone new.[21] Twentieth-century theologian Rudolf Bultmann similarly argued that the resurrection did not occur literally but, instead, is a mythic event intrinsically connected to the historical event of the cross. Very simply articulated, for him, the resurrection occurs when we hear the salvific word of the cross preached to us. When that happens, Jesus is resurrected as Lord in our hearts. Bultmann said the disciples encounter the risen Lord the same way we do—as he comes to us in the *kerygma*, or the preached word of God. Notice that Bultmann does not deny the resurrection of Jesus; he just believes that it happens spiritually, in the deepest recesses of the human heart. For him, the resurrection is also eschatological; it reminds us that death is not the end and that life has the final say.[22]

19. Wright, *Resurrection of the Son of God*, 553–54.
20. Grenz, *Theology for the Community of God*, 260.
21. Friedrich Schleiermacher, *The Christian Faith: A New Translation and Critical Edition*. Translated by Terrence N. Tice and Catherine L. Kelsey (Louisville, KY: Westminster John Knox, 2016), 419–21.
22. Rudolf Bultmann, *Kerygma and Myth: A Theological Debate*, ed. Hans Werner Bartsch (New York: Harper and Row, 1961), 417–20.

As we have seen above, however, other thinkers attest to the historical literal-ness of the resurrection by appealing to the New Testament witness. The early Christians claimed that Jesus of Nazareth, by the power of God, literally rose from the dead. Although it was steeped in Jewish forms of worship, the fact that the early church changed their day of worship from Saturday to Sunday to focus on and celebrate the resurrection provides a clue to its significance (Acts 20:7). Indeed, the Gospels, Paul, and the author of Hebrews all attest to the historicity of the resurrection: according to Scripture, many people saw Jesus alive after his death and burial (Matt 28:9; Mark 16:9–14; Luke 24; John 20; 1 Cor 15:5–8; Heb 13:20). This appeal to living witnesses of the historical resurrection lends significant weight to its authenticity. Because we have a text that attests to eyewitness accounts of the resurrected Jesus, I believe the burden of "proof" *against* a historical resurrection lies with those who say it did not happen.

Granted, two thousand years after the event we cannot prove the historicity of a literal resurrection of the crucified Jesus. We can, however, live according to the word of God preached to us in 1 Corinthians—the same word that Paul considered of first importance: "that Christ died for our sins in accordance with the scriptures, and that he was buried, and that he was raised on the third day in accordance with the scriptures, and that he appeared to Cephas, then to the twelve. Then he appeared to more than five hundred brothers and sisters at one time" (15:3–6). Whether we interpret the resurrection historically or spiritually, we can believe that because God raised Jesus from the dead, death is not the final destination. God will also raise us from the dead to live a new kind of life (Rom 6:3–11; 1 Cor 15:12–28). We will discuss that new, resurrected life in the last chapter.

The Humanity of Jesus

Incarnation and Kenosis

Any study of the person of Jesus must equally emphasize his humanity, for only through the human can we know the divine. In other words, we know God through the incarnation of Jesus of Nazareth. The word *incarnation* literally means "in (*in*) flesh (*carne*)." *Carne* gives us words such as chili *con carne* (chiles with meat—flesh), carnival (to put away flesh/meat—as in not eating it during Lent), or carnivore (a flesh/meat-eating animal). So, the Christian tradition claims that Jesus is God incarnate, or God in flesh. But how did the divine take on flesh and become human? The christological hymn in Philippians 2 remains one of the most provocative and significant passages in Scripture that helps us understand the incarnation. It tells us that Jesus, "though he was in the form of God, did not regard equality with God as something to be exploited [grasped], but emptied himself, taking the form of a slave, being born in human likeness. And being found in human form, he humbled himself and became obedient to the point of death—even death on a cross" (2:6–8).

Scholars call this section of Scripture the *kenosis* passage, because it explains the incarnation through the process of divine emptying (*kenosis* means "to empty"). The emptying of the Son into a humble human servant profoundly reveals to us the nature of God. Jesus's willingness to suffer humiliation and pain shows us his refusal to employ violence against his enemies.

Interestingly, according to Richard Rohr, the entire Trinitarian God embraced the act of self-emptying: "Like a waterwheel of divine love, the Father empties all of himself into the Son. The Son receives and empties all of himself into the Spirit. The Spirit receives and empties all of himself into the Father. The Father receives and the cycle continues."[23] In the Trinitarian community of unity, Father, Son, and Spirit have an equal voice, equal power, equal influence, and equal character, but Jesus the Son did not selfishly covet that place of privilege. Instead, he selflessly relinquished that position in order to live as a human being, voluntarily limiting himself by emptying himself into a human form. He became one of the poor, one of the marginalized, one of the "least of these" whom he instructs us to feed and clothe and love (Matt 25:31–46). He let go of the privileges of being God and of the unlimited exercise of divine attributes (such as omnipotence and omnipresence) incompatible with being a human and subjected himself to the limitations of the human condition. Although at times Jesus seemed to exercise omniscience—such as seeing Nathanael under the fig tree and knowing he had no deceit in his heart (John 1:47–48)—and omnipotence—such as calming the stormy sea (Mark 4:35–41)—it seems he does so only on occasion in order to fulfill God's intentions. At the same time, however, Jesus retained the divine moral attributes such as love and mercy.[24] He fed the hungry, healed the sick, ate with sinners, offered mercy to the poor, and taught through both actions and words that love and mercy define the ethics of God's kingdom.

While the divinity of Jesus gave him the power to perform miracles, it did not diminish the effects of being human. As fully human, Jesus was born to a poor Jewish family in first-century Israel, so he was steeped in a certain culture and religious heritage; he had to learn and grow, both spiritually and intellectually, just like any other child (Luke 2:52). He had to learn to obey his parents (Luke 2:51); he struggled with real temptations (Matt 4:1–11; Heb 4:15); he suffered hunger, thirst, grief, fatigue, and pain (Heb 2:14). He also experienced normal human emotions such as joy, anger, and sadness (John 11:35). As a human being he knew he would experience death, the constraints of twenty-four-hour days, inclement weather, and blistered feet. Had he lived beyond thirty-some years, he would have endured the joint pain, body aches, wrinkles, and disease so common in old age. As a man, Jesus encountered all the same limitations we encounter as finite humans. The difference between Jesus in the flesh and every other human being is that Jesus did

---

23. Richard Rohr, *The Divine Dance: The Trinity and Your Transformation* (New Kensington, PA: Whitaker, 2016), 90–91.
24. Grenz, *Theology for the Community of God*, 306–7.

not sin (1 Pet 2:22; 2 Cor 5:21; Heb 4:15). His intimacy with God and his obedience to God reveal to us a new type of humanity—one that he promises to us. He now serves as the model for us to imitate (1 Pet 2:21) and brings to us the potential for a new humanity, a new being, and a new community. We will discuss these topics in more detail in chapters 9 and 10, "The Church" and "Humanity."

The New Adam

Theologian Paul Tillich maintains that Jesus came to us as "the manifestation of the New Being in time and space."[25] Through Christ, God revealed to us God's original intent for the human race. And, according to Tillich, as soon as we recognize Jesus as the Christ, as God-for-us, we realize also our "existential estrangement and raise the question of the New Being"—the new beings that we, too, can become.[26] The apostle Paul articulates Tillich's assertion a bit differently, by claiming that Jesus is the new Adam, or second Adam. He writes, "'The first man, Adam, became a living being': the last Adam became a life-giving spirit" (1 Cor 15:45). He explains this notion in more detail in Romans, telling us that "just as one man's trespass led to condemnation for all, so one man's act of righteousness leads to justification and life for all. For just as by the one man's disobedience the many were made sinners, so by the one man's obedience the many will be made righteous" (5:18–19). Although, contrary to the will of God, the first human being, Adam, lived a life of spiritual ignorance in disobedience and therefore suffered separation from God, the second and last Adam, Jesus, existed as God intended humanity to exist—in perfect communion and intimacy with God, in obedience to the divine will and without sin. As the New Being, the last Adam, Jesus transfers his righteousness and its reward to a fallen humanity and, consequently, enables us to partake with the Father, Son, and Spirit in an intimate relationship in which God's very being becomes ours. As new beings in Christ, we can also live as God first intended for all humanity. We have here a beautiful image of redemption from the curse of spiritual ignorance and sin into the new life (2 Cor 3:18; 5:17; Gal 2:19–20; Eph 4:24; Phil 2:5; Col 3:10). We will discuss this concept in more depth in the next chapter, "Salvation and Atonement," about the work of Jesus.

God's Goals for Jesus

As the new Adam, Jesus set out to accomplish various goals or to fulfill a divine mission. Many Christians believe that dying on the cross was the crux of his mission.

---

25. Paul Tillich, *Systematic Theology*, vol. 2 (Chicago: University of Chicago Press, 1975), 97. Jesus did not stop emptying himself after he took on a body; he emptied himself of power when the bleeding woman touched him in the crowd and was healed. He emptied himself as he bled on the cross and died, and he emptied himself when he gave us his Holy Spirit at Pentecost.
26. Tillich, *Systematic Theology*, vol. 2, 100.

While Jesus did die on the cross as the precursor to his crowning achievement as a resurrected savior, his mission and goals included much more.

Jesus came as a *prophet*. In line with the Jewish expectations, Jesus as Messiah ("anointed one" of God) functioned as a prophet. God's people waited expectantly, through decades of silence, for God to send another prophet and Jesus fulfilled that role (Matt 21:11, 46; Mark 6:15; Luke 7:16; 24:19; John 6:14; Heb 1:1–3). Historically, prophets ministered as intermediaries between God and human beings, proclaiming the will and plans of God to the people. As God's prophet, Jesus preached the good news of new life, of restored relationships with God and others, and of the inauguration of the kingdom of God on earth. Jesus even suffered the fate of many of the earlier prophets in the Hebrew Bible: rejection, ridicule, and death.

Jesus came as a *priest*. While prophets typically served God outside the rules and regulations of institutionalized religion, priests served within those structures in order to lead the people in worship, "to offer gifts and sacrifices for sins" (Heb 5:1) and to teach them the ways of God. The book of Hebrews describes Jesus as just such a priest, yet a priest superior to any other, whose priesthood lasts forever and who mediates eternal reconciliation between God and humanity (Heb 2:17). Whereas other priests offered the blood of bulls and goats all year long, every year, to atone for sin, Jesus offered his own blood on the heavenly altar one time, for all time, for all people (Heb 5:1–6; 7:11–19; 9:11–22). In so doing, he brings all people to God through his sacrificial life revealed through his shed blood on the cross. Jesus acts as the highest of the high priests, the eternal priest to the temporal priests, the one whose sacrificial offering pleases God and restores a fallen humanity to God forever.

Jesus came as a *king*. The Hebrew Bible tells of the coming of a king in the line of David who will establish a government of peace, justice, mercy, and love (Isa 9:7; 32:1; Jer 23:5). The New Testament tells us that Jesus came as that king. Just as kings have power to rule over a kingdom, Jesus rules over the kingdom of God. Just as kings have the power to save the people from harm, Jesus has the power to heal and to save humanity from its spiritual ignorance and slavery to sin. Even Pilate, the Roman prefect for the province of Judea under the emperor Tiberius, referred to Jesus as "the King of the Jews" (John 19:19) Although he used the title in order to mock Jesus, he spoke the truth. His followers considered Jesus "the blessed and only Sovereign, the King of kings and Lord of lords" provident over an "eternal dominion" (1 Tim 6:15–16; see also Rev 17:14; 19:16). All of these kingly characteristics led the Jewish population to look forward to a messiah, one who would one day bring peace and justice to their land. The time was ripe for the coming of this messiah.

Jesus came as the *Messiah*. We see Jesus's most emphatic affirmation of his role as Messiah in Mark. Before Jesus's crucifixion, the high priest asks him whether he is "the Messiah, Son of the Blessed One." Jesus answers, "I am" (14:61–62). In addition, all three synoptic Gospels (Matthew, Mark, and Luke) mention Peter's confession that Jesus is the Messiah. In none of these accounts does Jesus deny the title. In fact, Matthew records Jesus praising Peter for his insight (Matt 16:16–17; Mark 8:29; Luke 9:20).[27] In addition to the testimony found in the Bible, we know that the earliest Christians, most of them Jewish converts, believed that Jesus fulfilled prophecies about the long-awaited Messiah. N. T. Wright contends, "Early Christianity was thoroughly messianic, shaping itself around the belief that Jesus was God's Messiah, Israel's Messiah."[28] Even though this early community did not envisage a suffering and dying Messiah, the resurrection proved their faith a fitting response to the life and work of Jesus.

Of course, forced by circumstances, the early church changed its ideas about how a messiah should behave. The execution and resurrection of Jesus the Messiah caused them to reject the common belief that a messiah would come to save them from Roman rule. They had to expand their concept of the saving work of their messiah to include salvation from the human condition and the oppression caused by spiritual ignorance and sin, rather than by governments, and focus on the war fought on the spiritual level rather than that of literal clashing armies. They saw that Jesus the Messiah acted to liberate them from the condemnation of the law of Moses and to set them free to live according to the law of love and grace. This Messiah won the eternal battle for souls rather than the temporal battle for cities. In so doing, Jesus revealed God's kingdom, which he rules, and God's community, which he creates.

In addition, as we will discuss more in chapter 9, "The Church," Jesus the Messiah, the Prince of Peace, also reveals the manner in which Christians can appropriately respond to the systemic sin of governments, rulers, and religious leaders. He confronts the powers-that-be with the counteractions of love, grace, and peace, providing us with an example to follow as we, too, confront abusive powers in our lives.

Jesus Reveals God as Loving and Nonviolent

Most Christians believe that Jesus is divine. That means in Jesus, God had a human body that experienced everything a human being experiences. But at the same time God experiences humanity, humanity experiences divinity. Through the man/God Jesus, God reveals God's self to the world. In fact, Jesus pulls aside that veil that obscures God from mere mortals and shows us who God is, how God acts, and what God desires. He reveals God as a Father who, out of love, begets a son; he reveals God as Spirit through his conception and by living his human life empowered

---

27. Scholars have argued *ad infinitum* over whether Jesus possessed a messianic consciousness. Those arguments lie outside the scope of this text as a preliminary introduction to theology. For in-depth studies on the topic see, for example, Raymond E. Brown, "How Much Did Jesus Know? A Survey of the Biblical Evidence," *The Catholic Biblical Quarterly* 29, no. 3 (July 1967): 315–45; Michael F. Bird, *Are You the One Who Is to Come? The Historical Jesus and the Messianic Question* (Grand Rapids, MI: Baker, 2009); Geza Vermes, *Jesus the Jew* (London: SCM, 1973); James D. G. Dunn, *Jesus Remembered: Christianity in the Making*, vol. 1 (Grand Rapids, MI: Eerdmans, 2003); Dale C. Allison, *Jesus of Nazareth: Millenarian Prophet* (Minneapolis: Fortress, 1988).
28. Wright, *Resurrection of the Son of God*, 554.

by that Spirit. Jesus is the window through whom we see the triune God. He is the decisive clue for all other theological construction, and therefore, we anchor all theology in God's revelation in Jesus Christ.[29] Theologian Richard Rohr aptly asserts that "in Jesus, God was given a face and a heart. God became someone we could love. While God can be described as a moral force, as consciousness, and as high vibrational energy, the truth is, we don't (or can't) fall in love with abstractions. So God became a person 'that we could hear, see with our eyes, look at, and touch with our hands.'"[30] Indeed, Jesus says, "Whoever who has seen me has seen the Father" (John 14:9). To see Jesus, then, is to see God, because Jesus is God in the flesh. And since Jesus reveals the triune God, we need to look at his life, teachings, actions, death, and resurrection to understand and know that God.

What, we may ask, did Jesus reveal to us about God? First, Jesus reveals God as love, the "all-encompassing compassionate heart of God."[31] In fact, as God in the flesh, the central feature of Jesus's mission is to mediate God's love to the world. Indeed, as we have seen before, Jesus took all 613 Jewish commandments and reduced them to just two: love God and love others as yourself. He summed up all of the law, all of the prophets, all of the teachings of the rabbis into one imperative: love. This comprehensive distillation of the law into love corresponds to the description of God in 1 John 4:8: "God is love." Remember our categories of "ontological" versus "functional" ways of understanding Jesus? We see here both the ontological and the functional connection of Jesus to God and to humanity. Jesus is God ontologically, and Jesus functions as God practically. God is love in God's essence; therefore, Jesus is love ontologically in essence. God acts in love functionally; therefore, Jesus acts in love practically. Accordingly, Jesus reveals God's character of love ontologically, through the hypostatic union, and functionally, by healing the sick, showing mercy to the needy, raising the dead, confronting the oppressive systems of government and religious rule, and dying because of our sin—not with violence, but with peaceful words and actions. He includes Samaritans and sinners, prostitutes and the poor, tax collectors and commoners, the marginalized and the mentally ill in his kingdom built on love. Jesus tells his disciples (and we are his disciples if we love others [John 13:35]) that as God has loved him, so he loves them. He loves all humanity so deeply that he voluntarily exhibits the greatest of all kinds of love and lays down his life for all people (John 15:9–13). Since Christians affirm that Jesus is fully divine, we can accurately say that God sent God the Son in order to redeem, reconcile, and restore us all to a right relationship with the Father, Son, and Holy Spirit, and that Love sacrifices all to restore all to God.

29. Daniel Migliore, *Faith Seeking Understanding* (Grand Rapids, MI: Eerdmans, 2004), 163.
30. Richard Rohr, *Franciscan Mysticism: I AM That Which I AM Seeking*, disc 3 of multi-disc CD set (Center for Action and Contemplation: 2012).
31. Grenz, *Theology for the Community of God*, 347–48.

Second, and intimately connected to love, Jesus reveals God as nonviolent.[32] Jesus tells Pilate that his kingdom is not of this world. We can interpret his statement to mean that his kingdom, a kingdom of heaven, of divine rule, differs greatly from the kingdoms of the earth. The world's kingdoms trade in violence and oppression while the kingdom Jesus claims as his own (and ours) hinges on peace, mercy, redemption, and love (John 18:36). Through his teachings and actions, Jesus spends his life and ministry revealing to us the kingdom of God and the God of the kingdom. Instead of wielding a sword, Jesus washes feet (John 13:3–5); instead of praising Peter for chopping off the enemy's ear, Jesus tells him to put away his sword and restores the ear of his enemy (Matt 26:51–52; Mark 14:47; Luke 22:50–51; John 18:10). Peter learned his lesson well, for in his letter to Christians scattered around the Roman Empire he praised the nonviolence of Jesus, writing that when Jesus was abused, "he did not return abuse; when he suffered, he did not threaten" (1 Pet 2:23). Even in the face of oppression and pain, Jesus responded peacefully rather than violently.

We have stated that the actions of Jesus reveal God. If Jesus is divine, as Christians have long proclaimed, then God acts the way Jesus acts. If we ever wonder what God would do in a certain situation, we have the perfect example to show us—Jesus. For instance, we may ask, What would Jesus do when confronted with an enemy? Jesus does not destroy those who reject God. He does not swing a sword, chop off heads, or spill blood in a fit of anger. He is not hell-bent on vengeance. His petition from the cross reveals that fact to us, as he hung there in pain and prayed for God to forgive those who did not know what they were doing (Luke 23:34). He taught us to love our enemies, not harm them. One of my theology students came to class one day wearing a T-shirt that said: "When Jesus told us to love our enemies, he probably didn't mean kill them." His T-shirt spoke the truth. Jesus did not tell us to do something he himself did not do. This command is not a parental cop-out of "Do what I say, not what I do." Jesus loves his enemies to the point of asking God to forgive them while they were in the process of executing him. Additionally, in the Sermon on the Mount, Jesus reverses any notion of vengeance as he exhorts his followers to turn the other cheek, to pray for their enemies, and even to love their enemies (Matt 5:38–48). Jesus practiced what he preached. He was beaten, slapped, whipped, spit upon, mocked, and executed unjustly, yet he never responded with violence; he always sought to redeem.

In his reading in the synagogue in Nazareth (Luke 4:16–21), Jesus not only proclaims the work God has for him to do on earth, but he also covertly, yet poignantly, counteracts the idea of violence and reveals his own nonviolent character, which is also God's. When Jesus enters the synagogue in Nazareth and begins to read from

---

32. I am aware of the arguments in favor of a violent Jesus, such as those advanced by some theologians and fictional works such as the Left Behind series, but when taking into consideration the teachings and actions of Jesus as a whole, one is hard-pressed to defend violence in the name of Jesus. Even in the book of Revelation, Jesus returns to redeem. His sword (in his mouth) symbolizes the word of God and the good news of reconciliation. Jesus does not use this sword to smite, but to save.

the Scriptures, we find that he stands, opens the book of Isaiah, and reads: "The Spirit of the Lord is upon me, because he has anointed me to bring good news to the poor. He has sent me to proclaim release to the captives and recovery of sight to the blind, to let the oppressed go free, to proclaim the year of the Lord's favor" (Luke 4:18–19). He then *closed the book and sat down.*

By closing the book at that point and sitting down, Jesus delivers a significant message to his hearers. His reading comes directly from Isaiah 61:1–2, but Jesus does not read the entire passage, as expected. He stops reading and closes the book right before the next line, which says, "and the day of vengeance of our God." His omission reveals that Jesus reads his Scriptures through a lens of peace and redemption rather than violence and vengeance. Jesus reinterprets God's message. His omission of "the day of God's vengeance," his closing the book, and his sitting down all emphasize this. "Through Jesus, God will bring not a sword but salvation, not revenge but redemption, not the violence of force but the compassion of forgiveness. All throughout the New Testament, we see Jesus, by word and deed, exhorting us to live in peace by loving enemies, reconciling with those who have something against us, healing the sick, and taking care of the poor."[33]

Although in the next chapter we will discuss a few more ways in which Jesus reveals God, for now we see that through his life of nonviolence, teachings on peace and forgiveness, and death on behalf of all creation, Jesus reveals God as nonviolent. He shows us the character of a God more interested in reconciling than in ravaging, in forgiving than in fighting, in mercy than in malevolence. Because Jesus taught against violence, lived in peace, and died without retribution, we see that God deals in restorative justice and unlimited mercy to redeem and reconcile all humanity into an everlasting relationship with the triune God.

33. Sharon Lynn Baker, *Razing Hell: Rethinking Everything You've Been Taught about God's Wrath and Judgment* (Louisville, KY: Westminster John Knox, 2010), 59–60.

7. Salvation and Atonement

. . . suffered under Pontius Pilate,

was crucified, died, and was buried;

he descended to the dead.

> In the world, violence is met with counterviolence; in the Kingdom [of God] it is met with forgiveness.
>
> —John D. Caputo, *After the Death of God*

> God is not revealed in the New Testament as an infinite Shylock demanding his pound of flesh before he will exercise mercy.
>
> —W. T. Conner, *The Gospel of Redemption*

I once walked into a basilica in Rome and saw a magnificent sculpture that, for me, articulates the work of Jesus on the cross more profoundly than any other piece of art I have seen to date.[1] He hung in the apse. With wide open eyes and arms extended outward toward a sinful humanity and upward toward a gracious God, the dying Jesus looked straight at me. His long, thin arms embrace the world with the love of God, and his eyes plead for a response. This sounds fairly typical except for the fact that, in this modern sculpture, Jesus hangs in mid-air—a crucifix without a cross! Now, "a crucifix without a cross" may sound counterintuitive or contradictory, but this unconventional representation of the death of Jesus profoundly and provocatively expresses the mystery, majesty, and meaning of the passion event.

As Jesus stares at us from this cross-less crucifix, his eyes seem to beckon us to die with him, to crucify our human lust for sinful ways of life and live instead empowered by the eternal life of the living God. In the silence of his summoning stare, Jesus beseeches us to come to him, to lay down our heavy burdens, and find rest in his love. Hanging between heaven and earth, he promises salvation from sin and invites us all to rest in the presence of God.

But how? How does "the cross" accomplish *for us* and apply *to us* the life of God in Christ?[2] How exactly does the work of Jesus manage such an extreme and

---

1. This sculpture, *Cristo Lux Mundi* (Christ, the Light of the World), by Alfiero Nena, resides in the Basilica of Santa Maria del Popolo in Rome, Italy, next to the main altar. The bronze artwork was presented on May 25, 1990, to the basilica in the presence of Council President [Prime Minister] Giulio Andreotti. It is the first new work of art installed in the basilica in two hundred years.
2. For me, the phrase *the cross* is not limited to the event of the crucifixion, but includes the entire life, teachings, death, and resurrection of Jesus.

extravagant accomplishment? The work of Christ, traditionally called *soteriology*, includes the topics of salvation and atonement. Specifically, the doctrine of salvation or atonement refers to the Christian claim that through his life, death, and resurrection, Christ saves us from spiritual ignorance and sin and reconciles us to God. Notice that the doctrine simply makes the claim *that* Christ saves us. It does not tell us how. This is where theories of the atonement come into play. A theory tries to explain *how* Jesus's life, death, and resurrection save us. We will survey various philosophical accounts of salvation (as it is conceived in the Eastern Orthodox tradition) and atonement (as it is called in Western Christianity) and assess the merits and weaknesses of each account. We can then look at the relationship of various theories of atonement to violence, a topic that has excited much theological speculation, especially in the last twenty-five years.

In Western Christianity, the word *atonement* points to the reconciling of relationships between God and human beings. Theologians first used it in the early 1550s. It literally means "at-one-ment"—to be "at one" with God or others. When we say, "Jesus atoned for our sins" or "Jesus saves us," we refer to the means by which we are brought into an intimate relationship with God through the work of Jesus during his life, death, and resurrection. We attempt to describe the sacrificial event of the incarnation of God and the results of Christ living life as a finite human being. We also refer to the work Jesus did to redeem, reconcile, and restore us to oneness with God. It sounds simple, but as we will see, salvation and atonement prove complicated given their many theories, metaphors, and motifs. We'll start by taking a look at several of the most popular, traditional theories of atonement in the West.

Traditional Western Theories of Atonement

We glean most of our ideas about the atonement from the New Testament. The problem, as we mentioned in the first two chapters, is that we must *interpret* the biblical text. The fact that the New Testament describes the cross event with so many diverse metaphors and images makes interpretation tricky; the text we have already assimilates a multitude of traditions. First, the New Testament never focuses on just one vision of the cross or one theory surrounding the work Jesus accomplished with his life, death, and resurrection. Christian theology has never held uniformly to one universal doctrine of salvation. The Bible uses many images, metaphors, and types to help its readers understand the cross. So we have to navigate through these images and try to understand what the people of earlier times might have understood about the atonement when they heard or read them. We should also take into consideration that the earlier church did not actually develop a full-blown doctrine of redemption or atonement. Early Christians simply adopted the New Testament language without attaching any doctrinal statements or theories to it. Using the language of "sacrifice" and "redemption," they worked their ideas about the atonement into their devotional practices, their music, and their preaching without attaching to it any formal doctrinal significance. Even so, we can still spot theological tendencies that later helped construct church doctrine.

Christus Victor, or Ransom Theory

Although the twentieth-century Swedish bishop Gustaf Aulén coined the official term *Christus Victor* (the "Victory of Christ"), this motif of the atonement stretches back to the early church's understanding of the cross. The ancient theologians thought of it in terms of paying a ransom to set sinners free from the devil's grasp (Matt 20:28). The early church fathers and St. Augustine favored this view and made it popular for their communities. Throughout the passage of time, theologians worked with and reinterpreted the metaphor of the "Victory of Christ" to make it more plausible and relevant for their cultural contexts. In our own day, we may have heard of this ancient motif because C. S. Lewis used it in his popular children's series The Chronicles of Narnia.[3] Many of the church fathers and patristics held to a form of *Christus Victor* or ransom theory, including Irenaeus, Origen, Justin Martyr, Athanasius, Basil the Great, Gregory of Nyssa, Gregory of Nazianzus, John of Damascus, John Chrysostom, Ambrose, Augustine, and Gregory the Great. Each of these early theologians interpreted the theory a bit differently. Irenaeus thought of it in terms of recapitulation, in which all fell into sin through the first Adam and all were rescued from sin through Jesus, the second Adam. Gregory of Nyssa thought of the theory in terms of a ransom paid by God to the devil. In this version, Jesus served as the ransom—God gives the devil Jesus in exchange for humanity. Only after killing Jesus did the devil realize that Jesus was really God in the flesh. Unable to bear the presence of God's Son, he spewed him out and Jesus took all humanity with him in victory over sin and death. Gregory of Nyssa uses the arresting image of Jesus acting as the bait on the fishhook that the devil swallowed whole.

Even though Christians, historically, have articulated various forms of *Christus Victor*, we do see some commonalities among them. For example, *Christus Victor* models of atonement often use the image of a cosmic battle between Jesus and the devil. In this rendition, the devil tempted humans to sin—a temptation we succumbed to, thus provoking a battle for souls between the two opposing forces of good and evil, God and Satan. Some explain the model as follows:[4] God created

---

3. C. S. Lewis, *The Chronicles of Narnia*, complete series (San Francisco: HarperCollins, 2010; individual books originally published 1950, 1951, 1952, 1954, 1955, 1956 by C. S. Lewis). C.S. Lewis himself did not have atonement theories in mind when he wrote this popular theory. See David Downing, *Into the Wardrobe* (Hoboken, NJ: Jossey Bass Publishers, 2005), 78–79.

4. For a history of Patristic thought, see L. W. Grensted, *A Short History of the Doctrine of the Atonement* (Eugene, OR: Wipf & Stock, 2001); Inna Jane Ray, *The Atonement Muddle: An Historical Analysis and Clarification of a Salvation Theory*, Journal of Women and Religion 15 (Berkeley: The Center for Women and Religion, 1997). For a contemporary theological view on the victory-of-Christ theory, see J. Beilby and P. R. Eddy, eds., *The Nature of Atonement: Four Views* (Downers Grove, IL: InterVarsity, 2006), 23–49; see also Joel B. Greene and Mark D. Baker, *Recovering the Scandal of the Cross: Atonement in New Testament and Contemporary Contexts* (Downers Grove, IL: InterVarsity, 2000), 116–25.

us with a free will for intimate relationships with both God and one another (and with all creation). We belong to God and to God's kingdom. Yet we willfully chose to turn our backs on our relationship with God, and we fell into sin. Our sin enabled the devil to steal us from God's kingdom and hold us captive in his domain of darkness (see Eph 2:1–3; Col 1:13). Because "the wages of sin is death" (Rom 6:23), not only were we held captive to sin in the dominion of evil; we were also held captive to death (2 Tim 2:26; Col 1:12–13). Thus, Satan (or evil) held us in slavery to sin and death; we could not set ourselves free.

Out of compassion for us, God sent Jesus to rescue us from evil and bring us back into God's kingdom, for which God created us (Col 1:13–14). Because Jesus as God's Son never sins, he does not deserve death as his wages. But the devil orchestrates the death of Jesus, thinking he has won the victory over us and over God. But because Jesus, as God, never sinned, death cannot hold him in the grave. Consequently, Jesus rises from the dead, proving and proclaiming his victory over sin and death.

When Jesus rises from the dead, several things happen. First, the devil realizes his grave error (so to speak) in killing God's Son. Second, because Jesus never sinned and therefore did not deserve death, he wins the victory over sin and death for all humanity. Just as through the first Adam (the representative of all humanity) sin and death applied to all humans, so through Jesus, the second Adam (and also representative of all humanity), the victory over sin and death applies to all humanity. The devil loses the cosmic battle—and he is angry, to say the least (just watch the final few scenes of Mel Gibson's film The Passion of the Christ!). God wins the battle for our souls and we are released from sin, spiritual death, and the power of the devil (evil) to hold us captive. We have victory in Jesus (1 Cor 15:54–57). Of course, theologians throughout the ages have reworked and nuanced this theory, some leaving the devil out of the equation. Others have talked about our release from the power of evil as a ransom paid by Jesus to the devil and, later in the tradition, a ransom paid to God.

Strengths and Weaknesses

All variations of the Christus Victor model of atonement have their pros and cons, a few of which are important for our conversation in this book.[5] Some have pointed out that Christus Victor is less of a full-blown philosophical theory than a recurring biblical motif or powerful set of images.[6] Either way, let us explore the major strengths of this motif/theory.

---

5. For a more detailed treatment, see Gustaf Aulén, Christus Victor: An Historical Study of the Three Main Types of the Idea of Atonement (Eugene, OR: Wipf & Stock, 1931), and J. Denny Weaver, The Nonviolent Atonement (Grand Rapids, MI: Eerdmans, 2001).
6. Robin Collins, "Girard and Atonement: An Incarnational Theory of Mimetic Participation," in Violence Renounced: René Girard, Biblical Studies, and Peacemaking, Studies in Peace and Scripture 4, ed. Willard M. Swartley (Telford, PA: Pandora, 2000), 149.

First, this model of atonement deals with sin objectively and on a cosmic level. In other words, the life, death, and resurrection of Jesus effected a universal or overall change in the status of all humanity (and all creation [Rom 8:20–22]). We move from a position of captivity to sin to one of liberation from sin. We need only to grasp through faith the victory and liberation that God in Christ has already won for us. Second, the *Christus Victor* model powerfully focuses on liberation from death, sin, and the devil (evil). Jesus accomplishes something that affects us in profound ways as we walk in the power of the Spirit, rather than in the flesh. Third, this motif emphasizes the resurrection, whereas many of the other models emphasize the death of Jesus almost to the exclusion of the resurrection. Fourth, some of the nuanced forms of *Christus Victor* stress the importance of the life and teachings of Jesus as well as the passion event: Through his obedience to God, Jesus repaired the damage done by the first Adam. Through faith, we partake of the healing Jesus made possible and participate in a life of obedience as well. Fifth, many in the early church, those nearest to the actual happenings, favored this theory. So *Christus Victor* has significant strengths as well as a wealth of biblical evidence in its favor.

Now, let us look at some of the weaknesses of this motif. Some say the *Christus Victor* model of atonement splits the universe into dual realms, one good and one evil, smacking too heavily of ancient Near-Eastern Zoroastrian mythology. In its earliest versions, the cosmic battle takes place between unseen angelic and demonic creatures fighting an invisible war with the devil for our souls, if you will. The devil plays too prominent a role for some theologians.

Along those same problematic lines, depending upon which version of the story we read, God deceives the devil in order to win the victory through Jesus. Or, as some have it, God must pay the devil a ransom to get us back. Either way, the devil enjoys a good bit of power over the fate of creation, and God must be complicit with deception in order to win us back. God must also contradict the concept of justice by requiring the death of an innocent man in order to win the battle with the devil (evil). Even in our own justice systems, we consider it unjust to make an innocent person suffer for someone else's crime. Along those same lines of thought, some pacifist theologians, such as J. Denny Weaver and Michael Hardin, believe that this model of atonement portrays God as needing the violent death of Jesus in order to win the victory over sin and death.[7] Even though the *Christus Victor* motif, with its defeat of evil, suffering, and death, resonates well with people suffering oppression and abuse, this view potentially puts God in collusion with violence and injustice because of the divine requirement for the violent death of an innocent man.

Another possible weakness in *Christus Victor* concerns the diminished role of forgiveness. Although liberation includes forgiveness, the diverse forms of the *Christus Victor* theory do not explicitly focus on it. The theory by itself downplays

7. See Weaver, *The Nonviolent Atonement*, and Michael Hardin, *The Jesus Driven Life: Reconnecting Humanity with Jesus* (Lancaster, PA: JDL, 2013).

forgiveness by emphasizing instead the victory of liberation from sin, death, and the devil. Forgiveness and its more relational aspects are overshadowed by the story of a cosmic battle between evil and God.

Finally, many have taken the motif too literally, causing debate over who paid what to whom: Did God pay the devil off with Jesus's blood? Did the devil hold so much power over God that God could not gain our release from sin in any other way? Or did Jesus pay God in some sort of intra-Trinitarian charade?

The work of contemporary Anabaptist theologian J. Denny Weaver solves many of these problems with the *Christus Victor* model. His *Narrative Christus Victor* model eliminates the cosmic battle between God and Satan by focusing instead on the biblical story of Jesus and his peaceful resistance to the religious and political systems of abuse. Through his life, death, and resurrection, says Weaver, Jesus protested the systemic evil inherent in the institutions in the Roman government and legalistic forms of Judaism. By imitating Jesus, we, too, can resist those powers in our own lives and in evil, abusive systems of government and religion. Weaver's model of atonement not only puts the responsibility for evil squarely on human systems, but it also clears God from any complicity with the violent death of an innocent man.

Scriptural Support

Each of the theories we will discuss in this chapter has support in Scripture, some more strongly than others. Scripture explicitly expresses the *Christus Victor* model, especially the ransom motif in various passages. We do not even have to stretch the meaning of the verses to fit our theory (as we do with some of the other theories). For instance, Colossians 1:13 says God "has rescued us from the power of darkness and transferred us into the kingdom of his beloved Son." The language of rescue denotes victory. Another passage in Colossians tells us God disarmed the rulers and authorities and triumphed over them through the cross of Christ (2:14–15). My favorite is Paul's great statement in 1 Corinthians 15:54b–57: "'Death has been swallowed up in victory.' 'Where, O death, is your victory? Where, O death, is your sting?' The sting of death is sin, and the power of sin is the law. But thanks be to God, who gives us the victory through our Lord Jesus Christ." These powerful verses form one of the choruses in Handel's musical masterpiece, *Messiah*. And, of course, in Hebrews we see that Jesus claimed the victory over temptation—a victory that belongs also to us (2:14–18).

The Satisfaction Theory

In the fourth century, Christianity won the favor of the Roman emperors and, therefore, no longer struggled with persecution by imperial powers. Christians enjoyed the perks of political and religious prominence to the point that the cosmic battle between God and Satan no longer mirrored the social conditions of the church. Consequently, the *Christus Victor* model of atonement diminished in significance, and eventually, new ways of explaining the cross event took its place as favored theories. One of these views, still popular in some form or other today, is the satisfaction theory of atonement expressed by St. Anselm of Canterbury in the eleventh century and by Thomas Aquinas in the thirteenth.

In 1098, Anselm, the archbishop of Canterbury, wrote a book entitled *Cur Deus Homo?* (*Why the God-Man?*), in which he definitively denied that the devil had any rights over us or that Jesus had to pay some sort of ransom to Satan to free us from sin and death. As we just learned, these were some of the theological inconsistencies surrounding the *Christus Victor* and ransom theories favored by the early church. Anselm's view of God would not allow him to believe that the devil could possess enough power not only to capture and keep us in his domain, but also to force God's hand in sending an innocent man to die in order to win us back.[8] So he had to reinterpret the Bible and his tradition in order to reconstruct a theory of atonement more in line with his view of God and more relevant to Christians living in Europe in the eleventh century. Consequently, he made use of metaphors from his own culture, images with which the people would be very familiar.

During Anselm's lifetime, the feudal system operated as the popular form of government. Vassal lords lived in castles surrounded by the village folks who paid homage in words, deeds, and money or goods. In return, the lords offered protection against roaming bands of vandals or other lords seeking to add to their lands and wealth through war. The vassal lords kept the community in order and maintained justice and the rights of the people. Yet, if a villager defied the lord through words, actions, or withholding payment, he would offend the lord's honor and incur a debt. Only by paying off the debt could the villager restore the lord's honor, and if he did not pay, he would suffer punishment. The debt had to be "satisfied."

I am not saying that Anselm deliberately decided to take images from his own culture or that he even thought to himself, "I need to make atonement theories more relevant to people, so I will borrow ideas from the feudal system." Nonetheless, as is true of all theologians, Anselm gleaned his theological ideas from and framed his theological beliefs according to what was most familiar to him—the worldview and presuppositions of his own culture and society. The satisfaction model, reworked and built upon in various ways by learned clergy from the eleventh century onward, has profoundly influenced what we believe today about the cross.[9] It was also the most philosophically sophisticated theory to date. The basic premises of the satisfaction theory of atonement are as follows:

---

8. Anselm of Canterbury, *Cur Deus Homo*, 1.7.
9. For a nice historical treatment of the theory, see Rita Nakashima Brock and Rebecca Ann Parker, *Saving Paradise: How Christianity Traded Love for This World for Crucifixion and Empire* (Boston: Beacon, 2008). See also Weaver, *The Nonviolent Atonement*.

God, as the sovereign Lord, created the universe to exist in perfect balance, according to a certain divine order. God created us to trust, love, honor, and obey God as Lord. Yet we disobeyed God in the garden. Variations of this view of atonement stress the legal obligations dictated by God's law. For instance, an offense against God is also an offense against the law. We, therefore, have broken the law, set the order of the universe spinning out of kilter, and dishonored God. In order to escape eternal punishment, we must satisfy the debt due God's offended honor so God can restore the normal order of the universe. For Anselm, then, the clincher is this: we must satisfy God's honor or suffer eternal punishment for the offense.[10]

We have a major problem, however: as human beings, we cannot ever hope to satisfy God's honor. For Anselm, an offense against an infinite God equals an infinite offense, which cannot be satisfied by finite human beings. Only another infinite person can satisfy the infinite offense against the infinite God and restore God's infinite honor. If this does not happen, we are doomed to suffer infinite punishment for our infinite sin. But since only an infinite person can make the necessary satisfaction for God's offended honor and since only God is infinite, God is the one who must make satisfaction. The problem with this, of course, is that God did not offend God's honor; human beings did. So at the same time, only a human being can and should make satisfaction.[11]

Since only God *could* make satisfaction and only a human *should* make satisfaction, God sent the God-man Jesus to do it for us. By dying on the cross, Jesus, as a man, satisfied God's honor. As God, the second member of the Trinity, he provided the infinite payment necessary to satisfy an infinite debt. Jesus's obedience and death satisfied God's honor so we do not have to suffer eternal punishment. Satisfaction eliminates the need for punishment. The order of the universe is now restored, and we who trust and obey God through the work of Jesus on the cross will enjoy eternal fellowship with God.[12]

Strengths and Weaknesses

As we have seen, every theory has strengths and weaknesses; despite its popularity, the satisfaction theory is no different. Here are the major strengths of this model: The satisfaction theory deals with sin in an objective way, on a cosmic level. Through his death, Jesus solves the problem of our disobedience and sin in a manner that affects all of creation for all time. By satisfying our debt for offending God's honor, Jesus restores order to the universe, which changes our status before God on a cosmic level.

Most people like logical explanations, and the satisfaction theory provides us with a logical, systematic explanation of what Jesus accomplished on the

10. Anselm of Canterbury, *Cur Deus Homo*, 1.9, 13, 15, 19; 2.1.
11. Anselm of Canterbury, *Cur Deus Homo*, 1.14, 19; 2.5–6, 8, 18.
12. Anselm of Canterbury, *Cur Deus Homo*, 1.24–25; 2.6–9, 18, 19.

cross and why God deemed such a death necessary. This was a step up from the ransom theory, which was not as systematic and logical. The satisfaction theory makes better sense to our human perceptions of right and wrong, guilt and innocence, punishment and pardon. In that way, the satisfaction theory provides a psychologically plausible means for us to deal with guilt. In addition, the satisfaction theory is not as negative as it looks. What Anselm first systematically conceived and constructed, other thinkers took and modified. For instance, St. Thomas Aquinas, disagreeing with Anselm's notions of necessity, reconceived the theory to suit his ideas about God's sovereignty and providence, nuancing and softening the necessity of God acting in any certain way to redeem creation. In addition, Colin Gunton makes the point that although the feudal system was the common form of government in Anselm's day, Anselm did not liken God to an arbitrary or oppressive ruler, as we sometimes think about feudal lords—in fact, just the opposite. God, as with feudal lords, maintained order, civil rights, and civil obligations so society could function satisfactorily. Although still in a retributive framework, this view of God is in keeping with God as the giver of the law in the Hebrew Bible.[13]

Now for a few weaknesses. The satisfaction theory of atonement makes God seem subservient to the order of the universe. An offense must be punished or satisfied for the universe to remain ordered and in harmony with itself and with God. For order and restoration to occur, God requires satisfaction and, therefore, must redeem humans through the death of the God-man Jesus—the only one capable of repairing the offense. No other way suffices, according to the laws God set in motion at the creation of the universe. Because the satisfaction theory hinges on the notion that "we did something bad to God, so God must make someone suffer in return," our redemption through grace seems more of an economy of *quid pro quo*—a Latin phrase meaning "something for something." So in the satisfaction theory, a *quid pro quo* works like this: You offend, you pay. You pay, God redeems. In this case, however, an innocent person pays the debt—shouldn't that alone set the order of the universe out of kilter? This theory also raises the problem of God seeming to pay God in order to forgive sin. But why couldn't God just forgive the debt without human beings having to pay for it in the form of satisfaction? And how can a finite offense justly amount to an infinite debt? All of these problems seem like they would put the universe out of kilter worse than the original offense.

---

13. See Colin Gunton, *The Actuality of Atonement* (Grand Rapids, MI: Eerdmans, 1989), 89. For a very good treatment of the honor/shame, retributive mindset of people living during Anselm's time, see John Philip Jenkins, *Jesus Wars: How Four Patriarchs, Three Queens, and Two Emperors Decided What Christians Would Believe for the Next 1500 Years* (San Francisco: HarperOne, 2011), 28–31. Of course, as with all scholarship, some historians do not believe that Anselm was all that influenced by his cultural surroundings but that he constructed his theory of atonement based upon his reading of Scripture alone. I think this is a naïve perspective that fails to realize that we are always influenced by our culture. I'm not saying that theologians didn't also pray, read Scripture, and interpret according to how the Spirit led them at the time. I am saying, however, that our perceptions, perspectives, and consequent theological constructions develop out of the society and culture we are thrown into. Our contexts and our reading of Scripture and tradition work together to form our theology.

Along those same lines, in order to redeem us, in the satisfaction theory of atonement God needs satisfaction through the torturous death of an innocent person. Someone must die a violent death in order to satisfy our Lord's offended honor. Only after God is satisfied does God forgive sin. Philosopher Robin Collins has a reading of the parable of the prodigal son translated into the language of the satisfaction theory in which the elder brother offers to die to pay for the sin of the prodigal, only after which the father in the story is satisfied. Obviously, the theory makes the parable of the prodigal son absurd and goes against its central message of unconditional forgiveness.[14] So the Satisfaction theory compromises the nature of forgiveness. God cannot forgive sin without first getting something in return—the blood of the innocent (sinless) Son of God. Jesus must balance the cosmic accounts before God will forgive. But what is there to forgive if the debt has been paid *quid pro quo* and the books balanced?

We can find an even worse objection. The death of Jesus was extremely violent and painful. Thomas Aquinas actually calls it a crime, a result of evildoing. Taking that idea a step further, some contemporary theologians argue that requiring the torturous death of an innocent man makes God complicit with the evil and violence of those who killed Jesus. If the death of Jesus was a crime and God required the death, does not God also, then, participate in a criminal act? Although God does not directly kill Jesus, God is the one who needs it, ordains it, and sees it through to the end. For some theologians, however, it is very difficult to swallow any theory that aligns God with evil and violence in this way.

Scriptural Support

Unlike the *Christus Victor* theory, it is difficult to find Bible verses that directly support the satisfaction theory of atonement. But if we stretch the meaning and skip taking into consideration the original language and historical context, we can find some passages that seem to fit. For example, Hebrews talks about Jesus as the high priest offering a blood sacrifice in the heavenly temple once and for all. In this way Jesus secures our redemption (9:7, 11–12). We find another passage in Romans, which tells us God put Jesus "forward as a sacrifice of atonement by his blood, effective through faith" (3:21–25). But as we'll see later in this book, neither of these passages ever mentions Jesus making satisfaction for sin. In the original Greek, these and other passages do not even allude to such a concept.

14. Robin Collins and spouse Rebecca Adams jointly wrote this satirical parable. Robin Collins, "A Defense of Nonviolent Atonement," *Brethren in Christ History and Life* 35, no. 1 (April 2012): 185–86.

Penal Substitution Theory

Closely related to the satisfaction theory is the theory of penal substitution, developed a bit later, also in a European context. Although theologians over the centuries allude to what we now know as the penal substitution theory of atonement, Protestant Reformer John Calvin (1509–1564) formalized it and made it popular. Again, as with all theological developments, Calvin's social context significantly influenced how he expressed his theology. By Calvin's day, a gradual shift had taken place, from the feudal system with its emphasis on paying a financial debt, to a focus on criminal law and the punishment of the guilty. Calvin, trained as a lawyer, expresses the legal ramification of sin, using language characteristic of the criminal-law theory common in his community. He calls God a "stern judge, a strict avenger of sin," and says God will punish all sinners who disregard God's law.[15] With the growth of the nation-state in the thirteenth and fourteenth centuries, civic leaders transferred judicial power from the local community to the state. This change in venue for trying criminals introduced the prison system as punishment for crime. Some of the Protestant Reformers, including Calvin, focused on sin and guilt because these were preoccupations in their culture. They interpreted the doctrine of the atonement through the lens of punishment and justification made popular by the institution of newer penal civil law. Thus, the "penal" image served as an explanation for the cross. Note that like the Satisfaction theory, this is a theory based on what is called the Retributive theory of justice, in which the purpose of justice is to punish (not rehabilitate or restore) the offender.

Although there are many variations of the Penal Substitution theory, it begins with the idea that all of us have sinned and fall short of the glory of God (Rom 3:23). The penalty for sin is death. Because of sin, we deserve eternal punishment (for many theologians, this punishment takes place in hell). But out of extravagant love for us, God desires to save us from that punishment, sending Jesus to suffer our penalty for sin on the cross. Jesus acts as our substitute, taking on our sin and suffering our punishment.[16] Those who have faith in Jesus and his substitutionary death are saved. One variation believed by strict Calvinists is that, relatively speaking, God elects only a small number of us for salvation. In their view, Jesus died only for the elect, and their faith is already preordained by God. So if you are not one of the elect, you go to hell.[17]

---

15. John Calvin, *Commentary on the Book of Psalms*, vol. 1, trans. James Anderson (Edinburgh: Calvin Translation Society, 1845), xl–xli.
16. John Calvin, *Institutes of the Christian Religion*, ed. John T. McNeill, trans. Ford Lewis Battles (Louisville, KY: Westminster John Knox, 1960), 2.1.4; 2.1.8. Calvin asserts that human sin, beginning with Adam, was so great that it "provoked God to inflict such fearful vengeance on the whole human race" (2.1.4).
17. Calvin, *Institutes of the Christian Religion*, 2.16.

Strengths and Weaknesses

There are two main strengths of the penal substitution theory. First, as with the *Christus Victor* and satisfaction models, it deals with sin in a concrete way and on a cosmic level. Jesus's death balances the heavenly accounts for sin's debt—again, a nicely cut-and-dried system that explains the work of Jesus on the cross. Many people like the neatness of the penal theory. Similar to the mindset in Calvin's society, we also like the fact that it satisfies our psychological need for a sense of retribution, or the idea of payback, for sin and helps us deal with our guilt and shame.[18]

But there are far more weaknesses connected to this theory. First, God requires the violent death of an innocent man before God can forgive sin, casting salvation as an economic transaction between God the Father and God the Son. Like the satisfaction theory, there is a *quid pro quo*, an across-the-board exchange of one thing for another. Second, the penal substitutionary model appears to assert that Jesus must save us from God or, in other words, that God the Son must save us from God the Father, pitting two members of the Trinity against each other. God punishes God's self, and then God appeases God's self. It also pits God against us as God's enemies. Yet, Romans 5:8–10 tells us that even though we were God's enemies, God loved us and sent Jesus to reconcile us to God's self.

Third, in this theory, the logic leads us to believe that God the Father needs the sacrifice to forgive sin, while God the Son does not. But how is that logical? In fact, while hanging from the cross, Jesus asks the Father to forgive us. If Jesus can just forgive our sin, why can't God? If God cannot forgive sin until Jesus pays the price for it on the cross, what does that say about the nature of forgiveness? According to the penal model of atonement, God will not forgive unconditionally. Someone must first take the punishment for sin, and that someone is Jesus the Son. Is that truly forgiveness? If Jesus has taken the hit, paid the price, and balanced the accounts, what does God have left to forgive? These problems are similar to the ones raised by the satisfaction theory. Fourth, as with the satisfaction theory, by condoning or, worse, requiring a crime by punishing an innocent man, the penal substitutionary theory makes God seem complicit with evil. Theologian Gregory Love criticizes the model for this very reason. He writes: "[In this theory] God works in and through evil human hearts and deeds to bring about the divinely willed effect—the salvation of the world."[19]

---

18. Calvin, *Institutes of the Christian Religion*, 3.21.7.
19. Gregory Anderson Love, *Love, Violence, and the Cross: How the Nonviolent God Saves Us Through the Cross of Christ* (Eugene, OR: Cascade Books, 2010), 32–38.

Scriptural Support

As with the satisfaction theory of atonement, the Bible does not explicitly support the penal substitution model of the cross. But if we stretch Scripture a bit and read it through the lens of John Calvin's theology, we can find certain verses to fit this theory. For instance, 1 Thessalonians 5:9–10 says that "God has destined us not for wrath but for obtaining salvation through our Lord Jesus Christ, who died for us, so that whether we are awake or asleep we may live with him." Nothing in this verse, however, speaks of punishment, and we have no reason to think "wrath" indicates a penal consequence. Here's another one: "Whoever believes in the Son has eternal life; whoever disobeys the Son will not see life, but must endure God's wrath" (John 3:36). Those who support the penal image of the cross assume that if we are not destined for wrath because Jesus died for us, then Jesus must have suffered the wrath. They equate "wrath" with punishment. However, as we shall see, this is not the only reading of the term "wrath" in Scripture. We will return to this point in more detail shortly.

Although we can find other verses to squeeze into the mold needed for the penal theory to work, they require a bit of a stretch. They also speak more about our redemption, reconciliation, and restoration to God than they do about a penal model of the cross. For instance, 1 Peter 1:18–19 tells us that we were not redeemed with "perishable things like silver or gold, but with the precious blood of Christ, like that of a lamb without defect or blemish." (The image of blood meant life in the ancient world.) Note that although Christ's blood is mentioned as the vehicle of redemption, nothing in this verse remotely indicates either satisfaction or penal images of the cross. Although at first glance these verses might appear to refer to substitution at the very least, they really don't support either one of these traditional, Western theories.

Moral Influence Theory

The moral influence theory takes the act of atonement in a direction different from Anselm and Calvin. In protest of Anselm's satisfaction theory of atonement, medieval monk and theologian Peter Abelard (1079–1142) developed yet another model more in tune with the ideas of courtly love that were popular in his day. A near contemporary of Anselm, Abelard objected to Anselm's idea that Jesus's death paid for or satisfied God's offended honor.[20] For Abelard, we did not need to assuage an angry, affronted God. Jesus did not need to die to change God's mind about punishing

---

20. Abelard was not the only one to push back against Anselm's satisfaction theology. In the thirteenth century, the Franciscan scholastic John Duns Scotus offered a view of atonement rejecting any retributive theory and stressing the incarnation. Franciscan theologian Richard Rohr says, "While the Church has never rejected the Franciscan position, it has remained a minority view." "At-one-ment, Not Atonement," Center for Action and Contemplation, February 5, 2020, https://tinyurl.com/y8dslx2l.

us. Instead, Jesus lived, died, and rose again to change *our* minds about rejecting God. Rather than perceiving God as angry, judgmental, and retributive, Abelard wanted his listeners to think about God as loving, compassionate, and merciful.[21] Consequently, in Abelard's theory Jesus lived, died, and rose again in order to reveal God's love to us. Everything Jesus said or did served as an example not only of how God behaves but of how we should behave. Abelard reminds us that God's love for us motivated God to send the Son to redeem us from sin. Further, Jesus lived and died not only to show the depth of God's love for us but also to convince us that we must love God (and others) in return.[22] Let's first go over the basics of this view, then move on to its strengths and weaknesses.

According to Abelard, we sinned and separated ourselves from God's love, losing sight of how to live according to God's will. But God sent Jesus to fully reveal and demonstrate God's love to us, giving us a perfect example of how to live. By dying on the cross, Jesus demonstrated the extravagance of divine grace and the lengths to which God will go to redeem us. Abelard directly refutes any thought that leads us to believe God holds someone else accountable to suffer for our sin. In no way, he insists, would God allow Jesus to suffer in our place. In Abelard's view, that is not justice.[23]

Now, according to Abelard, when we look upon the cross of Christ, we see God's incredible love for us and we desire union with that love. Our desire acts as an invitation to the Holy Spirit, who then fills and empowers us. Through the Holy Spirit, God pours the divine love into our hearts (Rom 5:5) and, by doing so, justifies us (makes us right with God) by forgiving our sin. Because of the power of God's Spirit, we then live our redeemed lives in imitation of God's love revealed in Jesus. Jesus thus serves as a moral exemplar to follow.

Strengths and Weaknesses

The moral influence theory has some real strengths. It embraces the life, teachings, and death of Jesus. Because it focuses on the love of God, it helps us do the same

21. In his commentary on Romans 3:19–26, Abelard writes: "Indeed, how cruel and wicked it seems that anyone should demand the blood of an innocent person as the price for anything, or that it should in any way please him that an innocent man should be slain—still less that God should consider the death of his son so agreeable that by it he should be reconciled to the whole world!" See Abelard, *Epistle to the Romans*, 3:21–23, in *A Scholastic Miscellany: Anselm to Okcham*, ed. Eugene R. Fairweather (Philadelphia: Westminster, 1954), 283.
22. See Paul S. Fiddes, *Past Event and Present Salvation: A Study on the Christian Doctrine of Atonement* (Louisville, KY: Westminster/John Knox, 1989), 145. Two of the most excellent treatments I've found on this subject are Stephen Finlan, *Problems with Atonement* (Collegeville, MN: Liturgical, 2005) and his work *The Background and Content of Paul's Cultic Atonement Metaphors* (Atlanta: Society for Biblical Literature, 2004). Another great source is Peter Schmiechen, *Saving Power: Theories of Atonement and Forms of the Church* (Grand Rapids, MI: Eerdmans, 2005), esp. 5–55.
23. Abelard, *Epistle to the Romans*, 3:21–23, in Fairweather, *A Scholastic Miscellany*, 278–79. Cf. Colin Green, "Is the Message of the Cross Good News for the Twentieth Century?" in *Atonement Today: A Symposium at St. John's College, Nottingham*, ed. John Goldingay (London: SPCK, 1995), 223; C. Behan McCullagh, "Theology of Atonement," *Theology* 91, no. 743 (September 1988): 399.

rather than focusing on the retributive actions of God that we see in some of the other theories. God does not need to punish the innocent Jesus in order to forgive. Neither does God need any sort of satisfaction to appease God's offended honor. But through love, God forgives our sin if we receive God's love through the Holy Spirit. Forgiveness, then, truly is unconditional in that it is given freely, without the need for payback first. Moreover, if we live our lives intent on following Jesus in the way of love, we will treat others the way God asks us to—by loving them, even if they are enemies. Additionally, the moral influence theory places a significant emphasis on the work of the Holy Spirit, which was unusual for the early thirteenth century.

Now for the weaknesses of this theory. Many argue that this view does not deal with sin in an objective way, on a cosmic level. In other words, the atonement does not change God, or the entire human race, all at once, once and for all. Rather, the Holy Spirit infuses those who ask on an individual basis. Nothing has happened on a universal level as in the other theories we have discussed, making the moral influence theory too subjective for some Christians. We could even argue that this theory implies that any good person could have died and as long as we follow their example, we can secure our own redemption. Subsequently, we can easily misrepresent the moral influence theory as a works-based salvation when, in actuality, Abelard intended to say that salvation occurs through the power of God as we receive the Holy Spirit. For him, salvation takes both God's grace and our acceptance of that grace. In other words, it takes two.

One of the most important weaknesses, and one that the moral influence theory has in common with the other models we discuss in this book, is that Jesus still must die a torturous death in order to demonstrate God's love and provide an example for our behavior. And God still requires that Jesus die in this manner. So, although the theory does not trade in retributive or penal justice, it still makes God complicit with violence. God still needs the death of an innocent man in order to give us an example to follow and the motivation to love others. This theory, popular through the last millennium with more liberal Christians, contains many intriguing and inspiring (as well as biblical) elements that still leave it seeming inadequate as a theory. Theologian J. Denny Weaver constructs the narrative *Christus Victor* theory combined with the moral influence theory to correct these inadequacies. In doing so, he perhaps solves the problem of divine violence and subjectivity that we find in Abelard.[24]

Scriptural Support

We can find a number of Bible verses that tell us Jesus came as an example for us to follow (John 13:15; Phil 2:1–11; 1 Pet 2:21–25). But 1 John 3:16 says it best: "We know love by this, that [Jesus] laid down his life for us—and we ought to lay down our

24. See, for example, Weaver, *The Nonviolent Atonement*.

lives for one another." We also see support for the salvific effect of the Holy Spirit in Romans 5:5, which says: "God's love has been poured into our hearts through the Holy Spirit that has been given to us." In addition, the moral influence theory finds broad support for its loving view of God and inspiring example of Jesus throughout his life and teachings.

The Problem of Divine Violence

We have a lot at stake in different theories of the atonement because they claim to show us certain things about God. The very nature of God is wrapped up in how we interpret the life, death, and resurrection of Jesus. For instance, if we hold to the *Christus Victor* theory of atonement, we may at the same time believe (consciously or unconsciously) that just as the devil practiced deception to enslave us and subject us to sin, God practices deception to liberate us and win us back! If we believe Anselm's satisfaction theory we must imagine God as retributive, requiring violence in order to forgive; we must believe God considers it just to kill an innocent man to satisfy someone else's sin. If we go with Calvin's penal substitutionary theory, we have to believe that God must punish someone for sin before forgiving it—even if the one suffering the punishment never sinned; because Calvin's view draws a huge chasm between justice and love, we must also believe that retribution takes precedence over mercy, not something taught generally in the Bible. So, each of these theories damages God's reputation in one way or another, and each also provides us with justification to take part in violence against others. What we see God doing, we will do to others. In order to decrease religious violence, many theologians are committed to rethinking, reinterpreting, and reconstructing our fondly held Western theories of atonement in favor of a model that will motivate us to love our enemies and that will reveal the true nature of God's extravagant, unconditional forgiveness even in the face of our most heinous sin.

All the Western models we have discussed have weaknesses; all of them also require us to believe something in particular about God that, ultimately, we may not want to accept. The consequences and theological implications of holding some of the above views are profoundly significant. If what we believe about God affects how we behave, then what we believe about God matters—in fact, it could be a matter of life and death. Unfortunately, people have used the theology of a violent God to justify suffering, torture, and death during the various crusades and inquisitions. Such theology has fueled pogroms and the genocides of entire peoples, even in recent history. For all these reasons we need to reexamine our options and presuppositions about how we think about God.

The Nonviolent God

Since most of the traditional Western theories of atonement give us an image of God as violent and retributive, many contemporary theologians have worked to construct scripturally based theories that more adequately understand the redemptive work of God through the lens of love, mercy, and forgiveness—all major characteristics of the God Jesus reveals. What in our traditional theories negates those divine characteristics? Several inconsistencies arise when comparing the God of Anselm and Calvin to the God Jesus reveals. For example, quantitative, law-based notions of retribution and payment of a debt to society, as exemplified in our judicial system, differ considerably from the biblical interpretation of the God of love who seeks justice tempered with mercy. Where human justice is often retributive, quantitative (*quid pro quo* or tit for tat), and destructive of relationships, God's justice is restorative, qualitative, and intent on building relationships. Even the seemingly retributive parts of the law in the Hebrew Bible serve the purpose of teaching the people to resist violence by limiting the justification of its use. These texts, therefore, really function as a means of restoration in the long run.

Conceptions of divine justice as restorative and relational rather than quantitative and retributive carry significant and profound implications for the work of Jesus in redeeming a fallen human race. Retributive justice sticks to the letter of the law, requiring payment or repayment and, therefore, depends on the exchange of something in order to forgive sin. Conversely, divine restorative justice seeks neither payment nor retribution. Restorative justice emphasizes the rehabilitation and redemption of offenders (and reconciliation with their victims). Divine justice seeks restoration, peace, and the fore-giving[25] of pardon so that restoration and qualitatively new relations can take place between offended parties. In other words, divine justice restores through forgiveness. Mercy permeates every aspect of divine justice. Rather than holding mercy and justice in polarity, the Bible speaks of divine justice and mercy as synonyms, one describing the other, one serving the other so that to be merciful is to be just and to be just is to be merciful. Richard Rohr, in his commentary on the book of Job, writes that "the general belief in the Scriptures . . . is that God's justice is not achieved by punishment, but by the divine initiative we call grace."[26] So, given the image of God as loving, merciful, redemptive, and restorative, what does the atonement look like?

---

25. *Fore-giving* expresses the notion of "giving beforehand" or giving something before a person repents or pays back a debt.
26. Richard Rohr, *Job and the Mystery of Suffering: Spiritual Reflections* (New York: Crossroad, 2005), 57. The Hebrew word *hesed*, often translated "mercy," expresses the biblical concept of justice.

Participatory Theories of Salvation and the Atonement

For help with this, we need look no further than another major sector of the Christian church, the Eastern Orthodox tradition. Rather than speaking about the term *atonement*, the Eastern Orthodox Church typically speaks instead of *salvation* and its effects. In this section we will discuss the ancient Orthodox view of salvation, some of the motifs of Western atonement worth preserving, and some modern reconstructions of this important doctrine. By putting these all together and drawing on the best of them, I hope to offer a view that best harmonizes with a central image of God as a God of love who desires nothing more than to restore us to an eternal relationship in Trinitarian love with all creation—a God who decides to come to us in bodily form in order to reveal the divine character and will.

The Eastern Orthodox Understanding of Incarnation, Recapitulation, and Theosis

Some of the thinkers of the ancient church had very different ideas from those of our legal structures in the West. The Eastern Orthodox doctrine of salvation begins with the incarnation of Jesus, instead of thinking about this central Christian theme as if it were an afterthought. As we discussed above, the doctrine of the incarnation says that God came to the world "in the flesh." And although "God with us" in the flesh forms the essential component for effecting our redemption, the Western theological tradition places more emphasis on Jesus's divinity, which can seem to diminish the importance of Jesus's incarnation for salvation. The Eastern Orthodox tradition, however, makes an essential link between the incarnation and the atonement. Because of the incarnation, something tangible happens on a cosmic level to change our relationship with God and with each other. When "God made human flesh his own,"[27] God descended into the human condition by becoming one of us with a human body and mind.

Early church father Irenaeus (130–200) frames the incarnation and its significance for our atonement in terms of the idea of "recapitulation." *Recapitulation* literally means to "do over." In Irenaeus's thought, the human and divine natures were united in the one person, the Son of God, Jesus. God became human through Jesus of Nazareth. And Jesus took what belonged to him—the life of God—and gave it to human beings, to us. Jesus also took to himself what belonged to us—humanity—and healed it, restored it, and transformed it into what God had created us to be. In other words, Jesus recapitulated or "did over" the human condition. He "re-did" humanity from a state of unrighteousness to one of righteousness. Through the new humanity evident in the incarnation of God in Christ, Jesus

27. Cyril of Alexandria, *Commentary of St. Cyril, Patriarch of Alexandria, upon the Gospel of St. Luke*, 2:4.

reversed the condemnation passed down to us all through the first human and gave us righteousness and new life in its place (Rom 5:10–19). Jesus participated in humanity and, in the process, healed and reconciled human nature so humanity could participate in God. Jesus's work actually lifted human nature into the Godhead (Eph 2:6). We could say that God descended to us in our humanity so we could then ascend to the life of God.[28]

Early church fathers in the East spoke of the work of Jesus (salvation or "at-one-ment") as union with God or as *theosis*. And Eastern Orthodox Christians still believe that Jesus was made human so that humans could be made divine. Now, the Orthodox Church does not teach that humanity will actually *be* God or be *equal to* God. But it does teach that we will become so like Jesus, so united (so at-one) with God, that we will be one, relationally speaking. In Jesus, who descended to us, we ascend to God. We unite with God and participate in the love relationship with the Father, Son, and Holy Spirit. Through our unity with Jesus, our human nature is remade into its original beauty, reborn to new life. "So if anyone is in Christ, there is a new creation: everything old has passed away; see, everything has become new! All this is from God, who reconciled us to himself through Christ" (2 Cor 5:17–18). In the Eastern Orthodox view of Jesus's saving work, through the perfect unity of the divine and human in Jesus, God participates in the life of humanity. Through that perfect union in Jesus, we also participate in the life of God.[29]

The metaphor of participation, of God participating in our humanness and our participating in God's divinity, captures the beauty of reconciliation and the restoration of our relationship with God. Through Jesus, we actually participate in God's nature and God in ours. As 2 Peter 1:4 tells us, we become partakers of the divine nature, liberated from our corrupt nature through the work of Jesus. Jesus, then, acts as the true mediator between God and humans (and all creation) by uniting the human and divine into one, so that we are "at-one." At-one-ment gives new meaning to "Immanuel, God with us." God is *really* with us. In us. One with us—never forsaking us because we are at-one. The at-one-ment of God's nature and ours through Jesus means that God's heart becomes ours; God's desires, God's purposes, and God's kingdom vision are ours as well. For us, at-one-ment means that to live is Christ (Phil 1:21). No longer do we live, but Christ lives within us (Gal 2:20). The Eastern Orthodox tradition articulates salvation in these terms as the very nature of at-one-ment. Sprinkled with the life-giving, shed blood (life) of Jesus Christ, we are cleansed, purified, forgiven, and made at-one with God so that we,

28. Vladimir Lossky, *The Mystical Theology of the Eastern Church* (Crestwood, NY: St. Vladimir's Seminary Press, 1976), 143–47; Stephen Finlan and Vladimir Kharlamov, eds. *Theōsis: Deification in Christian Theology*, Princeton Theological Monograph Series (Eugene, OR: Pickwick, 2006), 162–64; Christoforos Stavropoulos, "Partakers of Divine Nature," in *Eastern Orthodox Theology: A Contemporary Reader*, ed. Daniel B. Clendenin (Grand Rapids, MI: Baker Academic, 2003), 183–92.

29. Horace Bushnell, *The Vicarious Sacrifice: Grounded in Principles of Universal Obligation* (Hicksville, NY: Regina, 1975), 523. See also Finlan and Kharlamov, *Theōsis*, 1–15. There is so much scriptural evidence for this theory that I'll just list a few references here: Job 32:8; Ps 82:6; John 3:6; 10:34; 14:7, 12; Rom 8:16, 29; 12:2; 2 Cor 3:18; Eph 4:24; 5:1–2; Phil 3:21; 2 Pet 1:4; 1 John 3:2.

too, in imitation of Christ, can offer our own lives as living sacrifices acceptable to God. The Scriptures tell us this is the nature of true worship (Rom 12:1).

The Motif of Substitution

A number of theologians who oppose penal substitutionary theories of atonement prefer to eliminate the language of substitution altogether. I prefer to keep that traditional language. Although I see it somewhat differently than do proponents of the penal model, I believe substitution plays an important role in how Jesus saves us. The apostle Paul uses different ideas about substitution in the biblical text, and not all of these harmonize with one another. So what are we to make of the idea of substitution?

To understand the workings of substitution, we need to look at how the people before and during the time of Jesus and Paul might have understood it. In 4 Maccabees 5:1–6:30 (a book in the Apocrypha accepted by the Roman Catholic Church as scriptural), we have a story about Eleazar, a priestly leader during the Maccabean Revolt. The tyrant king, Antiochus, knowing that the law forbade Jews to eat pork, commanded Eleazar to eat a pig. Of course, as a devout Jew, Eleazar refused. Consequently, Antiochus tortured him by flogging him until his flesh hung in bloody strips from his body. He kicked Eleazar and beat him, burned him with fire, and poured horrid liquids into his nose. Finally, Eleazar spoke his last words before dying. He lifted his eyes to God and said: "You know, O God, that though I might have saved myself, I am dying in burning torments for the sake of the law. Be merciful to your people, and let our punishment suffice for them. Make *my* blood *their* purification, and *take my life in exchange for theirs*" (6:27–29; emphasis mine).

What did Eleazar mean in this story? In essence, he's suggesting that *his* suffering substitutes for those who persecuted him, that *his* shed blood purifies *them*, and that *his* life is given so they don't have to give theirs. Finally, we see in the story that "the tyrant [Antiochus] was punished, and the homeland purified—[Eleazar and other martyrs] having become, as it were, a ransom for the sin of [the] nation. And through the blood of those devout ones and their death as an atoning sacrifice, divine Providence preserved Israel" (4 Macc 17:21–23). Now this does not mean that Eleazar, as a martyr, paid the price for the sin of the nation, or that he was punished in the place of the people. The writer is using the metaphor of substitution and ransom in order to communicate an important truth. The deaths of those like Eleazar expose the violence and sin of the oppressors, and that exposure leads to their downfall and the cessation of sin and violence against the people. His suffering (and that of other martyrs like him) helps stop the suffering of people in the future. By exposing the cycle of violence in those times, he has helped end it. Essentially, Eleazer died so that many others did not have to.

Thinking about modern-day martyrs, we can begin to understand substitution in a productive way. What Rev. Dr. Martin Luther King Jr. or those four little girls killed in the Birmingham church bombing in 1963 have in common with Eleazar is that they all died substitutionary deaths that were in some way redemptive for the oppressed black people in the country. Each of these martyrs exposed the evil of oppression, abuse, and violence. They enabled their communities to see human sin at its worst and, in so doing, brought the horrific nature of these evils to light, forcing the guilty to confront the atrocities they committed.

I am not saying God willed these deaths—in fact, quite the opposite. These deaths occurred because of sinful persons acting outside of God's will. These martyrs exposed that sin. In uncovering the sin of the abusers, their deaths served not only as wake-up calls but also as catalysts that set the wheels of peacemaking rolling. Their deaths worked to stop the flow of further violence. They suffered so others after them did not have to. Mark Thiessen Nation puts it aptly: "Some of us may never have truly known the depth and breadth of racism without the extraordinary lives of King, Perkins, Rosa Parks, Fannie Lou Hammer and countless others."[30] We might say that the suffering of these Black martyrs served as a substitute for all who might have continued to die horrible deaths at the hands of wrongdoers had the martyrs not died instead. Their deaths provide vicarious salvation from further violence.

So we can see from the examples in these stories that Jesus saves us from living life shrouded in the horror of abuse by suffering that horror and abuse himself. Like Eleazar or those four little girls in the Birmingham church, Jesus, by exposing the human tendency to rationalize unmitigated violence upon another person, race, or nation, opens the way for us to change. He transforms us not only by a replacement of sinful human nature with the pure nature of righteousness, but also by exposing the horrendous nature of sin. He transforms those who suffer by standing with them in solidarity as a fellow sufferer. In fact, one of the ways to talk about vicarious (substitutionary) suffering is to see it as suffering *with* rather than suffering *instead of*. We can call this "inclusive place-taking," which means sharing the place of others. Jesus included himself *with* us in our suffering the consequences of sin. We can apply this concept whether we think of sin as something we have done wrong and are guilty for, or as something we suffer as victims. This "place-sharing" reaches to the center of our being as we take on the life of Christ.[31] Because Jesus endured horrendous suffering on our behalf, we can entrust our grief to him. We can cast our cares upon him. We can exchange our heavy burden for his lighter one—because he carries ours.

---

30. Mark Thiessen Nation, "'Who Has Believed What We Have Heard?' A Response to J. Denny Weaver's *The Nonviolent Atonement*," *Conrad Grebel Review* 27, no. 2 (Fall 2009): 26; in the article Nation articulates this form of substitution in connection to the death of Jesus. See also Finlan, *Problems with Atonement*, 52–55, where he discusses substitution as a "noble death" motif. See also Elizabeth A. Johnson, "The Word Was Made Flesh and Dwelt among Us," in *Jesus: A Colloquium in the Holy Land*, ed. Dorothy Donnelly (New York: Continuum International, 2001), 158–60.
31. See Finlan, *Background and Content*, 178–79.

In addition, Mark Thiessen Nation believes the passion predictions in Scripture point only to the *inevitability* of Jesus being killed after being rejected by the chief priests and scribes, not as a penal substitutionary sacrifice (see Mark 8:31; 9:31; 10:33; Matt 20:18–19; Luke 18:32).[32]

The circumstances surrounding Jesus's death suggest he suffered as a scapegoat. A significant development of the idea of atonement along these lines in recent decades comes from the philosopher and literary critic René Girard.[33] Girard emphasizes, through his reading of myths and of the biblical text, how Jesus served as a scapegoat, a substitute for the sins of the community. Girard says the biblical text (as opposed to many myths) represents the scapegoat as innocent of wrongdoing. Just as we saw with martyrs during the civil rights movement, the community executes a scapegoat, a person or persons who stand in as a synecdoche for the entire community. The persecuting community gathers together in solidarity around a scapegoat, who they believe represents the problems evident in their society. In a show of unity, they execute that scapegoat in an attempt to solve their social problems. Girard argues that this pattern goes back to the very beginning of human culture. But he also believes that in the experience of those who saw Jesus, and in the biblical accounts of his death and resurrection, Jesus, as the scapegoat, revealed not only his innocence but also the human violence that underlies all of human culture. Consequently, Jesus stripped the scapegoat mechanism and the communal violence of its efficacy. The scapegoating mechanism no longer works, Girard says, when we see that the victim is innocent: "Once the violent foundation of the human communities of the Principalities and Powers is revealed, they are visible on the Cross with Jesus, and thus lose their cathartic power."[34] Through his life, death, and resurrection, Jesus unmasked the scapegoat mechanism so it no longer functions to unify the community. He exposed the scapegoating tendencies of the people so they can no longer pretend that the violence of scapegoating others, of forcing others to substitute for us, stems from a divine command. Instead, Jesus revealed that the violence comes from the scapegoating community.

Girard believes we must repent and become imitators of God and of Jesus to save ourselves from the cycles of violence that can lead to the total destruction of the human race. Like Abelard, he also puts an emphasis upon the Holy Spirit, in this case as the defender of innocent victims and as the one who enables us to imitate

---

32. Nation, "'Who Has Believed What We Have Heard?'" 23.
33. For Girard as a theoretician of the atonement, see Jeremiah Alberg, Sherwood Belangia, and Matthew Taylor, "René Girard and Atonement: A Dialogue," *The Bulletin of Christian Culture Studies*, Kinjo Gakuin University, 21 (2018): 1–20. For a very simplified and conversational introduction to Girard's essential ideas in his own words, I refer the beginning reader to Michael Hardin, ed., *Reading the Bible with René Girard: Conversations with Steven E. Berry* (Lancaster, PA: JDL, 2015). For a comprehensive but basic introductory overview of Girard's thought excerpting primary source material, see James G. Williams, ed., *The Girard Reader* (New York: Crossroad, 1996). For a good secondary introduction, see Michael Kirwan, *Discovering Girard* (Cambridge, MA: Cowley, 2005). Kirwan is the first secondary-source book to present Girard's work to a wider audience.
34. Hardin, *Reading the Bible*, 132.

or participate in God, in whom there is no violence. Girard actually says, "Good imitation [as initiated by the Holy Spirit] is always moving against the violence, the bad imitation that ends in murder, and is moving toward the Father, the Trinity, becoming part of the Trinity, joining the Trinity in a way."[35] As the scapegoat who suffers the violence of the community, Jesus exposes the genesis of the violence, through that exposure ends the cycle, and thus fulfills the prophetic stories and emphases found all through the Hebrew Bible that tend to cry for mercy instead of sacrifice (Hos 6:6), redemption instead of retribution. So while we may repent of violence through seeing the innocence of the scapegoat, the Girardian viewpoint causes some to question the necessity of Jesus's death. To overcome this objection, we must emphasize Jesus's unique dual human and divine nature. Through his life, death, and resurrection, Jesus not only exposes the human cycles of violence; he does something that no one else can do—he conquers the spiritual ignorance and sin that give birth to evil and liberates us from a life of imitating evil into the freedom of imitating Christ instead.

In many ways, Girard's theory can be read as a modern, promising version of the moral influence theory, with both its strengths and its drawbacks.[36] Contemporary philosopher Robin Collins has articulated a new atonement theory that combines Eastern Orthodox participatory notions, Girardian ideas, and elements of the moral influence theory to produce what he calls the incarnational theory of the atonement.[37] This theory is a strong reworking of both Girardian and moral influence theory that overcomes the charge of subjectivism and other weaknesses of their thought. Despite any possible limitations, Girard's basic theory of substitution, whether in martyrdom or scapegoating, remains a powerful, biblical, and ethically compelling motif. Through the work of Girard, Collins, and others, we see that we are not alone; Jesus lives in solidarity with us and shares our pain. And we can see meaning in the lives of those who suffer, as they reveal the innocence of the victims of scapegoating and in some sense substitute for the lives of others in unmasking and stopping future violence.[38]

35. Hardin, Reading the Bible, 156.
36. For work comparing Girard's views and the moral influence theory, see Michael Hardin, "Practical Reflections on Nonviolent Atonement," in Violence, Desire, and the Sacred: René Girard and Sacrifice in Life, Love and Literature, vol. 2, ed. Scott Cowdell, Chris Fleming, and Joel Hodge (London: Bloomsbury, 2014), 247–58.
37. For a simplified version of Collins's incarnational argument, originally designed for an evangelical/pacifist audience, see Collins, "A Defense of Nonviolent Atonement." For the fully developed theory written from a Girardian perspective, see Collins, "Girard and Atonement."
38. I am indebted to my editor, colleague, and friend Rebecca Adams for her work on Girard. Her scholarly contributions to this chapter as a Girardian scholar have added significantly to its thesis and clarity.

Liberation from the Cycle of Violence

Girard claims that Jesus liberates us from a cycle of sacred violence and erroneous notions about God as its source. Not only does Jesus stand in solidarity with us in times of crisis, oppression, and suffering; he also exposes the cycles of violence that cause so much grief and injustice in the world. Jesus's radical solidarity with us challenges conceptions of the atonement that stress the idea of redemptive violence—the idea that the violent death of an innocent man will serve to redeem us through the appeasement of a violent deity who requires the payment of a debt or our punishment. Doing violence doesn't bring about peace. As Girard points out, the "peace" a scapegoat brings is temporary: scapegoating keeps the cycle of retribution in motion and gives birth to continued violence—and God considers that violence a sin. But, then, what do we make of the violence of the cross and Jesus's reaction to it?

Traditionally, we've been taught that Jesus could have called legions of angels down on his persecutors and saved himself from suffering a torturous death, not to mention giving himself the satisfaction of seeing the angels smite his enemies in one fell swoop. People passing by the cross as he hung dying taunted him, saying, "He saved others; he cannot save himself. Let the Messiah, the King of Israel, come down from the cross now, so that we may see and believe" (Mark 15:31–32). But he didn't. Jesus stayed there on the cross, and rather than call down an army of angels, he prayed for our forgiveness. Jesus revealed the opposite of retribution by entering into our suffering while, at the same time, neutralizing and exposing violence and redeeming both perpetrators and victims.

While Jesus hung dying on the cross, he prayed and asked God to forgive those who murdered him. This prayer, uttered in a state of intense suffering, expresses a desire for forgiveness rather than retaliation from God, pardon rather than a balancing of the books. While the evil of humanity reached a climax in crucifying Jesus, he himself reached out and sought the opposite of revenge. In the Hebrew Bible, an-eye-for-an-eye justice had limited the unlimited cycle of retaliatory violence for a time. But Jesus goes much further through his refusal to enact revenge at all and puts a stop to the violence. The great injustice of the cross culminates in compassionate restoration, a loving embrace that brings shame to the human structures of life. God has granted this forgiveness on a cosmic level. In other words, God forgives all people universally, without condition and without exception, something objective and concrete that applies to everyone. When we embrace that forgiveness, we are reconciled with God. We are at-one.

By asking God to forgive us, Jesus reveals the heart of God, showing us that the way to God is not a warpath, but a peace-path, the way of forgiveness and reconciliation. In Girard's thought, Jesus exposed and interrupted the cycle of violence that we never seem able to escape on our own. Through Jesus, God entered into our world, suffered the natural consequences of our enslaving attachment to violence, and, by not resorting to violence himself, reversed the retributive cycle of violence into a cycle of forgiveness, reconciliation, restoration, and peace. Theologian Mark Heim states it beautifully: "God was willing to be a victim of that bad thing [scapegoating] we had made apparently good, in order to reveal its horror and stop it."[39] With our traditional Western theories of atonement, in which God requires a certain kind of sanctioned "sacred violence" in order to bring peace, we have made violence a good thing, seen it as a redemptive thing.[40] In opposition to that way of thinking, Jesus reveals the horror of human violence and dies as the ultimate, once-and-for-all victim in an effort to put a stop to it. Jesus's resurrection from the dead reveals his innocence and the power of God to overcome violence, sin, and death.

In his famous play *The Merchant of Venice*, Shakespeare shows us a character named Shylock, who, under the law, is entitled to carve away a literal pound of flesh from a man to make him pay for a transgression. Shylock insists on payment; there is no arguing with him. In the play, the hero is saved from death only when another comes in and shows mercy. But unlike the violent payment Shakespeare's Shylock demanded, Jesus reveals to us and initiates us into God's restorative justice. As W. T. Conner says, "God is not revealed in the New Testament as an infinite Shylock demanding his pound of flesh before he will exercise mercy."[41] Since the death of Jesus occurred as the result of human sin, because he as the second Adam represented all of humanity to God and overcame death for all humanity, Jesus's prayer was a prayer for God to forgive all humanity[42] and revealed God's gracious desire to transform the violence of human existence into compassion, love, and forgiveness. God's act of forgiveness reveals the true nature of divine justice as merciful, reconciling, and restorative. The love of God discloses the greatest sacrifice that forgives humanity its sin without condition and without keeping accounts. God in Jesus sacrifices the right to vengeance or punishment. God suffers the loss by forgiving us the debt. God truly was "in" Christ reconciling the world to himself by "not counting [our] trespasses against [us]" (2 Cor 5:19). This divine forgiveness gives expression to the radically nonviolent, fully loving nature of God who seeks to save those who are trapped in strictures and structures of injustice—what conflict studies theorist Vern Neufeld Redekop has named "structures of violence."[43] And as we have seen, various structures of violence in the world are often

---

39. S. Mark Heim, "Saved by What Shouldn't Happen: The Anti-Sacrificial Meaning of the Cross," in *Cross Examinations: Readings on the Meaning of the Cross Today*, ed. Marit Trelstad (Minneapolis: Augsburg Fortress, 2006), 223.
40. Girard coined the phrase "sacred violence."
41. W. T. Conner, *The Gospel of Redemption* (Nashville: Broadman, 1945), 95–97.
42. In Christ's becoming sin for us, as Thomas Aquinas states in reference to 2 Cor 5:21, his prayer for forgiveness of that sin can be thought to cover all who have sinned. ST III, q. 46, a. 4, ad 3.
43. For this phrase and concept, see Vern Neufeld Redekop, *From Violence to Blessing: How an Understanding of Deep-Rooted Conflict Can Lead to Paths of Reconciliation* (Ottawa: Novalis, 2002).

justified by mistaken notions of God, even when talking about the doctrine of the atonement itself.[44]

A Costly Sacrifice

In this view of atonement, Jesus as a scapegoat still made a very costly sacrifice because of us and on our behalf. The death of Jesus, orchestrated not by God but by human beings, does not detract from the idea of sacrifice. Remember, Jesus shed his blood—that is, Jesus gave his life—*for us* and *to us* out of love. St. Thomas Aquinas clearly considers the sacrifice of Jesus a sacrifice of love. He writes that "on the part of those who put Jesus to death, the passion was a crime; on the part of Jesus, who suffered out of love, it was a sacrifice."[45] The active ingredient, therefore, that made the passion of Jesus a loving (not a violent, retributive) sacrifice was the internal condition of Jesus's heart and mind, his willing love, not the material elements of death such as the pain, the shed blood, or the nails through his hands and feet.[46] The violence of the passion did not please or satisfy a wrathful God; it was a crime. The true sacrifice of Jesus lies not in the literal shedding of blood but in the inward condition of his heart of love revealed by the outward giving of his life, symbolized by his blood.[47] As we have discussed, for the ancient Hebrews "the life of the flesh [was] in the blood"; that is, blood was a symbol of life.[48] Jesus, therefore, did sacrifice something. With a heart freely offered to God and to humanity in love, he sacrificed the right to take his pound of flesh; he sacrificed receiving back (as God) what was owed by humanity for the offense and condition of sin.

What Jesus offers, therefore, is the sacrifice of love and obedience by completely identifying with humanity and the consequences of human sin as he suffers in solidarity with the oppressed and abused throughout time. British theologian Paul Fiddes says that Jesus "plumbs the bitter depths where broken relationships run out into desolation and nothingness. He hangs on the cross at the end-point of human sin, at the focus of all human self-destruction."[49] Through his loving obedience, sacrificial in both life and death, Jesus integrates us into the kingdom of God, "re-socializes us, that is to say, he makes us citizens of his kingdom."[50]

---

44. René Girard says, "The Gospels can be read in a sacrificial [violent] way, if you don't want to understand them, which is what some people still do." Hardin, *Reading the Bible*, 55.
45. Aquinas, ST III, q. 48, a. 3, ad 3: "*Passio Christi ex parte occidentium ipsum fuit maleficium; sed ex parte ipsius ex charitate patientis fuit sacrificium.*"
46. Aquinas, ST III, q. 14, a. 1, ad 1.
47. Abelard, *Ethics*, ed. D. E. Luscombe (Oxford: Clarendon, 1971), 97.
48. Lev 17:11; Gen 9:4; Deut 12:23. See Vincent Taylor, *Jesus and His Sacrifice* (London: MacMillan, 1939), 54–75, and E. L. Mascall, *Corpus Christi: Essays on the Church and the Eucharist* (London: Longmans, 1955), 89.
49. Fiddes, *Past Event and Present Salvation*, 91. Dumas calls Christ's sacrifice "costly communion," as an act of solidarity through love. André Dumas, "La Mort du Christ n'est-elle pas Sacrificielle? Discussion d'objections contemporaines," *Etudes Théologiques et Religieuses* 56 (1981): 590.
50. Dorothee Sölle, *Christ the Representative*, trans. David Lewis (Philadelphia: Fortress, 1967), 118–19. Cf. C. F. D. Moule, *Forgiveness and Reconciliation and Other New Testament Themes* (London: Lynx Communications, 1998), 20. The work of Christ results in reconciliation, which demands the sacrifice

It takes one to forgive and two to reconcile. Although God freely forgives all of us without condition, we can choose whether to enter fully into the equation in order for reconciliation with God to happen. This reconciliation takes place as we turn back to God. God lifts us up into the life of God, and we participate joyfully in our new life in Christ. We can interpret the cross of Jesus as at-one-ment that does away, once and for all, with notions of a violent God bent on retributive justice. We see that the justice of God is love, and that love forgives, transforms, and seeks to create new and harmonious relationships. Through the forgiveness of God, a way is opened for the transformation of all humanity. Through the cross of Jesus, we are forgiven without condition, accepted as we are. Through repentance we are reconciled with God and transformed into those who live in the power of divine love. Divine justice, therefore, loves and forgives with a bottomless, endless, profound, even absurd level of forgiveness that reaches out in love to all humankind. Our "response-ability" is only to receive it, to enter into the forgiveness of God, reconciled and restored.

Scriptural Metaphors and Motifs and Participatory Models

Beginning with Eastern Orthodoxy, we have explored what we might call participatory models of salvation or the atonement. Abelard's theory also falls partially into this category. Participatory accounts start with the idea of God sharing our suffering and human life situation through the incarnation and attempt to show how we participate in God's life through what Jesus did in his life, death, and resurrection, and how this saves us.[51]

As if our redemption, reconciliation, and restoration were not enough, the work of Jesus continues as we live our lives. Sometimes theologians refer to salvation as the process of "justification" and "sanctification." Remember, the Western tradition and the Eastern tradition view things differently. The term *justification* comes from Western traditions and presuppositions that assume some sort of legal framework in which Christ's work on the cross *justifies* us by taking the form of an economic transaction among the persons of the Godhead, and then God *sanctifies* us as a separate process. The word *salvation* in the Eastern church, in contrast, has to do with more of a seamless whole in which justification (what Christ did on the cross to make us righteous before God) and sanctification (the work Christ does in our lives through the Holy Spirit) are more continuous in bringing us into the divine life. This latter view overcomes some of the objections to Abelard's moral influence

---

of obedience that works itself out in community living. See John Howard Yoder, *The Politics of Jesus: Vicit Agnus Noster*, 2nd ed. (Grand Rapids, MI: Eerdmans, 2008), 157. Cf. Timothy Gorringe, *God's Just Vengeance: Crime, Violence, and the Rhetoric of Salvation* (Cambridge: Cambridge University Press, 1996), 77.

51. Robin Collins, "Girard and Atonement," 132–56.

theory as merely subjective, because we do not just look at Jesus's example from a subjective perspective but actually participate objectively in his life. With all this in mind, let's look at a few of the theological motifs in Scripture and see how they illuminate and support nonviolent and participatory views of salvation and atonement.

Jesus Transcends the Law

We see from various New Testament passages that the law originally given by God to Moses and other writers in the Hebrew Bible did not fully reveal God to us. God gave the law in its original context as a teaching tool, relevant to the culture and context of the people hearing it for the first time. In fact, in Romans 2, Paul indicates that God sent the law to teach us, but by condemning sin. It revealed the nature and universality of sin, clearly expressing the need for a remedy to heal people from its infection. Additionally, some of its prohibitions were designed to limit the violence we could do to one another. After all, the idea of "an eye for an eye, a tooth for a tooth" is better than unregulated violence in uncontrolled retaliation, which served as the norm in cultures millennia before Paul's. In this way, even some of the seemingly retributive justice we see stressed in the Hebrew Bible tends ultimately toward peaceful ends. The law and the Hebrew prophets also pointed toward a messiah who would come to fulfill God's will on earth. Consequently, the people knew that God meant the law as a life-giving instrument (Lev 18:5).

As an observant, upstanding, and socially influential Jew, the apostle Paul clearly understood and valued the law, but he also saw its limitations. The law could only do so much. In some of his letters he develops a theology focused on the limitations of the law and how Jesus did not abolish but fulfilled the law and its original intent on our behalf. Paul describes in Romans 2 and elsewhere how the life, death, and resurrection of Jesus reinterpreted the old law and revealed something new about God. Jesus fulfilled the law, breaking down its barriers that, due to sin, separate us from God. Jesus set us free from the law's constraints, which had served a purpose but were now fulfilled in Jesus. He showed us a better way to God—a way of walking in love, forgiveness, and grace. Some of the Hebrew prophets had already stressed that God does not desire sacrifice (in the temple), but exhorts people instead to show mercy (Hos 6:6). In Micah's words, "What does the Lord require of you? To act justly and to love mercy and to walk humbly with your God" (6:8 NIV). The Hebrew Bible was thus already reinterpreting the law as restorative rather than merely retributive. Jesus stands within this prophetic tradition of interpreting the life-giving word of God to the people. In his teaching, Jesus summed up the law with two commandments that encompass and reinterpret everything else: the whole of the law, he says, is to love God and to love others, which obviously precludes violence and retribution (Matt 22:37–40; Rom 13:10; Gal 5:14).

Paul argues that the law cannot save us, however, because it does not go so far as to bring forgiveness. As we see in the Hebrew Bible, the body of the law relies largely on retributive justice that punishes rather than redeems (Deut 28). Whereas it was good at showing and condemning sin and thus served a vital purpose in God's revelation, now, Paul says, the grace and love of God have forgiven sin through Jesus—something the law itself did not accomplish. We see Jesus, as God in the flesh and as God's representative on earth, forgiving sin in his earthly life before he hung on the cross (Matt 9:1-8; Mark 2:1-12; Luke 5:17-26). And of course, Paul expresses the fact that God in Christ reconciled us to God's self through Jesus by "not counting [our] trespasses against [us]" (2 Cor 5:19). That is to say, God has redeemed us through the forgiveness Jesus prayed for from the cross. Mercy, grace, and love transcend the law that could only ultimately bring condemnation and death in favor of forgiveness that brings reconciliation and new life.[52] Because we are free in Christ, we no longer need to keep externally the many particular cultural laws given in the Hebrew Bible or to enact the rituals there. We obey and participate in the law of love at a higher, inner level of understanding and spiritual reality.

Jesus Bears Our Burdens

The Bible makes it clear that Jesus bears our burdens. And if we believe that the Hebrew Bible contains hints of the incarnation of Jesus and of his work, we see burden-bearing even there. For instance, we can rejoice with the Psalmist, singing, "Blessed be the Lord, who bears our burden day by day, The God who is our salvation! Selah." (Ps 68:19 AMP). Or we can lament with Isaiah over the pain of an innocent man and recite: "Surely he has borne our infirmities and carried our diseases; yet *we accounted* him stricken, struck down by God, and afflicted" (Isa 53:4; emphasis mine). Let us use the hermeneutical skills and principles we have developed and notice that just because *the biblical writers* thought God must have been the one who struck him down, that doesn't mean God really was the one doing the afflicting. Isaiah is describing an innocent who has been struck down by

---

52. How do we explain all the passages about retributive justice in the Hebrew Bible? Do we say they were not actually given by God and were human constructions? Or can we say that God gave them and that revelation was limited, but always tending toward a broader interpretation? Or might we say that God gave the law, but cultural context influenced its (mis)interpretation? I take the latter view and believe it's the view Paul takes. We have to be careful with these ideas or run the risk of charges of anti-Semitism and supersessionism, of which Paul has sometimes been accused. I believe he is critiquing legalistic forms of Judaism and expanding Judaism from within it, not rejecting Judaism. I find this approach helpful for these issues. See Matthew Pattillo, "Creation and Akedah: Blessing and Sacrifice in the Hebrew Scriptures," in *Sacrifice, Scripture and Substitution: Readings in Ancient Judaism and Christianity*, ed. Ann W. Astell and Sandor Goodhart (Notre Dame, IN: University of Notre Dame Press, 2011), 26. See also Sharon Lynn Baker, *Executing God: Rethinking Everything You've Been Taught about Salvation and the Cross* (Louisville, KY: Westminster John Knox, 2014), and *Razing Hell: Rethinking Everything You've Been Taught about God's Wrath and Judgment* (Louisville, KY: Westminster John Knox, 2010).

others unjustly—and it is the human community that creates just such scapegoats. God does not violently kill scapegoats—we do. Notice our tendency, even in the biblical writers, to attribute our own violence to God! We have to keep an eye out for this kind of thinking.[53]

In the New Testament we see that Jesus "bore our sins in his body"—after all, in our sinfulness, we nailed him to the cross (1 Pet 2:24). We can say with the writer of Hebrews that Jesus offered himself one time in order to bear the sins of all people (9:28). Jesus carried the burden of our sin by allowing us, in our sinfulness, to put him to death. And we can almost feel his compassion for us as he says, "Come to me, all you that are weary and are carrying heavy burdens, and I will give you rest" (Matt 11:28). The idea of a burden here implies both burdens caused by the guilt of wrongdoing and burdens incurred through undeserved suffering. So Jesus saves both perpetrators of violence and their victims, taking on their burdens.

As the embodiment of God's love, and true to the nature of that divine love, Jesus entered into all our human miseries. He took upon himself all the burdens of our human condition, suffered in solidarity with us, and, out of love and compassion, identified with our sufferings, adversities, pains, and evils. He plunged himself into the depths of all the misfortunes brought upon us and upon him by our sin.[54] Jesus revealed that he shares our burdens by spending his life healing and working miracles on behalf of the downtrodden. He takes on our infirmities and bears our sicknesses (Isa 53:4). He partook of our sins by bearing the consequences for them. These metaphors do not have to mean that Jesus took on our sin or our infirmities as a mysterious imputation required by God or had our punishment transferred to his person and, consequently, by his suffering satisfied the justice of God. (Remember, those are Western penal and legal ideas of sin.) Instead, Jesus took upon himself our sinning enmity by bearing all the abuse we handed out to him. He takes on our illnesses, the suffering we endure. He was painfully burdened by our fallen and broken condition, and he agonized with us in the most profound way possible—he suffered on account of *our* sin.[55]

Sin includes not only moral guilt but also our human failings and weaknesses, anything that causes our estrangement from the shalom God intended for us. Jesus knows how to treat his enemies (all those estranged from God)—he suffers with them (us) as a friend. He suffers both our frailties and our wickedness and violence toward him in order to win us with his love. Later in history, as we have seen, Abelard's theology emphasizes the heart of God that seeks to win us over with love.

---

53. This is a good example of Girard's concept of a "text in travail" in the Hebrew Scriptures. Notice how the passage contains reference to the solidarity of God with us and the innocence of the suffering servant, yet simultaneously contains hints of punishment, or at least the idea that the people believe that it is God who strikes people down or requires affliction, right in the same text. For an explanation of this concept, see Michael Kirwan, *Discovering Girard*, 92, and James Williams, *Girardians: The Colloquium on Violence and Religion 1990–2010* (Hamburg: Lit Verlag, 2013), 134.
54. Bushnell, *Vicarious Sacrifice*, 42
55. Bushnell, *Vicarious Sacrifice*, 46, 473–74.

The apostle Paul tells us that Jesus took the burden of our sin, the heavy weight that sin incurs as he suffered our sinful "wrath" on the cross—not God's wrath, but our wrath. Ephesians 2:3 calls human beings "children of wrath." We've most often interpreted this verse backwards, thinking it means we are sinners who will suffer God's wrath. But if we read it in context, we see that the wrath applies to us—it is our wrath toward one another (and even toward all creation), our wrath that works itself out through violence and especially scapegoating. We are given over to violence; we are captive to the cycles of violence that never seem to end. We suffer wrath. God absorbed this in Jesus. Yes, as much as we don't like to admit it, we are children of wrath who resort to violence whenever the opportunity or the whim strikes us.[56] We make innocent victims pay. We aimed our violence at Jesus. And we sinned by killing him. Our sin put him there. Our sin cursed him to suffer an unjust, horrific death, with no retaliation. He suffered our violence out of love for us and in order to reveal the greatness of God's grace, love, and desire to save us from the sin that executed him. By exposing the violence that is sin, Jesus redeemed it. By loving us, Jesus forgave it. By submitting to it, Jesus stands in solidarity with all who suffer—he bears our burdens in a redemptive way—by exposing and hindering the cycle of sin and violence.[57]

Jesus exposes the nature of human brokenness and our inclination to resort to violence against scapegoats at every turn. He identified with the scapegoats and let human beings execute him. He didn't run away; he didn't call down myriads of angels to smite the Romans or the Jewish leaders; he didn't fight back with his own sword or let Peter lop off anyone's head. He even fastened a soldier's ear back on after Peter's first attempt and told Peter to stop the retaliation. Instead, Jesus "fights" back with peaceful protest and allows himself to be killed by the world's wrath—by the children of wrath. In doing so, he exposes the hidden nature of our sin and forces into the light the things that have been done in darkness so they no longer have any power. Jesus takes the moral wrongdoing and the suffering we experience as children of wrath upon himself and liberates us from those oppressive burdens forever.

Jesus Gives Life

In the second century, the church father Irenaeus used the term *recapitulation* to describe a "great reversal" in which Jesus serves as the second Adam. We (humanity)

---

56. For the interpretation of Ephesians 2:3, see also David B. Miller, "God in the Hands of Angry Sinners: The Misdiagnosis of Wrath in Ephesians 2," in *Peace Be with You: Christ's Benediction amid Violent Empires*, ed. Sharon L. Baker and Michael Hardin (Telford, PA: Cascadia, 2010), 234–42.

57. See Stephen Finlan, *Options on Atonement in Christian Thought* (Collegeville, MN: Liturgical, 2007), 46–47. Although many scholars turn to the curses in Deuteronomy 27 to explain the curse in Galatians 3:13, Finlan argues against this theory. He doesn't believe there is sufficient evidence to warrant such an interpretation of the Galatians passage. In fact, there is no other soteriological formula in Paul's writings that would remotely point to a Deuteronomic reading of the cross.

were dead in our sins. But God is life. So when "the Word became flesh"—that is, human—Jesus brought the life of God into human flesh, and in so doing, he restored life to us and brought us back into communion with God (John 1:14). In giving humanity God's life, the incarnation broke the stranglehold that death had over us. As a result, we can all have communion with the God of eternal life because that life is now in us through the human Jesus. Not only did he break the stranglehold of death, but because Jesus defeated sin in the flesh, he also liberated us from the slavery of sin through forgiveness and passed on to us the power to defeat sin (see this logic in Rom 5:12–21; 1 Cor 15:21–22). In other words, through the first Adam, all humanity suffered the propensity to sin and remained captive to sin's deadly hold on us. Like Adam, we all sin (or, we could say, participate in the systems and structures of violence), which makes us slaves to sin and the spiritual death that goes with it. But Jesus, the second Adam, defeated sin and death (releasing us from these systems). Through him and the life of God in the flesh, we inherit the power to defeat sin and death. Jesus passed his righteousness and his eternal life on to us. So, like a new, cosmic Adam, Jesus presents to God the totality of the universe restored to unity in him. Irenaeus says powerfully that by descending to us (as a human being), Jesus lifts us to God (as divine).[58] Of course the incarnation and our participation in it as the body of Christ on earth profoundly influence the way we should live our lives.

Jesus reversed the path that Adam started us on by living a life of love in total obedience to God, including the fact that he saw it through to the end by dying on the cross. Not only that, but Jesus reclaimed all of humanity and all of creation and put it all back on the path toward fulfilling the purpose for which it was created—namely, union and communion with God. Where Adam brought death, Jesus brought the reverse—life. Jesus's obedience displaced Adam's disobedience, or falling away from God's original intent of goodness and shalom for us. Adam experienced death because he had sinned, but Jesus didn't participate in sin and therefore didn't have to die. By submitting himself to sin and dying voluntarily and rising from the dead, he broke the hold of sin and death. He brings life to all who love him. Consequently, Jesus has overcome all the results of Adam's sin for all creation, for all time and eternity.[59]

Jesus Acts as Our Mediator

To act as a mediator for someone means to intervene on their behalf or to stand in the middle and harmonize both sides of an argument. A mediator bridges the gap between estranged and conflicting parties in order to reconcile them and restore their relationship. Jesus does this for all creation. He mediates between God and

58. Payton, *Light from the Christian East: An Introduction to the Orthodox Tradition* (Downers Grove, IL: IVP Academic, 2007), 122–24.
59. Lossky, *Mystical Theology*, 137, 148.

humans by reconciling us and restoring our relationship (1 Tim 2:5–6). In Hebrews we're told that Jesus is the mediator of a new covenant of peace and reconciliation between God and all creation. How did he mediate? He shed his blood (think: life) in a manner "that speaks a better word than the blood of Abel" (Heb 12:24). Now what does that mean?

Abel's death was anything but reconciling, and it brought severe consequences to his brother Cain for killing him. Notice, however, that even in the case of Cain, God does not kill him in return but sets a seal upon his forehead to warn others to leave him alone, limiting retribution against him and showing mercy. Although Jesus and Abel might have been murdered for similar psychological reasons (anger, fear, jealousy), Jesus's death brings life. It reveals to us the way to reconciliation and restoration between God and all creation. Although Abel's blood cried out from the ground for vindication and retribution, Jesus cried from the cross, "Father, forgive them!" He mediates by asking God to forgive those who do not know what they are doing—a mediation that includes the entire human race. As the representative of all humanity, Jesus asks God to forgive all humanity (Rom 5:8–10). And in the face of torturous injustice Jesus doesn't call out for vengeance. He takes the loving mercy of God shown by God to Cain and illustrates it even further than simply refusing to return violence for violence. He actually loves and identifies with his enemies so extravagantly that he acts as the mediator between God and human beings, becoming the bridge between us and God's unending life in the Trinity.

Jesus Reconciles Us to God and Each Other

We've talked quite a bit about reconciliation but haven't really defined it in terms of Jesus and the cross. What does it mean to say that through Jesus we are reconciled to God? First, according to the *Oxford English Dictionary*, *reconciliation* indicates "the action or an act of bringing a thing or things to agreement, concord, or harmony." Reconciliation restores estranged parties back to friendship. Jesus has done just that for us (and for all creation).

Amazingly, as we have seen, Jesus reconciled us to God while we were still enemies. We went our own way against the wishes of our creator and, as a result, made ourselves God's enemies. Even though God sought us, forgave us, and longed for a loving relationship with us (Isa 30:18), we continued to flaunt our slavery to spiritual ignorance and sin—what we now call "freedom"—and live apart from the will and the friendship of God. But through the life of Jesus, God sought to bring us back into harmony, to reconcile us.

Romans 5:10–11 puts this into words: "For if while we were enemies, we were reconciled to God through the death of his Son, much more surely, having been reconciled, will we be saved by his life. But more than that, we even boast in God through our Lord Jesus Christ, through whom we have now received reconciliation." We see that through the life of Jesus, we receive forgiveness from sin and reconciliation with God. By allowing sinful human beings to kill him publicly, Jesus revealed to us the fathomless, extravagant love of God. He stood in solidarity with us as sufferers and as sinners. He plunged himself into the depths of human despair and forgave us. As we tap into that life of love that Jesus extends to us, we reconcile with God and with each other.

We see this reconciliation again in 2 Corinthians:

> All this is from God, who reconciled us to himself through Christ, and has given us the ministry of reconciliation; that is, in Christ God was reconciling the world to himself, not counting their trespasses against them, and entrusting the message of reconciliation to us. So we are ambassadors for Christ, since God is making his appeal through us; we entreat you on behalf of Christ, be reconciled to God. For our sake he made him to be sin who knew no sin, so that in him we might become the righteousness of God. (2 Cor 5:18–21)

I love these verses. Through Jesus, God reconciles us. How? By not counting our sins against us—in other words, by forgiving us. Reconciliation comes through forgiveness. We who were once estranged from God are brought into harmony with God, repairing the breach that once separated us.

The same idea is expressed in Colossians 2:13–14, in which God forgives us by actually erasing the debt that sin held against us. To erase it means the debt was there . . . and then it wasn't. There's no balancing of accounts; no one had to suffer any punishment in order to make restitution. Just like I erase my whiteboard, God simply erased the debt. God forgave it. God nailed it to the cross. What we see in full measure from the cross is love, the love of God revealed fully through Jesus. Jesus expressed this love by saying, "Father, forgive them; they don't know what they are doing." Not "Father, release them from the debt now that I've paid the price for it." Not "Father, now you don't have to punish them because you've punished me."

Through the love and forgiveness of God, revealed and realized through the life, death, and resurrection of Jesus, two estranged parties, God and humanity, are brought back into harmony (John 15:14). As if that weren't enough, Jesus brought peace through reconciliation. We will discuss the implications of this momentarily.

Jesus Redeems Us

When theologians speak about salvation or the atonement, they often use the language of redemption. It's important to remember that the writers of the Bible used metaphorical language to talk about the "at-one-ment" Jesus brought about, and that's the case with the words usually translated "redeem" or "redemption" in the New Testament. This can sound like an economic metaphor or exchange, as when my mother used to redeem Green Stamps or when we redeem coupons at the grocery store. But the original Greek words serve as metaphors that give us the image of Jesus delivering us, liberating us, rescuing us from lives lived apart from God, and reclaiming us as God's own possession (Col 1:13). Sometimes the word conveys the idea of making good on a loss or making amends.[60] Another way to look at it is to say that Jesus, as the good shepherd, brought us back into the sheepfold, or that Jesus procured our adoption into God's family (John 10:1–16; Rom 8:15–17). We could also assert that we have a new owner (Rom 1:6; 7:4; Gal 3:29). Or we might analogize an exchange of some sort, in the sense that Jesus traded death for life, slavery for freedom, sin for righteousness, disobedience for obedience. By becoming human, he exchanged sinful humanity for the righteous humanity that characterized our nature before spiritual ignorance and sin entered the world. He exchanged the old spiritually ignorant condition for the new spiritually enlightened condition in the life of God (2 Cor 5:17). And he invites us to share in that life and all it entails.

Although we may believe that the words most often translated "redeem" or "redemption" indicate an economic transaction of some sort, others believe that the word in the New Testament speaks of the *fact* of our delivery from sin rather than of the *means* of that delivery.[61] In this case the metaphor points to our delivery from sin but shouldn't be taken literally as "Jesus paid the price for our deliverance." Taking redemption in the literal sense raises too many problems that theologians have struggled with for centuries, such as: Whom did Jesus literally pay? The devil? As we have seen, many objected to the *Christus Victor*/ransom theory because they couldn't believe God would have to submit to the devil in any way. Or, conversely, did Jesus pay God? Then what does that say about the nature of forgiveness? And how is that logical? We have already examined some of these problems. More importantly, wouldn't Jesus have said something if his death were a payment of some sort?[62]

If we say Jesus's sufferings were not penal but redemptive, then Jesus couldn't have paid God or the devil or anyone else in order to rescue, deliver, liberate, or reclaim us. The significance of this metaphor of redemption lies in the idea that through the incarnation, Jesus did rescue and liberate us from slavery to sin. He did deliver us from spiritual death. And in so doing, he reclaimed us for the kingdom of God. He exchanged death for life.

Jesus Brings Peace

Reconciliation through forgiveness brings peace between formerly conflicted parties—in this case, God and humanity. Ephesians tells us that Jesus proclaimed

---

60. Finlan, *Background and Content*, 164. See also Finlan, *Problems with Atonement*, 40. An in-depth study of ἀπολύτρωσις and λυτρόω are beyond the scope of this book written for a general audience.
61. Finlan, *Options on Atonement*, 20–21.
62. See Finlan, *Options on Atonement*, 39.

peace to those of us who were far from God and to those who were nearer to God (2:15-20). Jesus proclaimed this peace by something that speaks louder than words—his actions. Even though he suffered because of our sinful actions that put him to death, Jesus sought to forgive and to reconcile us to God, bringing peace, love, and restoration not only between God and humans but among those in conflict with each other—Jew, gentile, male, female, slave, free. Peace on earth, goodwill to all people! Isn't that what the angels declared at the birth of Jesus—peace for everyone God favors? And God favors everyone (Ezek 18:32; 2 Pet 3:9)!

We get the same message in Colossians 1:20: "And through him God was pleased to reconcile to himself all things, whether on earth or in heaven, by making peace through the blood of his cross." As we have seen, the ancient Hebrew people understood blood as a metaphor for or a way of talking about life. So yes, through the life (or blood) of Jesus we have peace with God. That peace brought unity to what formerly existed in disunity (Col 1:21-22). What's more, peace with God gives us the peace of God that passes all comprehension (Phil 4:7). This peace and God's life of love are given for all things, human and nonhuman, for ultimately all of creation is reconciled.

Jesus Reveals and Imparts Love

Through his life, death, and resurrection Jesus not only reveals God's love to us, but he also imparts that love to us. In John 15:13 Jesus tells us, "No one has greater love than this, to lay down one's life for one's friends." And Jesus did just that. Let's return to medieval theologian Peter Abelard, who believed that God's love as revealed in Jesus is the foundation for our salvation.[63] First, Abelard reminds us that God's love for us motivated God's sending the Son to redeem humanity from sin. In order for us to realize the profound depth of divine love, Jesus willingly lived and died, giving us both the revelation and the example of God's love. And in order for God to show the depth of God's love for us and to convince us that we must love God in return, Jesus willingly submitted to our sinful actions and allowed us to execute him on the cross.[64] Abelard explains the purpose of the cross: "'To the showing of his justice'—that is, his love—which, as has been said, justifies us in his sight. In other words, to show forth his love to us or to convince us how much

---

63. For Abelard, Christ's passion is efficacious for those under both the old covenant and the new covenant, although those under the new covenant are given a greater righteousness through the love of God manifested in Christ. Abelard states that "everyone becomes more righteous—by which we mean a greater love of the Lord—after the passion of Christ than before, since a realized gift inspires greater love than one which is only hoped for." Abelard, *Exp. in Epist. ad Rom.* ii.iii. Quoted in Richard E. Weingart, *The Logic of Divine Love: A Critical Analysis of the Soteriology of Peter Abailard* (London: Clarendon, 1970), 95. For the love of God revealed in Christ's life and death, see 123-24 in the same source.

64. Abelard, *Epistle to the Romans*, 3:21-23, in Fairweather, A *Scholastic Miscellany*, 278-79. Cf. Green, "Is the Message of the Cross Good News?," 223; McCullagh, "Theology of Atonement," 399.

we ought to love him who 'spared not his own Son' for us."[65] So the cross gives us profound knowledge and genuine assurance of the love God has for us and the extravagance of forgiving grace.

Second, Abelard also believes that Christ's passion not only reveals the depth of God's love, but that through this love, God saves us. Abelard writes: "Through this righteousness—which is love—we may gain remission of our sins."[66] For Abelard, then, love is the motivation behind the cross; the revelation of the cross is love; the source of forgiveness and, therefore, of salvation in the cross, is love. The cross symbolizes divine love, the revelation of God's love for us and for all creation. The extravagant depth of divine love led Jesus to the cross as a willing sacrifice of love. In fact, the cross enables us to understand the extent of God's love and inspires us to love God in return.[67]

Abelard helps us see that Jesus did not die to win God's love for us, but to win us over with God's love. God's love went to the limit for us, diving into the depths of the human condition, suffering the consequences of human sin by dying a terrible death as an innocent man. And in the midst of that suffering love, Jesus revealed the greatest love of all—forgiving his enemies—and he asks us to do the same.

65. Abelard, *Epistle to the Romans*, 3:24, in Fairweather, *A Scholastic Miscellany*, 279.
66. Abelard, *Exp. in Epist. ad Rom.* i.i quoted from Weingart, *The Logic of Divine Love*, 75–76. Abelard, *Epistle to the Romans*, 3:26 and Sol. in Fairweather, *A Scholastic Miscellany*, 277–79, 284.
67. See Michael J. Dodds, *The Unchanging God of Love* (Fribourg, Switzerland: Éditions Universitaires Fribourg Suisse, 1986), 305. See also Conner, *The Gospel of Redemption*, 105–8; Gunton, *The Actuality of Atonement*, 54.

8. The Holy Spirit

I believe in the Holy Spirit . . .

> Those in whom the Spirit comes to live are God's new temple. They are, individually and corporately, places where heaven and earth meet.
> —N. T. Wright, *Simply Christian*

> The Spirit is more than just one of God's gifts among others; the Holy Spirit is the unrestricted presence of God in which our life wakes up, becomes wholly and entirely living, and is endowed with the energies of life.
> —Jürgen Moltmann, *The Source of Life*

My husband and I jog together in the humid, sweltering summer heat in Alabama. One particular day, the temperature reached 95 degrees; the heat seemed to bounce off the street in quivering waves, the sun beat down on us with unrestrained brutality, and the air tortured us with stagnating clamminess. As we neared the final stretch of the run, we longed for even just a little waft of a breeze to help evaporate the rivulets of sweat drenching our bodies. With no relief in sight, I did not think I could continue one more step and, longing for even a hint of cool air, was ready to quit. But then, in that moment, I felt the refreshing gust of a rogue breeze blowing amid the heat and humidity. It blew welcoming new life into my mind and body, revitalizing me enough to finish the run. Such a cool breeze reminds me of the Holy Spirit, who acts as a renewing force, a wind or breath that revitalizes us like a refreshing zephyr that brings new life on its wings. In fact, the Hebrew word for "spirit," *ruach*, in the Old Testament literally means "wind" or "breath." The word, when applied to the Spirit of God, denotes an active power, a windy energy, the principle of life, representing the activity of the Holy Spirit that brings on its wings the creative gust of new life.[1] The wind of the Spirit may describe a soft breath (John 20:22), a sheer silence (1 Kgs 19:11–13), a gale-force wind (Exod 15:8), or a gentle breeze (Gen 3:8). In theology, the study of the Holy Spirit is called "pneumatology," from the Greek *pneuma*, meaning "wind."

In Scripture, the Holy Spirit appears not only as a wind or breath, but also as a dove with wings gliding on the air currents to gift the world with the refreshment of renewed life, divine grace, and restoring love. For millennia, artists have represented the Holy Spirit with the image of a dove in icons, frescoes, oil paintings,

---

1. H. Wheeler Robinson, *The Christian Experience of the Holy Spirit* (London: Nisbet, 1928), 8, 20–21.

and sculpture, such as the one painted on the ceiling of the Basilica of Santa Maria del Popolo in Rome. This painting, surrounded by the divinely inspired artwork of Caravaggio, imagines the dove of the Holy Spirit with outspread wings that appear to be beating in the breeze, moving the air around it with an energy of divine power.[2]

As popular as this wind-winged representation of the Holy Spirit was throughout history, the Christian church's first nineteen hundred years of conversations sorely lack engagement with a doctrine of the Holy Spirit. Even in the creeds and confessions of both Eastern and Western churches, mention of the Holy Spirit is sparse and often follows the liturgical worship of God the Father and Son almost as an afterthought.[3] The Apostles' Creed merely states a bare belief in the Spirit, without amplification: "I believe in the Holy Spirit." Moreover, the first articulation of the Nicene Creed merely states that "We believe . . . in the Holy Spirit." Period. That's it. Church leaders such as Basil the Great (329–379) soon realized that language about the Holy Spirit needed to advance out of obscurity and ambiguity into the clarity and substance necessary to build theological unity in the church. The newly added language of the Spirit included a brief pneumatological description inserted into the Nicene Creed's faith statement during the Council of Constantinople in 381: "[We believe] in the Holy Spirit, the Lord and giver of life, who proceeded from the Father, who with the Father and Son together is worshiped and glorified, who spoke by the prophets."[4] But then the church largely ignored the Holy Spirit until almost a millennium and a half later. Although this neglect may not seem theologically significant, overlooking the work of the divine Spirit diminishes our understanding of God as immanent—as with us and in us. Instead, God can seem distant and unconnected from everyday life.

Fortunately, according to theologian of the Spirit Amos Yong, "the recent appearance of a variety of pneumatologies from biblical, theological, and other perspectives is a testimony to the fact that the once 'silent' and 'shy' member of the Trinity is silent and shy no longer."[5] Study of the divine Spirit tells us much about the mind and actions of God in triune form as well as about how we live our lives as Christians. First, just what does this "shy" member of the Trinity tell us about the triune God?

2. On a recent trip to Rome, my husband (B. Keith Putt) and I visited numerous basilicas, cathedrals, and museums. He photographed this painting, *The Holy Spirit and the Evangelists*, by Giovanni Battista Ricci on the ceiling in the anteroom of the Cerasi Chapel in the Basilica of Santa Maria del Popolo in Campo Marizo, Rome: https://tinyurl.com/y9h8pa8g.

3. Clark H. Pinnock, *Flame of Love: A Theology of the Holy Spirit* (Downers Grove, IL: InterVarsity, 2002), 10.

4. Christopher A. Hall, *Learning Theology with the Church Fathers* (Downers Grove, IL: InterVarsity, 2002), 103.

5. Amos Yong, *Spirit-Word-Community: Theological Hermeneutics in Trinitarian Perspective* (Hants: UK: Ashgate, 2002), 28, 43.

Naming the Spirit

Articulating the Spirit introduces a particular challenge. Our language does not truly furnish us with adequate words to describe such an ephemeral entity. Clark Pinnock asks: "How does one render that reality that is wind, fire, breath, life—tangible yet intangible, invisible yet powerful, inexpressible yet intimate, powerful yet gentle, reliable yet unpredictable, personal yet impersonal, transcendent yet immanent?"[6] Because the Holy Spirit acts dynamically and powerfully in many different ways, Scripture offers various names for the Spirit, depending on the context. Each of these names tells us something significant. For instance, the words "holy spirit"[7] occur three times in the Hebrew Bible, generally in opposition to sin (Ps 51:11; Isa 63:10–11), and more than ninety times in the New Testament. The word *holy* communicates to us that the Spirit is set apart from creation and its fallenness, and exists in the purity of holiness and righteousness. The term "spirit of God" occurs thirteen times in the Hebrew Bible and twelve in the New Testament, designating the Spirit as divine and as part of the Godhead—a discussion that becomes significant in the fourth and fifth centuries. The name "Spirit of the Lord" occurs over twenty times in the Hebrew Bible and five times in the New Testament and expresses the Spirit's power of sovereignty and providence as the giver of life who nurtures and cares for all creation. "Spirit of Christ" appears two times in the New Testament, and "Spirit of Jesus Christ" and "Spirit of his Son" appear once each. Yong asserts that "this genitive [grammatically possessive] structure denotes the adjectival character of Spirit who calls attention not to herself but instead to the other persons of the Godhead."[8] For example, the "Spirit of Christ" directs our attention to Christ and his activity in the world and in the lives of all people. The "Spirit of Truth," occurring once, reminds us that whether through prophets, words of God, Scripture, or Jesus, God's Spirit always and only reveals divine truth.[9] All of these names emphasize an understanding of the Spirit that refers to the mutual love, oneness, and gift of the Spirit by the Father and the Son.

The Holy Spirit in the Hebrew Bible

The Hebrew Bible tells us quite a bit about the actions of the Holy Spirit that, in turn, reveal the character, purposes, and mind of God. Although the actions we will discuss in what follows do not exhaust the work of the Spirit, they do provide

---

6. Pinnock, *Flame of Love*, 11.
7. Uppercase and lowercase distinctions of the Holy Spirit did not occur in the Hebrew or Greek. The NRSV renders "spirit" in lowercase letters in the Old Testament and in uppercase letters in the New Testament. So perhaps those distinctions are not as significant as their use in the English language suggests. The number of occurrences in the Hebrew Bible and New Testament vary depending on the version of the Bible.
8. Yong, *Spirit-Word-Community*, 64.
9. Fisher Humphreys, *Thinking about God: An Introduction to Christian Theology* (Covington, LA: Insight, 2016), 131–32.

valuable insight for perceiving the work of God from creation until the present day. We see that the Holy Spirit is the source of creation, life, renewal, wisdom, and divine presence, among other gifts.

The Source of Creation

Although it denotes an immateriality, the word *spirit* in the Bible refers more to the power of wind that we cannot tame and to the invisible reservoir of life that we cannot exhaust.[10] In fact, the word for "spirit," *ruach*, occurs in the Hebrew Bible 378 times and denotes a wind-like energy, an elusive yet penetrating presence, a supernatural power, a breath, or the vital, dynamic activity that creates and sustains life. The Spirit of God is God's power in action, in creation, and in bringing about new life.[11] We see a close connection between *ruach* and the breath or wind that ignites new life. This energetic wind "infuses life, fertilizes matter, and engenders life."[12] Starting in Genesis 1:2, the Spirit of God, as a fertile wind, "swept over the face of the waters," moving, hovering, and, in partnership with Trinitarian activity, dancing with creative contemplation over the as-yet unformed universe. Through the breath of the divine Spirit, the choreographer of the dance, God speaks. From God's Spirit-inspired Word, chaos turns into cosmos and the entire creation comes forth into existence.[13]

Truth, goodness, beauty, and the gift of creation dwell in the purview and person of the Spirit of God. Consequently, the entire universe—its unfathomable expanse of stars, planets, and galaxies, the loveliness of the "pale blue dot," the beauty of mountain ranges, the power of the oceans, the serenity of a sunset, the hope expressed by the sunrise bringing a new day, and the continual rebirth of spring after a cold winter—all communicate the universe as a sacrament (a visible manifestation of invisible grace) of God's loving presence evident in the omnipresence of the Holy Spirit.[14]

We may assert that creation springs forth from the loving relationships between Father, Son, and Spirit as an expression of God's generosity.[15] In the act of creation, we see the love of God overflow through the Spirit into the universe and embrace something other than God. Creation reveals the Spirit's desire to love, share, and communicate the presence of God with us, to foster loving relationships, unity, and

---

10. Pinnock, *Flame of Love*, 25.
11. Richard J. Plantinga, Thomas R. Thompson, and Matthew D. Lundberg, *An Introduction to Christian Theology* (Cambridge: Cambridge University Press, 2010), 285.
12. Boris Bobrinskoy, *The Mystery of the Trinity: Trinitarian Experience and Vision in the Biblical and Patristic Tradition*, trans. Anthony P. Gythiel (Crestwood, NY: St. Vladimir's Seminary Press, 1999), 26. See also Yong, *Spirit-Word-Community*, 47.
13. See also Pinnock, *Flame of Love*, 56; Yong, *Spirit-Word-Community*, 35; Stanley J. Grenz, *Theology for the Community of God* (Grand Rapids, MI: Eerdmans, 2000), 361–62; James Leo Garrett Jr., *Systematic Theology: Biblical, Historical, and Evangelical*, vol. 2 (Grand Rapids, MI: Eerdmans, 1995), 131–35.
14. Plantinga, Thompson, and Lundberg, *Introduction to Christian Theology*, 308.
15. Pinnock, *Flame of Love*, 55.

reciprocal participation in the work of God in our lives. The Spirit of God reveals to us the mind of God, who desires peace in community with all creatures and in nurturing care for the world. The conflicts and violence that so affect our world have no place in such a community formed by God's Spirit of peace in our lives.

The Source of Life

That first instance of life-giving creativity defines the action of the Holy Spirit in the history of the universe and in the work of God for the redemption of all creation. We see in Scripture that the Holy Spirit does not hoard life but generously gives it to the world to cultivate communion with other living beings. Our very lives are gifts of God's Spirit. From God's mouth to Adam, the outflow of divine breath caused the dirt of the ground to spring to life (Gen 2:7).[16] Humanity, then, partakes of the breath of God and lives. That divine breath within us enables us to commune with others, love others, and understand others—all characteristics of the image of God in us. We might say that the breath (Spirit) of God not only turns mud into living flesh but also endows all human beings with the very image of God—the life of God that enables humanity to live life in harmony with God and to carry out the purposes of God.

In addition to the Genesis passages about the life-giving Spirit, Job cries out while questioning his existence, "The spirit of God has made me, and the breath of the Almighty gives me life" (33:4). The Psalmist echoes Job in a reprisal of joy, singing to God, "When you send forth your spirit, they are created; and you renew the face of the ground" (104:30). All living things exist only because of the work of the Spirit giving, sustaining, nurturing, renewing, and preserving life (Gen 1:2; 2:7; Job 34:14-15; Ps 33:6; 104:29-30; 2 Cor 3:6).[17]

The Source of Renewal

In the Hebrew Bible, the Holy Spirit not only gives and sustains life but also renews life in the midst of death and destruction. Noah's dove, returning to the ark with a freshly plucked olive branch proving the rebirth of new life after the flood, provides us with a beautiful symbol of God's life-giving renewal and restoration (Gen 8:10-11). Of course, we find the most vivid example of renewal in the story of the dry bones coming to life (Ezek 37). As Ezekiel looks over a valley littered with thousands of dry old bones, God says to him, "Mortal, can these bones live?" The only logical and possible answer would be "Not a chance!" But human logic is not always divine logic, and where we claim impossibility, God reveals new possibilities. God tells Ezekiel to speak these divine words of life to the dry bones: "Thus says

16. Pinnock, *Flame of Love*, 50, 55.
17. See Paul Tillich, *The Shaking of the Foundations* (New York: Charles Scribner, 1955), 137. Tillich states, "The Spirit is life. It is creative life."

the Lord God to these bones: I will cause breath to enter you, and you shall live. I will lay sinews on you, and will cause flesh to come upon you, and cover you with skin, and put breath in you, and you shall live; and you shall know that I am the Lord" (37:5–6). From death, God's Spirit recreated renewed life. With nothing other than breath, the divine Spirit created muscles, flesh, and skin on dry, dead bones and then breathed life into the vast multitude of newly created people, "and they lived, and stood on their feet" (v. 10). And as we will see in the New Testament, God's Spirit carries that creative act of renewal into the life of all human beings through Jesus Christ so that we, along with the Psalmist, can ask God to create in us a clean, renewed heart and put a new spirit within us (51:10).

The Source of Wisdom

The Bible also describes the Holy Spirit as the source of divine wisdom: The Holy Spirit is "intelligent, holy, unique, manifold, subtle, mobile, clear, unpolluted . . . [and] is a breath of the power of God . . . [who] renews all things" (Wis 7:22, 25, 27).[18] That Spirit-induced wisdom rests upon Jesus, supporting the New Testament's description of his baptism (Isa 11:2; Matt 3:16). God's Spirit also granted wisdom and knowledge to certain Hebrew people so they could construct the temple in the wilderness (Exod 31:3–11). The divine Spirit possessed Samuel so he could speak God's wisdom to the prophets (1 Sam 10:10). Filled with the Spirit of wisdom, Daniel interpreted dreams and spoke God's words to those in power during the Babylonian captivity (5:10–16). Indeed, whenever God gives words, knowledge, understanding, or discernment to persons in the Hebrew Bible, we also see the Holy Spirit at work endowing them with divine wisdom to carry out their tasks. As the book of Wisdom in the Apocrypha asks us, "Who has learned your counsel, unless you have given wisdom and sent your holy spirit from on high?" (9:17); it also tells us, "The spirit of the Lord has filled the world" (1:7).

The Source of Divine Presence

The Hebrew Bible portrays God as omnipresent, infiltrating and filling the entire universe with the divine presence, life, and the power of God to speak, act, and relate to all of creation (Jer 23:23–24; Prov 15:3). As we saw, the divine Spirit hovers over the chaos, present in the formless void, before God created the universe. Psalm 139 proclaims that God's Spirit dwells in the lowest depth of the sea, in the highest expanse of the heavens, in the darkest corners of the earth, and in the deepest confines of Sheol (the traditional Hebrew name for the realm of the dead). We cannot run or hide from God's Spirit. No place we go is beyond the presence of

18. See Yong, *Spirit-Word-Community*, 36.

God. The Holy Spirit is present everywhere at all times, exerting power, pouring out love, manifesting creativity, revealing wisdom, and bringing new life.

The Source of Gifts

When the Hebrew people wandered in the wilderness, God commanded them to build a tabernacle so they could worship, offer sacrifices, and house the ark of the covenant (indicative of the divine presence). Since the people had no experience of this sort, nor the abilities to build such a structure or to make the furniture and instruments necessary for proper worship, the Spirit gave them gifts to accomplish the task—gifts of intelligence, skill, creativity, and artistic talent (Exod 31:1–11; 35:31). The Spirit also gave certain people in the Bible the ability to provide leadership so the community could function in an orderly fashion (Judg 3:10; 11:29; 1 Chr 12:18; Num 11:25; Job 32:8; Zech 4:6). In addition, the divine Spirit grants God's prophets the gifts of words and understanding so they can speak to the people for God (Isa 6:9; Jer 1:7; Neh 9:30).

Interestingly, the actions of the Spirit in the Hebrew Bible differ from those in the New Testament in one significant way. In the Hebrew Bible, God sends the divine Spirit to individuals for a certain task or function. The Spirit's presence is transitory and selective, given to a very few.[19] In the New Testament, God sends the Spirit to every follower of Jesus, whether Jew, Greek, slave, free, male, or female. The Holy Spirit of Christ dwells in everyone who confesses Jesus as Savior. This community of Spirit-filled people makes up the body of Christ, all called to exercise the gifts of the Spirit for the furtherance of God's kingdom and for God's glory—a topic we will develop in the next chapter.

The Source of Hope

The Holy Spirit also extends hope to a fearful, downcast people. When the people of Judah end up in captivity in Babylon, God promises to pour out the Spirit upon them. This divine promise encourages them to hope for a better future, for deliverance from the evils they presently suffer (Joel 2:28–32). When the time comes for the Israelites to leave Babylon, return to Jerusalem, and rebuild the temple, God sends the Spirit to give them hope and courage to move forward. As a result, they completed their task despite much difficulty and hardship (Hag 2:4–5). Indeed, all the way through the Hebrew Bible we read about the people of Israel on a journey with their God through times of oppression, war, famine, and captivity, with seemingly impossible tasks set before them, yet instilled with the life-giving hope of the Spirit for a renewed and better life ahead, by the gracious power of God.

---

19. Grenz, *Theology for the Community of God*, 364.

The Source of Justice

God sends the Spirit to promote justice in the land. The prophet Isaiah speaks of a time when God will send the divine Spirit to judge the poor and decide with fairness, wisdom, understanding, and righteousness in order to restore justice to all people (11:1–5). Isaiah continues with this theme several chapters later, prophesying a deliverer upon whom God's Spirit rests and who "will bring forth justice to the nations. . . . He will not grow faint or be crushed until he has established justice in the earth" (42:1–4). Isaiah reveals what this Spirit-led justice will look like: The Spirit will deliver "good news to the oppressed" and will "bind up the brokenhearted," bringing "liberty to the captives and release to the prisoners." This justice will give oppressed people the "oil of gladness instead of mourning, the mantle of praise instead of a faint spirit" (Isa 61:1–3).

In many ways throughout the Hebrew Bible—more than we have discussed in this brief chapter—God's Spirit acts as the creative source of healing, justice, hope, wisdom, renewal, and life. The Holy Spirit empowers individuals with gifts to serve God and brings hope to the hopeless, joy to the joyless, and liberty to those bound in captivity.[20]

The Holy Spirit in the New Testament

In addition, the Spirit plays a significant role in the creation of a new community in the New Testament, first in Jesus, and then in the lives of those who follow him. The Spirit works consistently to conceive, confirm, commission, and consummate the work of God on earth through Jesus Christ, God's Son.

At the start of his Gospel, Luke discloses the first instance of the Holy Spirit's interaction in the life of Jesus with the words spoken to Mary by the angel Gabriel: "The Holy Spirit will come upon you, and the power of the Most High will overshadow you; therefore the child to be born will be holy; he will be called Son of God" (1:35). In keeping with the Spirit as the giver of life, the Holy Spirit actively and creatively conceives the union of human flesh and divine *Logos*, in the life of Jesus of Nazareth. As we have discovered, this new life, wrought by God's Spirit, transforms the world with Spirit-led words and actions from birth to resurrection.[21]

Theologian Clark Pinnock asserts that the Holy Spirit functions as the most significant aspect not only of Jesus's conception but also of his confirmation as the Son of God and his commission to save creation.[22] Indeed, we see this first at his baptism as the Spirit confirms the identity of Jesus as God's beloved son (Luke 3:22; John 1:32–34). Here, the Holy Spirit affirms the union of the divinity and humanity of Jesus through the united participation of earthly water and divine

---

20. Daniel Migliore, *Faith Seeking Understanding* (Grand Rapids, MI: Eerdmans, 2004), 227.
21. See Grenz, *Theology for the Community of God*, 365; Pinnock, *Flame of Love*, 50, 86, 112.
22. Pinnock, *Flame of Love*, 80.

Spirit at baptism.[23] Immediately after the baptism, the Spirit leads Jesus out into the wilderness and provides him with the strength to resist the devil's temptations to misuse the divine power at his disposal (Luke 4:1–13). The Holy Spirit also commissions Jesus by endowing him with the divine power to fulfill his mission in the world (Acts 10:38). When Jesus heals the sick, walks on water, feeds five thousand, casts out demons, and raises the dead, the Holy Spirit acts as the superintendent of Jesus's life and ministry, as the instrument of empowerment for every act.[24] Even in Jesus's death, the Holy Spirit works to maintain the bond of love between the Father and Son so that when Jesus dies he gives the Spirit back to the Father, stating, "Into your hands I commend my Spirit" (Luke 23:46).

Because of the Holy Spirit, however, death does not have the final say. The Spirit of life, with the power of creation, makes the dead live again and resurrects Jesus from the grave. The apostle Paul emphasizes this work of the Spirit in the resurrection, saying that by the power of the Spirit, God raised Jesus from the dead. This one act brings to consummation the birth, life, teachings, and death of Christ by fulfilling the entire purpose of God in the redemption of all creation (Rom 1:4; 8:11). The life-giving act of the Spirit transforms Jesus and inaugurates the transformation of the world into a new creation in which death no longer has the last word (1 Cor 15:45; 1 Tim 3:16).[25] As the first-fruits of a new humanity, raised by the Spirit of God, we now live a new life in Christ through the power of the Holy Spirit (2 Thess 2:13; Jas 1:18).

The Holy Spirit Today

In addition to empowering Jesus of Nazareth from conception to ascension to fulfill the divine plan, the Holy Spirit actively works today in each person to bring about God's purposes for creating new life, transforming the world, and redeeming all creation. Below, we discuss a few of the ways the divine Spirit moves in the lives of people and in creation to accomplish God's goals.

The Spirit Bestows the Divine Presence

In the Hebrew Bible, a pillar of cloud and fire represented God's presence with the people, and sometimes God sent the Spirit out temporarily to individuals for specific purposes. And we have seen how the Spirit actively worked in every aspect of Jesus's life from conception to ascension. In these later days, since Pentecost, the Holy Spirit bestows a permanent divine presence on a community of believers. The Spirit, as Gordon Fee aptly says, "is God's way of being present, powerfully present, in our

---

23. Pinnock, *Flame of Love*, 87.
24. For example, see Matt 12:28; Luke 4:18; Acts 10:38. See also Pinnock, *Flame of Love*, 81, 112.
25. Pinnock, *Flame of Love*, 100; Wolfhart Pannenberg, *Systematic Theology*, vol. 1, trans. Geoffrey W. Bromiley (Grand Rapids, MI: Eerdmans, 1991), 315.

lives and communities as we await the consummation of the kingdom of God."[26] Through the Holy Spirit, God's face turns toward us with the promised power to transform the world and bring the divine plans to completion. "The Spirit is the form and power of [God's] presence."[27] So wherever love abounds, whenever acts of mercy occur, whatever brings about transformation of lives for good, however boundaries are dissolved to unite a diverse humanity in peaceful relationships, the presence of God is there through the Spirit, actively spreading hope, making peace, healing wounds, forgiving sin, and creating new life.

The Spirit Creates New Life

As we have already discussed, the Holy Spirit is the agent of creation, blowing divine breath over the nothingness of unformed matter (Gen 1:1-2). Moreover, the wind of the Spirit created new life out of dry, dead bones in the valley of the shadow of death (Ezek 37). And when Jesus died on the cross, giving his Spirit back to the Father, death did not have the final word; the Spirit of God never breathes a last breath but continually, always, blows forth new life—with the resurrected Jesus as the first-fruits of a new humanity, and then within God's new community, the church. "This new life reaches into the depths of the human condition and constitution,"[28] creating a new heart and a new humanity crafted in Christ so that Paul can say with faith, "If anyone is in Christ, there is a new creation: everything old has passed away; see, everything has become new!" (2 Cor 5:17). The Nicene Creed echoes Paul, calling the Holy Spirit "the Lord, the giver of life."[29] Indeed, just as the Spirit raised Jesus from death to new life, our baptism in the Spirit now raises us to live as Christ's body in the world (1 Cor 15:20-22; Titus 3:5). Thus begins the creation of a new community in which the Spirit of God has taken up residence, empowering believers to live lives of peace, to pour God's love out to all creation, and to serve as the body of Christ in a world sorely in need of the good news of new life. Indeed, Clark Pinnock exclaims that because of the Spirit, the power of creation breathing new life into the world, "God is closer to us than we are to ourselves."[30]

Actually, the love of God creates new life and brings into existence everything that exists. Without divine love, life would not exist at all.[31] As part of the Trinitarian "bond of love," the Holy Spirit continues the work of Jesus, breathing renewal into all creation and working to sustain life in every form—human and nonhuman,

---

26. Gordon D. Fee, *God's Empowering Presence: The Holy Spirit in the Letters of Paul* (Peabody, MA: Hendrickson, 1994), xxi.
27. Pannenberg, *Systematic Theology*, vol. 1, 269.
28. Yong, *Spirit-Word-Community*, 45-46.
29. Nicene Creed, *Evangelical Lutheran Worship* (Minneapolis: Augsburg Fortress, 2006), 104. This wording first published by English Language Liturgical Consultation in *Praying Together*, 1988.
30. Pinnock, *Flame of Love*, 61-62.
31. Catherine Mowry LaCugna, *God for Us: The Trinity and Christian Life*. San Francisco: HarperSanFrancisco, 1973, 265.

plants and animals, rivers and lakes, oceans and seas.[32] As theologian Jürgen Moltmann attests, the works of the Spirit give and affirm life, universally, in every created thing.[33]

In addition to serving as the agent of creation, the Holy Spirit re-creates human beings in ways that transform us into new persons, crafted according to the will of God. This process begins in the creation of a new heart: as the Psalmist beseeches, "Create in me a clean heart, O God, and put a new and right spirit within me. Do not cast me away from your presence, and do not take your holy spirit from me" (51:10–12). Indeed it is the Spirit who makes new and right and clean, so whenever we see a person transformed into something new and right and clean, we see the Spirit of God at work.[34] In addition, the Spirit works through us to heal the sick and wounded, to comfort the suffering and oppressed, to redeem and reconcile the estranged, and to unite people for fulfilling God's purposes.

The Spirit Indwells Us

Yet the Spirit is more than merely the presence of God. The Holy Spirit brings about renewed activity and dwells within us as the power of God's presence, creating new life and transforming the old into the new. How does this happen? John the Baptist tells us, crying out that Jesus will baptize us with the Holy Spirit (Mark 1:8; Luke 3:16)—a beautiful symbol for the saving act of God "whereby estranged humanity is brought back into proper relationship with the creator" by the gentle power of the Spirit abiding in us and claiming us as God's own.[35] Through baptism in the Spirit, first seen at Pentecost (Acts 2:1–4), we see the closure of the gap between God and humanity. Followers of Jesus enter into a relational life indwelt by God's Spirit, "clothed . . . with Christ," born to "walk in newness of life," and adopted as sons and daughters of God (John 14:17; Gal 3:27; Rom 6:4; 8:11–15). As sharers in the sonship of Jesus, and as participants in the divine nature (2 Pet 1:4), we now belong to a new community that shares in the work of the kingdom in the presence of the Father, through the life and work of the Son, by the indwelling power of the Holy Spirit.[36]

The Spirit Justifies, Sanctifies, and Glorifies

The Spirit-infused new life begins with justification, with the gracious divine acts of forgiving our sin, making us righteous, and repairing our broken relationship with God. Theologian Daniel Migliore describes this divine justification as "God's free,

32. Mark Wallace, *Finding God in the Singing River* (Minneapolis: Fortress, 2005), 6. John Calvin, *Institutes of the Christian Religion*, ed. John T. McNeill, trans. Ford Lewis Battles (Louisville, KY: Westminster John Knox, 1960), 1.13.14.
33. Jürgen Moltmann, *The Spirit of Life: A Universal Affirmation* (Minneapolis: Fortress, 1994), 7–9.
34. Rom 1:3–4; 5:5; 8:2; 14:17; 15:16; Gal 5:16–26; Eph 3:16; 4:22–24; Phil 1:27; 2:1–2; Heb 9:14; 1 John 3:24.
35. Yong, *Spirit-Word-Community*, 30–31.
36. LaCugna, *God for Us*, 363; Pannenberg, *Systematic Theology*, vol. 1, 267.

unconditional, and unmerited acceptance of us in spite of our sin and alienation from God, from others, and from ourselves."[37] Justification by the Spirit, therefore, means that by faith we stand before God forgiven and righteous. It means that as human beings made in the image of God, in right standing before God because of the work of Christ and the Spirit, we can drop all our negativity surrounding our humanity. In accord with the sentiments of Rev. Dr. Martin Luther King Jr. and Rev. Jesse Jackson, we are "somebodies" before God because we are children of God for whom Jesus lived, died, and rose from the dead. Justification before God "is the basis of our dignity, our worth, our human rights, and our human responsibilities."[38]

Karl Barth firmly connects justification to sanctification, another work of the Holy Spirit in believers, asserting that through the Spirit, God sees us as a "new form of existence of a faithful covenant-partner who is well-pleasing to Him and blessed by Him: 'I will be your God' is the justification of [humanity]. 'Ye shall be my people' is [our] sanctification.'"[39] Similarly, John Wesley affirms that "exactly as we are justified by faith, so we are sanctified by faith," indicating that the work of the Spirit first justifies and then sanctifies us in Christ.[40] Jürgen Moltmann expands our discussion and writes that "sanctification today means first of all rediscovering the sanctity of life and the divine mystery of creation. . . . Life comes from God and belongs to God, so it has to be sanctified through the people who believe in God."[41] Since in the context of personal redemption *sanctification* means "to make holy," Barth, Wesley, and Moltmann join voices and exhort us to live holy lives in imitation of Christ, to be holy because God is holy (1 Pet 1:16). Fortunately for us, God provides the means to our sanctification as a gift of the Holy Spirit; we do not have to lead holy lives all on our own. This gift in the power of the Spirit functions as the dynamic agent of transformation as we grow daily in the image of Jesus Christ so that, eventually, we can say with the apostle Paul, "It is no longer I who live, but it is Christ who lives in me" (Gal 2:20). Through the process of sanctification, God gloriously unites us with the life, death, and resurrection of Christ so that we can "do the works that [Jesus did] and, in fact, [even] greater works" (John 14:12). In other words, God raises us up into the Godhead, inviting us to participate in the Trinitarian work of God in Christ, through the power of the Spirit, to transform the world for God's glory (Eph 2:6; 2 Thess 2:13; 1 Pet 1:12).[42]

---

37. Migliore, *Faith Seeking Understanding*, 236.
38. Migliore, *Faith Seeking Understanding*, 239. In a speech, Rev. Jesse Jackson recited this poem by Rev. William H. Borders Sr., entitled "I Am Somebody": "I am somebody. I may be poor, but I am somebody. I may be young, but I am somebody. I may be on welfare, but I am somebody. I may be small, but I am somebody. I may make a mistake, but I am somebody. My clothes are different, my face is different, my hair is different, but I am somebody. I am black, brown, white, I speak a different language, but I must be respected, protected, never rejected. I am God's child. I am somebody."
39. Karl Barth, *Church Dogmatics*, vol. 4.2, ed. Geoffrey W. Bromiley and Thomas F. Torrance (Edinburgh: T & T Clark, 1958), 499.
40. John Wesley, "The Scripture Way of Salvation," in *John Wesley's Sermons: An Anthology*, ed. Albert C. Outler and Richard P. Heitzenrater (Nashville: Abingdon, 1991), 376.
41. Moltmann, *The Spirit of Life*, 171.
42. Yong, *Spirit-Word-Community*, 32.

Indeed, the Holy Spirit justifies and sanctifies us for another reason, one more other-worldly yet just as significant—glorification. The gift of the Spirit permanently seals us as God's children and serves as a down payment for the glorification to follow this life on earth (Rom 8:30; Eph 1:13–14). Amos Yong sums it up well: "The Spirit, in short, is the presence of God which graces human life, reconciles humankind to God, and, finally, brings humanity into that eschatological reunion with its creator."[43]

The Spirit Brings Unity in Diversity

God creates humanity to share in union with the Trinitarian life of God. Through sanctification, we enter into union with God, in Christ, through the Spirit, and begin our journey toward a transformed life. Friedrich Schleiermacher maintains the notion that "all who are living in the state of sanctification are conscious of an inner drive to become increasingly at one in a common co-operative and mutually interactive existence, this driving force being viewed as the common Spirit of the new life founded by Christ."[44] Indeed, Jesus united himself to humanity and now unites humanity to God, bringing together people who otherwise would not gather together, making possible a meeting of minds and hearts for the furtherance of God's kingdom in the power of the Spirit. The Spirit of God animates the life of every follower of Jesus to create a community in union with God and one another.[45] Through the very act of creation, God expresses the divine will for a community of newly re-created, Spirit-filled people, bound together by Jesus Christ, united in love, and committed to sharing in the life and purposes of the triune God (Eph 4:1–6).

Eastern theologians talk about this union with God as theosis, a becoming so united with God that we actually share God's life. Peter affirms the notion of theosis, stating that we are "participants of the divine nature" (2 Pet 1:4). Theologian Olivier Clément describes this unity, writing that theosis "established full communion between God and humanity . . . not by emptying out our human nature but by fulfilling it in the divine life, since only in God is human nature truly itself."[46] So although theosis includes eternal life in unity with God, it also involves living our lives in the world. Eastern Orthodox theologians often describe this union with God as "synergy," a "working together" of divinity and humanity to accomplish God's purposes. Through synergy with and in the Holy Spirit we respond freely to divine grace; we work with the Spirit and walk in the ways of God. God's will and the human will work together to spread love, forgiveness, and grace to

43. Yong, Spirit-Word-Community, 31–32.
44. Friedrich Schleiermacher, The Christian Faith: A New Translation and Critical Edition, trans. Terrence N. Tice and Catherine L. Kelsey (Louisville, KY: Westminster John Knox, 2016), 1565.
45. Pinnock, Flame of Love, 81, 105. See also Yong, Spirit-Word-Community, 40; LaCugna, God for Us, 298; as well as John 6:63 and 2 Cor 3:6.
46. Olivier Clément, The Roots of Christian Mysticism, 2nd ed. (Hyde Park, NY: New City Press, 2013), 37.

the world.[47] Thus, we partner with the Spirit to gather together "what has been sundered—races, nations, persons. . . . The Spirit who animates the praise of God incorporates persons into the deepest regions of divine life."[48]

The Spirit Enables Communication

As the medium for divine/human interaction and the source of rationality, the Spirit enables communication between God and God's creatures.[49] Paul tells us that the Holy Spirit reveals the wisdom of God to us and that, accordingly, "we have the mind of Christ" (1 Cor 2:10, 16). In our union with God, the Spirit gives us an understanding of the otherwise unsearchable and unknowable things of God (1 Cor 2:11–12) so we may know God and God's will. The Holy Spirit also teaches us truth. In fact, John calls the third person of the Trinity the Spirit of truth (14:17; 15:26; 1 John 5:6), who will guide us in truth, expand our knowledge, illuminate our thoughts, and help us apply those truths to our lives (John 16:12-15; Rom 9:1; Heb 9:8).[50] Moreover, Calvin regards "the Spirit of God as the sole fountain of truth" without whom we cannot know anything about God or truth at all and through whom we know Jesus Christ.[51]

The Holy Spirit communicates to us in many ways, extending comfort and encouragement to those who suffer. The divine Spirit serves as our *paraclete* (a Greek word meaning "advocate," a lawyer for the defense), as one who comes alongside and grieves with us, suffers with us, hopes with us, and instills us with joy (John 14:16; Acts 13:52; Gal 5:22; Eph 5:18–19; 1 Thess 1:6). Catherine LaCugna beautifully expresses this work of the Spirit, proclaiming that "the Spirit lifts up our hearts, holds the hand of the infirm, brings us to perfection."[52] Just as the Spirit communicates to us, through that same divine power, we communicate the love of God to others (1 Cor 2:4; 12:3; Eph 2:18; 3:5-6).

The Spirit Aids in Prayer and Praise

The community of believers is, first of all, a worshipping and praying community, and the presence of the Holy Spirit serves as the key to both (1 Cor 14:6–26; Eph 6:18). Indeed, the Spirit helps us to pray in accordance with God's will by interceding for us as a mediator between the divine and the human (Rom 8:26). When we pray, we do so by the power of the Spirit (Eph 6:18; Jude 20). Likewise, the "Spirit

---

47. James R. Payton, *Light from the Christian East: An Introduction to the Orthodox Tradition* (Downers Grove, IL: IVP Academic, 2007), 151–52.
48. LaCugna, *God for Us*, 362, 296–300.
49. Pannenberg, *Systematic Theology*, vol. 1, 266; Hall, *Learning Theology with the Church Fathers*, 102; Yong, *Spirit-Word-Community*, 35, 40, 42; Schleiermacher, *The Christian Faith*, 1568.
50. Yong, *Spirit-Word-Community*, 41.
51. Calvin, *Institutes of the Christian Religion*, 2.2.15: 273.
52. LaCugna, *God for Us*, 119.

inspires and activates our doxology" and points us to God in Christ.[53] Whenever we seek God through prayer and whenever we lift our hearts to God in praise, the Holy Spirit leads, intercedes, and inspires us to worship in the presence of God, according to the will of God (Jude 20).

The Spirit Endows Gifts

Whenever we love someone, we enjoy showing that love by giving him or her gifts in order to bring joy. Likewise, God showers us with gifts of the Spirit that bring joy and enable us to work effectively in partnership with God to transform the world. Through the gifts of the Spirit we participate in the power of God to love others and to reveal Christ to them. Paul speaks to the church in Corinth about the gifts of wisdom, knowledge, faith, healing, miracles, prophecy, discernment, tongues, and interpretation of tongues (1 Cor 12:7–10). Others have added to that list with gifts of teaching, mercy, and exhortation (encouragement). No one gift is more important than any other; all are needed to work in partnership with God in the world. But most importantly, Paul makes it clear that even though the Spirit gives many and various gifts, they come from one and the same Lord for the common good of the whole body of Christ. It takes an entire body, the one people of God in Christ, to do the work of God in the power of the Spirit. Even though no one person receives all the gifts, the Spirit gives one gift in particular to all people—the gift of love (1 Cor 13).

The Spirit Pours Out Love

Romans 5:5 tells us that "God's love has been poured into our hearts through the Holy Spirit that has been given to us." Considering Paul's concentration on the importance of love and the fact that Jesus condensed all 613 Jewish laws into two commandments to love God and love others, we can easily surmise that God emphasizes love above all other gifts, actions, and motivations. It makes sense that the gift of love, coming from the God of love, would also be the main characteristic of those who, through the Spirit of love, become partakers of and participants in the divine love of the triune God. "We are always and forever the conduits, the instruments, the tuning forks, the receiver stations. We slowly learn the right frequencies that pick up the signals from the Lover" so we can then pour God's love into the world, into others sorely in need of new life.[54]

---

53. LaCugna, God for Us, 363.
54. Richard Rohr, The Naked Now: Learning to See as the Mystics See (New York: Crossroad, 2009), 22–23, 138.

The Spirit Instills Hope

The Bible says quite a bit about hope and often connects that hope to the work of God's Spirit in our lives. For example, the power of the Spirit causes us to abound in the hope of our inclusion in God's plan for salvation (Rom 15:13), because through the Spirit, God has "given us new birth into a living hope through the resurrection of Jesus Christ from the dead" (1 Pet 1:3). Because of Jesus's resurrection, we participate in his new life as God's children and therefore can, like Jesus, legitimately call God "Father" (Rom 8:14-17). This hope includes an eternal inheritance reserved for us in Christ. In addition, the Holy Spirit serves as the Spirit of liberation and instills hope in us, saving us not only from spiritual ignorance and sin in the inward, moral sense, but also from the oppression and abuses that infect and stain contemporary society. God's Spirit accomplishes this work through the incomprehensible bond of love poured out into the unified body of Christ.[55] Indeed, through the Spirit, God comes to us in the midst of brokenness and gives us hope and empowerment for new life.[56] The Spirit empowers Christ's followers to stand in solidarity with those who suffer, to influence civil powers to act with justice, to love others by feeding and clothing them, and to worship God "in spirit and truth" (John 4:24).

The Spirit Equips Christians for Service

The first thing the resurrected Jesus did when he came face to face with his disciples was to breathe out the Spirit of God into them and send them into the world to accomplish God's mission.[57] The Holy Spirit inspires our action in service to God through the transpiration of gifts that equip us to complete the task (1 Cor 12). Church father Basil the Great acknowledges this power, telling us that "the Spirit is the vehicle, the power, the 'that by which'" we do the works of God.[58] The Spirit works in us not with coercive force, but with a gentle prodding, an impression in our minds, or a nagging thought that will not disappear. This gentle urge from the divine Spirit comes to us as a call, an invitation to participate in the work of God in the world. And with this petition and power, the Spirit also gives us the freedom to serve or not to serve, the power to say "yes" or "no." Consequently, we have the power to do God's works; all we need is the will. And, as St. Augustine claims, if we love God, we can do what we will because we will desire to do what God wills.[59] In order to will what God wills, the apostle Paul exhorts us to follow the lead of the Spirit: "Do not get drunk with wine, for that is debauchery; but be filled with the Spirit" (Eph 5:18). In other words, he tells us, do not be filled and controlled

55. James H. Cone, *Black Theology of Liberation* (Philadelphia: J. B. Lippincott, 1970), 122.
56. Pinnock, *Flame of Love*, 74.
57. Pinnock, *Flame of Love*, 113.
58. LaCugna, *God for Us*, 362.
59. Augustine, "Homilies of 1 Jn. 7.8," in *Augustine: Later Works*, ed. John Burnaby (Philadelphia: Westminster, 1955), 316.

by alcohol—that's the broad way that leads to destruction in this lifetime—but be filled and controlled by the Holy Spirit, which leads to the narrow way of fruitful living now. He says this so we will actively serve God in Christ through the power of the Holy Spirit and work in partnership with the Father, Son, and Spirit in the quest to transform the world for God's glory as we work toward justice, peace, and reconciliation between enemies.

Because the indwelling of the Spirit recreates believers in the righteousness of Christ (Rom 5:19), our lives should reflect the character, attitudes, and behavior of God in Christ as we serve God by serving the world.[60] In actuality, as we serve in the power of the Spirit, we participate in the Son's obedience to the Father; all of our service reflects the literal working of Jesus in us—our activity is Jesus's activity in the world.[61]

Fortunately, according to Paul, the Holy Spirit provides the means so we can be "filled with the knowledge of God's will in all spiritual wisdom and understanding, so that [we] may lead lives worthy of the Lord, fully pleasing to him, as [we] bear fruit in every good work" (Col 1:9–10). That we may live a life pleasing to God, Paul urges us to "live by the Spirit . . . and [to] not gratify the desires of the flesh" (Gal 5:16). Interestingly, Paul wrote this passage in the context of love. Through the Spirit of God, we can best serve God by loving others as God loves them—which might be why Galatians lists love as the first-fruit of the Spirit and 1 Corinthians exhorts us to exercise all the gifts of Spirit with love. When we love others, we love and serve God (Gal 5:22; 1 Cor 13).

Black theologian James Cone articulates the major priority that motivates us in doing the work of the Father, in the name of Christ, by the power of the Spirit. He insists that "the Holy Spirit is the Spirit of the Father and the Son at work in the forces of human liberation in our society today."[62] Since Jesus made oppression, marginalization, and discrimination his own by becoming human, we too should serve God by making the oppressed condition our concern, by living alongside those who suffer and encountering poverty, abuse, and oppression with them. People of God can stand in solidarity with "the least of these" (Matt 25:40) by imitating Jesus in feeding the hungry, clothing the poor, and liberating the oppressed with our time, energy, money, and votes. We do God's work by caring for communities, longing for justice, caring for the sick, and making peace, not war. And we know that wherever peace reigns, wherever harmony unites hearts and minds, wherever forgiveness and generosity flourish, wherever people love one another, there presides the Spirit of God in Jesus Christ.

---

60. Fee, *God's Empowering Presence*, 877.
61. Schleiermacher, *The Christian Faith*, 1567–69; Pinnock, *Flame of Love*, 97–98.
62. Cone, *Black Theology of Liberation*, 122.

The Spirit Makes Peace, Not War:
Nonviolent Love and the Holy Spirit

Finally, the Holy Spirit reveals to us the character and nature of God as a God of peace. In the Trinitarian life there is no room for violence; therefore, the same is true in the life of God's Spirit-filled people. As the third person in the Trinitarian dance of love, the Holy Spirit functions as the divine bond of love. That love, emptied out into human form, was conceived and born as Jesus of Nazareth, the Son of God. Zechariah prophesies about Jesus, pronouncing that he will "guide our feet into the way of peace" (Luke 1:79). And the angels sing at Jesus's birth, proclaiming that he will bring peace on earth and goodwill among people (Luke 2:14). Before his death, Jesus promised his disciples that he would send us the Holy Spirit as his presence on earth, saying, "Peace I leave with you; my peace I give to you" (John 14:27). These prophecies and proclamations continue to work as God's Holy Spirit leads us perpetually on the path of peace, negating the violence of the world.

In addition, "the fruit of the Spirit is love, joy, *peace* . . ." (Gal 5:22), indicating that the Spirit of God instills the divine quality of peace within all who follow Jesus. Peter exhorts us to "turn away from evil and do good; . . . seek peace and pursue it" (1 Pet 3:11). We are the people of God who "let the peace of Christ rule in [our] hearts, to which indeed [we] were called in the one body" (Col 3:15). Benedictive phrases that call on "the God of peace" to be with us, sanctify us, and make us complete grace the pages of the New Testament several times (Phil 4:7, 9; 1 Thess 5:23; Heb 13:20). Who is with us always? Who sanctifies us? Who makes us complete? The Holy Spirit—the Spirit of peace. The Spirit brings peace between humanity and God and works to make peace between people previously separated by peace-prohibitive boundaries (Eph 4:3).

So that we may serve as peacemakers in the world, "God's love has been poured into our hearts through the Holy Spirit that has been given to us" (Rom 5:5). We therefore have the power to set our minds on the Spirit, who brings us life and peace, rather than on the flesh that brings violence, chaos, and death (1 Cor 14:33; Rom 8:6). The Spirit hurts as we do and struggles with us against the powers of darkness that desecrate and devastate the world. We rejoice because we receive the Spirit as "a beloved guest in our hearts" who turned chaos into cosmos at creation, who continues to bring life out of death, who impregnates the world with peace, working patiently for the birth of God's kingdom in every place where people suffer, where violence reigns, and where poverty persists.[63]

Thankfully, the Holy Spirit is not confined to the walls of the church but, like wind, blows everywhere, pouring the love of God into the dark, abysmal, peace-less corners of existence, bringing peace, working for justice, and creating harmony

---

63. Pinnock, *Flame of Love*, 78.

among all people.[64] The Spirit knows no boundaries, brooks no prejudices, and drives out no differences. Instead, the Holy Spirit overcomes these divisions and barriers among people with the peace that only Spirit-led transformation can accomplish, creating and reconciling a world where there no longer exists Jew or Greek, male or female, free or slave, straight or gay, rich or poor, black or white—and, most significantly, where there is no longer violence or war (Gal 3:28; Col 3:11; Acts 10:34–35). Violence has no purchase in a kingdom created by God, ruled by Christ, and set apart by the Holy Spirit, because violence does not exist in the character and nature of the triune God. Through the work of the Spirit of the nonviolent, loving God, justice and shalom prevail, and renewal and love triumph over the meaninglessness of violence. Paul Tillich reminds us that "when for us the Spirit is present, desire is transformed into love and will to power into justice," and justice is born when peace rules. Love and peace are fruits of the Spirit, and when we listen to the still, small voice of God's Spirit, we will act in love and strive for justice, harmony, and peace in the world.[65]

---

64. Migliore, *Faith Seeking Understanding*, 234.
65. Tillich, *The Shaking of the Foundations*, 136.

9. The Church

. . . the holy catholic church, the communion of saints . . .

> The True Church can never fail / for it is based upon a rock.
>
> > —T. S. Eliot, "The Hippopotamus"

> The kingdom of God is not going to be defined by people filling churches, but by people in our churches being filled with God.
>
> > —Howard Spring

The New Testament refers to the new community of believers who gathered together to worship God through Christ in the power of the Holy Spirit as the *ecclesia*. The word derives from the Greek *kaleo* ("to call") and *ek* ("out of")—meaning an assembly or congregation "called out" to meet together for a specific purpose. The word *church* comes from the Greek word *kurios*, meaning "Lord" or "master," which developed further into the word *kuriakon*, or "Lord's house."

While we commonly use *church* to describe a building where Christians meet to worship, it more powerfully indicates a diverse body of people called "the body of Christ," who love God and others and who serve God by serving the world for God's glory. In other words, the church serves as the incarnation of Jesus Christ on earth, living as Jesus lived, loving as Jesus loved, preaching and teaching as Jesus taught and preached. So if the world sees a body of Christians in action, the world is seeing Jesus Christ. Medieval mystic St. Teresa of Ávila beautifully describes this earthly incarnation:

> Christ has no body but yours. No hands, no feet on earth but yours. Yours are the eyes through which he looks on this world. Yours are the feet with which he walks to do good. Yours are the hands through which he blesses all the world. Yours are the hands, yours are the feet, yours are the eyes, you are his body. Christ has no body now on earth but yours.[1]

This body of Christ takes many forms and includes people from diverse cultures, races, economic strata, and educational levels. Just as God ordained diversity in creation, God ordained diversity in the church. Everyone is invited, and everyone is welcome in this kingdom of God made visible on earth. This view of the church may seem idealistic given the Christian history of such things as crusades, inquisitions,

---

1. This saying is attributed to St. Teresa, but the source is unknown.

and exclusive doctrines that reject and judge others. Nonetheless, we see in Scripture that God calls us to participate in the kingdom of God through our presence in the church, with one faith, as one body, empowered by one Spirit, serving others in love with extravagant grace and hospitality (Rom 12:4–5; 1 Cor 12:27; Eph 4:1–6).

The Church and Its Sacraments

Images of the Church in the New Testament

The New Testament describes the church in over ninety different ways, using images and metaphors from family, biology, chemistry, architecture, agriculture, geography, temple, and civic life. For example, the church is portrayed as the body of Christ (1 Cor 12:27); the bride of Christ (Rev 21:9); the salt of the earth (Matt 5:13); a building on a rock (Matt 16:18); fishers for people (Mark 1:17); the temple of God (1 Cor 3:16); the household of God (Eph 2:19), God's own people, a royal priesthood, and a chosen race (1 Pet 2:9); strangers and foreigners (Heb 11:13); a new Jerusalem (Rev 21:2); and much more. We also see in the New Testament that God binds us to God as servants (Eph 6:6); calls us to act with graciousness, mercy, compassion, patience, peace, and love (Col 3:12–14); exhorts us to forgive freely (Matt 18:21–22); commands us to tear down the boundaries that typically separate and divide people and to preserve unity in the bond of peace (Gal 3:28; Eph 4:3); and asks us to love one another unconditionally (John 13:35; 1 John 4:11). Whereas God once dwelt in a temple made with human hands, through Christ God now dwells in a temple created with the blood (life) of Christ and with the power of the Holy Spirit, not a building but a fellowship of God's people.[2] We, as the church, serve as God's ministers of reconciliation, ambassadors for Christ, entreating those with whom we come in contact to receive divine forgiveness and healing and to be reconciled to God (2 Cor 5:18, 20).

Marks of the Church

Theologians typically talk about the church as a place "marked" by love, forgiveness, reconciliation, unity, and peace. The Apostles' Creed, however, names two other general marks of the church: *holy* and *catholic*. The Nicene Creed adds two additional marks to this short list: *one* and *apostolic*. First, the church is *holy*. This means God has set the church apart throughout history to accomplish God's purposes in the world in the name of Christ and by the power of the Holy Spirit. God sets apart the members of the body of Christ on earth to glorify God and to

---

2. Stanley J. Grenz, *Theology for the Community of God* (Grand Rapids, MI: Eerdmans, 2000), 467.

spread the good news of forgiveness of sin and reconciliation with God, as well as to communicate the hope of the future when God will be all in all.[3]

Second, the church is *catholic*. That means the church exists universally across all borders. It transcends all languages, cultures, races, nationalities, and economic levels. It extends across time and includes all followers of Jesus throughout all of history until the end of time. God has called out one universally united church and set it to work in diverse ways. This diversity in no way hinders the catholicity or universality, which leads us to the third mark: the church is *one*. Ephesians describes the church as "one body and one Spirit," with one calling, as well as "one Lord, one faith, one baptism, one God and Father of all" (4:4-6). The word "one" sticks out in these verses, communicating that even though many denominations dot the landscape of what we call "church," every single church is united with the others in the one body of Christ on earth, living and moving and having our being in one God, for one purpose, in one accord (at least theoretically!).[4]

Fourth, the church is *apostolic*. In other words, we continue the faith of the apostles, and the church reflects the beliefs of these earliest Christians. We see this reflection in the construction and use of the Apostles' Creed, which expresses the theology of the apostles of Jesus Christ. Apostolicity finds expression in various ways within the church. For followers of Jesus in the time of the early church fathers, bishops served in direct connection to the apostles as successors of them. Today "apostolic succession" describes the notion of bishops carrying on the apostles' teachings. Of course, for the Roman Catholic Church the pope (the bishop of Rome) leads that succession as the direct inheritor of the seat of the apostle Peter, in whom Jesus entrusted the church in Matthew 16:18—"You are Peter, and on this rock I will build my church."[5] Some Protestant denominations also accept a strong notion of apostolic succession, however, without holding to the primacy of the bishop of Rome. In any event, with Jesus's proclamation of apostolic succession, Scripture includes the act of preaching, or proclamation, as central to the church's mission.[6]

Proclamation

As representative of the kingdom of God, as the incarnated body of Christ on earth, the church has a responsibility to proclaim the revelation of God, through Christ, in the power of the Holy Spirit to a world sorely in need of the good news that brings hope, joy, and love. According to Karl Barth, the proclamation of the church, spoken by people guided by Scripture, must always "make the promise [of

---

3. Daniel Migliore, *Faith Seeking Understanding* (Grand Rapids, MI: Eerdmans, 2004), 271; Roger E. Olson, *The Mosaic of Christian Belief: Twenty Centuries of Unity and Disunity* (Downers Grove, IL: InterVarsity, 2016), 295.
4. Migliore, *Faith Seeking Understanding*, 271–72; Olson, *Mosaic of Christian Belief*, 290, 295.
5. Richard J. Plantinga, Thomas R. Thompson, and Matthew D. Lundberg, *An Introduction to Christian Theology* (Cambridge: Cambridge University Press, 2010), 347.
6. Don Thorsen, *An Exploration of Christian Theology* (Grand Rapids, MI: Baker Academic, 2008), 321.

God] given to the church intelligible . . . to the [community of people] in [our] own time."[7] The proclamation of the church consistently reminds us that God promises God's constant presence, the divine "I will be with you," as both a present and a future reality. It also continually reminds us that God's presence both *with* us and *in* us results directly from the life, death, and resurrection of Jesus, which ensure the forgiveness of sin and liberation from the spiritual ignorance that enables sin's hold on us. Accordingly, with words gleaned from Scripture and through lives lived as "little Christs,"[8] we proclaim God's promises and purposes to those who have ears to hear and eyes to see. This incarnational life of the church begins with the good news of God's promise of forgiveness and healing, both divine and human. Through forgiveness and acts of healing, we make manifest the love of God, reveal the heart of God, and start a chain reaction of love that can grow and spread to affect the whole world for God's glory.

Not only does the church have the responsibility to proclaim the gospel of love, healing, and forgiveness through Jesus Christ, but theologian James Cone exhorts us also to proclaim "the reality of divine liberation . . . to be out there in the world, not as an endorser of its oppressions but as the visible representative" of the Lordship of Christ, who sets captives free with truth, justice, and peace.[9] We proclaim God's presence with all creation, working to reconcile enemies, end violence, and usher in the divine kingdom of peace through the empowering of the Holy Spirit.[10] In doing so, the church works with God to establish "one new humanity" (Eph 2:15), a newly reconciled people who have overcome our estrangement and alienation from God and one another and now have the potential to live in the glow of healed relationships and just societies in harmony and peace. Thus, the proclamation and enactment of divine forgiveness and healing by the church have not only personal but also social and political implications, challenging and transforming the status quo. Both an inner personal liberation and a collective social liberation result from the proclamation of the good news in Christ.

Sacraments

The sacraments of the church remain one of the ways the church visibly apprehends, or signals, divine grace. The sacraments and their meanings differ across denominational traditions, but first, we need to discuss the meaning of the term

---

7. Karl Barth, *Church Dogmatics*, vol. 1.1, ed. Geoffrey W. Bromiley and Thomas F. Torrance (Edinburgh: T & T Clark, 1956), 59.
8. Although Martin Luther often mentioned Christians as being Christ to the world, C. S. Lewis picked up on this notion and applied the term "little Christs" to followers of Jesus. For him, all Christians should live as Jesus lived, loving others and serving God through their actions. All Christians should be able to say with Paul, "It is no longer I who live, but it is Christ who lives in me" (Gal 2:20). See C. S. Lewis, *Mere Christianity*, in *The C. S. Lewis Signature Classics: An Anthology* (New York: HarperOne, 2017), 144, 155, 159.
9. James H. Cone, *Black Theology of Liberation* (Philadelphia: J. B. Lippincott, 1970), 230, 237.
10. Barth, *Church Dogmatics*, vol. 1.1, 59.

sacrament. Church father Tertullian (ca. 155–ca. 240) translated the Greek word *musterion*, which means "mystery," into Latin as *sacramentum*, which found its way into Jerome's early Latin Vulgate (the Latin translation of the Bible). For the rest of Christian history, it has served as the label we apply to sacraments of the church. The term itself means "to consecrate" or "to set apart," and refers to the rites that the church sets apart to make visible the presence and purpose of God in Christ. St. Augustine says that sacraments are "visible signs of an invisible grace," although, as we will see, for many denominations the rites accomplish more in the life of the Christ-follower than merely serving as signs; they actually function as objective rituals that bestow grace.[11] But for the church as a whole, the sacraments "are palpable enactments of the gospel by means of which the Spirit of God confirms to us the forgiving, renewing, and promising love of God in Jesus Christ and enlivens us in faith, hope, and love."[12] So, what are these sacraments, what do they symbolize, and how do they administer grace?

The early church, for the first twelve hundred years, performed various rituals to enact the meaningful symbols and the grace of God. But by the thirteenth century the Roman Catholic and Greek Orthodox churches practiced seven sacraments: baptism, confirmation, Eucharist, penance (reconciliation), ordination (holy orders), marriage, and anointing of the sick (or last rites). These believers emphasized the "objective reality" of the sacraments, such that when properly administered, they effectively extend and instill the grace needed for salvation. In the sixteenth century, believing the church should only practice the sacraments instituted by Jesus himself in Scripture, the Protestant Reformers significantly reduced the number to two: baptism and the Eucharist (or the Lord's Supper).[13] Some denominational traditions that arose from the split between Roman Catholicism and Protestantism still held to more objective beliefs surrounding baptism and the Lord's Supper, while others moved toward a more symbolic interpretation of these two sacraments.

Baptism. The sacrament of baptism is considered the "initiation" into the life of the church and the beginning of the journey of becoming like Christ.[14] All church traditions recognize that Jesus not only commands the rite of baptism for those embarking on the Christian life, but also submitted to baptism himself (Matt 3:13–17; 28:19–20; Mark 1:9–11; Luke 3:21–22; John 1:29–34). The beautiful imagery of dying and rising with Christ accompanies the sacrament of baptism (Rom 6:3–4). The sprinkling with or immersion in water reenacts dying with Christ, the cleansing from sin, and the death of the old, sinful person. Rising up out of the water corresponds

---

11. Augustine, "To Boniface: Homily on Common Prayer and Sacraments," *Short-Title Catalogue* 13675, Renaissance Electronic Texts 1.1, ed. Ian Lancashire (Toronto: University of Toronto, 1994). In this context, the "sign" points us toward the body and blood of Jesus. The "symbol" stands in the place of the reality of the body and blood of Jesus and helps us participate in that reality.
12. Migliore, *Faith Seeking Understanding*, 271; Olson, *Mosaic of Christian Belief*, 280.
13. Migliore, *Faith Seeking Understanding*, 280–81.
14. Migliore, *Faith Seeking Understanding*, 283.

to rising with Christ to a renewed, resurrected life as a follower of Jesus. Baptism also illustrates the rebirth through the Holy Spirit and the incorporation of the person into the body of Christ, the church.

Channeling St. Augustine and the Nicene-Constantinopolitan Creed, respectively, the Roman Catholic and Eastern Orthodox churches view baptism as a means of securing grace that actually washes away the taint of original sin (more about this in the next chapter). Anglican, Lutheran, and some Methodist churches, as well as Churches of Christ, refer to baptism as more than a merely symbolic act and believe in addition that through this sacrament, the Spirit of God begins the process of transforming the individual into Christ-likeness. Christians in other Protestant traditions, such as Baptist, Anabaptist, Presbyterian, and many Pentecostal churches, practice baptism as a symbol for dying with Christ through the descent into the water and rising with Christ through the ascent out of the water. For them, baptism serves as an outward symbol of an inward reality of faith. In all cases, however, Christians perform the sacrament of baptism into the body of Christ in the name of the Father, the Son, and the Holy Spirit in obedience to the command of Jesus and as an expression of faith, a promise of love, and the expectation of a future hope.

Eucharist. Second, the church universally observes the sacrament of the Eucharist (meaning "thanksgiving"), also called the Lord's Supper or communion.[15] Jesus instructed the disciples on the practice of the Eucharist with his words at the Last Supper in the upper room, which he shared with his disciples just before his betrayal. He took the bread, gave thanks, and said, "Take, eat; this is my body." Then Jesus took the cup, gave thanks, and said, "Drink from it, all of you; for this is my blood of the covenant, which is poured out for many for the forgiveness of sins. I tell you, I will never again drink of this fruit of the vine until that day when I drink it new with you in my Father's kingdom" (Matt 26:26–29). Paul adds to those words and tells us that Jesus directs Christians to partake of the Lord's Supper in remembrance of Jesus and that, by doing so, we "proclaim the Lord's death until he comes" (1 Cor 11:23–26). The sacrament of the Eucharist, therefore, provides us with a profound image of the work of Jesus, allowing us to remember his salvific accomplishments on our behalf as we eat the bread and drink the wine or grape juice, commonly referred to as the "elements." In partaking of the elements, we remember the crucifixion of Jesus and its effects for Christians in the present, while looking ahead to the future fulfillment of the promises of Christ to forgive, reconcile, and restore us to God for all eternity. The Eucharist therefore serves as a means of grace.

15. There are a few exceptions to this, most notably in the Quaker and Salvation Army traditions. Quakers do not celebrate any sacraments, including the Eucharist. They believe these practices distract from the focus on God. The Salvation Army contends that the meaning of the Eucharist has caused divisions in the church.

The church, however, disagrees about how the sacrament disperses that grace and how it affects our standing before God. The Roman Catholic and Eastern Orthodox traditions believe in *transubstantiation*, affirming a corporeal presence of Christ with the bread and the wine turning into the actual body and blood of Jesus. *Trans* means "across" and *substantia* means "substance," so the substances of the bread and wine are transferred, or cross over, into the actual substance of the body and blood of Jesus. The "accidents," or physical appearance, of the bread and wine stay the same so that the elements maintain the appearance of bread and wine. For Christians in these traditions, partaking of the body and blood of Jesus literally infuses the believer with the grace of salvation, over and over again, every time they celebrate the Eucharist. So, baptism washes away original sin and initiates the cleansed believer into the kingdom of God, and the Eucharist maintains the salvific effects of Jesus's death and resurrection with the infusion of grace.[16]

Protestant churches in the Lutheran and Anglican traditions hold to the doctrine of *consubstantiation* when celebrating the Eucharist. Put simply, *con* means "with" and *substantia* means "substance." These denominations believe the body and blood of Jesus exist alongside, or "in, with, and under," the bread and the wine.[17] In addition to Lutherans and Anglicans, other Protestant traditions, such as Reformed, Presbyterian, and Methodist churches, believe in the *real presence* of Christ in the bread and the wine. These groups believe the elements are more than mere "signs" and serve as the conduit for strengthening the faith of those who partake. They are true symbols, in the sense that a symbol participates in the reality it describes. The bread and wine, therefore, convey the real spiritual body and blood of Christ to those who partake of the elements. In these traditions, the presence of Christ infuses the entire eucharistic celebration and unites believers to Christ, through the power of the Holy Spirit, for the upbuilding of faith and Christian community.[18] Calvin explains his view on the Eucharist, saying that the entire sacrament surpasses his ability to understand completely, but he does know that "in his sacred supper [Christ] bids me take, eat, and drink his body and blood under the symbols of bread and wine. I do not doubt that he himself truly presents them, and I receive them." Calvin asserts that the presence of Christ in the Eucharist "manifests itself . . . with a power and effectiveness so great that it not only brings undoubted assurance of eternal life . . . but also assures us of the immortality of our flesh."[19] In this view, the presence of Christ's body and blood infuses the bread and wine, giving a stronger faith that the promises of God to forgive, redeem, and restore, revealed in the cross of Christ, will find fulfillment now and in the future.

16. Olson, *Mosaic of Christian Belief*, 300–1.
17. Olson, *Mosaic of Christian Belief*, 301.
18. Migliore, *Faith Seeking Understanding*, 290; Olson, *Mosaic of Christian Belief*, 301.
19. John Calvin, *Institutes of the Christian Religion*, ed. John T. McNeill, trans. Ford Lewis Battles (Louisville, KY: Westminster John Knox, 1960), 4.17.32.

Other Christian traditions, such as Baptist, Anabaptist, and some nondenominational churches, follow the thought of the more radical Swiss Reformer Zwingli, and interpret the Eucharist as a sign or a memorial during which believers remember the life, death, and resurrection of Jesus in the present time and look forward to the future fulfillment of God's salvific promises. In these traditions, celebrating baptism and partaking of the Eucharist remind Christians of their commitment to follow God through Christ, in the power of the Spirit. The sacraments essentially retell the story of Jesus and his saving work, reminding people of their own participation in the life of Christ and their identity as Christians.

In every tradition, celebrating the Eucharist reminds followers of Jesus that they now live Christ's life (Gal 2:20) and have the help of Christ's Spirit to fulfill their responsibility to make manifest the kingdom of God on earth and to transform the world for God's glory. And, significantly, Richard Rohr reminds us that when we partake of the bread/body and wine/blood of Jesus, we announce our solidarity with every person whose blood has been unjustly shed on earth: "In the act of drinking the blood of Christ at this Holy Meal," Rohr says, "we are consciously uniting with all unjust suffering in the world, from the beginning of time till its end. Wherever there was and is suffering, there is the empathy and healing justice of God—and we are joining with God insofar as we can."[20] Participating in the body and blood of Jesus, in whichever way our tradition interprets it, empowers Christians and reminds us to walk in Jesus's steps, to live his life doing justice with mercy. It helps us remember we are now members of a different kingdom, one in which we live a new and transformed life, proclaiming in word and deed the kingdom promise of forgiveness, justice, peace, and love, now and forever.

The New Marks of the Church: The Visible, Nonviolent, Loving Manifestation of the Kingdom of God on Earth

Now that we have discussed the traditional marks of the church and the sacraments, we need to understand exactly what sort of community we belong to and how it works in the world. The New Testament articulates the realm of the kingdom of God, in which Christians reside, and over which Jesus Christ rules (1 Cor 3:11; Eph 2:19–22; 4:15). As the body of Christ here on earth, we rule in this kingdom *with* Christ, *as* Christ, and *for* Christ. So even though the church is not the kingdom itself, through ruling with Jesus, the church manifests the kingdom of God on earth. "The church . . . is called forth by the proclamation of the kingdom of God," says theologian Stanley Grenz. "It is the *product* of the kingdom, produced by the obedient response to the announcement of the divine reign."[21] In living in

20. Richard Rohr, *The Universal Christ: How a Forgotten Reality Can Change Everything We See, Hope For, and Believe* (New York: Convergent, 2019), 134–35.
21. Grenz, *Theology for the Community of God*, 465; Perry B. Yoder, *Shalom: The Bible's Word for Salvation, Justice, and Peace* (Nappanee, IN: Evangel, 1987), 478.

obedience to God, the church continues the movement that Jesus started when he called his first disciples to follow him. As contemporary disciples of Christ, we serve in that same line of succession and work to model the life of Jesus in the kingdom of God.[22]

What is the kingdom of God, and what does that mean for its members? The New Testament describes the kingdom as a present reality, as God's kingdom on earth (Matt 11:2–6; Mark 1:14–15; Luke 4:21; 17:20), in which Satan is defeated and Jesus Christ is victorious (Matt 12:28–29; Luke 10:9, 18, 20; 1 Cor 15:57; Col 2:15). Because of this, followers of Jesus live and serve in a community where anger is overcome with reconciliation (Matt 5:21–26); lust is kept under discipline (Matt 5:27–30); marriage is honored through lifelong fidelity (Matt 5:31–32); language is simple and honest (Matt 5:33–37); retaliation is renounced (Matt 5:38–42); and love replaces hate (Matt 5:43–48). Most importantly, however, Christians participating in the kingdom of God function as nonviolent peacemakers (Matt 5:9, 38–48; 7:12).[23] This kingdom behavior points us not only toward some utopian future but also to a present time. In the kingdom, God creates a new way of living life, and therefore, we follow the kingdom teachings of Jesus now as members of his body who are filled with God's Spirit.

Although Jesus calls us into the kingdom of God for this present time, Jesus also describes the kingdom as a future reality, an almost-but-not-yet realm that will find fulfillment at the end of time as we know it (Luke 21:31). As members of God's heavenly kingdom, we look forward to a hope for a future in which God will wipe away every tear, eliminate mourning and pain, and dwell among us (Rev 21:3–4). In the meantime, however, "we see in a mirror, dimly, but then we will see face to face"; right now we "know only in part," but then we "will know fully" (1 Cor 13:12). Even so, "faith, hope, and love abide" *with* us, *in* us, and *for* us, but love is the greatest of all (1 Cor 13:13). For now, God calls us into the kingdom of God to reveal the extravagance of divine love to all the world through our love and compassion for others (John 13:35).

Given the new kind of life God calls Christians to live, the church should mark itself out in unique ways in the world. So, although we have previously discussed the traditional marks of the church, and those marks still articulate the characteristics of the church, we need also to emphasize a few other, new "marks" of the church that relate directly to Christian behavior as peacemakers and lovers of others—even of enemies.

---

22. Grenz, *Theology for the Community of God*, 465; Yoder, *Shalom*, 136.
23. Richard B. Hays, *The Moral Vision of the New Testament: Community, Cross, New Creation; A Contemporary Introduction to New Testament Ethics* (San Francisco: HarperSanFrancisco, 1996), 321. See also Eric A. Seibert, *Disarming the Church: Why Christians Must Forsake Violence to Follow Jesus and Change the World* (Eugene, OR: Cascade, 2018), 64.

The Kingdom Calls

Just as the divine word calls things into existence in the first act of creation in Genesis 1, the divine word keeps on calling forth new creations, re-created human beings, to new life. The divine call issues from the creation story in which God's act of calling the new life of creation into being out of the chaos echoes continually throughout history. In the midst of death and disorder, God calls for the re-creation of life and order, of goodness and shalom, rather than hatred and evil. God calls from across an infinite distance to affirm and reaffirm the good creation and new life.

As we discussed in chapter 5, "Creation," God has never finished the act of creating, but keeps in play the ongoing process of recreation. God continually says "yes" to life and the creation of new life, justice, and peace, keeping the future open to the possibility of a good new creation in which Jesus Christ rules. God recurrently calls us with the paradoxically yielding force of love, soliciting us, inviting us to take part in the kingdom, in the continual act of creating new life as we work with God to transform lives and the world in the name of Jesus.

The kingdom call claims us unconditionally in an appeal not from a coercive power and authority, but from God, who lovingly advocates for new birth, for something unexpected to happen amid chaos, for an event that interrupts the status quo with the transformative power of God. The kingdom of God calls us out of the world that is already there, just as God called a new creation out of the elements swirling chaotically in the deep and called it "good" (Gen 1).[24] We have the responsibility to heed the call of God, reckon with it, and respond to it. God calls, and in response, like Isaiah, we open ourselves to God and answer, "Here am I; send me" (Isa 6:8). By making ourselves available to God we become partakers of a new life in Christ who seek to further the kingdom of God through reconciling love and forgiveness.

A Kingdom Where "Weakness" Rules

Theologian and philosopher John D. Caputo talks about the divine kingdom in terms of "weakness." He fashions his conceptions of the kingdom of God according to the Pauline passage in 1 Corinthians 1:25, 27–28, where the apostle Paul characterizes the kingdom of God as one of "great reversals" in which the wisdom of the world is foolishness and the foolishness of God is wisdom. Paul reverses the common structures of worldly power, in which the rich and powerful rule the less fortunate through coercion and violence, in favor of the kingdom of God, in which the cultural nobodies, the lowly poor, and the oppressed unprivileged rule alongside

24. John D. Caputo, *The Weakness of God* (Bloomington: Indiana University Press, 2006), 15, 37, 53–86, 105. For a profound treatment of God creating the universe from out of the deep, the *tehom*, see Catherine Keller, *Face of the Deep: A Theology of Becoming* (London: Routledge, 2003).

Christ in love. Whereas the world's powers demand that we act like adults, the kingdom requests we come as children. Whereas the world's justice punishes sin, the kingdom's justice forgives and heals it. Whereas the world builds its wealth on the backs of the underprivileged, the kingdom promises the wealth and riches of Christ and advocates for a community that works together for the wealth and good of all.[25] In the kingdom, where our weakness results in the power of love, God rolls out the red carpet for the disenfranchised, the weak, the poor, and the oppressed, giving them the royal treatment, a welcome worthy of kings. In the kingdom, God creates something out of nothing; God takes people the world thinks nothing of and makes them something by giving them an inheritance that will last forever.[26] These little ones proclaim the possibility of what, in the world, seems impossible—the (im)possibility of the "weak" power of divine love to melt hardened hearts, to forgive the unforgivable, to love the unlovable, to breathe new life into the dead, to "revive the spirits of the dispirited," and to offer peace in a world at war.[27]

Although some Christians may feel uncomfortable talking about a "weak" God, as the apostle Paul teaches, the weakness of God as love and forgiveness merely *seems* like weakness to a world bent on the view of coercion and force as "strong" power. Force pushes its agenda with such things as guns in hand and the threat of bombs from the air. But in truth, the weak power of God is a strong power for redemption, reconciliation, and restoration, for peace and justice that do away with the need for the world's "strong" power through the gentle power of divine love. So, the "weak" power of love actually serves as the strongest power we can know. As people empowered by the divine Spirit, we can say with Paul, "Whenever I am weak [with the divine power of love], then I am strong [with the power to transform the world through the love of God in Christ]" (2 Cor 12:10).

Theology of weakness finds its strength in the theology of the cross. The kingdom of God is a kingdom of the crucified Christ who, in his abandonment to horrendous suffering, utters a prayer for the forgiveness of his persecutors. The incarnated Christ embodies the "weak" force of divine love. Christians embody the Spirit of Christ, live according to the weak power of the cross, and stand with Jesus in his protest against violence and injustice by reversing the world's ideas of power—loving rather than hating, forgiving rather than condemning, welcoming rather than rejecting, allowing justice and peace to flow like water over the land.[28]

---

25. Caputo, *Weakness of God*, 12.
26. Caputo, *Weakness of God*, 23–40. Cf. René Girard, *I See Satan Fall Like Lightning*, trans. James G. Williams (Maryknoll, NY: Orbis, 2001), 14. See also René Girard, *Things Hidden Since the Foundation of the World*, trans. Stephen Bann (Stanford, CA: Stanford University Press, 1987), 197–98.
27. Caputo, *Weakness of God*, 14–17.
28. Caputo, *Weakness of God*, 42–54.

Transformation

The call of God begins with a call for transformation, not a physical transformation from this earthly body to some heavenly, ephemeral, wispy existence, but with the practical "*transformability of our lives* . . . in which we and all things are made new."[29] God creates in us a new mind and a new heart. God calls us to a newness of life that hearkens back to Genesis 1 and God's call to the unformed chaos "to be" light, and stars, and plants, and animals, and human beings. This divine call triggers an astounding transformation that forever changes the face of the earth, one that re-creates the chaos into something ordered and new. The same type of creative event occurs every time a person answers God's call to follow Jesus and take up residence in the kingdom of God. And we are all called to participate in this amazing transformation.[30] The kingdom of God is the open space "in which the relationship with the world and with others" is played out. In the kingdom, the relationship with the other is released from the confines of the world's values and obsession with power and becomes instead a relationship ruled by the kingdom ethics of love.[31] In the kingdom of God, the only law is the transformative law of love.

Gift-Giving

The kingdom of God hinges upon the gift of unconditional love—that is, upon love that gives service to others without the meeting of any prior condition on the part of the beloved. In the kingdom of God, gifts of love rule rather than duty to laws.[32] In fact, Jesus revealed the precedence of love over law by continually shocking his disciples and other listeners with his so-called defiance of the law when he healed the sick on the Sabbath, when he turned his back on the religious leaders in favor of healing lepers, and when he, with his disciples, plucked grain on the Sabbath because they were hungry. Whether giving the gift of healing or forgiveness or food or release from psychological torment, Jesus shocks the powers of the world with the kingdom rule of gift-giving (Matt 12:1-8, 9-13; John 9:1-25).[33] Likewise, when we give a gift, when we give *more* than duty requires, more than ethics dictates, more than self-interest permits and do not expect a payback, we give the way

29. Caputo, *Weakness of God*, 206; Abelard, "Epistle to the Romans," in Eugene R. Fairweather, A *Scholastic Miscellany: Anselm to Okcham* (Philadelphia: Westminster, 1954), 283.
30. B. Keith Putt, "What Do I Love When I Love My God? An Interview with John D. Caputo," in *Religion with/out Religion: The Prayers and Tears of John D. Caputo*, ed. James Olthuis (New York: Routledge, 2002), 170–71.
31. John D. Caputo, *Prayers and Tears of Jacques Derrida: Religion without Religion* (Bloomington: Indiana University Press, 1997), 228–29.
32. John D. Caputo, *More Radical Hermeneutics: On Not Knowing Who We Are* (Bloomington: Indiana University Press, 2000), 187, 185–86.
33. B. Keith Putt, "Faith, Hope, and Love: Radical Hermeneutics as a Pauline Philosophy of Religion," in *A Passion for the Impossible: John D. Caputo in Focus*, ed. Mark Dooley (Albany: SUNY Press, 2003), 247; "What Do I Love," 167. Anthony Bartlett, *Cross Purposes* (Norcross, GA: Trinity Press International, 2001), 242–45, 250–51, 256.

Jesus gave. We give as incarnations of the body of Christ in the kingdom of God. Gift-giving in the kingdom of God, therefore, marks the divine excess of love and grace, a mark that contradicts our own narcissistic human tendencies.

A human example of gift-giving that totally surprises onlookers is that of the widow giving her small gift of a "mite." In Jesus's parable, she had nothing much to her name; she did not give from an abundance but from her poverty. Her gift cost her something; it was a real sacrifice. By giving sacrificially and unconditionally, she shatters "the horizon of expectation" with an event that breaks through time and expresses the madness of kingdom giving (Luke 21:1–4).[34] In the heavenly kingdom on earth, God suspends every tit-for-tat economy, every transactional sense of justice and love, by giving the gifts of unconditional love and selfless service through the incarnation of Christ—God in flesh. And as members of the divine kingdom, we work with God to give selflessly, to love selflessly, and to manifest to one another and to the world God's rule—the rule of love and justice, not of condemnation and law. The kingdom of God is where the gift of love rules.[35] This is the new law we are called by God to follow.

Forgiveness

We cannot separate forgiveness from the act of kingdom gift-giving. The Jewish notion of sin portrays a picture of shackles, something that binds us or paralyzes us in bondage to a debt. Forgiveness of sin means "to release," to break the shackles of sin, much like a person who is sick is healed and released from illness. In English, the word *forgive* means "to give away" or "to release" something we have against someone else. We give away the debt, release them from the debt we have a right to collect. In the same way, God releases us through forgiveness. For example, when Jesus told the paralyzed man who was lowered through the roof that his sins were forgiven, he meant that the man was healthy again and no longer held down or impaired with the shackles into which that sin had locked him (Mark 2:1–12). Jesus was a healer of both souls and bodies. By his potent form of forgiving, giving away the debt of sin and not collecting the payment, he shocked and scandalized those intent on payback for the debt of sin and who do not want to let sinners "take a walk." Jesus offers this radical teaching to us both as good news and as a cure—good news because he rescues us from sin's consequences, and a cure because in the forgiveness of sin, Jesus heals us from our suffering due to sin,[36] both as something we need rescue from in the moral sense and as healing from something we suffer.

In the kingdom of God, forgiveness serves as a catalyst for reconciliation and renewal of a relationship with God and others. Through newly reconciled

---

34. Caputo, *Prayers and Tears*, 176–78.
35. Caputo, *Weakness of God*, 260–78.
36. Caputo, *More Radical Hermeneutics*, 189; Caputo, *Weakness of God*, 186–95. Cf. Bruce Chilton, *Rabbi Jesus: An Intimate Biography* (New York: Random House, Doubleday, 2000), 110.

relationships, the Spirit of God seeks to transform sinners into saints and saints into servants for the furtherance of the kingdom, the reign of God in our midst on earth. In this manner, unconditional love and forgiveness effectively break open vicious, closed economic circles of retributive "justice" and the logic of the *quid pro quo*. Forgiveness remains the most amazing gift of all, one that disturbs our sense of law and order. In forgiving, we unconditionally give away our rights for payback and for perpetuating the cycle of vengeance, retribution, and debt; we unencumber others from any debt owed to us as recompense for a wrong committed by letting it go, giving it away, pardoning it through forgiveness.[37]

Some Christians may feel scandalized by this notion of radical forgiveness. We sometimes gain more comfort in believing that God actually does require a divine pound of flesh from Jesus before offering forgiveness to God's offenders. But forgiveness operates as another form of the "great reversal" we discussed above—Jesus reverses the cycle of retribution for sin and instead offers unconditional redemption. The notion of God's unconditional forgiveness shocks the logic of a world that turns on a "heartless system of accounting or of balanced payments, where scores are always being settled. In the logic of the world, nobody gets off scot free." According to the logic of our world "offenders are made to pay for their offense and every investor expects a return. Every equation must be balanced" before God (and we) can offer forgiveness.[38] But Jesus reveals a God who abhors violence and injustice (1 Pet 2:23; Luke 22:50–51), who forgives and heals without condition (Isa 43:25; 1 John 1:9), so we may reasonably object to theological constructions in Christian circles that understand forgiveness as a function of a closed economy, in which God sets conditions upon forgiveness with the need to balance accounts and set the record straight before extending the gift of grace. We have already discussed this with regard to the atonement. Unconditional forgiveness is, indeed, what the kingdom of God is all about. There is no sin so great that God cannot, or will not, freely and unconditionally wipe it away.[39]

In fact, the entire crux of the kingdom of God turns on notions of forgiving and forgetting (Matt 26:28).[40] Jesus exhorts us to "turn the other cheek," to break the cycle of retribution implicit in the law's command of "an eye for an eye," and to renounce getting even, all through forgiveness. Jesus asks his followers to dismiss their debtors by forgiving those who offend them, by releasing them from any

---

37. Caputo, *Prayers and Tears*, 178, 227. To pardon means "to give" (*do*) "forward" or "toward" (*par*).
38. Caputo, *Weakness of God*, 107. See also Raymond G. Helmick and Rodney L. Petersen, eds., *Forgiveness and Reconciliation: Religion, Public Policy, and Conflict Transformation* (Philadelphia: Templeton Foundation, 2001); Howard Zehr, *Changing Lenses: A New Focus for Crime and Justice* (Scottsdale, PA: Herald, 1990); Gorringe, *God's Just Vengeance*.
39. Anselm, *Proslogion*, in Fairweather, *A Scholastic Miscellany*, 4.
40. Caputo, *Prayers and Tears*, 178, 222–23; *Weakness of God*, 223; Putt, "Prayers of Confession and Tears of Contrition," 74, 136–37; René Girard, *The Scapegoat*, trans. by Yvonne Freccero (Baltimore: John Hopkins University Press, 1986), 212. Walter Wink places forgiveness in the same category as miracle, emphasizing its importance for transformation and restoration. Walter Wink, *When the Powers Fall: Reconciliation in the Healing of Nations* (Minneapolis: Fortress, 1998), 14–18.

requirement to right the wrong or from the threat of punishment in order to receive forgiveness. Jesus asks his followers to extend grace. Furthermore, Jesus does not ask us to forgive unconditionally only one time. He sets an example by multiplying forgiveness in an unending cycle, asking us to forgive repeatedly, "seventy-seven times"—or in some translations, "seventy times seven" times—figurative for without calculation or limit (Matt 18:22). Likewise, we continually ask God to forgive us, entering a kingdom of positive, constructive repetition, of reciprocal forgiving. In forgiving as God forgives, we enter into the "madness" of the kingdom, the "mad" alternative economy of forgiving.[41] In the kingdom of God, forgiveness is never "one and done"; we keep on saying, "I forgive you," over and over again. As we forgive seventy times seven, we imitate God's re-creative activity, forgiving what goes awry in life and opening up the creative possibility of newly restored relationships.[42] Indeed, Jesus calls us to openly embrace others in relationship.[43]

As members of the heavenly kingdom on earth, we are called by God to imitate the forgiveness modeled by Jesus Christ. The kingdom of God is one where the gift of forgiveness reigns—forgiveness given now, in the present—it cannot wait!—to heal and transform the past and to give the future new life. Forgiveness, and the healing that goes with it, is God's justice.

Justice

Inasmuch as gift-giving is inseparable from forgiveness, forgiveness is inseparable from justice. Jesus reveals that divine justice is not retributive (tit for tat) but instead is restorative (healing the relationship). The life, example, and exhortation of Jesus to give without return or reserve and to respond to others with love, forgiveness, compassion, and healing without any desire for reimbursement are synonymous with the restorative justice in the kingdom of God.[44] Unfortunately, contrary to its purpose to make manifest the kingdom of God, the church all too often takes part in the injustice of the world. Rather than forgiving the unforgivable and loving the unlovable, movements of grace that serve as acts of justice, the church has allowed injustice, in the name of justice, to flow like detritus over the land. The church too often has joined the world to follow the stampede of public opinion and to fan rising resentment against minorities, women, immigrants, and the LGBTQ+

---

41. Caputo, *Weakness of God*, 210–11.
42. Caputo, *Weakness of God*, 146–54; Caputo, *Prayers and Tears*, 227–29; B. Keith Putt, "Prayers of Confession and Tears of Contrition: A Radically Baptist Hermeneutic of Repentance," *Religion with/out Religion: The Prayers and Tears of John D. Caputo*, James Olthuis, ed. (New York: Routledge, 2002), 64–66. Anthony Bartlett, *Cross Purposes*, 219–20, 207–8.
43. Although God calls us to forgive those who wrong us, God does not call us to remain in abusive relationships.
44. Putt, "Faith, Hope, and Love," 244; John D. Caputo, "The Good News about Alterity: Derrida and Theology," *Faith and Philosophy* 10 (1993): 453–70; John D. Caputo, "Reason, History and a Little Madness: Towards a Hermeneutics of the Kingdom," *Proceedings of the American Catholic Philosophical Association* 68 (1994): 27–41.

community. The church has historically also too often appealed to the greed of the wealthy and aligned itself with nationalist hatred of others.[45] It has judged spirituality and salvation based on the outward appearance of religion, such as attendance in church, certain political leanings, and whom we exclude. Contrary to this egregious affiliation with the kingdoms of the world, the kingdom of God stands for justice over and above religious ritual, spiritual jargon, shows of piety, church attendance, and political opinions. The kingdom of God deals in feeding the hungry, clothing the poor, standing in solidarity with minorities, seeking justice for the oppressed, and including in the realm of blessing those the world normally excludes. The prophet Amos reminds us that God does not desire our festivals and sacrifices, our loud songs and solemn assemblies. Instead, God wants restorative "justice [to] roll down like waters" over the land (Amos 5:24).[46] Unless our justice serves the world for good and works toward the prosperity of the "least of these" (Matt 25:40), our offerings do not please God.

As our example, Jesus preached justice as a mark of the kingdom of God. He poured all his energies—his entire life, death, and resurrection—into remedying social injustice, standing on the side of justice by standing on the side of the marginalized, the widow, the orphan, the diseased, and the social outcast. Just as Jesus tells the parable of the good shepherd who leaves the ninety-nine sheep to search for the one (Luke 15:4–7), justice does the same. In searching for the one in one hundred, the good shepherd seeks to reconcile and restore the one, leaving us with a sense of divine justice as restorative and reconciling rather than retributive. Retributive justice may have had its place in human society as a way of holding back violence in the Hebrew Bible, but it can bring no true peace or creativity or restoration. As those responding to the call of the kingdom of God, we too imitate Christ's justice, seeking out the one—one by one—as ambassadors of reconciliation (2 Cor 5:19), effecting restorative justice in the land.[47]

If the time of the kingdom is now, the time of justice is always now as well. The urgent demand for justice comes to us from every byway, from the homeless in our cities and the poor and the ill and the stranger. Every time we respond to the call for justice with an open hand and an open heart, the kingdom of God is manifest in that moment as justice interrupts the status quo. When justice calls, it is God calling, and our responsibility as participants in the kingdom of God and as a messianic people is to do justice; we are to be "bent into the service of justice."[48] In this manner, we help bring about the kingdom, or messianic time, the epoch of the Messiah in which God's love rules. Indeed, the kingdom of God hinges upon love, acceptance, and hospitality toward all peoples whether they carry certain

45. Caputo, *Prayers and Tears*, 125–26.
46. Caputo, *Prayers and Tears*, 338–39.
47. Caputo, *Weakness of God*; *Prayers and Tears*, 247.
48. Caputo, *Prayers and Tears*, 150, 80–81, 98, 114; John D. Caputo, *On Religion* (New York: Routledge, 2001), 28. See also Jacques Derrida, *Rogues*, trans. Pascale-Anne Brault and Michael Naas (Stanford, CA: Stanford University Press, 2005).

documentation or recite a particular creed. The kingdom of God, as a kingdom of justice, is also a hospitable kingdom.

Hospitality

The kingdom of God is also a kingdom of hospitality. Those who follow Jesus open themselves up to the other. Unlike the world's form of hospitality, which Caputo stresses is "carefully calculated and practiced under strict conditions, extended only to those who are on the list of invited guests . . . who can be counted on to reciprocate," kingdom hospitality lets outsiders in. It pushes against the limits of worldly hospitality, practicing unconditional hospitality instead.

In the kingdom of God, everyone is welcomed without discrimination, like the prodigal son whose father receives him with open arms and like the one lost sheep who counts as much as the ninety-nine who did not stray (Luke 15:11–32; 15:4–7). In the kingdom of God, everyone is invited to the wedding feast (Matt 22:1–10).[49] Hospitality so rules in the kingdom of God that *doing* hospitality *constitutes* membership in the kingdom.[50] Consequently, in God's kingdom, hospitality generates community, "a city without walls, a nation without borders, unconditional hospitality without sovereign power."[51] In this community, breaking down barriers and tearing down walls draw all persons toward God and one another and bind us together in peace.

Peacemaking

Paul tells us in Romans that "the kingdom of God is . . . righteousness and peace and joy in the Holy Spirit" (14:17). Accordingly, as evidenced in the life and teachings of Jesus, God calls the members of the divine kingdom to serve as peacemakers. Indeed, the New Testament teaches us that as God behaves, so should we behave. And according to Jesus, God "is kind to the ungrateful and the wicked" (Luke 6:35), "makes [the] sun rise on the evil and on the good, and sends rain on the righteous and on the unrighteous" (Matt 5:45). Even the Hebrew Bible supports a view of the peace-loving God who hates violence and exhorts us to seek peace. For example, "[God's] soul hates the lover of violence" (Ps 11:5), and "[God] will abolish the bow, the sword, and war from the land" (Hos 2:18). God also exhorts people to choose the way of nonviolence (Prov 3:31), to "do no wrong or violence" (Jer 22:3), and to "put away violence and oppression, and do what is just and right" (Ezek

---

49. Students sometimes want to know what to do with the parable of the wedding banquet, in which a person who does not have the right wedding garment is excluded from the celebration. The operative idea is that this guest disrespected the generosity of the host by trying to control the terms on which he would enter the feast. Thus, the rejected guest was not ready in some way, or tried to circumvent the generosity of the host. He excluded himself.
50. Caputo, *Weakness of God*, 215, 232–33
51. Caputo, *Weakness of God*, 278.

45:9). Granted, the Hebrew Bible also supports divine violence in some passages, and Bible scholars interpret those stories in various ways (see chapter 2, "Hermeneutics"). But in light of the revelation of God in Christ, violent behavior does not serve as our model. Jesus does.

Jesus steers clear of violence during his ministry, and his teaching reflects passages of the Hebrew Bible that reveal the peaceful character of God. Richard Rohr points out that when Jesus "does quote Scripture, the only Hebrew Scriptures that he quotes are those that move toward mercy, justice and inclusivity. [Although] there *are* Scriptures that present God as punitive, imperialistic or exclusionary . . . Jesus never quotes them. . . . In fact, he speaks against them."[52] Jesus also lived nonviolently, working to heal rather than to harm. For example, he resisted violent measures against a woman caught in adultery even though the law demanded her death (John 7:53–8:11); he did not respond with violence in the garden at his betrayal (Luke 22:47–51); and as he hung on the cross, in inconceivable pain, he rejected violence in favor of forgiveness, "making peace through the blood of his cross" (Luke 23:32–34; Col 1:20). Jesus only spoke harsh words to those who oppressed others, especially with onerous spiritual requirements.[53]

Now that Christ-followers are his body on earth, God calls us to act as peacemakers. In so doing, we will be blessed, "for [we] will be called children of God" (Matt 5:9). Eric Seibert explains the significance of this statement in Matthew: "The reason Jesus says peacemakers 'will be called children of God' is because people who make peace reflect God's character. . . . Since peacemakers facilitate reconciliation, the same kind of work God does, they bear a 'family' resemblance and are aptly called God's children."[54] And this kingdom is not like the kingdoms of the world where violence serves as the norm. In God's kingdom, peace rules the realm. As we discussed earlier in this chapter, the teachings of Jesus call us as members of the kingdom and as God's children to a life of shalom, or peacemaking. Consequently, the message of shalom should infiltrate our proclamation and model the message of peace on earth to all people.[55] This means dealing creatively, through the discernment and power of the Holy Spirit, with violent situations and people as we resist simply replicating the violence presented to us. We are called to affirm a "new normal" of peacemaking love in the realm of the kingdom, interpreting over and over what this means within our own times, places, and circumstances. Living out a life of shalom does not come easily. Nonetheless, empowered by the Holy

---

52. Richard Rohr, "The Bible: A Text in Travail," *Hierarchy of Truths: Jesus' Use of Scripture*, lecture presented in 2013, available on CD or MP3 from Center for Action and Contemplation, https://tinyurl.com/ya3ytcgm.
53. People sometimes use the instance of Jesus cleansing the temple to prove that he was a violent man, or that we should similarly feel free to kick around God's enemies. But what Jesus does in the temple is not retaliation, nor an act against enemies, but is instead an act of resistance to religious corruption. Jesus models righteous, yet nonviolent, anger at the injustice he sees in the practice of price-gouging the poor and in the commercialized selling of animals in the Temple courtyard.
54. Seibert, *Disarming the Church*, 65.
55. Yoder, *Shalom*, 137. See Seibert, *Disarming the Church*, 79.

Spirit and supported by the community of Jesus-followers, we are called to the work of shalom in real-life situations. Living lives intent on peacemaking, however, requires that we love others, including our enemies. And indeed, the kingdom of God is especially marked by love.

Love

John Caputo reminds us that religion, as practiced in the kingdom of God, is for lovers.[56] In fact, we might say that gift-giving, forgiveness, justice, hospitality, and peace are synonymous with love. Just as the kingdom of God is always at hand, the love of God is always at hand, forgiving, bringing justice through reconciliation, inviting all to come to the feast, healing and changing hearts, loving those who make love difficult. As with God's forgiveness, justice, and hospitality, God loves without any expectation of return, without counting the cost, with a passion that seems impossible to those used to the world's way of loving. The kingdom of God, therefore, hinges on God's love for all creation and on all creation's love for God. God loves without remainder, unconditionally, and without measure. No one is excluded. God's love is hospitable and just (Matt 22:37–40).[57]

Since God's love opens itself to the other, it serves as a template or ideal for how we should behave. Jesus motivates us to open ourselves to the other, always attempting to respond to the call of the kingdom in the voice of the suffering other. Just as love flows in excess from God, as we see in the life and death of Christ, we must grapple with the call of love, discerning our responsibility to ensure that love also flows in excess from us. Love is not a closed, miserly economy that keeps track of what is rendered and what is returned. Although this may pose quite a challenge to us, we love without concern for gain and without expectation of return. As medieval mystic Meister Eckhart says, we are to love "without why."[58] Søren Kierkegaard describes the love that Jesus promotes: "The lover forgets himself in order to think of another, forgets his sufferings in order to think of another's, forgets himself and forgets what he loses in order lovingly to consider another's loss, forgets his advantage in order lovingly to look after another's advantage. . . . In this way love reduplicates itself."[59] Love, therefore, enters into endless positive or constructive repetition, what René Girard calls a "good mimesis" (imitation or participation) that counteracts or reverses the structures of mimetic violence in which we so often find ourselves enmeshed—violent structures of closed repetition

---

56. Caputo, *On Religion*, 13.
57. Caputo, *More Radical Hermeneutics*, 183–84, 225–26; *On Religion*, 138. Paul Fiddes comments that infinite love is a part of God's character, and as a result, God overflows with an excess of love that finds its satisfaction in loving others. Paul Fiddes, "Creation Out of Love," in *The Work of Love: Creation as Kenosis*, ed. by John Polkinghorne (Grand Rapids, MI: Eerdmans, 2001), 170.
58. Quoted in Caputo, *More Radical Hermeneutics*, 183–84.
59. Søren Kierkegaard, *Works of Love*, trans. by Howard and Edna Hong (New York: Harper & Row, 1962), 262.

that lead only to envy, rivalry, and scapegoating of ourselves and others. Once it is unveiled, we easily see that scapegoating brings no true, lasting peace, having the character of negative, violent repetition. God sets this alternative, good repetition in motion by first loving us.[60] We then repeat that gesture to others, knowing that our needs will be met from the abundance of God's grace.

The scope of Christ's love and the boundlessness of his forgiveness not only provide reconciliation to God but also serve as an example to live by. Christ enables us to live a new kind of life, loving the unlovable and forgiving the unforgivable, promoting peace and justice rather than violence and abuse, standing in solidarity with those less fortunate, with the lepers of today's society: the LGBTQ+ community, people of color, Jews, Muslims, immigrants, poor people—in short, all whom the powerful in our culture denigrate, abuse, or forget. Through words and actions Christ called forth the kingdom and set it in motion on earth. Jesus proclaimed that the kingdom of God "has come near" (Matt 4:17); it is here, now—a kingdom made of all who hear God's call to justice, love, and peace.

Lest talking about the unconditionality of love and forgiveness runs the risk of sounding too good to be true, we must remember that God calls us to this ideal as Christ's body in the world. Followers of Jesus must discern how to embody Christ creatively in our own day, using the power of the Holy Spirit within us. In the past, some highly influential theologians such as St. Augustine and Martin Luther evaded this responsibility by advocating what they called a "two-kingdom" approach. In this view, the ethics of the church differ from those of the secular—especially the political and social—world, which the church has sometimes seen as the unredeemed realm of Satan. These theologians argued that Jesus's radical commands about forgiveness, hospitality, love, and non-retaliation apply only to private, interpersonal relationships and cannot be translated into the social, the communal, and especially the political realm. But the early church did not think of the world as two separate kingdoms. For the first three hundred years of the church, for instance, Christians refused to serve in the military, expressing concern for victims of war on all sides. One of the ancient and contemporary marks of the church as a manifestation of the kingdom of God on earth is indeed concern for victims of oppression and violence, echoing the long tradition of the Hebrew prophets that Jesus affirmed and of which he is a part.

We must heed the cries of those abandoned to injustice, yet also seek to forgive the persecutors in acts of restorative justice, truly engaging in following the example of Jesus, in the power of the Spirit. God calls us to imitate Jesus in concern for the redemption and liberation of victims and perpetrators alike, remaining mindful of how we participate in these roles ourselves. (All of us do.) And God calls

60. For a more fully developed description of constructive, creative, or loving mimesis within a Girardian framework, see Rebecca Adams, "Loving Mimesis and Girard's 'Scapegoat of the Text': A Creative Reassessment of Mimetic Desire," in *Violence Renounced: René Girard, Biblical Studies, and Peacemaking*, ed. Willard M. Swartley (Telford, PA: Pandora, 2000), 277–307.

us to hear and live the truth in love, speaking up within our own social systems against inequity and injustice. Imitating the love and forgiveness of Jesus enables us to hear the other cry out, "I am thirsty, parched in a desert bereft of the healing waters of justice," or "I am sick, infected with the world's and religion's structures of violence," or "I am in prison, in the world's prison where violence rules."[61]

Only with ears to hear and hearts to act can we advocate for the less fortunate, empowering them and ourselves with the good news of God in Christ, who frees all captives. Indeed, we are all prisoners of spiritual ignorance, personal sinful patterns, and oppressive social structures, and Jesus has freed the entire human race. Those who realize this constitute the church and seek to live into Jesus's freedom as a reality in the world. Out of this new freedom we respond, as Jesus exhorted us, to all victims of injustice and people in need, as we would to Christ himself; in fact, in responding in love to those in need, we do respond in love to Jesus.

Inasmuch as we have a responsibility to act on behalf of and from within the situation of the other, we do not do so alone. René Girard links our advocacy for victims with the power of the Holy Spirit, who hovered over the face of the deep, working to create new life and a new kingdom order from out of the chaos.[62] The Spirit of God hovers in and near us, too, not only calling us to responsibility but giving us the response-ability to act. Recognizing both our own victimhood and at times our perpetration of violence, as redeemed people we can, nonetheless, continually enter into forgiveness and the deep healing of both ourselves and others.

61. Girard, *I See Satan Fall*, 177.
62. Girard, *The Scapegoat*, 207.

10. Humanity

. . . the forgiveness of sins . . .

My humanity is bound up in yours, for we can only be human together.

—Desmond Tutu

Be a sinner, and let your sins be strong, but let your trust in Christ be stronger, and rejoice in Christ who is the victor over sin, death, and the world.

—Martin Luther

But do Thou, O Lord my God, hear me and look upon me and see me and pity me and heal me, Thou in whose eyes I have become a question to myself: and that is my infirmity.

—St. Augustine, *Confessions*

Life is difficult. We constantly engage with moral dilemmas, right and wrong, good and bad, nice and nasty. We struggle with our choices. We sometimes feel enmeshed in deep patterns of addiction or craving. Why does our humanity seem so difficult to manage sometimes? Who am I and why do I do the things I do? Jesus revealed the answer to these questions as he hung from the cross, dying in extreme pain (Luke 23:34 KJV): "They know not what they do." He said we do not know what we are doing; perhaps that is because we do not know who we are. Jesus understood our human dilemma; he lived as a human, with other humans. And he knew that we will never know who we are or what we do until we know him, until we receive his new life and become new creatures. As we have seen, salvation allows this miracle of transformation. Character conflicts and moral decisions will always confront us, but through Christ, we will have the life of God to empower and guide us as we walk the tightrope between what St. Paul calls the "flesh" and the "spirit."

Contrary to how it might sound, *flesh* and *spirit* do not refer to a conflict between the physical body and an immaterial realm. Rather, in Paul's theology "the flesh" refers to our old "sin nature," or our spiritually ignorant, unredeemed selves. "The spirit" refers to the spiritual enlightenment and renewed nature we receive through Christ's work, which will ultimately result in our being united to God in theosis. Rather than articulating the movement from sin nature to new nature as an exchange of one nature for another, we may think about it as a move from "spiritual ignorance" to "spiritual enlightenment." In other words, sin brought about spiritual ignorance, but as we continually take on the life of Jesus, the light of the Spirit of Christ overcomes our ignorance until, one day, with fully enlightened spirit, we become new creatures in Christ and gain oneness with God (John 1:4–9; 8:12; 1 Cor 13:12; 1 John 3:2).

The transformation into a new creation does not come without internal struggle, as Paul reveals in Romans 7:14–25. After describing his own personal conflict between the flesh and the spirit, Paul exclaims, "With my mind I am a slave to the law of God, but with my flesh I am a slave to the law of sin" (v. 25). Paul also emphasizes in this same verse that Jesus has given us victory over this dilemma. Like Paul, we will have a hard time shedding our old identity with its propensity to sin, but the Holy Spirit calls, enlightens, strengthens, and sanctifies us so that we can, instead, be clothed with the new reality of our participation in the Spirit of Christ.

God created human beings to exist in an ideal relationship with God and with one another. But we obviously fall short of this ideal and, instead of living as God created us to, we live in sin. Theologians call the concept and the study of sin *hamartiology*, or the study of "missing the mark." While some theologians have stressed sin simply as individual conscious moral wrongdoing, sin and its consequences are far more complex than this. We can discuss sin using metaphors such as being in bondage to the devil, brokenness or incompleteness, lack of health, "missing the mark," spiritual ignorance, and being caught up in structures of violence. Or we can state simply that sin is anything that keeps us from an ideal relationship with God and with each other. But must we always struggle between "spirit" and "flesh" in an agonizing attempt to live into the life Christ has so graciously given us? How do we become the people God created us to be?

We see this restless conflict in St. Augustine of Hippo in his *Confessions* as he chronicles his struggles and subsequent anxiety concerning the numerous temptations that draw him away from God, leading him to pen the words "I have become a question [or a problem] to myself."[1] After decades of searching for answers surrounding his human identity, Augustine surrenders to God in Christ. When he finally discovers the truth his heart has so diligently sought, he offers God this prayer of affirmation: "You prompt us yourself to find satisfaction in appraising you, since *you made us tilted toward you*, and our heart is unstable until stabilized in you" (italics mine).[2] Indeed, St. Augustine can finally find his heart's rest in the knowledge that he only knows himself by knowing God. I find Garry Wills's translation of Augustine's words interesting and pertinent to our discussion on humanity: "You made us *tilted* toward you." God created human beings to naturally *tilt* or *lean* Godward. Before the problem of sin clouded and divided our hearts, our divinely given human nature inherently drew us and inclined us toward an intimate relationship with God. And, according to St. Augustine, we cannot find peace until we find God, until

---

1. Augustine, *Confessions of Saint Augustine*, trans. F. J. Sheed (New York: Sheed & Ward, 1943), X.33; 242–44.
2. Augustine, "Confessions," in *Saint Augustine's Childhood: Confessions*, Book One, trans. Garry Wills (New York: Viking, 2001), 29.

we clear away our own internal confusion and discover the true meaning of our being, made in God's image. But what is the image of God in us, exactly?

The Image of God in Genesis 1

For millennia, human beings have asked, What does it mean to be human? How are humans different from the rest of creation? And what is the image of God in us (the *imago Dei* in Latin)? Each question generates an assortment of answers. Let's explore a few.

First, some believe that the image of God in us points to our inner abilities to reason and, therefore, to our freedom to make decisions. Theologian Paul Tillich, for example, asserts that our *rationality* makes human beings different from all other creatures by structuring our freedom to make decisions and enabling us to discern between one choice and another, one idea and another.[3] The great medieval theologian Thomas Aquinas, who also argues that the key to the image of God lies in the capacity for human reason, claims that as the only creatures made in God's image, we participate in and reflect the *logos* (reason/rationality) of God, through which God created the world (translated "Word" in John 1:1).[4] Although the ability to reason certainly points toward the divine *logos* mirrored in human beings, we also see this same ability in other creatures, calling into question the claim that humans uniquely possess this quality. For instance, my cat knew that he could make my husband get up and feed him just by pounding his feet on the carpet when walking into the bedroom at five a.m. He also knew that when my husband was traveling, I would not get up to feed him, so he did not even bother walking into the room. Actually, we see instances of creatures in the animal world exercising reasoning abilities all the time. So, although humans may possess *advanced* reasoning capacity, other species also have an aptitude for rationality.

Second, some Christian thinkers believe that *freedom* explains the character of the image of God in us. The church father Irenaeus states that God created humanity with the power to choose to live according to or against the divine will. If we are bearers of the image of God, the freedom abiding inherently in the divine nature automatically becomes ours at creation. In fact, we communicate the existence of God in our every act of freedom. Since divine freedom finds its most explicit expression in humanity, every time we use our freedom to live within God's will and participate with God in love, we reveal God's existence through the display of divine freedom built into us as those who bear the divine image.[5]

Black theologian James Cone considers human freedom the distinguishing feature of the *imago Dei* in us. God does not merely *give* humans freedom; God creates humanity with inherent freedom to serve God by living lives that benefit

---

3. Paul Tillich, *Systematic Theology*, vol. 1 (Chicago: University of Chicago Press, 1973), 259.
4. Thomas Aquinas, *Summa Theologia*, 1.1.93, a. 4.
5. Irenaeus, *Against Heresies*, 4.37.1, 518.

others through justice and liberation from oppression. He states: "To be human is to be in the image of God—that is, to be creative: revolting against [any] threat that is opposed to humanity."[6] In other words, our innate freedom connects directly to God's injunction to "rule" over the earth and everything in it. This dominion or rule does not give us permission to lord it over creation, to use it for anthropocentric purposes, but to care for it, guard it, protect it, nurture it, and serve as God's image bearers revealing the divine love, compassion, and care for the entire creation. According to Cone, to be human, created in the image of God as free creatures, is to care for all creation, which also means protecting other humans from oppression and abuse. In accordance with Cone, Walter Brueggemann aptly articulates that "God is not imaged in anything fixed but in the freedom of human persons to be faithful and gracious," administering with love and care that which God entrusts to us.[7]

Third, as creatures who stand in freedom to participate with God in caring for the world, we also have the inherent free capacity to receive divine revelation, to *communicate* with God in the free expression of a love relationship. Our ability to commune with God in freedom animates us and motives us to tilt toward God in the intimacy of interrelational community with the Father, Son, and Holy Spirit. Through the image of God in us, we have the capacity for relationships in which we love others, are loved by others, and experience the love of others, including God. Analogously, with our innate ability to commune with God, we participate in the Trinitarian relational dance of love, leading us toward the knowledge of God as the lover (Father), the beloved (Son), and the love (Holy Spirit). The image of God, then, directly connects us to a communal relationship with the triune God.[8] God addresses us personally and calls us into an intimate relationship of covenantal communion, expecting us to respond to the divine offer of life.

From the beginning, when God declared that the first person needed someone to partner with him in the garden, God revealed the divine intent for community (Gen 2:18). We see that God created humanity to live in communion with one another, as equal partners, as persons who multiply and create communities and communion as a fact of life. To that end, as bearers of God's image, we find our true identity as we live in relationship with one another and with God: "to exist in relationships of mutual fidelity and mutual freedom."[9] In fact, the ability for human beings to communicate with and relate to each other on the temporal level enables us to mirror

6. James H. Cone, *Black Theology of Liberation* (Maryknoll, NY: Orbis, 2010), 99.
7. Walter Brueggemann, *Genesis*, Interpretation (Atlanta: John Knox, 1982), 32; J. Richard Middleton, *The Liberating Image: The Imago Dei in Genesis 1* (Grand Rapids, MI: Brazos, 2005), 236.
8. Augustine, "The Trinity," in *Nicene and Post-Nicene Fathers*, vol. 3, ed. Philip Schaff (Buffalo, NY: Christian Literature Publishing, 1887), 8.10.14.
9. Daniel Migliore, *Faith Seeking Understanding* (Grand Rapids, MI: Eerdmans, 2004), 141, 144.

the life of communion and relationship within the eternal, triune God. Through our relationships with each other, we (potentially) reveal God to the world.[10]

Fourth, God created both men and women in the divine image for *equal, bilateral, supportive relationships.*[11] When God says, "Let us make humankind in our image" (Gen 1:26), the Hebrew text uses the word for humankind in general, *adam.* Rabbinic scholars assert that this term applies to both male and female, indicating equality. And in Genesis 5:2 we see *adam* applied to both genders: "Male and female he created them, and he blessed them and named them *adam* when they were created."[12] Namely, as a statement of equality, God calls both male and female by the same "name," *adam,* a play on the word *adamah* for "ground" or "dirt." The texts in Genesis express no hierarchy in the relationship, no indication of gender superiority, but instead express total equality and harmony in relationships between men and women. Interestingly, the fact that *both* male and female characterize God's image teaches us something significant about God: specifically, the nature of God includes characteristics of both male and female.

According to philosopher Judith Butler, the essential quality of humanity as created in God's image lies in the human drive toward an ability to maintain relationships with God and others, not in gender specificity. Specific gender identification, not wrapped up in the being or essence of humans, arises from physical attributes as seen in the differences between bodies, but also emerges due to sociocultural influences and dispositions. For example, in my patriarchal culture, many people label women as the "weaker" gender or the more "nurturing" gender, whereas we label men as the "stronger" gender or the "leader" of all other genders. In addition, we often describe female physicality differently than we do for men. The media in our Western culture portray women as thin, with round buttocks and perfectly shaped breasts, and men as muscular, with broad shoulders and narrow hips. But not all men and women take those physical forms. Physical forms differ; therefore, they are not essential characteristics of our being. Feminist theologian Serene Jones, referencing Judith Butler, argues that "being a woman or a man is therefore not the expression of a natural predisposition or a biological fact; gender identities are better understood as 'performances' in which we put on the 'drag' of culturally generated gender/sex/body assumptions."[13]

For some, then, the idea that these distinctions derive from our being or essence serves as a myth and a distortion of the first creation story in Genesis 1.[14] In other

10. Meir Zlotowitz, trans. and comment., *Bereishis: A New Translation with a Commentary Anthologized from Talmudic, Midrashic, and Rabbinic Sources,* vol. 1a (Brooklyn: Mesorah, 1995), 67–70.
11. Zlotowitz, *Bereishis,* 73.
12. Zlotowitz, *Bereishis,* 69.
13. Serene Jones, *Feminist Theory and Christian Theology: Cartographies of Grace* (Minneapolis: Fortress, 2000), 31–32. See also Judith Butler, *Gender Trouble: Feminism and the Subversion of Identity* (New York: Routledge, 2006).
14. Migliore, *Faith Seeking Understanding,* 146.

words, God created both male and female in the image of God, which has everything to do with a created community, the desire and the ability to participate in intentional, freely consenting relationships, horizontally (with other humans) and vertically (with the triune God). Walter Brueggemann fittingly expresses the text's intended focus in the creation stories in Genesis, including our considerations surrounding the meaning of the image of God. Our concern for the meaning and practical application of these texts "is not finally the danger of sex, the origin of evil, the appearance of death, or the power of the fall. It is, rather, the summons of this calling of God for us to be his creatures, to live in his world on his terms."[15]

Fifth, as we discussed in the first few chapters, when we attempt to interpret a text from Scripture, we must consider the *cultural context*, the meaning of words, and how the people during the time of the first transmissions of the passage would have heard those words. What might people have heard when they first listened to these words: "Then God said, 'Let us make humankind in our image, according to our likeness. . . . So God created humankind in his image . . . ; male and female he created them" (Gen 1:26–27)? In his writings from the twelfth and thirteenth centuries, the medieval scholar and rabbi Maimonides discusses the use of plural pronouns in these verses, indicating they refer to God in consultation with the angels in heaven.[16] The use of pronouns may indicate that to stress the significance of this new creature, God holds a council meeting, a planning session, proposing (rather than commanding) the creation of humanity—the final climax of the divine creating enterprise.[17] This heavenly scene may have reminded the hearers of a Persian court scene in which the king confers with his advisors before taking action.

Of course, the image of God figures significantly into just such a scene. The Persian kings reigned over large territories with a palace in each region. Not able to be present in every palace at the same time, the king would stamp an image of himself on a large bronze disc, polish it to a high gloss, affix it to a long pole, and set it up as a standard on the roof of his palace while attending to business elsewhere. Whenever people saw that large image shining brightly as it caught the sun's rays, they knew the king was present even in his absence. Analogously, since we cannot "see" God visually or hear God audibly, God has "stamped" the divine image on all humanity so that we reflect the image of God in the world, proclaiming God's presence even in God's seeming absence. So through our ability to reason with intention, with the freedom to make choices according to God's plan, with the power to participate with God in ruling (caring for) the world, and with the capacity and drive for equal, loving relationships in communion with God and others, we "image" God in the world. God's presence is made known in us, God's very good creation.

15. Brueggemann, *Genesis*, 32; Middleton, *The Liberating Image*, 43–44.
16. Zlotowitz, *Bereishis*, 68.
17. Joseph H. Coleson, *'Ezer Cenegdo: A Power Like Him, Facing Him as Equal* (Indianapolis: Wesleyan/Holiness Women Clergy, 1996), 2–3.

Creation of Humanity in Genesis 2

Whereas in the first creation story in Genesis 1 God creates humanity in God's image, the text does not give us any information about humanity other than the instructions for partnering with God to take care of the world. In the second creation story in Genesis 2, however, God plays in the mud. With the divine hands, God molds and forms the dirt to create human beings, thereby distinguishing humanity from any other created being so far. *Yatsar*, the Hebrew word for "formed," indicates a hands-on, loving act, much like the potter who takes care to craft a vessel on the wheel. The text tells us that after creating the earth and the heavens, "the Lord God formed *ha adam* [the human being] from the dust of the ground, and breathed into his nostrils the breath of life; and *ha adam* became a living being" (Gen 2:7). Amazingly, the human being, formed by God from the dirt, attains the gift of life straight from the breath of God. We are "Dirtonians," so to speak, dry as dust and dead as dirt, until God gives us the breath of life. Medieval Jewish scholars believed that our creation out of both earthy dirt (*adamah*) and divine breath points to our lives in two realms—one here and now on earth and the other eternally with God in heaven.[18] Indeed, the transcendent, almighty God, who up until this point brought the universe into existence by a spoken word, intimately and lovingly molded and modeled the first human being and animated him/her with divine breath. Made out of dirt, we are not divine ourselves, but unlike the animals, we can say our very lives arose from the inspiration and expiration of the breath of God.[19]

As we discussed above, added to the combination of dirt and divinity as the creative ingredients for our existence, the Hebrew word for "human" in the text, *adam*, is a collective noun including both male and female. The eleventh-century rabbi Rashi explains that according to the Midrash (Jewish texts of commentary on the Hebrew biblical text), humanity was created with two faces, with male and female halves—one "person" both male and female.[20] As odd as this may sound, the text provides ample evidence for this viewpoint. We will discuss the more "traditional" popular view of this chapter later, but for now, stay with me while we discuss this more ancient interpretation.

All was well in paradise; in fact, after finishing the work, God declared that all was *very good* (Gen 1:31). Then, to our surprise, in the next chapter, God says, "It is *not good* for *adam* to be alone" (Gen 2:18). God realized that the *adam* needed a companion, a community other than God. So what did God do? The next verse in the chapter tells us God paraded all the animals before the *adam* and, in line with the divine command for humans to exercise dominion and rule over the earth, gave the *adam* the power to name all the animals. We can imagine each newly created animal coming before the human being one by one and receiving its name. But

18. Zlotowitz, *Bereishis*, 91.
19. Coleson, *'Ezer Cenegdo*, 9.
20. Zlotowitz, *Bereishis*, 72.

after the *adam* finished naming every creature, we can picture the *adam* turning to God and shaking his head. As the passage informs us, not one of those animals suited the *adam* as a companion.

At this point, knowing that God intended to find *adam*'s mate from among the animals, we may wonder what kind of mate God had in mind! Fortunately, the text tells us. God desired to give the *adam* an *ezer cenegdo*. Although many versions of the Bible translate these words as "helper suitable," the meaning differs significantly from that rendering. *Ezer*, used elsewhere in Scripture, means "strength" or "power." Depending upon which Hebrew root we choose, *ezer* can also mean "helper," but given its coupling with *cenegdo*, it likely indicates a person with strength or power. *Cenegdo* means "facing," standing in another's presence face-to-face, which carries important social significance. In Middle Eastern countries, facing someone and looking him or her in the eye connotes equality. So a simple, paraphrased translation of Genesis 2:18 might read like this: "To end the loneliness of the single human, I will make another *adam*, like the *adam*, a strong power facing the *adam* as an equal."[21]

Not finding the sought-for partner from among the animals, God went to work creating just such an *ezer cenegdo*. "So the Lord God caused a deep sleep to fall upon the *adam*, and he slept; then he took one of his ribs and closed up its place with flesh. And the rib that the Lord God had taken from the *adam* he made into a woman and brought her to the *adam*" (Gen 2:21–22). Although the theory that God crafted the woman from the man's rib predominates in traditional creation motifs, the text suggests other equally valid meanings. Whereas a common reading of the passage leads us to claim that God put the *adam* to sleep, took one of his ribs, and from it fashioned a woman, the translation of the Hebrew word into "rib" appears only here in Genesis. When used in other verses in the Hebrew Bible, it refers to the entire side of a building, mountain, or wall. Because the man called the woman (2:23) "flesh of my flesh" as well as "bone of my bones," we may conclude that God actually took not just one rib but the entire side of the *adam* in order to fashion the woman. In such a case, God actually did create the *adam* both male and female, one human being (*adam*) in one human body. When the animals did not suit the *adam*, God decided that splitting apart the female from the male would make the best companion for the *adam*. Indeed, not surprisingly, it seems God made the right decision. Because as soon as the man saw the woman, he said something like, "Woo-hoo! That's more like it, God! Yes!!" He declared with joy, "This time, finally, you have given me bone of my bones and flesh of my flesh! For this reason she shall be called 'woman,' because from 'man' she was taken" (Gen 2:23, paraphrased).

Interestingly, this interpretation of the story finds support in the fact that, for the first time, in Genesis 2 we see gender-specific words for a man and a woman, indicating that prior to the divine "surgery," *adam* was both male and female. The

21. Coleson, *Ezer Cenegdo*, 11–14.

newly separated couple can now enjoy a bilateral, companionable relationship joined back together in love. In fact, the next verse describes God's plan for human sexuality. What God separated, God now joins back together into one flesh—a beautiful image of a monogamous marriage relationship that resonates later with the revelation of Christ and the church (Eph 5:25). Remember, before God divided the one human into two, *adam* had only God for camaraderie, only God with whom to relate and to love. But after the one became two, we see a new type of relationship in paradise, one in which the two become one again in bilateral and equal unity.

Many of my students have questions about interpreting this text in light of contemporary issues surrounding gender and sexuality. As in parables, when we attempt to discern the meaning of a biblical passage, we should look for the main idea, the one significant message the text tries to communicate. The main focal point in Genesis 2 is the issue of relationships, first between God and the God-breathed human and, second, between humans living together in companionship and love. We can see that the ancient text, rather than making dogmatic assertions and unbending decrees about gender and sexuality that must apply forever across diverse cultures, focuses on the *quality* of relationships between human beings.[22]

Regardless of how we interpret the story of the divine creation of humanity, Genesis 2 speaks of the equality in decision-making, the sharing of responsibilities, and the delights of newfound intimacy between two people. Whether we interpret the text as historically accurate, literal accounts of creation, or as allegories that reveal profound truth, we see that sexuality is good; it is part of God's gift to us as we live in harmonious, committed, free, and equal relationships. We can celebrate with Adam, who, newly divided and reunited with his *'ezer cenegdo*, Eve, exults with a poem of thanksgiving and an invitation to every couple to celebrate the divinely ordained mystery and joy surrounding the pleasures of human gender and sexuality.[23]

Our Tasks

God created human beings for specific tasks. Although opinions differ concerning the nature of those tasks, in the Bible, three in general stand out as significant. First, we *multiply* (*create*). In Genesis 1, God blessed the *adam* and said, "Be fruitful and multiply, and fill the earth and subdue it; and have dominion over . . . every living thing . . ." (Gen 1:28). In Genesis 2, God "took the *adam* and put him in the garden of Eden to till it and keep it" (Gen 2:15). We see, then, that God intends for us to multiply, to rule, and to till (take care of creation). God spent six days creating the universe with its stars, planets, and moons; the earth with its oceans, lakes,

22. Brueggemann, *Genesis*, 32–35.
23. Coleson, *'Ezer Cenegdo*, 16–17.

mountains, valleys, and plains; and the living creatures, each after its kind. Finally, God created human beings in the divine image with a commission to serve God by continuing the creation process through multiplication.

God rests on the seventh day, not to cease all creation, but to delegate the responsibility to God's partners, human beings created in the divine image. Jewish scholars assert that the blessing for fruitfulness and multiplication means the new humans should "not be so engrossed in the spirit and intellect that [they] neglect the physical and thus destroy the world; [God's] desire is that [they] populate the world, not destroy it."[24] God takes a risk, blesses us with fertility and creativity, then allows us to exercise our new gifts as divine representatives in the world, continuing the divine creation process not only through procreation but also through art, architecture, agriculture, and ideas.[25] Accordingly, we care for the world by populating the world and sustaining its communal continuation.

Second, we *rule*. The fact that God invites humanity to continue the process of creation in partnership indicates that God also shares with us the divine power to rule (Gen 1:28).[26] Note that to rule does not give human beings permission to "lord it over" the rest of creation. Quite the contrary. In the past, Christians have sometimes thought God's command to rule over the earth meant we could simply use the earth's resources for our own benefit and prosperity, allowing us to justify polluting rivers and lakes with chemicals, clear-cutting forests in our desire to build bigger and better structures, contaminating the air we breathe with toxic fumes, even violating outer space around earth with an excess of 500,000 bits of orbital debris. But that form of "ruling" misinterprets and oversteps the divine/human partnership. Instead, God intends for us to administrate as God's representatives on earth and to imitate Jesus, who ruled through love, humility, and service (Isa 42:1; Mark 10:45; John 6:38; 13:12–17). We have dominion over the world for the *earth's* benefit, not for the sake of our own selfish desires that often lead to ecological violence. Just as God created without violence, so we continue the divine creative activity in peace, harmony, respect, and love. Our task is to participate in the universe as God's partners, to bless and benefit the world as God's stewards, who work toward a creation fully willed by God.[27]

Third, we *till*. Having dominion or rule over the world means that we care for it, guard it, protect it, "till" it like we work a garden. As partners with God in taking care of the universe, we "loosen the dirt," metaphorically speaking, so plant roots can penetrate the ground to gain nourishment; we "pull weeds" that threaten to choke out productive growth; we "water the garden" so plants can continue to live and grow. How does this garden analogy translate into contemporary action?

---

24. Zlotowitz, *Bereishis*, 74.
25. Middleton, *The Liberating Image*, 289, 291, 294–95.
26. Middleton, *The Liberating Image*, 287–88.
27. Brueggemann, *Genesis*, 33, 40; Hans Küng, *The Beginning of All Things: Science and Religion*, trans. John Bowden (Grand Rapids, MI: Eerdmans, 2005), 125.

As human beings created in God's image to serve the world as God's partners, we work continually to increase shalom on earth through ecological responsibility, to counter violence and evil with redemptive measures, to spread peace and harmony for the well-being of all life, to "water" the world with the reconciling love of God through Christ.[28] Our ruling in this manner allows God to work through us to transform all creation, to rid the world of evil, not through violent means but by conquering evil with love. Yet, even though God has made human beings in the divine image to work with God to care for all creation, we live in an overwhelmingly violent and polluted world.

Sin

So, what happened? We have a simple, but deceptively difficult, answer to this question: Sin happened. Theologians ancient and modern have attempted to define sin in many ways, but the fact of the matter remains—Genesis 3 tells us that in some primordial way, instead of staying true to God's command for living life in peaceful relationship with God and others, human beings decided to do their own thing, or strayed away from God's original intent. What, exactly, is "their own thing"? While some Christians are more familiar with the answer that we consciously, willfully rebelled against God through pride (how St. Augustine in Western Christianity defined sin), the church has not always understood sin in this way. The early church father Irenaeus, for instance, saw Adam and Eve more like children who didn't know what they were doing and thus fell tragically into the bondage of patterns of evil, which resulted in death through deception by the serpent, a biblical creature often interpreted as the devil. Rather than focusing narrowly, as St. Augustine does, on personal guilt, Irenaeus's view emphasizes our bondage to sin and Christ's work as a release from that bondage.

Others view sin as those patterns of addiction or structures of violence from which we need to be healed and redeemed. How we define sin matters, just as our theology of atonement and salvation from sin matters; the two issues connect intimately. Contemporary theologian Marjorie Suchocki has an interesting take on this: Although "sin has been considered primarily as rebellion against God throughout most of Christian history," at least in the West, she proposes a new, more nuanced definition, a view of "sin as the violence of rebellion against creation. Sin is unnecessary violence against any aspect of existence, whether through act or intent, whether consciously or unconsciously chosen or otherwise. Sin violates the creation, and therefore acts as a rebellion against creation's well-being."[29] Using the language we have used previously, sin is the opposite of shalom, of creative

---

28. Brueggemann, *Genesis*, 46.
29. Marjorie Hewitt Suchocki, *The Fall to Violence: Original Sin in Relational Theology* (New York: Continuum, 1995), 16.

peace and flourishing. Anything that falls short of God's original good intent for creation is sin.

As we read the ancient accounts of how our forebears sinned, we have to make choices about what we will emphasize. The text uses poetic and powerful imagery to describe what went wrong with the human race. Instead of focusing on arguments surrounding the literal, historical accuracy of the story in Genesis 3, which, according to Bruggemann, is not the point of the text, we will center our attention on the meat of the text, the main meaning of the act of sin, and explore some common definitions and aspects of sin suggested by the text.

First, the first *humans willed what God did not will*. God willed that they not eat from the tree of the knowledge of good and evil, and the humans willed to do so.[30] In other words, human beings sin when, either knowingly or unknowingly, they seek to satisfy their desires outside the will of God. For example, whenever we ignore God's will to love others by committing violence against them physically, psychologically, or spiritually, we will what God does not will and, therefore, participate in sin. Anytime we will to do, say, or even think (Matt 5:28) anything that falls outside the will of God, we sin. And God always wills shalom, the flourishing of all creation.

Second, *sin is failing to reflect God's image* and, therefore, is the denial of our created selves. The gifts and abilities given through the *imago Dei* can be corrupted. For instance, reason, which we need in order to rule in dominion, take care of creation, and live in peace, can turn into a means to oppress people instead of a motivation to resist oppression and abuse.[31] Our freedom, as an extension of the *imago Dei*, can deviate into inflicting slavery and injustice, taking away the freedoms of others. Instead of using our obeying the commands of God to act with justice, mercy, and love, we can distort our freedom and spread violence, injustice, and hatred.[32] In so doing, we reflect an *imago sui*, the image of a self of our own making, separated existentially from the *imago Dei* and the destiny of shalom appointed to us by God. We depend on ourselves and other human beings for meaning, satisfaction, and the flourishing of our lives, but we find them in distorted ways and from a limited point of view.

Third, *sin is absence of love through the rejection of divine grace*. This absence of love results in a refusal to live in harmonious relationship in community with God and others. Sin not only causes us to deny our created selves, but also produces a denial of our fundamental connectedness to others. Sin is "the depth of human intolerance for difference" in others, a refusal to live respectfully, hospitably, and gratefully in community with those who differ from us.[33] It disrupts our relationship

---

30. Brueggemann, *Genesis*, 47–48.
31. Cone, *Black Theology of Liberation*, 165.
32. Migliore, *Faith Seeking Understanding*, 148.
33. Susan Thistlethwaite, *Sex, Race, and God: Christian Feminism in Black and White* (New York: Crossroad, 1989), 59.

with others and with God, evoking a life deficient of the divine grace that enables us to love God and others as Jesus commanded (Luke 10:27, 36–37). Indeed, when we refuse to live in shalom relationships with God and others, we say "no" to the divine grace that draws us together in one body. We say "no" to a life serving God in partnership with others. We say "no" to a life that invites others into our community of friendship and love, and therefore, we say "no" to living lives based on justice, peace, and liberation for all.[34]

In addition, the consequences for sin in Genesis 3 profoundly and adversely affect the relationship between partners committed in love to live their lives together. God tells the woman her desire will be for her husband and he will "rule over" her (Gen 3:16). If this arrangement did not occur until after the first sin, we can assume such hierarchical order is not part of God's original good creation. As an equal partner ('ezer cenegdo) with each other, the male and female carry equal importance, equal decision-making power. But, as the story goes, after the woman made the unilateral choice to eat the fruit of the tree, seemingly without the bilateral support of Adam, the relational order between them took on new dimensions.

This event suggests that in the beginning, the subordination of women to men had no place in paradise, but the failure to live within the limits set by God provoked a significant disorder in the harmonious bilateral relationship between the man and the woman.[35] Whereas God wills mutuality and equality, human sin resulted in a struggle for control and an intrinsic disconnection in the relationship between two people.[36] As Genesis 3 indicates, then, this "no" to grace and God-ordained relationships profoundly affects the manner in which we relate to one another as life partners. Even though the story itself deals primarily with the marriage relationship, it also indicates that, because of sin, our relationships with the earth (ecology), our bodies (sexuality), and one another (society) also suffer. We can, therefore, apply its lessons more generally (Gen 3:15–19). As we will see below, our new creation in Christ releases us from those consequences.

Fourth, *sin is universal*. Everyone sins; "all have sinned and fall short of the glory of God" (Rom 3:23). Sin infiltrates and infects every person, every human institution, and every communal structure. Sin leaves its mark on everything, even the good we do. We cannot get away from the consequences of sin without the grace of God that, paradoxically, in sinning we tend to refuse. By our self-chosen or unintentional acts, sin corrupts and imprisons our wills so we "miss the mark" set for us by God as beings created in the divine image.[37] Sin sets us at a profound

---

34. Migliore, Faith Seeking Understanding, 150–57.
35. Mary Aquin O'Neill, "The Mystery of Being Human Together," in Freeing Theology: The Essentials of Theology in Feminist Perspective, ed. Catherine Mowry LaCugna (San Francisco: Harper SanFrancisco, 1993), 142.
36. Brueggemann, Genesis, 51.
37. See Martin Luther, The Bondage of the Will, trans. J. I. Packer and O. R. Johnston (Grand Rapids, MI: Baker Academic, 2012); John Calvin, Institutes of the Christian Religion, ed. John T. McNeill, trans. Ford Lewis Battles (Louisville, KY: Westminster John Knox, 1960), 2.2; Augustine, "On Original Sin," in

spiritual distance from God and from each other. This spiritual distance holds us in bondage to a life outside God's will.

Additionally, a multifaceted definition of sin can help us understand the profoundly disordered world in which we find ourselves. Rather than defining sin merely as wrongdoing for which we need forgiveness, we can *also* define it as a profound, pervasive bondage from which we need release, a disease from which we need healing, and spiritual ignorance that needs exposure to the light of Christ. This multifaceted definition helps us understand the profoundly disordered world in which we find ourselves.

Ancestral Sin and Original Sin

Theologians often refer to the universal and pervasive problem of sin in the created order as "original sin" or "ancestral sin."[38] These are two different concepts that must be distinguished. The Greek word used in the early church for "ancestral sin" or "ancestral inheritance" refers to the inheritance of *death* (not guilt) that all humanity suffers because of the sin of the first parents. In this understanding, we all suffer death because of sin, but we do not inherit the guilt of the first parents. The more specific theological idea of *original* sin as inherited, universal human guilt is a later doctrine first faintly articulated by Irenaeus and then developed by St. Augustine. The doctrine of original sin claims that our first parents' personal sin is our sin; their personal guilt is our guilt. The distinction between the two ideas of ancestral sin and original sin is important to Eastern Orthodox Christians.

For the first three hundred years of the church, there was no developed doctrine of original sin as inherited guilt. Rather, the Greek fathers articulated concepts of being in bondage to the devil and the power of death, from which Jesus releases us into life. They, like the apostle Paul, refer to the human inheritance from our first parents of a "sin nature" or a "propensity to sin," resulting in an inheritance of death. But these metaphors speak more about healing a disease and saving us from the power of death than about forgiving a guilty act we have committed along with Adam. Similarly, in Judaism there is no doctrine of original sin in the sense of inherited guilt. Jewish scholars call Genesis 3 "the garden story," having no doctrine of "the fall" in the sense of inherited, universal guilt that dooms us to eternal punishment for wrongdoing. Rather, in Judaism the stories about Adam and Eve and especially Cain and Abel serve as a kind of universal drama of the human dilemma, one that we all recapitulate by individually wrestling with the "evil urge" toward murder or the sinful behavior that overcame Cain. In Judaism, the *yetser hara* is the congenital inclination to do evil—an ancestral inheritance that leads

---

The Basic Writings of Saint Augustine, vol. 1, ed. Whitney J. Oates (New York: Random House, 1948), 652–53.

38. Serene Jones, *Call It Grace: Finding Meaning in a Fragmented World* (New York: Viking, 2019), 28–29; 37–48; 57–59.

to death if not resisted through the exercise of free will. To stay free of evil, every person must choose to live a life of divine shalom.

St. Augustine of Hippo on Original Sin and Guilt

St. Augustine of Hippo first developed a doctrine of original sin as *inherited human guilt* in the fifth century. By conflating sin and guilt, he posited that all humanity, at the moment of conception, inherits a literal, personal guilt (not just a sin nature or a propensity to sin) from the sin of our first parent Adam and is therefore condemned and doomed to die a physical and spiritual death (Rom 5:12). Sin and its consequential guilt, therefore, reside in our DNA, so to speak, as a mutation of God's original creation of a sin-free humanity.[39] The science of Augustine's time influenced his views and may have helped conflate sin with guilt. At that time, people believed the "seed" of the man contained a fully developed miniature human (or homunculus). This view was a primitive way of talking about how Adam's semen literally contained all of humankind, a sort of proto-theory of physical DNA.[40] In addition, Augustine argued that sexual intercourse propagated the inherited guilt of original sin. Although prominent in modern times within the Augustinian-Calvinist tradition, these ideas have struck many as odd or implausible (even ethically immoral), and have not found universal acceptance, by any means.[41] Orthodox theologian V. Rev. Antony Hughes points out that "the doctrine of ancestral sin naturally leads to a focus on human death and Divine compassion as the inheritance from Adam, while the doctrine of original sin [as interpreted by Augustine] shifts the center of attention to human guilt and Divine wrath."[42]

The doctrine of original sin (and how we interpret it) has major implications for other Christian ideas, such as baptism and the afterlife. As we have seen, for the first three centuries or so of Christianity, though they had no concept of original sin (guilt) yet, early Christians baptized believers as a mark of faith. Baptism initiated new adult Christians into the participatory life of God that liberated them from the consequence of Adam's ancestral sin—that is, death. When the church father Tertullian began to articulate an idea of "hell" in the late second century (an idea imported partly from the pagan culture's idea of an afterlife of punishment), Christians started baptizing infants so that if they died early, they would escape the flames of hell. But Tertullian himself objected to the practice of infant baptism and wondered how infants, who had never actually sinned, could be guilty of sin.

---

39. Augustine, "On Original Sin," 652–53.
40. Suchocki, *The Fall to Violence*, 21–22.
41. Richard Swinburne, "Responsibility, Atonement, and Forgiveness," in *Debating Christian Theism*, ed. J. P. Moreland, Chad Meister, and Khaldoun A. Sweis (New York: Oxford University Press, 2013), 361–71; and William Lane Craig, "Original Sin," Reasonable Faith, October 22, 2017, https://tinyurl.com/y84c9h68.
42. Antony Hughes, "Ancestral versus Original Sin: An Overview with Implications for Psychotherapy," https://tinyurl.com/y8qoop9c.

With the development of St. Augustine's doctrine of original sin in the fifth century, infant baptism became standard practice. In St. Augustine's interpretation of original sin as original guilt, *all* persons who die before being baptized spend eternity in hell. Notice the penal emphasis of this theory, even for infants. This theology caused a critical problem in St. Augustine's day and for centuries afterward because, unfortunately, infant mortality rates reached around 50 percent through the fifteenth century. Teachings about original sin, especially as interpreted by St. Augustine, have created much anguish and suffering over centuries for mothers and others discerning enough to detect the inherent contradictions within them.[43]

The early church, in contrast (in accordance with St. Paul), asserted that as in Adam all died, all shall be made alive in Christ, the second Adam. The Pauline theology in Romans 5 focuses not on the guilt of sin but on God's salvation from sin's consequences and, in chapter 6, the divine power to raise us up with Christ to new life. Remember, the early church believed salvation consisted of Jesus triumphing over the devil/evil that held us captive. They spoke of how Jesus saves us from the consequences of sin, and of death as separation from the original divine intention. In this way, their conception of sin (as opposed to guilt) is a way of talking about something gone wrong through inherited death rather than as humanity gone wrong through inherited sin and guilt. Eastern Orthodox Christians have, in fact, over the centuries never accepted Augustine's idea of inherited guilt, and the modern Roman Catholic Church rejects Augustinian and later Calvinistic ideas about how sin results in "total depravity," a term we discussed in chapter 4.

But St. Augustine's influence still deeply pervades Christian thought today. As we noted previously, for many Christians who maintain this Augustinian doctrine, the purifying waters of baptism cure the infection of original sin. Even though infant mortality rates have gradually improved with the invention of the microscope and other medical means, many Christian denominations still baptize babies in order to wash away the taint of Adam's original sin, often with the accompanying teaching that baptism serves as a way of saving people from hell. That said, many other Christian denominations, such as Lutheran, Methodist, some Presbyterian, and Reformed churches practice infant baptism as a sign of grace. For these Christians, baptism cleanses infants from the power of sin before the child actually sins, providing a clear witness to the fact that this grace is a free gift that cannot be earned.

43. Limbo and other solutions for infants were offered by the medieval Roman Catholic Church. For a modern scholarly evangelical treatment of the doctrine of inherited guilt in relation to infants, see Adam Harwood, *The Spiritual Condition of Infants: A Biblical-Historical Survey and Systematic Proposal* (Eugene, OR: Wipf & Stock, 2011). Harwood rejects the Augustinian-Calvinist view of original guilt and the idea that infants go to hell without baptism, without denying that infants can participate in an ancestral "sin nature" or tendency toward personal sin.

The Propensity to Sin

Pelagius (354–418), Augustine's theological nemesis and a monk and theologian in the British Isles, rejected the notion that infants, who have never sinned, should suffer eternal punishment in hell. In fact, in his view, no person experiences divine condemnation until he or she actually sins. Every person is born pure, without sin, and, if they choose, can live life in total righteousness. Yet, even Pelagius admits that most, if not all, people sin and that, as such, each person is responsible for his or her own sin, not the sin of past generations. Pelagianism typically interprets original sin as the "propensity" or "tendency" to sin, rather than as a literal infection all humans inherit from Adam.[44] Western theologians such as Abelard, Arminius, John Wesley, Vladimir Lossky, Paul Tillich, and Richard Rohr do not directly use the language of "original sin," but speak instead of every person being unable to resist the temptation to sin. For example, we could see Adam's sin in the garden story as merely symbolizing the sin of all humanity, showing us something that is typical of every person. All of us are guilty of our own sin just as Adam was guilty of his, but we do not inherit sin from our first parents. We inherit the propensity, or the leaning toward sin, but God holds us accountable for our own sin only.

We make a mistake when we believe that those who rejected (and continue to question in our own day) an idea of original, inherited guilt did not take sin seriously.[45] We all know, as they did, that sin adversely affects human character and influences the way we behave in the world. In that manner, sin is like an infection, poisoning every human thought and endeavor; infiltrating the structures and institutions we create; spreading evil, violence, suffering, and destruction on a universal level. Sin remains a powerful way of talking about the suffering and evil we see all around us. As Suchocki notes, sin, as going against shalom, is an even larger and more pervasive category than guilt. We have to see ideas of sin and the story of Adam and Eve in the garden as attempts to deal with questions related to what theologians call the problem of evil.

The Problem of Evil and Suffering

Many theologians throughout the ages have tried to explain the existence of evil in light of an omnibenevolent (all-good) and omnipotent (all-powerful) God. Traditionally, we can divide the problem of the existence of evil into moral evil—that created by the thoughts and actions of moral agents, which corresponds to sin—and natural evil—that created by natural disasters and processes that cause suffering.

---

44. Augustine, "On Original Sin," 634–35.
45. Pelagius's thought was found by one church council to be orthodox but then condemned as heretical by later councils. Yet many of the church fathers before Augustine—namely Justin Martyr, Theophilus, Irenaeus, and Clement of Alexandria—taught that humans have the power of free will and choice over good and evil.

Of course, the problem of evil causes us to question the nature of God and the created order. The problem, as articulated by philosophers and theologians is termed *theodicy* and, simply put, goes as follows: If God is all good, God will want to create a world in which evil does not exist. If God is all powerful, God has the power to create a world in which evil does not exist. But evil does exist. So, God must either be all powerful but not all good or all good but not all powerful.

Because of the influence of classical theism, we may find it difficult either to nuance or to dismiss omnipotence and omnibenevolence. Instead, theologians have often tried to find ways to justify God in the face of evil and suffering—a theological category of arguments called *theodicy*, from *dike* ("to justify") and *theos* ("God"). When we construct a theodicy, we attempt to explain or justify how God can be both all good and all powerful and still allow evil to exist. Scholars have crafted various solutions to this problem that claim varying degrees of clarity, coherence, and consistency with the claims of an all-powerful, all-good God. Given the space limitations, we can only briefly address the most common solutions.[46]

Soul-Making and Connection-Building Theodicies

First proposed by the second-century theologian Irenaeus and later modified and made popular by the twentieth-century philosopher and theologian John Hick, the Soul-Making Theodicy defends the idea that evil exists in order to help human beings use their freedom to develop into mature spiritual persons who eventually spend eternity united with God.[47] This theodicy claims that God specifically designed the best possible world in a way that would implement evil to build our characters, to bring our souls into a state of God-readiness. In this case, evil serves as a "greater good" that could not otherwise be accomplished.

Contemporary philosopher Robin Collins expands on the "greater good" model a little differently with his Connection-Building Theodicy. He explains that the evils in the world draw people not only toward God but toward one another in love. Through suffering the evils that infect our lives, we develop intimate connections to others. The benefits of these eternal connections, Collins claims, far outweigh the temporal suffering induced by evil.[48] Collins's connection-building view has the advantage of not wishing away sin and evil, but also not simply attributing them to free will or the chance for individual soul-building—explanations that can feel lacking to actual victims of violence. Rather, he shows how even the unfortunate

46. The brevity of this section on evil may motivate readers to do more research on the topic. For further reading, see Chad V. Meister, *Evil: A Guide for the Perplexed* (New York: Bloomsbury, 2018); Augustine, *On the Free Choice of the Will*, trans. Thomas Williams (Indianapolis, IN: Hackett, 1993); Stephen Davis, *Encountering Evil: Live Options in Theodicy* (Louisville, KY: Westminster John Knox, 2001); John Hick, *Evil and the God of Love* (London: Palgrave Macmillan, 2010); Richard Swinburne, *Providence and the Problem of Evil* (Oxford: Clarendon, 1998).
47. Hick, *Evil and the God of Love*, 253–56.
48. Robin Collins, "The Connection-Building Theodicy," in *The Blackwell Companion to the Problem of Evil*, eds. Justin P. McBrayer and Daniel Howard Snyder (Hoboken, NJ: Wiley Blackwell, 2014): 222–35.

existence of evil can work toward greater relationships and love in the universe. The Connection-Building Theodicy has also been called the Love Theodicy since it works well in explaining the experiences of those who have undergone oppression. We help each other within and moving forward out of oppression, and these connections of love, like love itself, abide forever.

Free-Will Defense Theodicy

Articulated by St. Augustine of Hippo in the fourth and fifth centuries, the Free-Will Defense Theodicy remains a widely accepted solution to the question of God's goodness and power in the face of evil and suffering. St. Augustine started out asking, "Where did evil come from?" Because he believed that only good can come from God, Augustine asserted that God could not have created or caused evil. Evil, then, must be a nonexistent negation of good, since God created everything that exists. But if God created everything that exists and created it all good, how did evil enter the world? St. Augustine believed that even though God created everything good, the world is still finite and changeable. Consequently, human beings, with their finite and changeable wills, turned away from the goodness of the divine will and, in so doing, brought evil into God's good creation. The blame for evil, therefore, in St. Augustine's opinion, falls squarely on human beings, whose acts, deprived of good, make space for evil.

Notice how St. Augustine's theodicy conflates evil (and sin) with moral wrongdoing or guilt. It simply does not account for natural evil or must implicitly attribute some major change in how the natural physical world behaves to the consequences of Adam's sin.[49] It also does not explain the problem of evil very well from the point of view of those who have historically been the primary victims (rather than the perpetrators) of sinful social structures.[50]

Philosopher Alvin Plantinga expounds on the notion of human freedom, asserting that a world in which God creates human beings with the freedom to make their own choices is far better than a world in which humans have no freedom at all. Since the freedom to choose automatically assumes we have choices to make, God must have created us to choose between good and evil. In creating authentically free creatures, God must allow us to make those choices without stepping in

49. Collins deals with numerous thorny issues that I do not have space to cover, particularly describing various historical views of the Genesis 3 text and exploring the implications of these theological questions given what we know about animal behavior and possible evolutionary beginnings. For different views of the historicity of the text, see Collins, "Evolution and Original Sin," in *Perspectives on an Evolving Creation*, ed. Keith B. Miller (Grand Rapids, MI: Eerdmans, 2003), 489–94. For the question of whether Adam and Eve were ever in a literal paradisial state, see p. 493. See also the treatment of the Garden Story in an evolutionary scenario in Raymund Schwager, *Banished from Eden: Original Sin and Evolutionary Theory in the Drama of Salvation* (Herefordshire, UK: Gracewing, 2006).
50. Robin Collins offers a general critique of this problem in "Evolution and Original Sin," 489–96. See also John Haught's discussion of natural evil and the problems of traditional theodicy in "Teilhard and the Question of Life's Suffering," in *Rediscovering Teilhard's Fire*, ed. Kathleen Duffy (Philadelphia: St. Joseph's University Press, 2010).

and preventing them—that would render our freedom meaningless. Unfortunately, human beings used their God-given freedom to choose evil, and as a result, we live in a world that struggles with evil in confrontation with good.[51]

Protest Theodicy

This theodicy finds voice in the book of Job, in various Psalms, and in the work of Jewish theologians.[52] In the face of evil, those who suffer honestly question God's total goodness, justice, and mercy. They lament and protest the evil that has so disrupted their lives. In the midst of suffering, they cry out to God, like Job, who continually proclaims his innocence (Job 23:10); like the Psalmist, who begs God to lift him out of his distress (Ps 13:1–4); like Jacob, who wrestles all night with God (Gen 32:22–32), or like Jesus, who from the cross exclaims, "My God, my God, why have you forsaken me?" (Mark 15:34). They remind God to remember them and to return them to the divine loving embrace. So, although Protest Theodicy never really provides answers or solutions to the problem of evil, it allows us to ask God questions that may otherwise seem irreverent. It allows us to exercise faith in the midst of great doubt—after all, the act of protesting against God indicates a measure of faith that God will listen and intervene. In addition, since we usually only complain to our closest, most loved friends and family, our laments against the divine in the face of evil demonstrate the existence of an intimate and dynamic relationship with God. Protest theodicy confronts the reality of evil head-on and, at times, even blames God for it. But it also recognizes that the heart of God desires always to redeem and restore, and that only God is finally able to overcome evil. And God, through Christ, seeks to overcome evil and give spiritual enlightenment, transforming all creation into something new.

Transformation to a New Creation— A New Nonviolent, Loving Humanity

Genesis 3 conveys a deep theological truth about how evil and suffering infiltrate our world in profoundly disturbing and disastrous ways. It recounts an ideal order that Adam and Eve violated, an ideal that may or may not ever have been realized, depending on how literally one interprets the ancient accounts. But, fortunately, sin and evil do not have the final say. From the beginning, from the time of that first human stepping outside the limitations of the divine will, God set out to redeem, reconcile, and restore. Walter Brueggemann affirms that the story in Genesis 3 tells us more about God's desire to redeem and restore than about the despair and

---

51. Alvin Plantinga, *God, Freedom, and Evil* (Grand Rapids, MI: Eerdmans, 1977), 30.
52. For example, Elie Wiesel, *Night* (New York: Hill & Wang, 1958); John K. Roth, "A Theodicy of Protest," in *Encountering Evil: Live Options in Theodicy*, ed. Stephen T. Davis (Atlanta: John Knox, 1981): 7–22.

hopelessness of our sinful situation: "The miracle is not that [humans] are punished, but that they live. . . . When the facts warrant death, God insists on life for his creatures."[53] God begins the redemptive, life-giving process with the symbolic act of clothing the man and woman. Since they cannot survive the wild new world without this God-given covering, clothing the two partners essentially symbolizes the divine act of giving them life. Having thus clothed the "first Adam" as an act of redemption, God continues the process of salvation and directs history and all creation toward the coming of the second Adam, Jesus of Nazareth (Rom 5:12–21).

As we discussed in chapter 7, "Salvation and Atonement," God redeemed humanity by redoing (recapitulating) the human condition. In other words, by giving us the life of Jesus Christ, the second Adam, God brings us back to the originally intended, spiritually enlightened condition in which we stood before sin entered the scene. In so doing, God reverses the consequences of sin and provides us with the power to live as "little Christs," representatives of Jesus in the world, for "it is no longer [we] who live, but it is Christ who lives in [us]" (Gal 2:20). Through Jesus, we become what God intended for us to be all along.

Recapitulation: The Divine Do-Over

So, what does this great reparative reversal look like?

We reflect God's image. The image of God in us is "the key to our human nature and the link that connects us to God. It is the clue to the whole question of human knowledge of God."[54] But tarnished by sin, God's image in us remains hidden until the cleansing power and new birth offered by Jesus Christ are manifested in our lives. Through his act of recapitulation, Jesus "scrubbed the tarnish off" the image of God given to us in Genesis 1 at the creation of humanity. We can liken the process of cleaning up our image with the metaphor of a goldsmith preparing raw gold for the creation of a beautiful piece of jewelry. The craftsperson puts a chunk of gold in a crucible and, under extreme heat, melts it until all the impurities rise to the surface. The craftsperson skims them off, allows the gold to cool, and repeats the process. He knows the process is completed when he can look into the melted gold, clear of impurities, and see his own image reflected back. In like manner, God can look at us and, in our new, reborn humanity, can see God's own image reflected back. With the impurities of sin cleansed away, we now reflect God's image for all to see, in the workplace, at home, and in public venues. God through Christ cleanses us of our impurities and allows us to reflect the divine light. Through the renewed image of God in us, "we have the mind of Christ" (1 Cor 2:16), and therefore, we have power through the Holy Spirit to reflect God and to

53. Brueggemann, *Genesis*, 44, 49–50.
54. Garrett Green, *Imagining God: Theology and the Religious Imagination* (San Francisco: Harper & Row, 1989), 84.

transform the world for God's glory.[55] "The Spirit is the one who makes us holy . . . restores the image of God in our souls, and discloses the invisible God. The Spirit lifts up our hearts, holds the hand of the infirm, brings us to perfection" so that we can serve as reflections of Jesus in the world.[56]

We have the freedom to will what God wills. With Jesus as our redeemer and example and with the Holy Spirit as our enabler, we live spiritually enlightened lives. We are released from the slavery to sin and have a new freedom for partnership with God and others to transform the world. We can return to our original created purpose and will what God wills by carrying out "the ministry of reconciliation" to which God has called us, working with God toward the ultimate goal of ushering in the kingdom of God on earth (2 Cor 5:18). We work alongside God to set others free from sin, unrighteousness, oppression, and injustice through the non-coercive, nonviolent power God reveals in the first creation story and gives to us through the Holy Spirit. We work to eliminate spiritual ignorance with the light of new life. As a new humanity, we will what God wills—the ability for all to flourish; we live in solidarity with those who suffer, and we invite others into God's kingdom of justice, mercy, and love.[57] James Cone reminds us that our human freedom "becomes a reality when [we] throw in [our] lot with the cause of the oppressed . . . and participate in a community of those who are victims of oppression."[58] We truly experience our originally created freedom when we seek "to emancipate" ourselves and others from the abuses and violence of injustice.[59]

We live as community-minded individuals. In chapter 5 on creation, we discussed the five ways God loves all creation. Those same forms of love inherently exist among the members of the kingdom of God, a redeemed humanity, as we live in community. We love as God loves because God first loved us (1 John 4:7–20). And if we believe that God is love, then that extravagant love, by its very nature, is self-giving. It loves unconditionally, intimately, affectionately, practically, and longingly. It seems self-evident, therefore, that we should love one another in the same ways.

We participate in the universality of redemption. We have examined different metaphors and images for sin. We could say that just as sin is like an infection within all of creation, so redemption is its cure—an antibiotic that destroys the intrusion of sin and re-creates us into new beings who imitate God in Christ. In fact, God tells John to write down the true and trustworthy words that say God is making

55. Tillich, *Systematic Theology*, vol. 1, 256.
56. Catherine Mowry LaCugna, *God for Us: The Trinity and Christian Life* (San Francisco: Harper-SanFrancisco, 1973), 119.
57. Migliore, *Faith Seeking Understanding*, 160.
58. Cone, *Black Theology of Liberation*, 171.
59. James R. Payton, *Light from the Christian East: An Introduction to the Orthodox Tradition* (Downers Grove, IL: IVP Academic, 2007), 98–99.

all things—all creation—new. Indeed, it is already done, finished, by the Alpha and the Omega, the first and the last. The one who began the work of redemption has finished it (Rev 21:5–6). We see a clear trajectory, a coherence between the beginning (creation) and the end (salvation) that offers all creation hope for final redemption and eternal life with God, that renews and recreates in this present time a community with undivided hearts, living out that hope for the world to see.[60] We, then, as people redeemed and recreated by the love and power of God, participate with God in transforming the world for God's glory. As the very present body of Christ, we live as Jesus on earth and, by loving others, work with God toward finally seeing *"every* knee . . . bend" and hearing *"every* tongue . . . confess that Jesus Christ is Lord, to the glory of God the Father" (Phil 2:10–11; emphasis mine).

60. Richard Rohr, *Eager to Love: The Alternative Way of Francis of Assisi* (Cincinnati: Franciscan Media: 2014), 209–10.

11. The Last Things

. . . and he will come to judge the living and the dead.

. . . the resurrection of the body, and the life everlasting.

> Through me the way into the suffering city,
> Through me the way to the eternal pain,
> Through me the way that runs among the lost.
> Justice urged on my high artificer;
> My maker was divine authority,
> The highest wisdom, and the primal love.
> Before me nothing but eternal things
> Were made, and I endure eternally.
> Abandon hope all who enter here.
>
> —Dante, *The Divine Comedy*

> It behoved that there should be sin; but all shall be well, and all shall be well, and all manner of thing shall be well.
>
> —Julian of Norwich, *Revelations of Divine Love*

> No eschatological perspective is sufficient which does not challenge the present order.
>
> —James Cone, *Black Theology of Liberation*

Doomsday. The end of the world. Fluffy clouds and pearly gates. For millennia, artists have fascinated our imaginations with depictions of what happens after death, as well as of the destruction of this world at the end of time. They either feed our fear of the unknown or stimulate our hope for the future. In his famous literary work *The Divine Comedy*, Dante Alighieri (1265–1321) paints a graphic depiction of the afterlife. He describes in horrific detail the eternal sufferings of hell, the temporary yet terrible punishments in purgatory, and the infinite happiness of those in heaven. For a visual representation, we can turn to Hieronymus Bosch's famous *Visions of the Hereafter*, four compelling panel paintings that illustrate the fate of the unfortunate hell-bound and the bliss of the blessed ones headed for heaven.[1] The many artworks, films, and literary works portraying the end of the world reveal our human curiosity about the "end times"—inquisitiveness that often

---

1. See Hieronymus Bosch, *Visions of the Hereafter*, https://tinyurl.com/yaaldlj2.

leads to apparently insatiable doomsday deliberations. We want to know how and when the end will occur and what, if any, type of life we will have after "heaven and earth . . . pass away" (Matt 24:35).

In theology the study of the "last things" is called *eschatology*, from the Greek word *eschatos*, meaning "last." Eschatology is concerned with things such as death, judgment, and the final destiny of the individual soul, but also with the fate of humankind as a whole and the final events of history. The existential curiosity of theologians and biblical scholars throughout the centuries has generated library shelves full of theories about God's eschatological plans for creation. Each theory presupposes a divine *telos* (ultimate purpose) for which God directs all creation toward the future, toward a glorious reign in fulfillment of God's ultimate will for the universe. Interestingly, the historic creeds, confessional statements, and formal doctrines of the main Christian traditions attach little weight to one theory over another. Each theory rests primarily on specific interpretations of the book of Revelation and parts of the book of Daniel, and most of these interpretations differ quite significantly. Consequently, we have a stunning amount of theological diversity surrounding the return of Christ and the reign of God in a new heaven and a new earth.[2] While admitting to the speculative nature of eschatological thought, most Christians agree on popular eschatological themes such as the return of Christ, the resurrection of the dead, the final judgment, and the new heaven and new earth, even if many spiritualize these events. But we need to remember the warning issued by theologian Reinhold Niebuhr against speculating on the exact "furniture of heaven and the temperature of hell."[3] That said, what are some of these speculations that have so excited Christians throughout the ages?

Eschatological Theories and Interpreting the Scriptures

Any responsible theology of the end times begins with a responsible reading and interpretation of the book of Revelation. We need to remember, however, that the church has never accepted any one reading of Revelation or one eschatological theory as the "official" interpretation. Because of this, we must approach this study with humility and graciousness, knowing we do not know how God will bring about the last days and what will happen afterward. Let's first discuss several of the ways the church has interpreted Revelation.

Many people believe that Revelation serves as a biblical code that discloses the future—an interpretation aptly known as *futuristic*. Those who hold this view believe the book points to a final, apocalyptic event at the very end of time as we know it. According to the futuristic understanding, all eschatological events in

---

2. See Roger E. Olson, *Mosaic of Christian Belief: Twenty Centuries of Unity and Disunity* (Downers Grove, IL: InterVarsity, 2016), 308, 334–35; Stanley J. Grenz, *Theology for the Community of God* (Grand Rapids, MI: Eerdmans, 2000), 608–9.
3. Reinhold Niebuhr, *The Nature and Destiny of Man*, vol. 2 (New York: C. Scribner's Sons, 1949), 294.

Revelation occur in the future. Others hold to the *preterist* approach to Revelation, believing that most of the events described already occurred in the first century. In this case, they could point to the destruction of Jerusalem in 70 CE as the apocalypse. The *historicist* view, on the other hand, believes that the symbols in Revelation reveal certain historical persons or events from when John wrote the book: for example, the antichrist was Rome or the Roman emperor, and the text spoke out against that worldly rule.[4] Others take a more eclectic approach to the symbols and images in Revelation, believing in an "already but not yet" perspective—the kingdom of God is here, but not completely; the time of the end is happening, but not yet fully; the salvation of God through Christ is finished, but not finally fulfilled. These interpreters read Revelation as a text that describes both events that have taken place and events that will occur in the future.

Regardless of how we perceive Revelation temporally, we still need to interpret the symbols, images, and events in the text, deciding whether to read the book as literal, historically accurate accounts or as figurative language and metaphors that point us toward profound truths about God's kingdom and the eschaton (the last days). Biblical scholars throughout history have taken various approaches. We will briefly discuss just a few of them. The first of these views deal with the second coming of Christ.

Postmillennialism

Prominent during the nineteenth and twentieth centuries and aligned with the Social Gospel movement, postmillennialism states that the return of Christ will occur at the end of a literal, thousand-year "golden age" of peace.[5] Those who hold this view believe that the gospel message will eventually reach all nations, including Jews. Salvation through Jesus will ultimately transform the world for God's glory, bringing in a utopian era of shalom and righteous living. Once the world reaches moral readiness, it will welcome the return of Christ. This viewpoint emphasizes the work of human beings empowered by the Holy Spirit to bring about God's will on earth. After the two world wars in the early twentieth century, however, this hopeful view fell into disrepute. Rather than heading toward a utopian perfection, humanity seemed to be speeding toward its own destruction.[6]

---

4. For a good explanation of these theories, see Olson, *Mosaic of Christian Belief*, 350–52.
5. For more about postmillennialism, see N. T. Wright, *History and Eschatology: Jesus and the Promise of Natural Theology* (Waco, TX: Baylor University Press, 2019).
6. Richard J. Plantinga, Thomas R. Thompson, and Matthew D. Lundberg, *An Introduction to Christian Theology* (Cambridge: Cambridge University Press, 2010), 399.

Dispensational Premillennialism

Dispensational premillennialists try to interpret Revelation as a literal, historically accurate text that predicts the future. These believers divide history into specific periods called "dispensations," claiming that God works differently throughout these ages of time and, most significantly, that the nation of Israel has a special eschatological purpose. Dispensationalist views claim the end of this age marks the beginning of the great tribulation (a time of persecution) for the Jewish people. The raptured church will celebrate the great marriage feast of the Lamb in heaven (Rev 19:1–10), while the antichrist wreaks havoc on earth and God prepares Israel to accept Jesus as the Messiah. The people on earth will suffer profound persecution that culminates in a major war, in the midst of which Christ will return with his heavenly armies, conquer the devil and his cohorts, and set up the literal millennium. All Israel will "look on the one whom they have pierced" and be saved (Zech 12:10). During these one thousand years, the nation of Israel will enjoy a time of peace and prominence, basking in the blessings of God.[7]

First articulated in the 1830s by John Nelson Darby, who believed that God must deal separately and differently with Israel, this theory has enjoyed prominence in evangelical media since 1970 with Hal Lindsey's book *The Late Great Planet Earth* and the Left Behind book series written by Tim LaHaye and Jerry Jenkins. These theologians propose that God devised one plan for Israel, which must take place in the literal land of Canaan, and another plan for the church, which takes place in heaven. Many scholars have legitimate problems with this view, contending that God would not separate the ethnic state of Israel from the multiethnic church for salvific purposes. In other words, contrary to dispensationalism, God does not save Israel any differently than God saves gentiles. Because of this focus on Israel, pastor Brian Zahnd argues that dispensationalism is a "thoroughly modern and deeply mistaken reading of the Bible."[8]

Historic Premillennialism

Historic premillennialism, another view that attempts to interpret Revelation as a literal account of the end of time, holds that Christ will return after a seven-year tribulation period and the battle of Armageddon depicted in Daniel and Revelation. At that point, he will set up his thousand-year reign on earth, a time of peace and prosperity for everyone until the final resurrection of the dead, the great judgment, and the ushering in of the new heaven and new earth. But according to this view, God does not deal separately with Israel. In fact, the church serves as the

---

7. See Grenz, *Theology for the Community of God*, 616–17; Plantinga, Thompson, and Lundberg, *Introduction to Christian Theology*, 400.
8. Brian Zahnd, *Sinners in the Hands of a Loving God: The Scandalous Truth of the Very Good News* (Colorado Springs, CO: Waterbrook, 2017), 148.

continuation of the nation of Israel as a "chosen race, a royal priesthood, a holy nation, God's own people" (1 Pet 2:9).

Many early church fathers held this view, including Justin Martyr, Irenaeus, and Tertullian. In his *Dialogue with Trypho the Jew*, however, Justin Martyr spoke of various views and concluded that even though he personally believed the millennium would be a literal one thousand years, other very pious and faithful Christians thought otherwise.[9]

A Word on the "Rapture"

In 1 Thessalonians 4:13–18, the apostle Paul describes an event during which believers in Christ will suddenly rise up to meet Jesus in the air. For eighteen hundred years of church history, most Christians saw this passage as an image of the second coming of Christ. Paul had written this passage to the church in Thessalonica, whose members worried about the fate of loved ones who had died before Jesus returned. Paul wrote to reassure the church that everyone, both dead and alive at the time of Christ's return, would partake in heavenly glory with the Lord. So, while Christians had an idea of a sudden event, the term *rapture* (which means, literally, a "kidnapping" or "taking away") never appears in the Bible.

John Nelson Darby claimed the revelation of a "new doctrine" in the early 1830s, with the teaching of a two-part return of Christ: first, a "secret" rapture event in which Jesus returns to the earth's atmosphere and takes the church up from the earth to be with him, then his actual second coming to the earth.[10] This view has gained popularity in evangelical circles, despite the fact that it is relatively recent and has no real precedent in church history. Contrary to this popular belief, the Roman Catholic Church, Eastern Orthodox Church, Anglican Communion, Lutheran tradition, and some Calvinist denominations do not hold an idea of the rapture as a preliminary return of Christ.

For Christians who interpret 1 Thessalonians 4 as describing a rapture, its timing relates to the great tribulation predicted in Daniel and Revelation, when they believe the antichrist will set up three and a half years of peace and then three and a half years of persecution, war, and chaos before Christ returns. Dispensationalists believe the rapture will occur *before* the tribulation (pre-tribulation rapture). Some historic premillennialists believe it will occur in the *middle* of the tribulation period after half of this literal seven-year period (mid-tribulation rapture). Other historic premillennialists believe the rapture will occur at the same time as Christ's second coming (a post-tribulation view). Most Christians through history, however, have not seen this passage as describing a separate event from Christ's second coming. We can only speculate what this very mysterious occurrence will

---

9. Justin Martyr, *Dialogue with Trypho the Jew* (Pickering, OH: Beloved, 2015), 97, chapter 80.
10. Donald J. Akenson, *Exporting the Rapture: John Nelson Darby and the Victorian Conquest of North American Evangelicalism* (Oxford: Oxford University Press, 2018), 40–48.

look like. What does seem apparent, however, is that our Christian hope remains intact. In one way or another, we can affirm, we will not get left behind; we will all be with Jesus Christ at the end.

Amillennialism

Amillennialism provides us with another, more plausible view that found popularity with the early church and with many theologians throughout history. This view treats Revelation as a book filled with symbolic, figurative language that, if taken literally, causes a number of awkward hermeneutical problems. Amillennialists believe that a literal interpretation of Revelation amounts to irresponsible hermeneutics, asserting that any competent and conscientious reading of Scripture includes the consideration of genre. We treat genres comprising apocalyptic, figurative language, packed full of imaginative metaphors and abstract symbols, differently than we do historical narratives or epistles.

For example, no one believes, as the book of Revelation asserts, that three frogs will literally lead a large army, or that a lamb with seven literal eyes and seven horns sits next to God, or that a beast with ten horns and seven heads will literally rise out of the ocean (Rev 16:13–14; 5:6; 13:1). At the same time, these strong symbols may point to very real events. As theologian Brian Zahnd says: "Both Armageddon and New Jerusalem are symbols, but they are true symbols of very real alternative fates. The way of the beast leads to Armageddon, while the way of the Lamb leads to the New Jerusalem."[11] So for Zahnd and many other scholars, such as the ancients Clement of Alexandria, Origen, and Cyprian, most medieval Catholics, and the Protestant Reformers, the most responsible way to read Revelation is to accept the fact that it describes significant events in figurative language. In fact, John Calvin says of those who attempt to interpret Revelation and the thousand-year period literally, "Now their fiction is too childish either to need or to be worth a refutation. . . . For the number 'one thousand' (Rev 20:4) does not apply to the eternal blessedness of the church but only to the various disturbances that awaited the church while toiling on earth."[12] Here, Calvin articulates a widespread view that equates the millennium with the period of time called the Church Age.

Amillennialism was also a hermeneutical method espoused by St. Augustine. He believed that the millennium symbolized all the events in history starting from Christ's first coming and ending with Christ's return.[13] According to this view, we already live in the millennium; we live in the midst of the reign of Christ on earth and the kingdom of God right now. Through the power of the cross and resurrection of Christ, God has defeated sin and death, transformed the human

---

11. Zahnd, *Sinners in the Hands of a Loving God*, 154.
12. John Calvin, *Institutes of the Christian Religion*, ed. John T. McNeill, trans. Ford Lewis Battles (Louisville, KY: Westminster John Knox, 1960), 3.25.5.
13. Augustine, *City of God*, ed. Henry Bettenson (New York: Penguin, 1984), 20.7.

condition, and inaugurated the divine kingdom. At the same time, the dominion of darkness still holds sway over the creation. Though defeated by Jesus, sin and death continue to stalk us, war and violence still ravage our nations, and disease continues to inflict suffering. The spirit of antichrist, the lawless one destined for destruction, continues to torment (1 John 4:3; 2 Thess 2:3). Said another way, the Spirit of Christ in the kingdom of God works to redeem and transform the world for God's glory, while the spirit of antichrist in the dominion of darkness works to deceive and destroy the world for the sake of evil. The Christian hope lies in the fact that Jesus has already won the victory; the kingdom of God is already here, with us, and we reign in the kingdom with Christ as his body on earth, working with God to bring peace on earth and good will to all people.

Of course, amillennialism also requires that we exist within the landscape of the "already but not yet." We live and work in God's kingdom now, but we look forward in hope to the final fulfillment of a future that has not yet come. Drawing on the chronology of World War II, theologians Benjamin Gladd and Matthew Harmon express this two-stage eschatology: "Christians live between D-day [invasion day] and V-day [victory day]. D-day was the first coming of Christ, when the opponent was defeated decisively; V-day is the final coming of Christ, when the adversary will finally and completely surrender."[14] In the meantime, our hope for the fulfillment of Christ's victory remains steadfast, as we recognize that the victory over sin, evil, and death has already come to pass.

Although in amillennialism the church reigns now in the eschatological kingdom, while awaiting the final fulfillment it has the responsibility to critique the status quo. We should remain uncomfortable with empires and worldly power structures that deceive and destroy, oppress and overpower, enthrall and enslave us. Revelation reveals a dramatic contrast between the Roman Empire and the kingdom of God in Christ. It expresses a clash between the "beastly empire of Rome and the peaceable reign of the Lamb of God." Jesus wins the victory, not through a violent bloodbath fought with weapons of destruction, but by the precious blood of the peaceable Lamb through his death on the cross and the resurrection to new life.[15] Revelation calls us to the peacemaking, compassionate, love-filled way of life modeled by Jesus, the Lamb of God who takes away the sin and violence of the world by redeeming and transforming it through self-sacrificing love. We can already sing with the voices in heaven: "The kingdom of the world has become the kingdom of our Lord and of his Messiah, and he will reign forever and ever" (Rev 11:15).

As Zahnd writes, Revelation "is perhaps the most important biblical text for the . . . church right now."[16] It magnificently, creatively, and provocatively serves as our guide to living in the world under the shadow of the unjust powers that be. It

---

14. Benjamin L. Gladd and Matthew S. Harmon, *Making All Things New* (Grand Rapids, MI: Baker Academic, 2016), 9.
15. Zahnd, *Sinners in the Hands of a Loving God*, 152–53, 162.
16. Zahnd, *Sinners in the Hands of a Loving God*, 150.

reminds us that the revelation of Jesus Christ truly is good news, that our hope is not in vain, and that God's will for the redemption of all creation will reach fulfillment in the future. But it also reminds us that as members of God's already very present kingdom, we have work to do in partnership with Christ in the power of the Spirit.

Salvation and the Afterlife

When I teach students about this "already" stance, they inevitably ask, "But what about salvation and the afterlife?" So before we discuss how we live eschatologically in the "now," we will explore theories surrounding the afterlife. Many students wonder what happens immediately after death: Do we go directly to heaven? Do we see Jesus at the end of that "tunnel of light" that near-death researchers have talked about? Theologians have varying views on this topic. Most of them agree that we will all stand before God for an eschatological judgment and that, in Christ, we will escape death and rest eternally in God's loving presence, where evil, darkness, and suffering are abolished. The main differences in theological circles arise when we consider the time period between death and the final resurrection.

Intermediate State

Based on the words of Jesus to the thief on the cross, "Today you will be with me in Paradise" (Luke 23:43), and Paul's affirmation that "to be absent from the body [is] to be present with the Lord" (2 Cor 5:8 KJV), the intermediate state holds that, at death, the immortal soul separates from the mortal body and goes to dwell with Jesus Christ in heaven. We then exist in a state of disembodied consciousness with God as we await the time of the final resurrection when our bodies and souls reunite and live eternally in the new heaven and the new earth in glory.[17] Roman Catholicism adds a variation to the intermediate state and claims that souls not quite holy enough to enter directly into the presence of God go first to a place of preparation called "purgatory," for a purifying time of suffering. *The Catechism of the Catholic Church* states that "all who die in God's grace and friendship, but still imperfectly purified, are indeed assured of their eternal salvation; but after death they undergo purification, so as to achieve the holiness necessary to enter the joy of heaven."[18] Purgatory, from words meaning "to purge" or "to purify," makes souls fit enough for heaven so that, eventually, they too enter into the glory of God

---

17. See Plantinga, Thompson, and Lundberg, *Introduction to Christian Theology*, 405; Grenz, *Theology for the Community of God*, 591.
18. Catholic Church, "The Final Purification, or Purgatory," in *The Catechism of the Catholic Church*, 2nd ed. (Vatican: Libreria Editrice Vaticana, 2012), §III.

in union with Christ.[19] This view says that eventually our mortal bodies are resurrected and our consciousness reunited with them.

Soul Sleep

Based on scriptures that speak of saints "falling asleep" to refer to their death, Protestant Reformer Martin Luther argued that when we die, we simply fall asleep until the final resurrection.[20] The soul enters into a state of unconsciousness and reawakens, totally unaware of the passing of time, at the resurrection of the dead.[21] Traditionally, Jehovah's Witnesses have also held this view.

Regardless of how we spend our time between death and final resurrection, Christians typically believe that "the darkness of death is accepted in the light of the hope of the resurrection."[22] Of course, thoughts of the afterlife and the final resurrection prompt us to ask questions about judgment, heaven, and hell—who goes to which place? Christians from every tradition have asked these types of questions for millennia, and the varying Christian traditions have come up with plenty of answers—some better than others. Since it seems the final resurrection occurs prior to any judgment and subsequent assignment to heaven or (God forbid!) hell, we will begin with the resurrection.

Resurrection

The Bible explicitly mentions the bodily resurrection of Jesus[23] and in connection to that refers to the future resurrection of all people.[24] The biblical witness, then, clearly teaches that just as God raised Christ from the dead, God will also raise us from the dead—we will share in Christ's resurrection and in eternal life.[25] Christ's resurrection begins the new creation, the divine project of making all things new and of ushering in the divine kingdom (2 Cor 5:17). Even though the new life created by Jesus's resurrection begins with our transformed lives in the present, the final resurrection forms the basis of our hope for the future when God will reconcile all things to God's self through Jesus Christ so that, finally, God will truly be all in all (Col 1:20; 1 Cor 15:28).

19. See Grenz, Theology for the Community of God, 591.
20. See Paul Althaus, The Theology of Martin Luther (Minneapolis: Fortress, 1963), 414–15. See, in NIV, 1 Cor 15:6, 18, 20, 51; 1 Thess 4:13–15.
21. Plantinga, Thompson, and Lundberg, Introduction to Christian Theology, 405; Grenz, Theology for the Community of God, 406.
22. John Polkinghorne, The God of Hope and the End of the World (New Haven: Yale University Press, 2003), 125.
23. Matt 17:9; 20:19; Mark 8:31; 10:34; Luke 18:33; John 2:19–22; Acts 2:24; 1 Cor 15:4.
24. Matt 22:23–32; Luke 14:14; Rom 6:4–5; 15:1–58; 1 Thess 4:14; Rev 20:5–6.
25. J. Richard Middleton, A New Heaven and a New Earth: Reclaiming Biblical Eschatology (Grand Rapids, MI: Baker Academic, 2014), 132.

Our bodily resurrection attests to the fulfillment of God's hope for creation as well. In fact, the earliest Christians considered the resurrection the beginning of God's plan for the ultimate completion of reconciliation and restoration of all things. The resurrection affirms the essential goodness of creation by overthrowing the tyrant called "death." It firmly establishes God's miracle of new life that embraces every part of the universe with divine love. N. T. Wright beautifully expresses Paul's narrative on the resurrection, writing that the apostle's "controlling narrative is constantly pointing to the way in which the creator finally brings his human, image-bearing creatures, and indeed the entire cosmos, through the impasses of the fall, of the thorns and thistles and the whirling, flashing sword, to taste at last the gift of life in all its fullness, a new bodily life in a new world where the rule of heaven is brought at last to earth."[26]

According to Wright, the resurrection turns the world upside down.[27] It demonstrates the reversal of injustice and reveals divine justice as restorative rather than retributive. The resurrection reverses the damage of sin, evil, and death that previously inhibited the restorative purposes of God for peace, prosperity, and limitless love. In other words, the final resurrection inaugurates God's plan for all creation so that the shalom of God will reign unhindered in the new heaven and new earth.[28] First, however, we must all stand before the judgment seat of God (2 Cor 5:10; Rev 20:11–15).

Judgment, Heaven, and Hell

Growing up a Baptist, I cannot count the number of times I sat in a pew watching a dark-suited preacher wipe sweat from his brow as he shouted out an old-fashioned fire-and-brimstone sermon. These types of messages have pervaded Christian churches like insidious horror stories, laced with terrifying verbal images that portray sinners standing before a terrible, large, angry God with a long gray beard, sitting upon a great white throne, pointing a judgmental finger in their direction. Trembling with fear, they await the final pronouncement that ordains where they will spend eternity—in the burning fires of eternal, conscious torment or in the idyllic paradise of heaven. True, many stern warnings about judgment "grace" the pages of Scripture, informing us that we all will stand before the judgment seat of Christ at the end of our lives.[29] We will encounter both the reality of God and the reality of our own existence. But will the final judgment truly entail such horrors?

St. Augustine thinks so. He says that we will stand before God who has the power to "ensure that all actions, good and bad, of every individual will be recalled to

---

26. N. T. Wright, *The Resurrection of the Son of God* (Minneapolis: Fortress, 2003), 373, 727–30. See also Middleton, *A New Heaven and a New Earth*, 155–56.
27. Wright, *Resurrection of the Son of God*, 138.
28. Middleton, *A New Heaven and a New Earth*, 143–54.
29. Matt 10:28; 13:37–43; 25:31–46; Rom 2:6–10; 2 Thess 1:5–10; Heb 9:27; Rev 20:11–15.

mind and presented to the mind's view with miraculous speed, so that each person's knowledge will accuse or excuse his conscience."[30] At that point, those who desire God (the "sheep" of Matt 25:31–46) will find ultimate fulfillment and bliss, and those whose desire opposes God (the "goats" of Matt 25) will experience eternal torment in hell. But the Christian tradition also has other views more in line with a nonviolent God of love.

Judgment

The Eastern Orthodox Christian tradition imagines the final judgment as a time of purifying. Although judgment will entail the pain of experiencing the exposure of our lives before God, the ultimate end of judgment is a process, not a verdict. According to this view, we stand before God as both the sheep and the goats described in Jesus's parable in Matthew, while the all-consuming fire of God burns away the impurities (the "goat" part of us) that infect our lives and leaves behind the purified sheep in each of us. As righteous new creations imbued with a new innocence, we will see the goodness and love of God and freely consent to enter the divine kingdom. The love of God will turn us all toward God so that, as St. Augustine says, we will find our true rest in God.[31] This purgation process will prepare us for eternal life with God, fulfilling the scriptural promise: "No eye has seen, nor ear heard, nor the human heart conceived, what God has prepared for those who love him" (1 Cor 2:9).

Judgment began with Jesus, the true light that came into the world to expose the darkness (John 3:19–21). In Eastern Orthodox thought, the final exposure of our darkness lies in the sanctifying light of divine fire, and in the purifying fire of judgment lies our hope for redemption. As John Polkinghorne writes, "Properly conceived, judgment is the divine antidote to human sin."[32] Indeed, Jesus revealed to us the outcome of that judgment when he spoke the words "Peace I leave with you; my peace I give to you. I do not give to you as the world gives. Do not let your hearts be troubled, and do not let them be afraid" (John 14:27). When we stand face-to-face before God in Christ, we will finally "be like him, for we will see him as he is" (1 John 3:2). We will all enjoy the peace of Christ through purification and the forgiveness of sin.

Many people have found the images of judgment in C. S. Lewis's *The Last Battle*[33] helpful for understanding how God compassionately judges us. In the afterlife, a young man stands before Aslan (the Christ figure in the *Chronicles of Narnia* series) and expects punishment because he has not worshipped and served the true God

---

30. Augustine, *City of God*, XX.20.
31. Augustine, *Confessions*, I.1.1; Polkinghorne, *The God of Hope*, 130–34.
32. Polkinghorne, *The God of Hope*, 130–32.
33. C. S. Lewis, *The Chronicles of Narnia*, complete series (San Francisco: HarperCollins, 2010. Individual books originally published 1950, 1951, 1952, 1954, 1955, 1956 by C. S. Lewis).

he sees before him now. He reviews his entire life and feels himself condemned, as he acknowledges he has served a cruel, bloodthirsty, smaller god in which he was taught to believe. Aslan reassures him that whatever good he has done in the name of his evil god and whatever true worship he has engaged in out of love have always been accepted as belonging to the true God of love. Similarly, the evil he has done belongs to the evil god. This is a form of separating the sheep from the goats. Lewis's imaginative portrayal in this scene could be seen as a form of purification theory, in which the young man sees his life clearly and painfully, yet gains a new perspective on its meaning at the same time, coming out whole and forgiven in the end.

Heaven

Of course, questions surrounding the last judgment raise other questions about heaven and hell. We all have images in our minds about what heaven is like—pearly gates, streets of gold, angels singing beautifully in the dazzling divine light of glory, or perhaps a bucolic paradise as we walk in the sunshiny cool of the day with Jesus, Moses, and Abraham. Actually, these images have only scant support in Scripture. The Bible describes heaven as a place beyond our imagination with many rooms or dwelling places (John 14:2; 1 Cor 2:7–9) and with angels in attendance (Matt 18:10). For us as transformed people of God, heaven will be our home in the presence of Jesus and will be filled with singing, praise, and worship (2 Cor 5:8; Phil 1:20–23; Rev 5:9–13). Revelation does mention golden streets and pearly gates (21:21), though in a context of symbolic language about many things. The pearls and gold and precious stones in the new heaven symbolize the purity of righteousness, the precious value and cost of redemption, the beauty of the divine presence, and the absence of evil and darkness. These symbols communicate a transformation from secular to sacred, impure to pure, perishable to imperishable, mortal to immortal, and death to life. They point to an existence of union, of oneness with Christ, in which God will be all in all (John 17:20–23).

For many Christians, human oneness with God in eternal bliss expresses the most poignant and intimate image of heaven. The image of oneness points us back to the atonement as "at-one-ment" and reveals our participation within the intimate, communal relationship of the Trinitarian dance with Father, Son, and Holy Spirit for all eternity. Our heavenly hope is a communal hope; "our human destiny is a collective destiny" the fulfillment of which "lies in our incorporation into the one body of Christ," forever and ever.[34]

Additionally, scholars such as Franciscan Richard Rohr believe that, as citizens of heaven already, we experience heaven on earth in this lifetime. Pope John Paul II

---

34. Polkinghorne, *The God of Hope*, 130–36.

(1920–2005) would have agreed with Rohr, asserting that heaven (and hell) are not physical places but, instead, the living relationship we have with God every day. The joy we feel, the peace that comes upon us during trying times, the companionship of a loved one, the praise and worship in community with others all bring heaven to earth for us. So, again, we have an "already but not yet" eschatological mindset, even when we think about our sojourn in heaven.[35]

Hell

But what about those who go to eternal damnation? We also have vivid pictures of hell in our imaginations. We can almost see the gates of hell, fire, brimstone, and ghoulish bodies screaming in pain while Satan looks on with glee. Thanks to Dante Alighieri's literary masterwork *The Divine Comedy*, this view of hell gained great popularity throughout Western Christendom starting in the fourteenth century, though it does not have strong support in Scripture. The apostle Paul makes little mention of hell—a strange lacuna if he considered it a central idea. And the early Christians did not preach the gospel as salvation from hell; for them, salvation meant life on earth in the divine kingdom. In fact, theologians Rita Nakashima Brock and Rebecca Ann Parker assert that "a divide of the afterlife to heaven and hell is absent from Christianity's visual world until the medieval period."[36] Surprisingly, the Christian tradition has no official view on hell, and views surrounding the topic differ widely throughout the vast theological streams of Christian thought. The doctrine of hell as eternal punishment was articulated for the first time in the early third century by the Latin church father Tertullian, but as theologian Edward Beecher has noted, for the first four centuries of the church there were at least six theological schools. Of these six, only Tertullian's school taught the eternal conscious torment.[37] Let's look at four of these views in turn.

Eternal Conscious Torment Theory (ECT). This understanding describes hell as a place of literal fire and brimstone with its inhabitants suffering eternal, conscious torment. Along with Tertullian, St. Augustine held this view, believing that unrepentant sinners suffer incessant bodily torture for all eternity.[38] Dante made this view popular in the Middle Ages, and it has held on strongly in the West, especially in evangelical and fundamentalist churches. Although preaching the torturous

35. Richard Rohr, *Teachings on Love*, ed. Joelle Chase and Judy Traeger (Maryknoll, NY: Orbis, 2018), 250–51; Pope John Paul II audiences on the topics of heaven (July 21, 1999) and hell (July 28, 1999). Full texts of these addresses can be found at https://tinyurl.com/ya7opxs2.
36. Rita Nakashima Brock and Rebecca Ann Parker, *Saving Paradise: How Christianity Traded Love for This World for Crucifixion and Empire* (Boston: Beacon, 2008), 13.
37. Edward Beecher, *History of Opinions of the Scriptural Doctrine of Retribution* (New York: Appleton, 1878).
38. Augustine, *City of God*, XXI.9.

dangers of hellfire seems to serve as a great marketing strategy for evangelizing, it tries to motivate faith through fear. We must ask, therefore, whether God desires fear-based devotion or love-based devotion.[39]

Annihilation Theory. This potentially more palatable view of hell depicts it as a temporary place of torture until it joins Hades (the place of the dead) and the devil in the lake of fire, as depicted in Revelation, whereupon hell and the people in it experience total annihilation.[40] People in hell still suffer torment, but do not do so eternally. The horrors of hell and their people's conscious existence end in the lake of fire (Rev 19:20; 20:10, 14–15; 21:8). Both ECT and annihilationism communicate an image of a punishing God who simply will not, or cannot, forgive sin and embrace all humanity.[41] Because God is nonviolent love, however, would God really operate an "eternal torture chamber" and call it just? Or kill off forever those God has created in the divine image? Does eternal punishment or annihilation for finite, temporal sin balance the scales of divine justice? Certainly it wouldn't in our human systems of justice! Nonetheless, many Christians, especially in the West, believe a just God must eternally punish the unrepentant sinner in some form. Fortunately, other viable views exist.

Hell as a state of existence now. Theologians such as Richard Rohr and Pope John Paul II believe we can experience hell during this lifetime. These scholars assert that Jesus, in his teachings and parables, pointed to hell in this lifetime rather than to any hell in the afterlife. He talked about the threat in *this* life, the misery that accompanies those who do not repent of their sin and turn toward God.[42] For example, the rich man suffering a great thirst in Hades in Jesus's parable never learned the love of God; he never learned to love, and in his loveless state, he thirsts for the water of love that only God through Christ can give. This parable in Luke 16:19–31 serves as a warning for people still outside the knowledge of God's love. Those who do not know Jesus Christ live in a hellish world filled with suffering, anxiety, and violence, without hope or joy or love. For them, this life is hell because they do not know the peace of God, the joy of salvation, or the hope of a redeemed future.[43]

---

39. Thomas Jay Oord, *God Can't: How to Believe in God and Love after Tragedy, Abuse, and Other Evils* (Grasmere, ID: Sacrasage, 2019), 151.
40. Hades, the traditional place of the dead in the Bible, should be distinguished from later ideas of hell as a place of retributive punishment. In the Apostles' Creed, the phrase that has sometimes been translated "He descended into hell" is better translated "He descended to the dead." Unfortunately, this cosmic event has been misleadingly named "the harrowing of hell." "The harrowing of hell" refers to Jesus descending to the place of the dead between the time of his crucifixion and resurrection and preaching the gospel to the souls there.
41. Plantinga, Thompson, and Lundberg, *Introduction to Christian Theology*, 409.
42. Zahnd, *Sinners in the Hands of a Loving God*, 124–25.
43. Rohr, *Teachings on Love*, 250–51; John Paul II, audiences (1999).

This view of hell talks about reaping the internal consequences of sin in everyday life and into the future, rather than about external future retributive punishment.

Purification Theory. Many Christians concerned about the image of God as nonviolent, trading in restorative rather than retributive justice, hold to the purification theory. For some, this model makes more sense given the power of God, the love of God, and the efficacy of the atonement for all creation. Theories of hell as a purifying fire go back to the earliest Christian traditions, including Eastern Orthodoxy. For these believers, God is an all-consuming fire (Heb 12:29) who desires all people to repent of sin and enter the kingdom of God (1 Tim 2:4), even if that occurs after the body dies. After death, at the final resurrection, every person stands before God, the fire of passionate love. Rather than a fire that punishes with retributive intentions, this fire burns away the impurities of sin with the intent to redeem and restore. This time enveloped in God's fiery love may cause the type of pain that always accompanies acknowledgment of sin, repentance, and restoration—it may serve as a type of "hell" or purgation for those going through it. But as a sinner draws nearer to God, the divine fire burns away all the wickedness, leaving behind a totally pure person who then has the choice to enter the heavenly kingdom because of the forgiveness and acceptance granted by God through Christ. A righteous person, no longer enslaved by sin, restored to the human condition imputed by the recapitulation accomplished through Jesus, and free to choose Christ, would naturally assent to eternal life with God in the kingdom. This vision of final purification or judgment as "hell" and the reconciliation and restoration of all created things brings glory to God in Christ, for "every knee [will] bend . . . and every tongue [will] confess that Jesus is Lord, to the glory of God the Father" (Phil 2:10–11).[44]

Hell as a moment of standing in the divine purifying fire squares significantly with the theology of a nonviolent God. Theologians who reject notions of divine retributive violence also reject for several reasons theories of the retributive violence of hell as eternal punishment. First, the teaching of Jesus rejects violence of any sort, especially in the Sermon on the Mount, which exhorts us to forgive, to go the extra mile, to love others, and to pray for enemies rather than persecute them (Matt 5). Surely God's goodness is even greater than the goodness Jesus calls us to practice. Second, the violence of eternal punishment for temporal sin not only seems unjust but contradicts the message of Jesus as the Prince of Peace who comes to bring peace on earth to all people (Isa 9:6; Luke 2:14). A loving, peaceful God would not allow evil to exist eternally in hell where souls that God loves

---

44. For a more complete treatment of this view, read Sharon Lynn Baker, *Razing Hell: Rethinking Everything You've Been Taught about God's Wrath and Judgment* (Louisville, KY: Westminster John Knox, 2010). See also scriptures claiming universal salvation for all creation: for example, Rom 8:20–21; 1 Tim 4:9–10; 1 John 2:1–2.

suffer in perpetual agony. The continued existence of such evil would be an ethical problem, but some theologians have even tried perversely to justify the delight of the saints in heaven who watch the torments of the damned in hell.[45] Third, a just God would not punish temporal sin for all eternity. A loving, nonviolent God, who desires all people to be saved (1 Tim 2:4) would never bring down an iron-clad curtain at the time of death, closing off any possibility of reconciliation in favor of an eternity of violent punishment. As John Polkinghorne says, "Surely the God of everlasting love is always ready, like the father in Jesus' parable, to meet the returning prodigal whenever he comes to himself and returns to his true home."[46] In C. S. Lewis's novel *The Great Divorce*, hell is represented as a dreary place of paralysis of the will for those who inhabit it, but a place where the door is "locked from the inside."[47] Those in hell may always repent, unlock their hearts, and walk out the door if they use what is left of their free will to do so. God will welcome them with open arms, like the father with the prodigal.

Ideas of hell that turn on vengeance and retributive justice originate in our human imaginations, not God's. The people who wrote the Hebrew Bible, though it speaks of judgment, had no concept of hell in the afterlife, and certainly not of eternal conscious torment. As innumerable passages in the Prophets and Psalms indicate, God deals in the peace of reconciliation, the balm of healing, the restorative justice of forgiveness, and the fiery purification of sin that only love can bring. Again and again, God asks people to return. And at times, God withdraws to let people suffer the consequences of their disobedience—but always with restoration in mind. After all, the inexpressible, boundless love of God serves as the powerful, purifying agent in the hearts of sinners and will not let us go until we repent (turn around). Yes, the pain of purification is the result of intense love, "for the sorrow caused in the heart by sin against love is more poignant than any torment."[48]

Ideas of Salvation

Our discussion of these various Christian views leads us to ask, Who is saved? As with all other doctrines we have discussed in this text, questions surrounding *soteriology* (the theological term for "study of salvation") have a variety of answers, some more responsible than others. Although Christian traditions articulate these views differently, we will explore a couple of the more common

---

45. Peter Lombard, *Sentences*, 4.43–50.
46. Polkinghorne, *The God of Hope*, 127–28.
47. C. S. Lewis, *The Great Divorce: A Dream* (San Francisco: HarperOne, 2001; originally published 1946). Quote from C. S. Lewis, *The Problem of Pain* (San Francisco: Harper SanFrancisco, 2001), 127.
48. Isaac the Syrian, "Homily 27," in *The Ascetical Homilies of Saint Isaac the Syrian* (Boston: Holy Transfiguration Monastery, 1984), 141. See also Andrew Louth, *Introducing Eastern Orthodox Theology* (Downers Grove, IL: IVP, 2013), 158.

expressions. All of the views, with the exception of pluralism, include the support of Scripture.

Exclusive view of salvation. This view claims that persons are saved only when they explicitly profess faith in the work of Jesus (Rom 10:9-10). St. Augustine concluded that after the final judgment, two cities with their own strict boundaries will still exist in the new heaven and the new earth. One city will belong to the devil and the other, the holy city, will belong to Jesus. The first will embrace evil, and its inhabitants (all who have not professed faith in Christ) will suffer punishment for eternity. The other city will embrace good, and its inhabitants (all who have explicitly professed faith in Christ in this earthly life) will enjoy an eternal paradise with God.[49] Many conservative Christians, especially evangelicals and fundamentalists, hold the exclusivist position. Some philosophers and theologians also call this view *Restrictivism*.[50]

Inclusive view of salvation. Some theologians believe in an inclusive view. This understanding holds that all people are saved through Jesus, but it differs from the exclusive view in that it does not require an outward, explicit profession of faith. Jesus eventually saves all people—but many do not experience this salvation until after the purification process in the presence of God's consuming fire of love (John 14:6; Rom 8:20-21; 2 Cor 5:19; 1 Tim 2:4; 4:9-10; 2 Pet 3:8-9; 1 John 2:1-2). Here we must emphasize the fact that in this view salvation is still *through Jesus Christ* only. Those who believe that Jesus saves all people stress the omnipotence and goodness of God. They assert that the efficacy of Jesus's life, death, and resurrection extends to all creation, including, eventually, every single person. Of course, according to Philippians 2:10-11, profession or confession of Christ as savior will occur for all people, but for some, it will be after death. Many Christians have held this view, including John Wesley, C. S. Lewis, Karl Rahner, Clark Pinnock, John E. Sanders, and Seventh-day Adventists. Even evangelist Billy Graham was an inclusivist, though he did not like to call it by that name because he thought people often confused inclusivism with universalism, and he did not consider himself a universalist. At one time, the Roman Catholic Church taught that "outside the church there is no salvation," a position of exclusivism; however, since the Second Vatican Council (1962-1965), inclusivism has become the official position of Roman Catholicism.

Pluralism. Pluralism argues for the salvation of every person, with or without profession of faith in Jesus. Despite the lack of scriptural support, this view is gaining popularity. Out of care and concern for the very devout practitioners of other faiths, some theologians simply cannot believe that God would not somehow

49. Augustine, *City of God*, 20.14-16.
50. John Sanders coined this term. See *No Other Name: An Investigation into the Destiny of the Unevangelized* (Grand Rapids, MI: Eerdmans, 1992).

save those who faithfully worship the divine within the context of other historical religions.[51] For example, we have already discussed how C. S. Lewis addresses this question, and contemporary philosopher and theologian John Hick developed a pluralist view in detail in the last decades.[52] The line between this position and that of some nuanced forms of inclusivism may be difficult to tease out, hinging on the issue of what John Sanders calls "post-mortem salvation," whether practitioners of other religions need ultimately to go through Jesus Christ to attain salvation, or whether their own religious traditions are adequate (though perhaps partial) paths to God. Some of our most important interreligious conversations (and disagreements) likely take place at this interface.

Universalism. Of course, soteriological conversations ultimately lead to questions about universalism. In this chapter we are specifically concerned with Christian universalism. Christian universalists believe that the exclusivist view—that God only saves those who explicitly profess faith in Christ during the short span of a lifetime—offers too small a soteriology.[53] Instead, this inclusivist view asserts that God saves all people, but through Jesus Christ alone. Universalism stresses the idea that *all* will eventually be saved. The early church father Origen held to Christian universalism in the second century and suggested that God would accomplish *apokatastasis* (the final restoration of all things) at the end of time.[54] Church fathers Gregory of Nazianzus (329–390) and Gregory of Nyssa (335–394) also both believed that God would reconcile all creation and creatures to God (Acts 3:21; Rom 5:15; 11:32; 1 Tim 2:4; 4:9–10; 2 Pet 3:9; 1 John 2:1–2). Many other theologians as well have believed in the final restoration of all creation—namely Søren Kierkegaard, Friedrich Schleiermacher, William Barclay, Karl Barth, Robin Parry, Marilyn McCord Adams, and nineteenth-century theologian and novelist George MacDonald, to name a few.

Christian universalists base their soteriology on faith in the unlimited, extravagant love of God that never ends, never gives up, and never fails (1 Cor 13:8, 13). Isaac the Syrian (613–700) expresses the extent of divine salvation when he writes, "There exists with [the Creator] a single love and compassion which is spread out over all creation, which is without alteration, timeless and everlasting. . . . No part belonging to any single one of (all) rational beings will be lost as far as God is concerned."[55] Diodore of Tarsus (?–390) believed that "not even the immense wickedness [of the

---

51. For a more comprehensive treatment of the various soteriological viewpoints, see John Hick et al., *Four Views on Salvation in a Pluralistic World* (Grand Rapids, MI: Zondervan, 1996); Paul F. Knitter, *Introducing Theologies of Religions* (Maryknoll, NY: Orbis, 2002), 27–59.
52. See John Hick, *Evil and the God of Love* (London: Palgrave Macmillan, 2010).
53. See Rob Bell, *Love Wins: A Book about Heaven, Hell, and the Fate of Every Person Who Ever Lived* (San Francisco: HarperOne, 2011); Richard Crane, "The Problem of the Plan of Salvation," in an unpublished manuscript, 2.
54. Origen, *On First Principles*, trans. Henri De Lubac (Gloucester, MA: Peter Smith, 1973), 52–65.
55. *Isaac the Syrian*, part II, 40.1, 7, A. S. Brock (Louvain: Peeters, 1995), 174–76.

demons] can overcome the measure of God's goodness."[56] Bishop Kallistos Ware, a modern Eastern Orthodox thinker, encourages Christians with these words: "Divine love is stronger than all the forces of darkness and evil within the universe, and in the end it will prevail. . . . This appeal to the invincibility of divine love is the strongest argument in favor of universal hope."[57]

Since divine love never coerces or overrules human freedom, Bishop Ware believes that at the time of judgment, God's effective love will win and every person will freely accept Jesus Christ as Savior. He says, "The power that is victorious is the power of loving compassion, and so it is a victory that does not overrule but enhances our human freedom."[58] For these theologians, God's eschatological *telos* (ultimate purpose) deals not merely in individual salvation but in the ultimate reconciliation of all people, the healing of all nations (Rev 22:2), and the restoration of all creation. Every tribe, every tongue, every nation will live in harmony with God, one another, and all creation.[59] These hope-filled Christians look forward to the time when "God may [truly] be all in all" (1 Cor 15:28). Indeed, every created being has a place prepared for them within the Trinitarian dance, or perichoresis. We will all participate in the dance of mutual love that transpires eternally among Father, Son, and Holy Spirit so we can say with medieval mystic Julian of Norwich and poet T. S. Eliot, "It behoved that there should be sin [or in modern translations, 'sin is necessary']; but all shall be well, and all shall be well, and all manner of things shall be well."[60]

Christian universalism makes sense in light of a nonviolent God of love—a God whose very nature *is* love. The whole story of Scripture climaxes with the completion of God's ultimate purpose for the history of the world—the redemption of the entire creation, the recapitulation and restoration of all things, the "rescue and transformation of the world that God so loves."[61] The Eastern Orthodox iconographic tradition paints a profoundly beautiful image of universal salvation as divine rescue in the depiction of Jesus's resurrection, which, of course, foreshadows our own. These Eastern icons differ significantly from resurrection icons in the West, where we see an empty tomb or, later on, images of Jesus standing in glory immediately after rising from the dead. In the East, however, Jesus stands atop a personification of Hades (the place of the dead) with broken chains and locks and shattered pieces of rock walls littering the ground around his feet. With his hands (sometimes one, other times both), Jesus reaches out to Adam, Eve, Moses, David, Judas, and other unidentified persons in order to rescue them out of hell. He lights

56. Louth, *Introducing Eastern Orthodox Theology*, 158.
57. Kallistos Ware, *The Inner Kingdom*, vol. 1 (Crestwood, NY: St. Vladimir's Seminary Press, 2000), 210.
58. Ware, *The Inner Kingdom*, vol. 1, 202.
59. Michael J. Gorman, *Reading Revelation Responsibly* (Eugene, OR: Wipf & Stock, 2010), 166.
60. Julian of Norwich, *Revelations of Divine Love*, trans. Barry Windeatt (Oxford: Oxford University Press, 2015), 74; T. S. Eliot, "Little Gidding," in "Four Quartets," *The Complete Poems and Plays 1909–1950* (New York: Harcourt Brace Jovanovich, 1971), 142, 146. See also Ware, *The Inner Kingdom*, 193.
61. Middleton, *A New Heaven and a New Earth*, 156, 206.

the sky around himself in sharp contrast to the empty darkness of the newly har-rowed hell. These arresting icons symbolize the doctrine of universal salvation so prevalent in the Eastern Christian churches and communicate to believers and unbelievers alike the hope we all have in a redeemed, reconciled, restored, and recapitulated existence with God in Christ for all eternity.[62]

Eschatological Living—Now: A Nonviolent, Loving Way of Life

We could say so much more about the "not yet" future when God, through Christ, brings all of history to its final consummation, when God is all in all and every knee bows in praise to worship the Lamb of God. But the most important eschatological question does not deal with an eternal tomorrow; it asks about the temporal reality of today. How are we to live eschatologically, today, right now?

First, we need to realize God has already partially answered the prayer "Thy kingdom come, thy will be done, on earth as it is in heaven" (Matt 6:10; traditional Lord's Prayer wording). Jesus Christ has reconciled the disastrous division between heaven and earth. The new heaven and the new earth are present realities, and we the church, as God's new creation transformed by the power of the Holy Spirit, reveal the love of Jesus to the world. Christians have a responsibility to create and promote the values of God's kingdom in our own societies, to reveal the heart of God to those around us. James Cone asserts, "No eschatological perspective is sufficient which does not challenge the present order."[63] In so doing, we stand in solidarity, like Jesus did, with those who suffer; we work, like Jesus did, to alleviate the hardships wrought through poverty, disease, and death; we speak against the abusive powers of governments and, like Jesus did, call out national leaders who corrupt their positions in order to promote greedy agendas. That means we live now as if Jesus has already returned. We live now as citizens of the millennial kingdom, loving God and others, spreading the good news of Christ as ministers of reconciliation (2 Cor 5:18, 20).[64]

Second, as we already discussed in chapter 9, "The Church," as participants in the divine eschatological kingdom, Christians initiate God's shalom in the world. Just as Scripture begins with a nonviolent creation of the cosmos, so the new crea-tion begins by spreading God's message of shalom, even and especially in a world permeated by violence.[65] We do not wage war, as this world does, with weapons of mass destruction or large-caliber automatic machine guns. The nonviolent God revealed by the nonviolent Jesus calls us to a compelling and more hopeful way

---

62. See John Dominic Crossan and Sarah Sexton Crossan, *Resurrecting Easter: How the West Lost and the East Kept the Original Easter Vision* (San Francisco: HarperOne, 2019).
63. James H. Cone, *Black Theology of Liberation* (Maryknoll, NY: Orbis, 2010), 241.
64. See Zahnd, *Sinners in the Hands of a Loving God*, 187–93.
65. David Neville, *A Peaceable Hope: Contesting Violent Eschatology in New Testament Narratives* (Grand Rapids, MI: Baker Academic, 2013), 80–81.

of combating evil. Jesus challenges us to proclaim and make manifest the divine kingdom of peace and justice through our own nonviolent forms of restorative justice, peacemaking, and unconditional love. Signs of the nonviolent reign of God, according to the gospel perspective, include feeding the hungry, clothing the poor, and liberating the oppressed (Zech 7:9–10; Matt 25:31–46).

In accordance with God's mandate of shalom on earth, we need to strive to beat our swords into plowshares and our spears into pruning hooks, stop resorting to easy militarization against other nations, and learn the ways of peace instead of war (Isa 2:4). In her latest work, *The Force of Nonviolence*, philosopher Judith Butler calls for rethinking nonviolence as a universal strategy, "not as an absolute principle" but by "pos[ing] the question of violence and nonviolence within a different framework, where the question is not 'What ought I to do?' but 'Who am I in relation to others, and how do I understand that relationship?'"[66] Standing before a crowd at the Masonic Temple in Memphis, Rev. Dr. Martin Luther King Jr. spoke these words on April 3, 1968—the night before his death: "The choice before us is no longer violence or nonviolence; it is nonviolence or nonexistence. That is where we are today." Changing our orientation is a matter of life or death. Our salvation is not just individual but collective. Much like a prophet calling to his people in the Hebrew Bible, King understood that the kingdom of God "invites us to turn from the violence of the world, a violence which has the capacity to destroy all humanity and the entire planet, and instead choose the spiritually explosive nonviolence of God, which can transform every human heart and the face of the earth into a new realm of justice, peace, and love."[67]

Third, struggling with how to live eschatologically, one of my students asked me how to balance imitating the nonviolent life Jesus led and taught with resisting the systemic powers that oppress people, that serve to make the poor poorer, and that use violent means to remain in power. Let's look first to the example of Jesus. During his time of temptation in the wilderness, Jesus waged battle with his words rather than with weapons (Matt 4:1–11). We also see that followers of Jesus can defeat the devil "by the blood of the Lamb and by the word of [our] testimony" (Rev 12:11)—our testimony about the power of God's love. We can speak truth to power, as Jesus did, but we season all our words with grace (Col 4:6) so they edify others rather than tear them down (Eph 4:29). We are empowered to forgive others freely, as Jesus did, bringing peace and love into every relationship. We can utter words of peace and speak the truth in love (Eph 4:15). Jesus was faithful to the end to his mission of bringing the kingdom of God, even if it meant death on a cross. God calls us to confront evil structures with acts of compassion and nonviolent resistance, looking to people such as King and Gandhi as our examples. Their lives and methods show us practical ways to engage in loving but effective civil disobedience toward unjust laws, should we feel called to this ministry in particular

66. Masha Gessen, "Judith Butler Wants Us to Reshape Our Rage," *The New Yorker*, February 9, 2020.
67. John Dear, *The God of Peace: Toward a Theology of Nonviolence* (Eugene, OR: Wipf & Stock, 2005), 85.

circumstances. And, as always, we bathe in prayer every endeavor to bring God's peace and restorative justice to the world. On the whole, the church exists for the good of everyone and, therefore, has the responsibility to bear witness to God's reign and to teach others about God's future eschatological hope of renewal and victory in which peace, love, and the joy of true life will be given to all creation.[68]

68. Gorman, *Reading Revelation Responsibly*, 169; Dorothee Sölle, *Thinking about God: An Introduction to Theology* (Philadelphia: Trinity Press International, 1990), 150.

Postscript
On Kingdom Ethics

Amen.

Amen literally means "Let it be so." We say it at the end of prayers or, in this case, the Apostles' Creed, with which we have been engaging in this book. I have systematically developed here the subject of nonviolence and a loving God who desires to reconcile with and restore all of creation, while at the same time covering the most essential doctrines of the Christian faith. I hope I have demonstrated the malleable nature of doctrine and the construction of theology. They are only as good as our hermeneutical techniques, our cultural context, and our presuppositions about God. I have tried to start with different presuppositions, examine the evidence, engage what many others have said, and come to some consistent conclusions based on both historic thought and modern scholarship.

By emphasizing love, its significance, and its relevance, I hope to add my voice to theologians and thinkers such as Abelard, René Girard, John Caputo, and Thomas Aquinas, all of whom place responsibility for violence in the hands of humanity—our hands—rather than in the hands and heart of God. Too often throughout history, theologians have attributed the need for, or existence of, violence to God, justifying it as necessary or sanctioned. We have thus created God in our own, violent image, an attribution Girard calls "sacred violence."[1]

In God's kingdom, violence is not the heart of the story, and violence is not at the heart of God; forgiveness and nonviolent, creative love are. We should not attribute violence to God—not even the obvious violence of the cross, as if this is something God required as a propitiation for sin. Violence instigates and contributes to the problem of sin; it does not serve as its solution. Theologian Walter Wink calls this archetypal and theological motif "the myth of redemptive violence," and we need to question it wherever we find it. This myth says we overcome "bad violence" through "good guys" wielding "good violence" to defeat "bad guys."[2] Furthermore, the myth of redemptive violence would have us believe that retributive justice is the main characteristic of God, above all else. Unfortunately, as we have discussed, some atonement theories reinforce this myth.

---

1. For an explanation of sacrificial substitution and scapegoating as "sacred violence," see an excerpt from *Violence and the Sacred* in "Part III: Sacrifice," in James G. Williams, ed., *The Girard Reader* (New York: Crossroad, 1996), 67–93.
2. This is a paraphrase of Walter Wink's thesis about how redemptive violence works in countless stories. For a more thorough treatment of the myth of redemptive violence, see his "Facing the Myth of Redemptive Violence," *Ekklesia*, November 15, 2014. https://tinyurl.com/2gqsml; and "The Myth of the Domination System," in *Engaging the Powers: Discernment and Resistance in a World of Domination* (Minneapolis: Fortress, 1992), 13–31.

But love, rather than violence, remains the key to the kingdom, the key to revealing the divine heart. As members of the human race, we have a responsibility to take that key of love in hand, do as Jesus did, and speak out against violence, hatred, and systemic abuse of people of every ethnicity, social status, sexual orientation, gender, religion, and nationality. We can work toward shalom between the earth and its inhabitants. As forgiven and transformed people, we hold the responsibility to forgive and transform structures of violence wherever we find them, seeking reconciliation with others, restoring relationships, and welcoming the stranger in our midst, just as Jesus taught and showed us by his example.

René Girard rightly asserts that the passion of Christ was nothing less than the community putting an innocent man to death, and that we should recognize it as such—as an act of human violence, a consequence of sinful behavior, and not something required by God to fulfill a retributive law of the universe. But we can go further than Girard's notion of the atonement as the unveiling of scapegoating and emphasize that Christ's entire life, death, and resurrection together constitute an indispensable event for our ongoing reconciliation to God. The atonement (salvation) is love in action, love that persists to the end in the face of violence and then overcomes violence and brings new resurrection life through nonviolent means. We can certainly agree with Girard that the rule of the kingdom of God and the unveiling of scapegoating it brings have life-or-death consequences and that we, working together as ministers of reconciliation, can overcome violence. But in order to succeed, all humanity must ultimately decide to abide by the kingdom rule of love, to choose the way toward life. In accord with the teachings of Jesus, Girard writes: "If all mankind offered the other cheek, no cheek would be struck. . . . If all men loved their enemies, there would be no more enemies" (John 15:13).[3]

Meanwhile, in the "already but not yet" kingdom, we live lives of creativity and peacemaking in loving witness to others and, when necessary, in resistance to evil. If we do not hear this call of the kingdom, if the call of our responsibility to what philosopher Emmanuel Levinas calls "the face of the Other"[4] falls on deaf ears and hardened hearts, we actually forget the meaning of Jesus's death, which unveiled the structures of mimetic violence within religion and society and gave us the way forward to loving union with God in theosis. Instead, we re-veil violence and its source and continue to live as if Jesus never died. We will then continue to solve the problem of violence violently, and work against the biblical promise that love never fails (1 Cor 13:8).

We must not let the anguished cries of our children and their children after them be drowned by heavy artillery, by the dominant voices of the world's powerful. Demand for retribution is everywhere in the world's value system—patterns we

---

3. René Girard, *Things Hidden Since the Foundation of the World*, trans. Stephen Bann (Stanford, CA: Stanford University Press, 1987), 211.

4. Emmanuel Lévinas, *Otherwise than Being, or Beyond Essence*, trans. Alphonso Lingis (Pittsburg, PA: Duquesne University Press, 1998), 12–13, 89–92, 145.

see continuing even from within theology itself, held captive to a violent religious intoxication that hinges upon theories of a violent God.[5] Girard claims that the only way to gain liberation from the structures of violence is to give up ideas of retribution: to give up on violent, "sacred" forms of retributive justice, false peacemaking (through scapegoating), militarized and racist forms of government, and many other behaviors we have often considered legitimate and necessary—even divine. This may involve the discipline of prayerfully giving up certain types of violent theology as well. Although these things have served our sense of identity and survival, they do not provide us with the true source of power we seek. Jesus gave up his right for self-defense and reprisals in the name of true justice. In the power of Christ's forgiveness and love, and through a new imitation of love, we too can give up our right for reprisal, retribution, and remuneration. We too can spread the good news of restoration and reconciliation through our actions in the world.[6]

God in Christ stands in solidarity with humanity against injustice and its violence that trapped, condemned, and killed Jesus. Jesus died because he loved God and his neighbor up to the very end, no matter what the cost. Jesus calls us to the same cause, the kingdom cause, causing the kingdom to rule on earth through surprising gifts of love. Jesus disturbed the world with a profound act of divine restorative justice, through the shocking reversal of the closed retributive economy with an event of forgiveness, and through an unexpected invitation of cosmic hospitality to return to God, like the prodigal, no matter who we are. At the center of non-retributive views of the atonement rules a "God who chooses to suffer violence rather than to sponsor it."[7] God has shown us through God's own Son that God suffers to the depths with the victims of violence and forgives and redeems violent persecutors as well. Ultimately, God nonviolently and lovingly rescues *all* victims of sin, taking that burden upon God's self and setting us free from these insidious categories and their power over us.

The gospel is truly good news, for all people. As Christians, we can proclaim that the life, death, and resurrection of Jesus Christ, as a unit, with its message of new life and victory over evil and death, resounds with a critical relevance for our contemporary situation. It is especially good news for all who have been oppressed, just as Jesus says (Luke 4:18). But at the same time, some theologians are now bringing the question of violence into the foreground (especially violence supposedly "condoned" by God), calling into question its practical implications, its supposed biblical support, and its benefits to a globe already overwhelmed with human violence, much less with violence ascribed to God. Certainly the powerless suffer from violent theologies more than do those who perpetrate them.

---

5. Robert G. Hamerton-Kelly, *The Gospel and the Sacred: Poetics of Violence in Mark* (Minneapolis: Fortress, 1994), 126; Gil Bailie, *Violence Unveiled: Humanity at the Crossroads* (New York: Crossroad, 1997), 59, 66.
6. Girard, *Things Hidden*, 198.
7. Bailie, *Violence Unveiled*, 66.

But a theology of nonviolent love provides us with the example of Jesus's life, death, and resurrection that enables us, through the inward transformation by the Spirit of God, to live a divinely empowered life in this present age, without exception. We show our gratitude and the overflowing love in our hearts by forgiving others as God has forgiven us, and through our actions we reveal to others the offer of redemption through Jesus Christ. We work to further the co-creative kingdom of God through acts of justice, mercy, and humility toward all, out of love for God and others. Redemption comes not just on an individual level but on a collective and cosmic level and puts the creation right, allowing us to live into the goodness that God has always intended for creation. To that we can certainly say "Amen, may it be so!"

Bibliography

Abelard, Peter. *The Christian Theology.* Edited by J. Ramsay McCallum. Oxford: Black-well, 1948.

———. *Ethics.* Edited by D. E. Luscombe. Oxford: Clarendon, 1971.

Adams, Rebecca. "Loving Mimesis and Girard's 'Scapegoat of the Text': A Creative Reassessment of Mimetic Desire." In *Violence Renounced: René Girard, Biblical Studies, and Peacemaking,* edited by Willard M. Swartley, 277–307. Telford, PA: Pandora, 2000.

———. "Violence, Difference, Sacrifice." In *Conversations with René Girard,* edited by Cynthia Haven, 51–71. London: Bloomsbury, 2020. Originally published as "Violence, Difference, Sacrifice: A Conversation with René Girard." In *Violence, Difference, Sacrifice: Conversations on Myth and Culture in Literature and Theology,* a Special Issue of *Religion and Literature* 25, no. 2 (Summer 1993): 9–33.

Akenson, Donald J. *Exporting the Rapture: John Nelson Darby and the Victorian Conquest of North American Evangelicalism.* Oxford: Oxford University Press, 2018.

Alberg, Jeremiah, Sherwood Belangia, and Matthew Taylor. "René Girard and Atonement: A Dialogue." *The Bulletin of Christian Culture Studies,* Kinjo Gakuin University 21 (2018): 1–20.

Allen, Bob. "Falwell on Terrorists: 'Blow Them Away in the Name of the Lord.'" EthicsDaily.com, October 29, 2004. https://tinyurl.com/uj6qnou.

Althaus, Paul. *The Theology of Martin Luther.* Minneapolis: Fortress, 1963.

Augustine. *City of God.* Edited by Henry Bettenson. New York: Penguin, 1984.

———. "Confessions." In *Saint Augustine's Childhood: Confessions,* book 1, translated by Garry Wills. New York: Viking, 2001.

———. *Confessions of Saint Augustine.* Translated by F. J. Sheed. New York: Sheed & Ward, 1943.

———. "On Original Sin." In *The Basic Writings of Saint Augustine,* vol. 1. Edited by Whitney J. Oates. New York: Random House, 1948.

———. *On the Free Choice of the Will.* Translated by Thomas Williams. Indianapolis: Hackett, 1993.

———. *On the Trinity.* Translated by Edmund Hill. Edited by John E. Rotelle. Brooklyn, NY: New City, 1991.

———. "To Boniface: Homily on Common Prayer and Sacraments." *Short-Title Catalogue* 13675, Renaissance Electronic Texts 1.1. Edited by Ian Lancashire. Toronto: University of Toronto, 1994.

———. "Tractate 29, John 7:14–18." *Tractates on the Gospel of John.* New Advent, n.d. https://tinyurl.com/yagp4efc.

———. "The Trinity." In *Nicene and Post-Nicene Fathers,* vol. 3. Edited by Philip Schaff. Buffalo, NY: Christian Literature Publishing, 1887.

Aulén, Gustaf. *Christus Victor: An Historical Study of the Three Main Types of the Idea of Atonement*. Eugene, OR: Wipf & Stock, 1931.

Bahnson, Fred, and Norman Wirzba. *Making Peace with the Land: God's Call to Reconcile with Creation*. Downers Grove, IL: IVP, 2012.

Bailie, Gil. *Violence Unveiled: Humanity at the Crossroads*. New York: Crossroad, 1997.

Baker, Sharon Lynn. *Executing God: Rethinking Everything You've Been Taught about Salvation and the Cross*. Louisville, KY: Westminster John Knox, 2014.

———. *Razing Hell: Rethinking Everything You've Been Taught about God's Wrath and Judgment*. Louisville, KY: Westminster John Knox, 2010.

Barth, Karl. *Church Dogmatics*, 4 vols. Edited by Geoffrey W. Bromiley and Thomas F. Torrance. Edinburgh: T & T Clark, 1956–58.

Bartlett, Anthony. *Cross Purposes*. Norcross, GA: Trinity Press International, 2001.

Bauckham, Richard. *The Theology of Jürgen Moltmann*. Edinburgh: T & T Clark, 1995.

Beecher, Edward. *History of Opinions of the Scriptural Doctrine of Retribution*. New York: D. Appleton, 1878.

Beilby, J., and P. R. Eddy, eds. *The Nature of Atonement: Four Views*. Downers Grove, IL: InterVarsity, 2006.

Bell, Rob. *Love Wins: A Book about Heaven, Hell, and the Fate of Every Person Who Ever Lived*. San Francisco: HarperOne, 2011.

Belousek, Darrin W. Snyder. "God, Evil, and (Non)Violence: Creation Theology, Creativity Theology, and Christian Ethics." *The Conrad Grebel Review* 34, no. 2 (Spring 2016): 155–79.

Bird, Michael F. *Are You the One Who Is to Come? The Historical Jesus and the Messianic Question*. Grand Rapids, MI: Baker, 2009.

Bloch-Smith, Elizabeth. "Cult Stands, 12th–10th Century BCE." In *Center for Online Judaic Studies*, https://tinyurl.com/see8x5p.

Bobrinskoy, Boris. *The Mystery of the Trinity: Trinitarian Experience and Vision in the Biblical and Patristic Tradition*. Translated by Anthony P. Gythiel. Crestwood, NY: St. Vladimir's Seminary Press, 1999.

Boff, Leonardo. *Introducing Liberation Theology*. Translated by Paul Burns. Maryknoll, NY: Orbis, 1987.

———. *Trinity and Society*. Translated by Paul Burns. Eugene, OR: Wipf & Stock, 2005.

Boyd, Gregory A. *The Crucifixion of the Warrior God: Interpreting the Old Testament's Violent Portrayals of God in Light of the Cross*. Vol. 1. Minneapolis: Fortress, 2017.

———. *God at War: The Bible and Spiritual Conflict*. Downers Grove, IL: InterVarsity, 1997.

———. *Satan and the Problem of Evil: Constructing a Trinitarian Warfare Theodicy*. Downers Grove, IL: InterVarsity, 2001.

Boyer, Paul. *When Time Shall Be No More: Prophecy Belief in Modern America*. Cambridge, MA: President and Fellows of Harvard College, 1992.

Brock, Rita Nakashima, and Rebecca Ann Parker. *Saving Paradise: How Christianity Traded Love for This World for Crucifixion and Empire*. Boston: Beacon, 2008.

Brown, Raymond E. "How Much Did Jesus Know? A Survey of the Biblical Evidence." *The Catholic Biblical Quarterly* 29, no. 3 (July 1967): 315–45.

Brueggemann, Walter. *Genesis*. Interpretation. Atlanta: John Knox, 1982.

Bruns, Gerald L. *The History of Hermeneutics.* New Haven, CT: Yale University Press, 1992.

Bub, Jeffrey. "Quantum Entanglement and Information." In *The Stanford Encyclopedia of Philosophy* (Spring 2019 Edition), edited by Edward N. Zalta. https://tinyurl.com/y9qsy2rx.

Bultmann, Rudolf. *Kerygma and Myth: A Theological Debate.* Edited by Hans Werner Bartsch. New York: Harper and Row, 1961.

Burnaby, John, ed. *Augustine: Later Works.* Philadelphia: Westminster, 1955.

Bushnell, Horace. *The Vicarious Sacrifice: Grounded in Principles of Universal Obligation.* Hicksville, NY: Regina, 1975.

Butler, Judith. *Gender Trouble: Feminism and the Subversion of Identity.* New York: Routledge, 2006.

Calvin, John. *Commentary on the Book of Psalms*, vol. 1. Translated by James Anderson. Edinburgh: Calvin Translation Society, 1845.

———. *Institutes of the Christian Religion.* Edited by John T. McNeill. Translated by Ford Lewis Battles. Louisville, KY: Westminster John Knox, 1960. Also at https://tinyurl.com/ybbz8qkv.

Caputo, John D. "The Experience of God and the Axiology of the Impossible." In *The Experience of God: A Postmodern Response*, edited by Kevin Hart and Barbara Wall, 20–41. New York: Fordham University Press, 2005.

———. "The Good News about Alterity: Derrida and Theology." *Faith and Philosophy* 10 (1993): 453–70.

———. *More Radical Hermeneutics: On Not Knowing Who We Are.* Bloomington: Indiana University Press, 2000.

———. *On Religion.* New York: Routledge, 2001.

———. *The Prayers and Tears of Jacques Derrida: Religion without Religion.* Bloomington: Indiana University Press, 1997.

———. "Reason, History and a Little Mad-ness: Towards a Hermeneutics of the Kingdom," *Proceedings of the American Catholic Philosophical Association* 68 (1994): 27–44.

———. *The Weakness of God.* Bloomington: Indiana University Press, 2006.

Catholic Church. "The Final Purification, or Purgatory." In *The Catechism of the Catholic Church*, 2nd ed. Vatican: Libreria Editrice Vaticana, 2012.

Celsus. *On the True Doctrine: A Discourse against the Christians.* Translated by R. Joseph Hoffmann. New York: Oxford University Press, 1987.

"The Chalcedon Formula." Anglicans Online, May 23, 2017. https://tinyurl.com/yb99sdwn.

Chilton, Bruce. *Rabbi Jesus: An Intimate Biography.* New York: Random House, Doubleday, 2000.

Clément, Olivier. *The Roots of Christian Mysticism*, 2nd ed. Hyde Park, NY: New City, 2013.

Coleman, J. J. "Biblical Inerrancy: Are We Going Anywhere?" *Theology Today* 31 (1975): 295.

Coleson, Joseph H. *'Ezer Cenegdo: A Power Like Him, Facing Him as Equal.* Indianapolis: Wesleyan/Holiness Women Clergy, 1996.

Collins, Robin. "The Connection-Building Theodicy." In *The Blackwell Companion to the Problem of Evil*, edited by Justin P. McBrayer and Daniel Howard Snyder, 222–35. Hoboken, NJ: Wiley Blackwell, 2014.

——. "A Defense of Nonviolent Atonement." *Brethren in Christ History and Life* 35, no. 1 (April 2012): 185–213.

——. "Evolution and Original Sin." In *Perspectives on an Evolving Creation*, edited by Keith B. Miller, 469–501. Grand Rapids, MI: Eerdmans, 2003.

——. "Girard and Atonement: An Incarnational Theory of Mimetic Participation." In *Violence Renounced: René Girard, Biblical Studies, and Peacemaking*, Studies in Peace and Scripture 4, edited by Willard M. Swartley, 132–56. Telford, PA: Pandora, 2000.

Cone, James H. *Black Theology of Liberation*. Philadelphia: J. B. Lippincott, 1970; Maryknoll, NY: Orbis, 2010.

——. *God of the Oppressed*. New York: Seabury, 1975.

Conner, W. T. *The Gospel of Redemption*. Nashville: Broadman, 1945.

——. *A System of Christian Doctrine*. Nashville: Southern Baptist Convention, 1924.

Cowles, C. S. "The Case for Radical Discontinuity." In *Show Them No Mercy: Four Views on God and Canaanite Genocide*, edited by C. S. Cowles, Daniel Gard, Tremper Longman III, and Eugene H. Merrill, 11–46. Grand Rapids, MI: Zondervan, 2003.

Craig, William Lane. "Original Sin." Reasonable Faith, October 22, 2017. https://tinyurl.com/y84c9h68.

Crane, Richard. "The Problem of the Plan of Salvation." In an unpublished manuscript.

Crossan, John Dominic, and Sarah Sexton Crossan. *Resurrecting Easter: How the West Lost and the East Kept the Original Easter Vision*. San Francisco: HarperOne, 2019.

Cullmann, Oscar. *Christology of the New Testament*. Translated by Shirlie C. Guthrie and Charles A. M. Hall. Rev. ed. Philadelphia: Westminster, 1963.

Davis, Stephen. *Encountering Evil: Live Options in Theodicy*. Louisville, KY: Westminster John Knox, 2001.

Dear, John. *The God of Peace: Toward a Theology of Nonviolence*. Eugene, OR: Wipf & Stock, 2005.

Derrida, Jacques. *Psyche: Inventions of the Other*, Meridian: Crossing Aesthetics 1, edited by Peggy Kamuf and Elizabeth Rottenberg. Stanford, CA: Stanford University Press, 2007.

——. *Rogues*. Translated by Pascale-Anne Brault and Michael Naas. Stanford, CA: Stanford University Press, 2005.

DeVries, LaMoine F. "Cult Stands: A Bewildering Variety of Shapes and Sizes." *Biblical Archaeological Review* 13, no. 4 (July/August 1987): 26–37.

Dodds, Michael J. *The Unchanging God of Love*. Fribourg, Switzerland: Éditions Universitaires Fribourg Suisse, 1986.

Downing, David. *Into the Wardrobe*. Hobeken, NJ: Jossie Bass Publishers, 2005.

Dumas, André. "La Mort du Christ n'est-elle pas Sacrificielle? Discussion d'objections contemporaines." *Etudes Théologiques et Religieuses* 56 (1981): 577–91.

Dunn, James D. G. *Jesus Remembered: Christianity in the Making*, vol. 1. Grand Rapids, MI: Eerdmans, 2003.

Eliot, T. S. *The Complete Poems and Plays 1909–1950*. New York: Harcourt, Brace, Jovanovich, 1971.

Evangelical Lutheran Church in America. *Evangelical Lutheran Worship*. Minneapolis: Augsburg Fortress, 2006.

Fairweather, Eugene R., ed. A *Scholastic Miscellany: Anselm to Okcham.* Philadelphia: Westminster, 1954.

Fee, Gordon D. *God's Empowering Presence: The Holy Spirit in the Letters of Paul.* Peabody, MA: Hendrickson, 1994.

Fiddes, Paul. "Creation Out of Love." In *The Work of Love: Creation as Kenosis,* edited by John Polkinghorne. Grand Rapids, MI: Eerdman's, 2001.

———. *Past Event and Present Salvation: A Study on the Christian Doctrine of Atonement.* Louisville, KY: Westminster/John Knox, 1989.

———. "Relational Trinity: Radical Perspective." In *Two Views on the Doctrine of the Trinity,* edited by Jason S. Sexton and Stanley N. Gundry, 159–85. Grand Rapids, MI: Zondervan, 2014.

Filaret (Metropolitan of Moscow). *Oraisons funèbres, homélies et discours.* Translated by A. de Sturdza. Paris, 1849.

Finlan, Stephen. *The Background and Content of Paul's Cultic Atonement Metaphors.* Atlanta: Society for Biblical Literature, 2004.

———. *Options on Atonement in Christian Thought.* Collegeville, MN: Liturgical, 2007.

———. *Problems with Atonement.* Collegeville, MN: Liturgical, 2005.

Finlan, Stephen, and Vladimir Kharlamov, eds. *Theōsis: Deification in Christian Theology.* Princeton Theological Monograph Series. Eugene, OR: Pickwick, 2006.

Fretheim, Terence F. *The Suffering God: An Old Testament Perspective.* Philadelphia: Fortress, 1984.

Gadamer, Hans-Georg. *Philosophical Hermeneutics.* Translated by D.E. Linge. Berkeley: University of California Press, 2004.

———. *Truth and Method.* Translated by G. Barden and J. Cummings. New York: Crossroad, 1980.

Garrett, James Leo. 1990–1995. *Systematic Theology: Biblical, Historical, and Evangelical,* 2 vols. Grand Rapids, MI: Eerdmans, 1990.

Gessen, Masha. "Judith Butler Wants Us to Reshape Our Rage." *The New Yorker,* February 9, 2020.

Gilkey, Langdon. *Maker of Heaven and Earth: A Study of the Christian Doctrine of Creation.* Garden City, NY: Doubleday, 1959.

Girard, René. "Generative Scapegoating." In *Violent Origins: Walter Burkert, René Girard, and Jonathan Z. Smith on Ritual Killing and Cultural Formation,* edited by Robert G. Hamerton-Kelly, 73–148. Stanford, CA: Stanford University Press, 1988.

———. *I See Satan Fall Like Lightning.* Translated by James G. Williams. Maryknoll, NY: Orbis, 2001.

———. *Sacrifice.* East Lansing: Michigan State University Press, 2011.

———. *The Scapegoat.* Translated by Yvonne Freccero. Baltimore: John Hopkins University Press, 1986.

———. *Things Hidden Since the Foundation of the World.* Translated by Stephen Bann. Stanford, CA: Stanford University Press, 1987.

Gladd, Benjamin L., and Matthew S. Harmon. *Making All Things New.* Grand Rapids, MI: Baker Academic, 2016.

Goldsworthy, Graeme. *Preaching the Whole Bible as Christian Scripture.* Grand Rapids, MI: Eerdmans, 2000.

Goodhart, Sandor. *The Prophetic Law*. Lansing: Michigan State University Press, 2014.

Gorman, Michael J. *Reading Revelation Responsibly*. Eugene, OR: Wipf & Stock, 2010.

Gorringe, Timothy. *God's Just Vengeance: Crime, Violence, and the Rhetoric of Salvation*. Cambridge: Cambridge University Press, 1996.

Green, Colin. "Is the Message of the Cross Good News for the Twentieth Century?" In *Atonement Today: A Symposium at St. John's College, Nottingham*, edited by John Goldingay, 222–39. London: SPCK, 1995.

Green, Garrett. *Imagining God: Theology and the Religious Imagination*. San Francisco: Harper & Row, 1989.

Greene, Joel B., and Mark D. Baker. *Recovering the Scandal of the Cross: Atonement in New Testament and Contemporary Contexts*. Downers Grove, IL: InterVarsity, 2000.

Grensted, L. W. *A Short History of the Doctrine of the Atonement*. Eugene, OR: Wipf & Stock, 2001.

Grenz, Stanley J. *Rediscovering the Triune God: The Trinity in Contemporary Theology*. Minneapolis: Fortress, 2004.

———. *Theology for the Community of God*. Grand Rapids, MI: Eerdmans, 2000.

Gunton, Colin. *The Actuality of Atonement*. Grand Rapids, MI: Eerdmans, 1989.

Haarsma, Deborah B., and Loren D. Haarsma. *Origins: Christian Perspectives on Creation, Evolution, and Intelligent Design*. Grand Rapids, MI: Faith Alive, 2011.

Hall, Christopher A. *Learning Theology with the Church Fathers*. Downers Grove, IL: InterVarsity, 2002.

Hamerton-Kelly, Robert G. *The Gospel and the Sacred: Poetics of Violence in Mark*. Minneapolis: Fortress, 1994.

Hanson, R. P. C. *Allegory and Event: A Study of the Sources and Significance of Origen's Interpretation of Scripture*. Richmond, VA: John Knox, 1959.

Hardin, Michael. *The Jesus Driven Life: Reconnecting Humanity with Jesus*. Lancaster, PA: JDL, 2013.

———. "Practical Reflections on Nonviolent Atonement." In *Violence, Desire, and the Sacred: René Girard and Sacrifice in Life, Love and Literature*, vol. 2, edited by Scott Cowdell, Chris Fleming, and Joel Hodge, 247–58. London: Bloomsbury, 2014.

———, ed. *Reading the Bible with René Girard: Conversations with Steven E. Berry*. Lancaster, PA: JDL, 2015.

———. "Sacrificial Language in Hebrews: Reappraising René Girard." In *Violence Renounced: René Girard, Biblical Studies, and Peacemaking*, edited by Willard M. Swartley, 3–119. Telford, PA: Pandora, 2000.

Hart, Ray L. *Unfinished Man and the Imagination: Toward an Ontology and a Rhetoric of Revelation*. New York: Seabury, 1979.

Harwood, Adam. *The Spiritual Condition of Infants: A Biblical-Historical Survey and Systematic Proposal*. Eugene, OR: Wipf & Stock, 2011.

Haught, John F. *God after Darwin: A Theology of Evolution*, 2nd ed. New York: Routledge, 2019.

———. "Teilhard and the Question of Life's Suffering." In *Rediscovering Teilhard's Fire*, edited by Kathleen Duffy, 53–68. Philadelphia: St. Joseph's University Press, 2010.

Hays, Richard B. *The Moral Vision of the New Testament: Community, Cross, New Creation; A Contemporary Introduction to New Testament Ethics*. San Francisco: HarperSanFrancisco, 1996.

Heim, S. Mark. "Saved by What Shouldn't Happen: The Anti-Sacrificial Meaning of the Cross." In *Cross Examinations: Readings on the Meaning of the Cross Today*, edited by Marit Trelstad, 211–24. Minneapolis: Augsburg Fortress, 2006.

Helmick Raymond G., and Rodney L. Petersen, eds. *Forgiveness and Reconciliation: Religion, Public Policy, and Conflict Transformation*. Philadelphia: Templeton Foundation, 2001.

Herman, Arthur. *The Cave and the Light: Plato versus Aristotle, and the Struggle for the Soul of Western Civilization*. New York: Random House, 2014.

Hick, John. *Evil and the God of Love*. London: Palgrave Macmillan, 2010.

Hick, John, Clark Pinnock, Alister E. McGrath, R. Douglas Geivett, and W. Gary Phillips. *Four Views on Salvation in a Pluralistic World*. Grand Rapids, MI: Zondervan, 1996.

Hildegard of Bingen. *Illuminations of Hildegard of Bingen*. Commentary by Matthew Fox. Rochester, VT: Bear and Company, 2002.

Hoffman, Thomas A. "Inspiration, Normativeness, Canonicity, and the Unique Sacred Character of the Bible." *Catholic Biblical Quarterly* 44 (1982): 447–69.

Holmes, Arthur M. *All Truth Is God's Truth*. Downers Grove, IL: Intervarsity, 1977.

Holmes, Stephen R. "Classical Trinity: Evangelical Perspective." In *Two Views on the Doctrine of the Trinity*, 25–48. Edited by Jason S. Sexton and Stanley N. Gundry. Grand Rapids, MI: Zondervan, 2014.

Hughes, Antony. "Ancestral versus Original Sin: An Overview with Implications for Psychotherapy." https://tinyurl.com/y8qoop9c.

Hughes, Richard. *Christian America and the Kingdom of God*. Chicago: University of Chicago Press, 2009.

Humphreys, Fisher. "The Revelation of the Trinity." *Perspectives in Religious Studies* (September 2006): 285–303.

——. *Thinking about God: An Introduction to Christian Theology*. Covington, LA: Insight, 2016.

Hurtado, Larry W. *How on Earth Did Jesus Become a God? Historical Questions about Earliest Devotion to Jesus*. Grand Rapids, MI: Eerdmans, 2005.

——. *Lord Jesus Christ: Devotion to Jesus in Earliest Christianity*. Grand Rapids, MI: Eerdmans, 2003.

Irenaeus. *Against Heresies*. Peabody, MA: Hendrickson, 1994.

Isaac the Syrian. "Homily 27." In *The Ascetical Homilies of Saint Isaac the Syrian*. Boston: Holy Transfiguration Monastery, 1984.

——. *Isaac of Nineveh (Isaac the Syrian): The Second Part, Chapters IV–XLI*. Translated by A. S. Brock. Louvain: Peeters, 1995.

Janzen, David. "The God of the Bible and the Nonviolence of Jesus." In *Teaching Peace: Nonviolence and the Liberal Arts*, edited by J. Denny Weaver and Gerald Biesecker-Mast, 53–63. Lanham, MD: Rowman and Littlefield, 2003.

Jenkins, John Philip. *Jesus Wars: How Four Patriarchs, Three Queens, and Two Emperors Decided What Christians Would Believe for the Next 1500 Years*. San Francisco: HarperOne, 2011.

John Paul II. Audiences. 1999. https://tinyurl.com/ya7opxs2.

———. *Laborem Exercens (On Human Work).* Papal encyclical. 1981.

Johnson, Elizabeth A. "The Word Was Made Flesh and Dwelt among Us." In *Jesus: A Colloquium in the Holy Land,* edited by Dorothy Donnelly, 158–60. New York: Continuum International, 2001.

Johnson, Luke Timothy. *The Creed: What Christians Believe and Why It Matters.* New York: Doubleday, 2003.

Jones, Serene. *Call It Grace: Finding Meaning in a Fragmented World.* New York: Viking, 2019.

———. *Feminist Theory and Christian Theology: Cartographies of Grace.* Minneapolis: Fortress, 2000.

Julian of Norwich. *Revelations of Divine Love.* Translated by Barry Windeatt. Oxford: Oxford University Press, 2015.

Justin Martyr. *Dialogue with Trypho the Jew.* Pickering, OH: Beloved, 2015.

Kaufman, Gordon. *In the Face of Mystery: A Constructive Theology.* Boston: Harvard University Press, 1993.

Kearney, Richard. *Anatheism: Returning to God after God.* New York: Columbia University Press, 2011.

———. *The God Who May Be.* Bloomington: Indiana University Press, 2001.

———. *The Wake of Imagination: Toward a Postmodern Culture.* London: Routledge, 1994.

Keller, Catherine. *Face of the Deep: A Theology of Becoming.* London: Routledge, 2003.

Kierkegaard, Søren. *Repetition.* Translated by Walter Lowrie. New York: Harper Torchbooks, 1941.

———. *Works of Love.* Translated by Howard and Edna Hong. New York: Harper & Row, 1962.

Kirwan, Michael. *Discovering Girard.* Cambridge, MA: Cowley, 2005.

Knitter, Paul F. *Introducing Theologies of Religions.* Maryknoll, NY: Orbis, 2002.

Küng, Hans. *The Beginning of All Things: Science and Religion.* Translated by John Bowden. Grand Rapids, MI: Eerdmans, 2005.

LaCugna, Catherine Mowry. *God for Us: The Trinity and Christian Life.* San Francisco: HarperSanFrancisco, 1973.

———. "God in Communion with Us: The Trinity." In *Freeing Theology: The Essentials of Theology in Feminist Perspectives,* edited by Catherine Mowry LaCugna, 83–114. San Francisco: HarperSanFrancisco, 1993.

———. "The Practical Trinity." *Christian Century* 109, no. 22 (July 15–22, 1992): 678–82.

Layland, Aleksandra. *The Feathered Crown.* Windflower Saga. Aleksandra Layland, 2016.

Lee, Aquila H. *From Messiah to Pre-existent Son: Jesus' Self-Consciousness and Early Exegesis of Messianic Psalms.* Tübingen: Mohr Siebeck, 2005.

Lévinas, Emmanuel. *Otherwise than Being, or Beyond Essence.* Translated by Alphonso Lingis. Pittsburg, PA: Duquesne University Press, 1998.

Lewis, C. S. *The Chronicles of Narnia.* Complete series. San Francisco: HarperCollins, 2010. Individual books originally published 1950, 1951, 1952, 1954, 1955, 1956 by C. S. Lewis.

———. *The Four Loves.* New York: Harcourt Brace Jovanovich, 1960.

——. *The Great Divorce: A Dream*. San Francisco: HarperOne, 2001; originally published 1946.

——. *Mere Christianity*. In *The C. S. Lewis Signature Classics: An Anthology*, 1–177. New York: HarperOne, 2017.

——. *The Problem of Pain*. San Francisco: Harper SanFrancisco, 2001.

Lossky, Vladimir. *In the Image and Likeness of God*. Crestwood, NY: St. Vladimir's Seminary Press, 1974.

——. *The Mystical Theology of the Eastern Church*. Crestwood, NY: St. Vladimir's Seminary Press, 1976.

——. "The Procession of the Holy Spirit in Orthodox Trinitarian Theology." In *Eastern Orthodox Theology: A Contemporary Reader*, edited by Daniel B. Clendenin, 163–82. Grand Rapids, MI: Baker Academic, 2003.

Louth, Andrew. *Introducing Eastern Orthodox Theology*. Downers Grove, IL: IVP, 2013.

Love, Gregory Anderson. *Love, Violence, and the Cross: How the Nonviolent God Saves Us Through the Cross of Christ*. Eugene, OR: Cascade Books, 2010.

Luther, Martin. *The Bondage of the Will*. Translated by J. I. Packer and O. R. Johnston. Grand Rapids: Baker Academic, 2012.

Mantzavinos, C. "Hermeneutics." In *The Stanford Encyclopedia of Philosophy* (Spring 2020 Edition), edited by Edward N. Zalta. https://tinyurl.com/yb5decpd.

Mascall, E. L. *Corpus Christi: Essays on the Church and the Eucharist*. London: Longmans, 1955.

McCall, Thomas H. "Relational Trinity: Creedal Perspective." In *Two Views on the Doctrine of the Trinity*, edited by Jason S. Sexton and Stanley N. Gundry, 113–37. Grand Rapids, MI: Zondervan, 2014.

McCullagh, C. Behan. "Theology of Atonement." *Theology* 91, no. 743 (September 1988): 392–400.

McFague, Sally. *The Body of God: An Ecological Theology*. Minneapolis: Fortress, 1993.

Meister, Chad V. *Evil: A Guide for the Perplexed*. New York: Bloomsbury, 2018.

The Message. Translated by Eugene H. Peterson. Colorado Springs: NavPress, 1993.

Middleton, J. Richard. "Created in the Image of a Violent God? The Ethical Problem of the Conquest by Chaos in Biblical Creation Texts," *Interpretation* 58, no. 4 (October 2004): 341–55.

——. *The Liberating Image: The Imago Dei in Genesis 1*. Grand Rapids, MI: Brazos, 2005.

——. *A New Heaven and a New Earth: Reclaiming Biblical Eschatology*. Grand Rapids, MI: Baker Academic, 2014.

Migliore, Daniel. *Faith Seeking Understanding*. Grand Rapids, MI: Eerdmans, 2004.

Miller, David B. "God in the Hands of Angry Sinners: The Misdiagnosis of Wrath in Ephesians 2." In *Peace Be with You: Christ's Benediction amid Violent Empires*, edited by Sharon L. Baker and Michael Hardin, 234–42. Telford, PA: Cascadia, 2010.

Miller, Keith B., ed. *Perspectives on an Evolving Creation*. Grand Rapids, MI: Eerdmans, 2003.

Molnar, Paul D. "Classical Trinity: Catholic Perspective." In *Two Views on the Doctrine of the Trinity*, edited by Jason S. Sexton and Stanley N. Gundry, 69–95. Grand Rapids, MI: Zondervan, 2014.

Moltmann, Jürgen. *The Church in the Power of the Spirit*. New York: Harper & Row, 1977.

——. *The Crucified God: The Cross of Christ as the Foundation and Criticism of Christian Theology*. New York: Harper & Row, 1974.

——. *God in Creation: A New Theology of Creation and the Spirit of God*. San Francisco: Harper & Row, 1985.

——. *The Spirit of Life: A Universal Affirmation*. Minneapolis: Fortress, 1994.

Mooney, Chris, and Brady Dennis. "The World Has Just Over a Decade to Get Climate Change Under Control, U.N. Scientists Say." *Washington Post*, October 7, 2018. https://tinyurl.com/y4n9jp72.

Moule, C. F. D. *Forgiveness and Reconciliation and Other New Testament Themes*. London: Lynx Communications, 1998.

Nation, Mark Thiessen. "'Who Has Believed What We Have Heard?' A Response to J. Denny Weaver's *The Nonviolent Atonement*." *Conrad Grebel Review* 27, no. 2 (Fall 2009): 17–30.

Neville, David. *A Peaceable Hope: Contesting Violent Eschatology in New Testament Narratives*. Grand Rapids, MI: Baker Academic, 2013.

Newbigin, Lesslie. *The Relevance of Trinitarian Doctrine for Today's Mission*. Edinburgh: Abingdon, 1984.

Niebuhr, Reinhold. *The Nature and Destiny of Man*, vol. 2. New York: C. Scribner's Sons, 1949.

Olson, Roger E. *Against Calvinism*. Grand Rapids, MI: Zondervan, 2011. Kindle digital edition, loc. 293.

——. *The Mosaic of Christian Belief: Twenty Centuries of Unity and Disunity*. Downers Grove, IL: InterVarsity, 2016, 308.

O'Neill, Mary Aquin. "The Mystery of Being Human Together." In *Freeing Theology: The Essentials of Theology in Feminist Perspective*, edited by Catherine Mowry LaCugna, 139–60. San Francisco: Harper SanFrancisco, 1993.

Oord, Thomas Jay. *God Can't: How to Believe in God and Love after Tragedy, Abuse, and Other Evils*. Grasmere, ID: Sacrasage, 2019.

Origen. *On First Principles*. Translated by Henri De Lubac. Gloucester, MA: Peter Smith, 1973.

Palaver, Wolfgang. "Sacrificial Cults as 'The Mysterious Centre of Every Religion': A Girardian Assessment of Abu Warburg's Theory of Religion." In *Sacrifice and Modern Thought*, edited by Julia Meszaros and Johannes Zachhuber, 83–99. Oxford: Oxford University Press, 2013.

Pannenberg, Wolfhart. *Systematic Theology*, vol. 1. Translated by Geoffrey W. Bromiley. Grand Rapids, MI: Eerdmans, 1991.

Pattillo, Matthew. "Creation and Akedah: Blessing and Sacrifice in the Hebrew Scriptures." In *Sacrifice, Scripture and Substitution: Readings in Ancient Judaism and Christianity*, edited by Ann W. Astell and Sandor Goodhart, 240–60. Notre Dame, IN: University of Notre Dame Press, 2011.

Payton, James R. *Light from the Christian East: An Introduction to the Orthodox Tradition*. Downers Grove, IL: IVP Academic, 2007.

Pinnock, Clark H. *Flame of Love: A Theology of the Holy Spirit*. Downers Grove, IL: InterVarsity, 2002.

Pinnock, Clark, Richard Rice, John Sanders, William Hasker, and Jason Basinger. *The Openness of God: A Biblical Challenge to the Traditional Understanding of God.* Downers Grove, IL: InterVarsity, 1994.

Piper, John. "Why I Do Not Say, 'God Did Not Cause the Calamity, but He Can Use It for Good.'" Desiring God. September 17, 2001. https://tinyurl.com/uu3blhe.

Plantinga, Alvin. *God, Freedom, and Evil.* Grand Rapids, MI: Eerdmans, 1977.

Plantinga, Cornelius, Jr. "Social Trinity and Tritheism." In *Trinity, Incarnation, and Atonement: Philosophical and Theological Essays,* edited by Ronald J. Feenstra and Cornelius Plantinga Jr., 21–47. Notre Dame, IN: University of Notre Dame Press, 1989.

Plantinga, Richard J., Thomas R. Thompson, and Matthew D. Lundberg. *An Introduction to Christian Theology.* Cambridge: Cambridge University Press, 2010.

Pliny the Younger, *Epistles* 10.96. In *A New Eusebius: Documents Illustrative of the History of the Church to A.D. 337,* edited by J. Stevenson, 20–24. London: SPCK, 1974.

Polkinghorne, John. *The God of Hope and the End of the World.* New Haven: Yale University Press, 2003.

Putt, B. Keith. "Faith, Hope, and Love: Radical Hermeneutics as a Pauline Philosophy of Religion." In *A Passion for the Impossible: John D. Caputo in Focus,* edited by Mark Dooley, 237–50. Albany: SUNY Press, 2003.

———. "Indignation toward Evil: Ricoeur and Caputo on a Theodicy of Protest," *Philosophy Today* 41, no. 3 (Fall 1997): 460–71.

———. "Prayers of Confession and Tears of Contrition: A Radically Baptist Hermeneutic of Repentance." In *Religion with/out Religion: The Prayers and Tears of John D. Caputo,* edited by James Olthuis, 62–79. New York: Routledge, 2002.

———. "What Do I Love When I Love My God? An Interview with John D. Caputo." In *Religion with/out Religion: The Prayers and Tears of John D. Caputo,* edited by James Olthuis, 150–79. New York: Routledge, 2002.

Rahner, Karl. *The Trinity.* Translated by Joseph Donceel. London: Continuum, 1970.

Ray, Inna Jane. *The Atonement Muddle: An Historical Analysis and Clarification of a Salvation Theory.* Journal of Women and Religion 15. Berkeley: The Center for Women and Religion, 1997.

Redekop, Vern Neufeld. *From Violence to Blessing: How an Understanding of Deep-Rooted Conflict Can Lead to Paths of Reconciliation.* Ottawa: Novalis, 2002.

Richard of St. Victor, *The Trinity.* Edited by Ruben Angelici. Eugene, OR: Cascade, 2011.

Ricoeur, Paul. "Biblical Hermeneutics," *Semeia* 4 (1975): 29–148.

———. *Essays on Biblical Interpretation.* Edited by Lewis S. Mudge. Philadelphia: Fortress, 1980.

———. *Freud and Philosophy: An Essay on Interpretation.* New Haven: Yale University Press, 1970.

Robinson, H. Wheeler. *The Christian Experience of the Holy Spirit.* London: Nisbet, 1928.

Rohr, Richard, "At-one-ment, Not Atonement." Center for Action and Contemplation, February 5, 2020. https://tinyurl.com/y8dslx2l.

——. "The Bible: A Text in Travail." *Hierarchy of Truths: Jesus' Use of Scripture*. Lecture presented in 2013, available on CD or MP3 from Center for Action and Contemplation. https://tinyurl.com/ya3ytcgm.

——. "The Blueprint of Creation." *The Cosmic Christ*, Week 1. Center for Action and Contemplation, March 28, 2017. https://tinyurl.com/yb23o6rn.

——. "Creation Reflects God's Glory." *Creation*, Week 2. Center for Action and Contemplation, February 18, 2018. https://tinyurl.com/y8ovwdvl.

——. *The Divine Dance: The Trinity and Your Transformation*. New Kensington, PA: Whitaker, 2016.

——. *Eager to Love: The Alternative Way of Francis of Assisi*. Cincinnati: Franciscan Media: 2014.

——. *Franciscan Mysticism: I AM That Which I AM Seeking*. Disc 3 of multi-disc CD set. Center for Action and Contemplation: 2012.

——. *Job and the Mystery of Suffering: Spiritual Reflections*. New York: Crossroad, 2005.

——. *The Naked Now: Learning to See as the Mystics See*. New York: Crossroad, 2009.

——. *Teachings on Love*. Edited by Joelle Chase and Judy Traeger. Maryknoll, NY: Orbis, 2018.

——. *The Universal Christ: How a Forgotten Reality Can Change Everything We See, Hope For, and Believe*. New York: Convergent, 2019.

——. "The World, the Flesh, and the Devil: The Spiral of Violence." Center for Action and Contemplation, October 21, 2015. https://tinyurl.com/yagr8eps.

Roth, John K. "A Theodicy of Protest." In *Encountering Evil: Live Options in Theodicy*, edited by Stephen T. Davis, 7–22. Atlanta: John Knox, 1981.

Sagan, Carl. *Pale Blue Dot: A Vision of the Human Future in Space*. New York: Random House, 1994.

Sanders, John. *The God Who Risks: A Theology of Providence*. Downers Grove, IL: InterVarsity, 1998.

——. *No Other Name: An Investigation into the Destiny of the Unevangelized*. Grand Rapids, MI: Eerdmans, 1992.

Schleiermacher, Friedrich. *The Christian Faith: A New Translation and Critical Edition*. Translated by Terrence N. Tice and Catherine L. Kelsey. Louisville, KY: Westminster John Knox, 2016.

Schmiechen, Peter. *Saving Power: Theories of Atonement and Forms of the Church*. Grand Rapids, MI: Eerdmans, 2005.

Schwager, Raymund. *Banished from Eden: Original Sin and Evolutionary Theory in the Drama of Salvation*. Herefordshire, UK: Gracewing, 2006.

Seibert, Eric A. *Disarming the Church: Why Christians Must Forsake Violence to Follow Jesus and Change the World*. Eugene, OR: Cascade, 2018.

——. *Disturbing Divine Behavior: Troubling Old Testament Images of God*. Minneapolis: Fortress, 2009.

——. *The Violence of Scripture: Overcoming the Old Testament's Troubling Legacy*. Minneapolis: Fortress, 2012.

Sexton, Jason S. and Stanley N. Gundry, eds. *Two Views on the Doctrine of the Trinity*. Grand Rapids, MI: Zondervan, 2014.

Sölle, Dorothee. *Christ the Representative: An Essay in Theology after the Death of God.* Translated by David Lewis. Philadelphia: Fortress, 1967.

———. *Thinking about God: An Introduction to Theology.* Philadelphia: Trinity Press International, 1990.

Solzhenitsyn, Alexandr. *The Gulag Archipelago.* New York: Harper & Row, 1973.

Stavropoulos, Christoforos. "Partakers of Divine Nature." In *Eastern Orthodox Theology: A Contemporary Reader,* edited by Daniel B. Clendenin, 183–92. Grand Rapids, MI: Baker Academic, 2003.

Stevens, Wallace. *The Collected Poems of Wallace Stevens.* New York: Knopf, 1990.

Suchocki, Marjorie Hewitt. *The Fall to Violence: Original Sin in Relational Theology.* New York: Continuum, 1995.

Swinburne, Richard. *Providence and the Problem of Evil.* Oxford: Clarendon, 1998.

———. "Responsibility, Atonement, and Forgiveness." In *Debating Christian Theism,* edited by J. P. Moreland, Chad Meister, and Khaldoun A. Sweis, 361–71. New York: Oxford University Press, 2013.

Taylor, Vincent. *Jesus and His Sacrifice.* London: MacMillan, 1939.

Thistlethwaite, Susan. *Sex, Race, and God: Christian Feminism in Black and White.* New York: Crossroad, 1989.

Thorsen, Don. *An Exploration of Christian Theology.* Grand Rapids, MI: Baker Academic, 2008.

Tillich, Paul. *A History of Christian Thought: From Its Judaic and Hellenistic Origins to Existentialism.* Edited by Carl Braaten. New York: Simon & Schuster, 1968.

———. *The Shaking of the Foundations.* New York: Charles Scribner, 1955.

———. *Systematic Theology,* vol. 1. Chicago: University of Chicago Press, 1973.

———. *Systematic Theology,* vol. 2. Chicago: University of Chicago Press, 1975.

Vermes, Geza. *Jesus the Jew.* London: SCM, 1973.

Wallace, Mark. *Finding God in the Singing River.* Minneapolis: Fortress, 2005.

Ware, Kallistos. *The Inner Kingdom,* vol. 1. Crestwood, NY: St. Vladimir's Seminary Press, 2000.

Weaver, J. Denny. *The Nonviolent Atonement.* Grand Rapids, MI: Eerdmans, 2001.

Weingart, Richard E. *The Logic of Divine Love: A Critical Analysis of the Soteriology of Peter Abailard.* London: Clarendon, 1970.

Wesley, John. "The Scripture Way of Salvation." In *John Wesley's Sermons: An Anthology.* Edited by Albert C. Outler and Richard P. Heitzenrater, 371–80. Nashville: Abingdon, 1991.

Westphal, Merold. *Whose Community? Which Interpretation? Philosophical Hermeneutics for the Church.* Grand Rapids, MI: Baker Academic, 2009.

Wiesel, Elie. *Night.* New York: Hill & Wang, 1958.

Wiles, M. F. "Origen as a Biblical Scholar." In *From the Beginnings to Jerome,* edited by Peter R. Ackroyd and C. F. Evans, 454–89. CHB 1. Cambridge: Cambridge University Press, 1970.

Williams, James G., ed. *The Girard Reader.* New York: Crossroad, 1996.

———. *Girardians: The Colloquium on Violence and Religion 1990–2010.* Hamburg: Lit Verlag, 2013.

Wink, Walter. "Facing the Myth of Redemptive Violence," *Ekklesia,* November 15, 2014. https://tinyurl.com/2gqsml.

———. "The Myth of the Domination System." In *Engaging the Powers: Discernment and Resistance in a World of Domination*, 13–31. Minneapolis: Fortress, 1992.

———. *When the Powers Fall: Reconciliation in the Healing of Nations*. Minneapolis: Fortress, 1998.

Wirzba, Norman. *The Paradise of God: Renewing Religion in an Ecological Age*. New York: Oxford University Press, 2003.

Woodley, Randy S. *Shalom and the Community of Creation: An Indigenous Vision*. Grand Rapids, MI: Eerdmans, 2012.

Wright, N. T. *History and Eschatology: Jesus and the Promise of Natural Theology*. Waco, TX: Baylor University Press, 2019.

———. *The Resurrection of the Son of God*. Minneapolis: Fortress, 2003.

Yoder, John Howard. *The Politics of Jesus: Vicit Agnus Noster*, 2nd ed. Grand Rapids, MI: Eerdmans, 2008.

Yoder, Perry B. *Shalom: The Bible's Word for Salvation, Justice, and Peace*. Nappanee, IN: Evangel, 1987.

Yong, Amos. *Spirit-Word-Community: Theological Hermeneutics in Trinitarian Perspective*. Hants: UK: Ashgate, 2002.

Zahnd, Brian. *Sinners in the Hands of a Loving God: The Scandalous Truth of the Very Good News*. Colorado Springs: Waterbrook, 2017.

Zehr, Howard. *Changing Lenses: A New Focus for Crime and Justice*. Scottsdale, PA: Herald, 1990.

Zlotowitz, Meir, trans. and comment. *Bereishis: A New Translation with a Commentary Anthologized from Talmudic, Midrashic, and Rabbinic Sources*, vol. 1a. Brooklyn: Mesorah, 1995.

Index